NEW CENTURY BIBLE

General editors

RONALD E. CLEMENTS

M.A., B.D., PH.D. (Old Testament)

MATTHEW BLACK

D.D., D.LITT., F.B.A. (New Testament)

The Gospel of Matthew

NEW CENTURY BIBLE

Based on the Revised Standard Version

The Gospel of Matthew

Edited by

DAVID HILL, B.D., S.T.M., Ph.D.

Department of Biblical Studies
University of Sheffield

OLIPHANTS

OLIPHANTS

MARSHALL, MORGAN AND SCOTT
BLUNDELL HOUSE
GOODWOOD ROAD
LONDON SE14 6BL

ISBN 0 551 00169 0

Printed in Great Britain by
Butler & Tanner Ltd., Frome and London

To
St Mary's College
in the
University of St Andrews
With gratitude and affection

CONTENTS

CONTENTS

PREFACE

The writer of a commentary on one of the Synoptic Gospels may consider that his primary responsibility is to reach and present conclusions concerning the historicity of the events and teaching recorded in that Gospel, or he may view his task as being primarily that of exposition, of making clear the religious message which the evangelist wished to convey to his readers through his narratives and by the arrangement of his Gospel as a whole. Both approaches are legitimate, but they are not exclusive alternatives, any more than the two different conceptions of revelation on which they are based—revelation as *act* of God in history, and revelation as *interpretation* of God's action for a specific situation or group of people—are mutually exclusive: both approaches to Gospel commentary are complementary, although most of the recent trends in Gospel criticism suggest that the second is more fruitful and more likely to do justice to the character of the material with which the commentator is concerned. This commentary on the Gospel of Matthew stresses interpretation: the way in which the Evangelist employed traditional material, his distinctive theological emphases, and the meaning of his teaching for the Church of his time are all matters which receive attention in the following pages. Nevertheless, questions about historicity and genuineness are not neglected: they are raised in a general way in the Introduction and considered more carefully at a number of places in the Commentary, especially in relation to some of the sections which are frequently regarded as secondary creations of the Church. Textual and grammatical points are not dealt with in any detail, because an adequate treatment of them would presuppose an audience of specialists, and to such this series of commentaries is not directed. It is hoped that clergy and laymen, as well as students, will be helped in their understanding of the Gospel by concentrating on its thought, teaching and theology.

Of the many commentaries and books on Matthew's Gospel to which this work is indebted, two deserve special mention: W. D. Davies's magisterial study, *The Setting of the Sermon on the Mount*, and the commentary by Pierre Bonnard, *L'Évangile selon Saint Matthieu*. The latter is the only available commentary which applies the method known as *Redaktionsgeschichte* ('tradition-criticism') consistently to the entire Gospel of Matthew, and the result is an excellent presentation of the Evangelist's meaning and theology. The work by Davies, on the other hand, reveals the signal importance of discovering the setting in which the specially distinctive Matthean Sermon may most fairly be interpreted, and the meticulous care with which this search is carried out provides indispensable guidance for the better understanding of the whole Gospel and its purpose.

As I acknowledge my indebtedness to previous commentators on the Gospel of Matthew and to a number of friends who helped me during the preparation of this commentary, I am conscious, at the same time, of what I owe to the college in which my academic study of the Bible and theology commenced. The dedication of this book is an expression of thanks for the stimulating introduction to the study of the New Testament which I received there.

D.H.

LISTS OF ABBREVIATIONS

BIBLICAL

OLD TESTAMENT (*OT*)

Gen.	Jg.	1 Chr.	Ps.	Lam.	Ob.	Hag.
Exod.	Ru.	2 Chr.	Prov.	Ezek.	Jon.	Zech.
Lev.	1 Sam.	Ezr.	Ec.	Dan.	Mic.	Mal.
Num.	2 Sam.	Neh.	Ca.	Hos.	Nah.	
Dt.	1 Kg.	Est.	Isa.	Jl	Hab.	
Jos.	2 Kg.	Job	Jer.	Am.	Zeph.	

APOCRYPHA (*Apoc.*)

1 Esd.	Tob.	Ad. Est.	Sir.	S 3 Ch.	Bel	1 Mac.
2 Esd.	Jdt.	Wis.	Bar.	Sus.	Man.	2 Mac.
			Ep. Jer.			

NEW TESTAMENT (*NT*)

Mt.	Ac.	Gal.	1 Th.	Tit.	1 Pet.	3 Jn
Mk	Rom.	Eph.	2 Th.	Phm.	2 Pet.	Jude
Lk.	1 C.	Phil.	1 Tim.	Heb.	1 Jn	Rev.
Jn	2 C.	Col.	2 Tim.	Jas	2 Jn	

DEAD SEA SCROLLS (*DSS*)

1QIs^a	First Isaiah Scroll
1QIs^b	Second Isaiah Scroll
1QLevi	Second Testament of Levi
1QpHab	Habakkuk Commentary
1QS	Rule of the Community (Manual of Discipline)
1QSa (= 1Q28a)	Rule of the Community (Appendix)
1QSb (= 1Q28b)	Collection of Benedictions
1QM	War of the Sons of Light against the Sons of Darkness
1QH	Hymns of Thanksgiving
4QFlor	Florilegium, Cave 4
4QpPs 37	Commentary on Psalm 37
4Qtest	Messianic Testimonia
CD	Fragments of a Zadokite Work (Damascus Document)
DSH	(now designated 1Qp Hab)

JEWISH WRITINGS

TRACTATES OF THE MISHNAH

Bab. Bath.	Baba Bathra	Meg.	Megillah
Bab. Metzia	Baba Metzia	Ned.	Nedarim
Berak.	Berakoth	Pes.	Pesahim
Eduy.	Eduyoth	San.	Sanhedrin
Hagig.	Hagigah	Shab.	Shabbath
Ket.	Ketuboth		

OTHERS

Ascen. Isa.	Ascension of Isaiah
Ass. Mos.	Assumption of Moses
B.	Babylonian Talmud
J.	Jerusalem Talmud
Jub.	Jubilees
LXX	Septuagint
M.	Mishnah
Mek.	Mekilta
M.T.	Massoretic Text
Pesik.	Pesikta
Ps. Sol.	Psalms of Solomon
R.	Midrash Rabbah
Test.	Testaments of the Twelve Patriarchs
Tes.	Tosephta
Vulg.	Vulgate

SELECT BIBLIOGRAPHY

AV   Authorized Version.

Abrahams   I. Abrahams, *Studies in Pharisaism and the Gospels*, Cambridge, 1917–1924. 2 vols.

Allen   W. C. Allen, *A Critical and Exegetical Commentary on the Gospel according to St Matthew*, 3rd ed., Edinburgh, 1912.

Arndt   W. F. Arndt and F. W. Gingrich, *A Greek–English Lexicon of the New Testament*, Cambridge, 1957.

Aux Sources   *Aux Sources de la tradition chrétienne* (Goguel Festschrift), Neuchatel–Paris, 1950.

BJRL   *Bulletin of the John Rylands Library.*

BKW   Bible Key Words series.

BNTE   *The Background of the New Testament and its Eschatology* (Dodd Festschrift), Cambridge, 1956.

Bull NTS   *Bulletin of the Studiorum Novi Testamenti Societas*, Nos. 1–3, Cambridge, 1963.

Bacon   B. W. Bacon, *Studies in Matthew*, New York, 1930.

Barrett, *JGT*   C. K. Barrett, *Jesus and the Gospel Tradition*, London, 1967.

Barrett, *The Holy Spirit*   C. K. Barrett, *The Holy Spirit and the Gospel Tradition*, London, 1947.

Benoit   P. Benoit, *L'Évangile selon Saint Matthieu*, Paris, 1961.

Black, *Aramaic Approach*   M. Black, *An Aramaic Approach to the Gospels and Acts*, 3rd ed., Oxford, 1967.

Black, *Scrolls*   M. Black, *The Scrolls and Christian Origins*, London, 1961.

Blair   E. P. Blair, *Jesus in the Gospel of Matthew*, New York, 1960.

Blass–Debrunner   F. Blass and A. Debrunner, *A Greek Grammar of the New Testament*, translated by R. W. Funk, Cambridge, 1961.

Bonnard   P. Bonnard, *L'Évangile selon Saint Matthieu*, Paris, 1963.

Bornkamm   G. Bornkamm, *Jesus of Nazareth*, London, 1960.

Box   G. H. Box, *The Gospel of St Matthew*, London, 1922.

Brown   R. E. Brown, *New Testament Essays*, London, 1965.

Bruce   F. F. Bruce, *Biblical Exegesis in the Qumran Texts*, London, 1960.

Bultmann, *HST*   R. Bultmann, *The History of the Synoptic Tradition*, translated by J. Marsh, Oxford, 1963.

Bultmann, *TNT*   R. Bultmann, *Theology of the New Testament*, 1, London, 1952.

Burney   C. F. Burney, *The Poetry of our Lord*, Oxford, 1925.

Burrows   M. Burrows, *The Dead Sea Scrolls*, New York, 1955.

CD   *See under* Dead Sea Scrolls.

Cross   F. M. Cross, *The Ancient Library of Qumran and Modern Biblical Studies*, London, 1958.

Cullmann, *Baptism*   O. Cullmann, *Baptism in the New Testament*, London, 1950.

Cullmann, *Peter*   O. Cullmann, *Peter: Disciple, Apostle, Martyr*, London, 1953.

DSH   *See under* Dead Sea Scrolls.

DSS   Dead Sea Scrolls.

Dalman   G. Dalman, *The Words of Jesus*, Edinburgh, 1902.

Daube   D. Daube, *The New Testament and Rabbinic Judaism*, London, 1956.

Davies, *COJ*   W. D. Davies, *Christian Origins and Judaism*, London, 1962.

Davies, *SSM*   W. D. Davies, *The Setting of the Sermon on the Mount*, Cambridge, 1964.

Davies, *Torah*   W. D. Davies, *Torah in the Messianic Age and/or the Age to Come*, Philadelphia, 1952.

Descamps   A. Descamps, *Les Justes et la Justice dans les évangiles et le christianisme primitif*, Louvain, 1950.

Dibelius   M. Dibelius, *From Tradition to Gospel*, London, 1934.

Dodd, *Acc. Scrip.*   C. H. Dodd, *According to the Scriptures*, London, 1952.

Dodd, *Parables*   C. H. Dodd, *The Parables of the Kingdom*, London, 1936.

Dodd, *Studies*   C. H. Dodd, *New Testament Studies*, Manchester, 1953.

ET   *Expository Times*.

Ellis   E. E. Ellis, *The Gospel of Luke*, London, 1966.

Eusebius   Eusebius, *Ecclesiastical History*.

FBK   P. Feine, J. Behm, W. G. Kümmel, *Introduction to the New Testament*, London, 1966.

Fenton   J. C. Fenton, *Saint Matthew*, London, 1963.

Filson   F. V. Filson, *A Commentary on the Gospel according to St Matthew*, London, 1950.

Fuller, *Foundations*   R. H. Fuller, *The Foundations of New Testament Christology*, London, 1965.

Fuller, *Introduction*   R. H. Fuller, *A Critical Introduction to the New Testament*, London, 1966.

Gaechter   P. Gaechter, *Das Matthäus Evangelium*, Innsbruck, 1964.

Gärtner *Die rätselhaften Termini*   B. Gärtner, *Die rätselhaften Termini Nazoräer und Iskariot*, Lund, 1957.

Gärtner, *Temple*   B. Gärtner, *The Temple and the Community in Qumran and the New Testament*, Cambridge, 1965.

Goppelt   L. Goppelt, *Christentum und Judentum im ersten und zweiten Jahrhundert*, Gütersloh, 1954.

Grant, *Gospels*   F. C. Grant, *The Gospels: their origin and their growth*, London, 1957.

Grant, *HI*   R. M. Grant, *Historical Introduction to the New Testament*, London, 1963.

Gundry   R. H. Gundry, *The Use of the Old Testament in St Matthew's Gospel*, Leiden, 1967.

Guthrie   D. Guthrie, *New Testament Introduction: the Gospels and Acts*, London, 1965.

HCNT   D. E. Nineham and others, *History and Chronology in the New Testament*, London, 1965.

HDB   *Hastings' Dictionary of the Bible*, one volume revised edition edited by F. C. Grant and H. H. Rowley, Edinburgh, 1963.

HTR   *Harvard Theological Review.*

Hare   D. R. A. Hare, *The Theme of Jewish Persecution of Christians in the Gospel according to St Matthew*, Cambridge, 1967.

Héring   J. Héring, *Le Royaume de Dieu et sa venue*, Paris, 1959.

Higgins   A. J. B. Higgins, *Jesus and the Son of Man*, London, 1964.

Hill   D. Hill, *Greek Words and Hebrew Meanings*, Cambridge, 1967.

Hooker, *Jesus*   M. D. Hooker, *Jesus and the Servant*, London, 1959.

Hooker, *SSM*   M. D. Hooker, *The Son of Man in Mark*, London, 1967.

Hoskyns and Davey   E. Hoskyns and F. N. Davey, *The Riddle of the New Testament*, 3rd edition, London, 1947.

Hummel   R. Hummel, *Die Auseinandersetzung zwischen Kirche und Judentum im Matthäusevangelium*, Munich, 1963.

IDB   *The Interpreter's Dictionary of the Bible*, New York and Nashville, 1962. 4 vols.

JBL   *Journal of Biblical Literature.*

JB Jerusalem Bible, London, 1966.
JTS Journal of Theological Studies.
Jeremias, *EW* J. Jeremias, *The Eucharistic Words of Jesus*, 2nd edition, London, 1966.
Jeremias, *Heiligengräber* J. Jeremias, *Heiligengräber in Jesu Umwelt*, Göttingen, 1958.
Jeremias, *Parables* J. Jeremias, *The Parables of Jesus*, 2nd edition, London, 1963.
Jeremias, *Prayers* J. Jeremias, *The Prayers of Jesus*, London 1958.
Jeremias, *Servant* J. Jeremias and W. Zimmerli, *The Servant of the Lord* (2nd edition), London, 1965.
Josephus, *Ant.* Josephus, *The Antiquities of the Jews.*
Josephus, *BJ* Josephus, *Bellum Judaicum.*
Josephus *Vita* Josephus, *Vita Flavii Josephi.*
Kilpatrick G. D. Kilpatrick, *The Origins of the Gospel according to St Matthew*, Oxford, 1946.
Kuhn K. G. Kuhn, *Achtzehngebet und Vaterunser und der Reim*, Tübingen, 1950.
Kümmel W. G. Kümmel, *Promise and Fulfilment*, 2nd edition, London, 1961.
Leaney A. R. C. Leaney, *The Gospel according to St Luke*, London, 1958
Lightfoot R. H. Lightfoot, *The Gospel Message of St Mark*, Oxford, 1950.
Lindars B. Lindars, *New Testament Apologetic*, London, 1961.
Lohmeyer E. Lohmeyer, *Das Evangelium des Matthäus*, completed by W. Schmauch, Göttingen, 1956.
Lohmeyer, *Temple* E. Lohmeyer, *Lord of the Temple*, translated by S. Todd, Edinburgh, 1961.
McNeile A. H. McNeile, *The Gospel according to St Matthew*, London, 1915.
Manson, *Jesus* W. Manson, *Jesus the Messiah*, London, 1943.
Manson, *Sayings* T. W. Manson, *The Sayings of Jesus*, London, 1947.
Manson, *SM* T. W. Manson, *The Servant Messiah*, Cambridge, 1953.
Manson, *Teaching* T. W. Manson, *The Teaching of Jesus*, Cambridge, 1935.
Marmorstein, *Doctrine* A. Marmorstein, *The Doctrine of Merits in the Old Rabbinical Literature*, London, 1920.

Marmorstein *Studies* A. Marmorstein, *Studies in Jewish Theology*, Oxford, 1950.

Marxsen W. Marxsen, *Der Evangelist Markus*, Göttingen, 1959.

Mélanges bibliques *Mélanges bibliques rédigés en l'honneur de A. Robert*, Paris, 1957.

Moule, *BNT* C. F. D. Moule, *The Birth of the New Testament*, London, 1962.

Moule, *Idiom Book* C. F. D. Moule, *An Idiom Book of New Testament Greek*, 2nd edition, London, 1959.

Moule, *PNT* C. F. D. Moule, *The Phenomenon of the New Testament*, London, 1967.

NEB *The New English Bible*.

NT *Novum Testamentum*.

NTE A. J. B. Higgins, ed., *New Testament Essay: Studies in Memory of T. W. Manson*, Manchester, 1959.

NTS *New Testament Studies*.

NT Apocrypha E. Hennecke, *New Testament Apocrypha*, English translation, edited by R. M. Wilson, London, 1963–5. 2 vols.

Neotestamentica *Neotestamentica et Patristica* (Cullmann Festschrift), Leiden, 1962.

Nepper-Christensen P. Nepper-Christensen, *Das Matthäusevangelium: ein juden-christliches Evangelium?*, Aarhus, 1958.

Nineham D. E. Nineham, *St Mark*, London, 1963.

Peake *Peake's Commentary on the Bible* (ed. M. Black and H. H. Rowley), London, 1962. (References are to paragraphs.)

Perrin N. Perrin, *Rediscovering the Teaching of Jesus*, London, 1967.

Pliny Pliny, *Naturalis Historia*.

Polybius Polybius, *History*.

RB *Revue Biblique*.

RSV *Revised Standard Version*.

Rawlinson A. E. J. Rawlinson, *The Gospel according to St Mark*, 2nd edition, London, 1927.

Richardson A. Richardson, *The Miracle Stories of the Gospels*, London, 1941.

Riesenfeld H. Riesenfeld, *The Gospel Tradition and its Beginnings*, London, 1957.

Rigaux B. Rigaux, *Témoinage de l'évangile de Matthieu* (Pour une histoire de Jesus II), Bruges–Paris, 1967.

SB H. L. Strack and P. Billerbeck, *Kommentar zum Neuen Testament aus Talmud und Midrasch*, Munich, 1922–8. 6 vols.

SEA *Svensk Exegetisk Årsbok.*

SG *Studies in the Gospels,* edited by D. E. Nineham, Oxford, 1957.

SNT *The Scrolls and the New Testament,* edited by K. Stendahl, London, 1958.

ST *Studia Theologica.*

Stud. Evan. *Studia Evangelica,* edited by K. Aland, Berlin, I, 1959; II, 1963.

Schechter S. Schechter, *Some Aspects of Rabbinic Theology,* London, 1909.

Schniewind J. Schniewind, *Das Evangelium nach Matthäus,* Göttingen, 1956.

Schrenk G. Schrenk *et al., Righteousness* (Bible Key Words series), London, 1951.

Schweitzer, *Quest* A. Schweitzer, *The Quest of the Historical Jesus,* London, 1911.

Schweizer, *LD* E. Schweizer, *Lordship and Discipleship,* London, 1960.

Stauffer E. Stauffer, *New Testament Theology,* London, 1955.

Stendahl K. Stendahl, *The School of St Matthew and its Use of the Old Testament,* Uppsala, 1954.

Strecker G. Strecker, *Der Weg der Gerechtigkeit,* Göttingen, 1962.

TB *Theologische Blätter.*

TIM G. Bornkamm, G. Barth and H. J. Held, *Tradition and Interpretation in Matthew,* London, 1963.

TLZ *Theologische Literaturzeitung.*

TWNT *Theologisches Wörterbuch zum Neuen Testament,* edited by G. Kittel and G. Friedrich, Stuttgart, 1933—(English translation: Grand Rapids, 1963—).

TZ *Theologische Zeitschrift.*

Tasker R. V. G. Tasker, *The Gospel according to St Matthew,* London, 1961.

Taylor V. Taylor, *The Gospel according to St Mark,* London, 1957.

Tödt H. E. Tödt, *The Son of Man in the Synoptic Tradition,* London, 1965.

Trilling W. Trilling, *Das wahre Israel, Studien zur Theologie des Matthäusevangeliums,* Leipzig, 1959.

Turner N. Turner, *Syntax* (J. H. Moulton, *A Grammar of New Testament Greek,* III), Edinburgh, 1963.

Walker R. Walker, *Die Heilsgeschichte im ersten Evangelium,* Göttingen, 1967.

ZNW *Zeitschrift für die neutestamentliche Wissenschaft.*
ZTK *Zeitschrift für Theologie und Kirche.*

The following are significant contributions to Matthean studies that have been published since this commentary was written.

F. W. Beare 'The Mission of the Disciples and the Mission Charge: Matthew 10 and Parallels', *JBL*, LXXXIX 1970, pp. 1–13.

C. E. Carlston, 'The Things that Defile (Mk 7.14) and the Law in Matthew and Mark', *NTS*, xv, 1968–9, pp. 75–96.

J. Carmignac, *Recherches sur le 'Notre Père'*, Paris, 1969.

W. Grundmann, *Das Evangelium nach Matthäus* (Theol. Handkomm. zum *N.T.*, 1), Berlin, 1968.

J. D. Kingsbury, *The Parables of Jesus in Matthew 13: a Study in Redaction-Criticism*, Richmond (Va.), 1969.

B. J. Malina, 'The Literary Structure and Form of Matthew 28.16–20', *NTS*, xvii, 1970–1, pp. 87–103.

R. P. Martin, 'St Matthew's Gospel in Recent Study', *ET*, lxxx, 1968–9, pp. 132–6.

E. Schweizer, 'Observance of the Law and Charismatic Activity in Matthew', *NTS*, xvi, 1969–70, pp. 213–30.

K. Tagawa, 'People and Community in the Gospel of Matthew', *NTS*, xvi, 1969–70, pp. 149–62.

H. T. Wrege, *Die Überlieferungsgeschichte der Bergpredigt*, Tübingen, 1968.

INTRODUCTION

to

The Gospel of Matthew

INTRODUCTION TO THE GOSPEL OF MATTHEW

1. EARLY TRADITIONS CONCERNING THE GOSPEL

THE ANCIENT WITNESSES

The position of the Gospel according to St Matthew as the first book in the New Testament and the first in order of the Gospels has tended to maintain the wide acceptance in popular thought of the view that it is the first of the Gospels in the order of their writing. The tradition that this is the case is very old, and rests mainly upon the statement of Papias (*c.* A.D. 135) quoted by Eusebius (III.xxxix.16): 'Matthew, however, compiled' [or 'arranged' (Greek *synetaxato*)] 'the *logia* in the Hebrew language' [or 'dialect'], 'and each one interpreted' [or 'translated' (Greek *hērmēneusen*)] 'them as he was able.' This statement of Papias (the interpretation of which we shall discuss at length below) is possibly the origin of Irenaeus' claim that 'Matthew also among the Hebrews published a book [Gospel] in their own dialect, when Peter and Paul were preaching in Rome and founding the church' (*Haer.*, III.i.1; Eusebius, v.viii.2–6). Clement of Alexandria (Eusebuis, VI.xiv.5) claims that Gospels which contain genealogies of Jesus (i.e. Matthew and Luke) were written first, and Origen says that he learned that 'the first Gospel was written by Matthew, who was once a tax-collector and afterwards an apostle of Jesus Christ, and it was prepared for the converts from Judaism and published in the Hebrew language' (Eusebius, VI.xxv.4). Eusebius himself (III.xxiv.5) appears to assume Matthew's priority, and both he (v.x.3) and Jerome (*de vir. illus.*, 36) narrate a story about Pantaenus, in the second century, finding the Gospel of Matthew in Hebrew letters (i.e. Aramaic) in India. Epiphanius claims that the Aramaic Gospel of Matthew existed in his day in the possession of an Ebionite sect, probably the Elkasites. Augustine writes that, of the Gospels, only Matthew was written in Hebrew (Aramaic), the others in Greek, and that Mark followed closely in Matthew's footsteps, as his imitator and epitomizer (*de cong. Evang.*, 1.ii.4).

Patristic traditions therefore seem to unite in the testimony that the first Gospel was written by the apostle and former tax-collector Matthew, and that it was originally produced in the Hebrew (Aramaic) language. It is clear that the corner-stone of this testimony is Papias's statement, although it seems to have been overlooked that Papias discusses Mark before Matthew. But we must proceed to investigate what Papias said, and then relate our findings to the later traditions.

THE INTERPRETATION OF THE PAPIAS TRADITION

The main point of discussion in Papias's statement is the meaning of the word *logia*, but it should be noted in passing that the verb *hērmēneusen*, appearing in the context of a linguistic description ('in the Hebrew dialect'), most probably means 'translated' rather than 'interpreted'. One view of the meaning of *logia* is that it refers to prophetic *oracles* concerning the Coming One, i.e. Old Testament *testimonia* which are embedded in Matthew's Gospel. This is the view favoured by Grant (*Gospels*, pp. 65, 144) who claims for it the support of Eusebius (III.xxxix.14) where *logia kyriaka* (the subject of Papias's exegesis, III.xxxix.1) are described as *oracles* of the Lord, precisely as in the Old Testament prophets (i.e. as divinely inspired utterances): he assumes therefore that Papias would not and did not confuse *logia* ('oracles') and *logoi* ('words'). But, if *hērmēneusen* means 'translated', surely no one would have been compelled to translate Old Testament *testimonia*, since there were already existing Greek versions of the Scriptures. It would seem, therefore, that the term *logia* must have a distinctively Christian content. The view that by *logia* Papias meant simply our canonical Matthew, or the Gospel in terms of the five great discourses incorporated in it (so Bacon), could be supported from Papias's remarks about Mark's Gospel (Eusebius, III.xxxix.15) where 'the things either said or done by the Lord' (i.e. the Gospel tradition) seem to be described immediately afterwards as 'the Lord's oracles (*logia*)'. The chief stumbling-block to the acceptance of this view is that it makes Papias's statement virtually valueless—and would Eusebius quote a tradition from one of whose intelligence he had a low estimate anyway unless he thought it valuable?—for our canonical Matthew is in Greek and uses Greek sources (Mark, and LXX in quotations) and cannot be considered to have existed as a whole at any time in a Semitic language. If, in spite of all this, it is claimed that Papias's *logia* refers to the Gospel (as recently and strongly by C. S. Petrie, *NTS*, xiv, 1967–8, pp. 15–33), then it has to be assumed either that there was confusion between the Gospel and some other Semitic work (like the *Gospel according to the Hebrews*), or that there was a Semitic translation of Matthew's work in existence at the time of Papias. Since neither of these assumptions carries much weight, attempts have been made to interpret 'in the Hebrew (Aramaic) dialect' in some quite unusual sense. For instance, J. Kürzinger (*NTS*, x, 1963, pp. 108–15) argues that the words ought to be understood in a literary rather than linguistic sense, i.e. that Matthew arranged his material in a Jewish-Christian literary form, which would naturally be dominated by Old Testament (Semitic) characteristics. Another suggestion is made by Munck (in *Neotestamentica*, pp. 249– 260) to the effect that the tradition about a 'Hebrew' Gospel of Matthew arose in connection with the formation of the Canon, and as a result of attempts to clarify the differences among the Synoptics. But these hypotheses do not seem well-founded, or even attractive, as attempts to defend Papias's testimony. It seems clear that, if Papias meant 'the Gospel (of Matthew)' when he spoke of the *logia*, his statement does not correspond to the literary facts of the case. We may either dismiss his evidence altogether (as *FBK*, pp. 44, 85), or we may agree that the tradition of Matthew's having written something in Hebrew or Aramaic is correct and search for another interpretation of what is meant by *logia*.

Is it possible that, however Papias and even Eusebius understood it, the word *logia* refers to oracles of Jesus, a collection of which (in Aramaic) was incorporated in the Gospel? This is the view espoused by T. W. Manson (*Sayings*, pp. 18ff.), and he, with many others, identifies this compilation of *logia* with Q, the collection of the sayings of Jesus used in different versions by Matthew and Luke.

The Q hypothesis—and it still remains a hypothesis—came into being to explain the fact that about 250 verses are common to Matthew and Luke which are not found in Mark. In many of these common verses the resemblance between the Matthean and Lucan versions is so close as to become almost identity, and there are also signs that the order in which both Matthew and Luke have used their common material is similar. It is mainly for these reasons that the existence of a common written source has been

suggested, but these agreements in wording and in order between
Matthew and Luke (when they are not employing Mark) could
have arisen either through Matthew's use of Luke as a second
source or through Luke's use of Matthew in addition to Mark. The
former possibility seems very unlikely: Matthew's emphases and
arrangement seem so independent of Luke's that it is hard to
believe that the author employed Luke as a written source, though
recently an attempt has been made to suggest that Matthew used,
with Mark, a primitive version of Luke, thus accounting for the
agreements of Matthew and Luke against Mark (H. P. West,
NTS, xiv, 1967–8, pp. 75ff.). The view that Luke used Matthew
(as well as Mark) has been seriously put forward, and most
recently by A. M. Farrer (in *SG*, pp. 55–88). Attractive though
this theory is, in that it disposes of the admittedly difficult problem
of the agreements of Matthew and Luke against Mark, it is open
to serious objection. Would Luke have broken up the well-
arranged Matthean discourses (especially the Sermon on the
Mount) to scatter the fragments in various places in his Gospel
and in settings which are usually inferior, even omitting some
parts of Matthew's tradition? Why did Luke take over none of
the Matthean additions to the Marcan text? The Q hypothesis
still seems to be the most reasonable explanation of the phenomena
for which it seeks to account. But the extent to which Q was a
written document (and presumably 'the *logia* compiled by
Matthew' would refer to a written document) is a matter of
dispute. The fact that in many passages in the material common to
Matthew and Luke the extent of verbal agreement is considerable
although far from total (as it is in other passages) makes it likely
that we are dealing, not simply with a common written Greek
source, but with alternative translations of earlier Aramaic
material as well. It is therefore extremely difficult to define with
any certainty what precisely is meant by Q. Perhaps it is best to
speak of Q material (i.e. the Matthew/Luke common traditions)
and, if the symbol Q is used, to recognize it as a means of indicating a (common) layer of tradition, partly written and perhaps
partly oral, rather than a single document (cf. Fuller, *Introduction*,
p. 72, and R. M. Grant, *HI*, p. 116). If this widely held view is
adopted, what becomes of the identification of the collected *logia*
(in Papias's statement) with Q? That an apostle, indeed, that the
apostle Matthew, should have collected sayings of Jesus in Aramaic

is in no way unlikely; in fact, quite recently H. Schürmann has suggested (in *Der historische Jesus und der kerygmatische Christus*, pp. 342–70) that some of the Q materials were collected in the time of Jesus and used by the disciples—a suggestion which, if valid, would strengthen the claim to authenticity of this sayings-material: that such a collection (by Matthew) was used at some stage in the production of the Gospel—thus eventually giving the name *kata Matthaion* to the work—is again likely, but it could have formed only a part (though probably an important part) of that material which we have designated by Q.

It is attractive therefore to suppose that Papias had a tradition about a work by Matthew in Aramaic—a Semitic apostolic sayings-collection which formed part of the Q material—and that he wrongly considered this to be the Gospel. Papias's mistake or confusion may be the ground for the later statements which claim that there was an original Matthew in Hebrew (Aramaic), and it was made plausible (according to Davies, in *HDB*, p. 631) by the existence in Palestine, in that period, of information about a document or documents actually existing in a Semitic tongue and bearing a more or less close resemblance to our Matthew. Irenaeus (*Haer.* i.22) claims that the Jewish-Christian sect of the Ebionites used only Matthew's Gospel, but, since they did not recognize the Virgin Birth of Jesus, this Gospel used by them cannot have been the canonical Matthew, though it may have resembled it: and Eusebius (iii.xxvii) mentions that a special group of Ebionites (who did recognize the Virgin Birth) used only the *Gospel according to the Hebrews*, and some of the extant fragments of that work may represent developments of special Matthean tradition. It may be noted that the existence in the first half of the second century of (i) the *Gospel of the Nazaraeans* (in Aramaic or Syriac, and attested by Hegesippus, Eusebius, Epiphanius and Jerome) which showed a close relationship with the canonical Matthew, and (ii) the *Gospel of the Ebionites* (quoted by Epiphanius, *Haer.* xxx xiii.2, and called by him the 'Hebrew Gospel') which is more closely related to Matthew than to any other of the canonical Gospels, may explain why Papias spoke of translations (or interpretations) of the *logia* which he incorrectly considered to be the Gospel. Both these Semitic Gospels are virtually targumistic renderings of the canonical Matthew.

The attempt to account for the ascription of the Gospel to

Matthew by reason of the incorporation in it of a Matthean
(apostolic) collection of sayings (which formed *part* of Q)—a view
favoured by Manson (*Sayings*, pp. 18ff.) and by Allen (pp. lxxx,
lxxxi)—is rejected by Kilpatrick, pp. 138f. Although he accepts
the view that in the statement about the *logia* Papias meant
the Gospel and therefore ascribed the authorship to Matthew,
Kilpatrick explains the tradition as a conscious community
pseudonym affixed by the Church that produced the Gospel in
order to commend the book and win acceptance for it. This theory
has as corollary the suggestion that the hypothesis of a translation
of the original Matthew was caused by the need to meet objections
being made to the apostolic authority of the book as it stood:
but the idea of a community pseudonym—convincing all other
churches as well!—is unparalleled and unlikely.

Another reinterpretation of the tradition is found in Stendahl's
idea of a 'school of Matthew' (see pp. 35-7 below). In this case,
the identity of the actual author is lost in the 'school' out of which
the Gospel grew: but since this school is considered to have
continued the tradition of Matthew's catechesis, the use of that
apostolic name for the Gospel would have seemed natural. This
theory need not be at odds with the view we favour; for within
Matthew's catechesis would not a collection of Jesus' *logia* have
been fundamental? In our opinion it is necessary, in any account
of how Matthew came to be and what it was for, to find room for
the persistent early tradition of a Semitic writing by the apostle
Matthew: in doing so, it is simplest and probably best to postulate
a Semitic apostolic sayings-collection (a part of the Q material,
and therefore lying behind Luke as well), and to assume that this
is what is witnessed to in the Papias tradition, although Papias
himself believed he was speaking of the canonical Gospel. If this
assumption is made, then it becomes possible that Papias's allusion
to diverse translated versions ('each one translated them as he was
able') may help to explain some of the differences between
Matthew and Luke in parallel passages (cf. Moule, *BNT*, pp. 88f.,
215-19).

THEORIES OF MATTHEAN PRIORITY

Since the later Fathers accepted Papias's statement that the
disciple/apostle Matthew collected the *logia*, it was natural for
them to assume that he must have been the first evangelist to

write. But, in doing so, they overlooked the fact that Papias himself, as quoted by Eusebius, discussed Mark before Matthew. And the priority of Mark is the foundation-stone of most recent Synoptic literary criticism. Nevertheless, there have been some attempts to maintain the priority of Matthew over against Mark. Following the suggestion of Augustine, J. J. Griesbach (in 1789) considered Mark as an epitomizer of Matthew, while Luke was regarded as also earlier than Mark. This theory, which is in flagrant opposition to Papias's view that Mark is based on Peter's reminiscences (Eusebius, III.xxxix.15) has been discounted, to a large extent, because it fails to do justice to the literary characteristics and independence of view-point found in Mark. To suggest, as this theory does (and it has been strikingly revived by W. R. Farmer in *The Synoptic Problem*), that Mark is a skilful selection and combination of material taken from Matthew (the first Gospel) and Luke raises the almost insuperable difficulty of postulating an adequate motive for the production of Mark in such circumstances. Is it simply a 'compromise' document? The judgment of E. A. Abbott (quoted from the *Encyclopaedia Britannica*, 1879, by Farmer, p. 75) still stands:

> To take two documents, to put them side by side and analyse their common matter, and then to write a narrative, graphic, abrupt, and in all respects the opposite of artificial, which shall contain every word that is common to both—this would be a *tour de force* even for a skilful literary forger of these days, and may be dismissed as an impossibility for the writer of the second Gospel.

In proposing the priority of Matthew, B. C. Butler also abandoned the Q hypothesis (*The Originality of St Matthew*, 1951). Luke, he argued, was dependent on Matthew for what was called Q material, and on Mark for the material which the two had in common. Much of the force of Butler's arguments depends on the assumed inadmissibility of appealing to Q as an explanation of cases where Matthew's text seems more original than, or in some other way superior to, Mark. But does not the order and arrangement of incidents in Matthew and Mark exclude Butler's view? (Cf. H. G. Wood, *ET*, LXV, 1953–4, pp. 17–19.) A detailed and, in its cumulative effect, convincing refutation of Butler's theory is given by G. M. Styler (Moule, *BNT*, pp. 223ff.)

The more usual modern form of the case for Matthean priority argues for a preliminary version of Matthew, shorter than the canonical Gospel, and written in Aramaic or Hebrew. Out of this 'proto-Matthew' Mark produced his Gospel, adding particulars from the Roman preaching of Peter: the Aramaic Matthew was then translated into Greek, and in the production of the canonical Matthew and Luke Mark was used together with a special source. But canonical Matthew remains the best witness to the primitive Aramaic Matthew. In slightly different forms this view is put forward by Benoit, pp. 27ff., L. Vaganay, *Le Problème synoptique*, 1952, and Pierson Parker, *The Gospel before Mark*, 1953. That part of the theory which maintains that our Greek Matthew and Luke depend on Mark would be very widely accepted, but to postulate a 'proto-Matthew' out of which Mark was formed in order to preserve the tradition of Matthean priority is an unproveable hypothesis, and in fact may be an unnecessary one, for the tradition of Matthean priority probably rests (as suggested above) on a misinterpretation of Papias's statement, or on Papias's misunderstanding of the actual matter to which he was referring.

2. LITERARY SOURCES AND SCRIPTURAL QUOTATIONS

SOURCES

Aramaic

To say that 'proto-Matthew' (i.e. a primitive Aramaic Gospel) is an unwarranted hypothesis is not to deny that Aramaic sources lie behind our Gospels: it is simply to deny that an Aramaic *Gospel* (and we would have some idea of what is meant by a Gospel if the word is to have meaning) lies behind our Gospels. We have already indicated our general acceptance of the theory that by Papias's *logia* in Aramaic is meant an Aramaic collection of sayings of Jesus, which formed part of the Q tradition, used by Matthew and Luke either in a direct translation (so perhaps for Luke) or in an already existing literary revision in Greek (so perhaps Matthew): see Black, *Aramaic Approach*, pp. 186ff. In his quest for Aramaic sources for the Gospels (rather than Aramaic originals) Black maintains that there is sufficient evidence to point to a sayings-source in Aramaic (Q, or at least part of the Q layer of tradition)—and if Jesus taught in Aramaic, then it may be assumed that some Aramaic background would be found in the tradition of his teaching (oral, written, and eventually translated) —but he does not think that Matthew's narrative sections show so much Aramaic influence as do those of Mark, although it must be added that the Semitic style of the latter does not necessarily point to an Aramaic source; it may simply be evidence of the kind of Greek which an Aramaic-speaking Jew would write (Black, *Aramaic Approach*, p. 271). Whether or not the Aramaic sayings-source, or presupposed tradition, was written or oral cannot be decided from the evidence. There are those who confidently claim that Aramaic predecessors of our Gospels are only to be accepted with certainty for the oral tradition (*FBK*, p. 45): but, if we give any weight at all to Papias's words, we must assume that at least some part of the Aramaic tradition (and of the Q material) was committed to writing.

Mark and Q

It is our opinion then that the basic sources on which the writer of Matthew drew are the Gospel of Mark and that layer of tradition, partly written and partly oral, which is conveniently designated Q: the latter circulated in Aramaic, but may have been available in a Greek version before its use by the author of the Gospel. That that author took over almost the whole of Mark (about nine-tenths) is surprising, because, as Davies points out (in *HDB*, p. 631), the point of view of Mark on crucial matters, e.g. the Law, is not that of Matthew (cf. Mk 7.1–23 and Mt. 15.1–20). That Mark was taken over, virtually *in toto*, by another writer suggests that the earlier work was regarded with profound respect, and this is vouched for by the fact that Matthew follows, to a large extent, the order in which material is found in Mark. But Matthew conflates Mark freely with other material (see chapter 12, where Mark alternates with Matthew/Luke common material) and this suggests that he had a familiarity with Mark, perhaps even to the extent of being able to use it from memory. (Grant, *Gospels*, p. 145, posits a familiarity of about twenty years: presumably there was free intercourse between Rome and Palestine or Syria where Matthew is probably to be located.) It is of interest and importance to note that Matthew very seldom alters the sayings of Jesus taken over from Mark, although he undertook to make consider-

able changes in Mark's narrative by means of rearrangement in
the interests of systematization, by means of quite substantial
abbreviation of Mark (particularly in the accounts of miracles),
and by reason of his (theological) emphases, e.g. on faith as the
presupposition for receiving Jesus' help (15.28, cf. Mk 7.29), on
the idealization of the disciples (cf. Mt. 13.16f. with Mk 4.13, and
Mt. 14.33 with Mk 6.52), on the exaltation of Jesus, as Lord:
abbreviation is caused also by removing or changing the accounts
of Jesus' emotions (cf. Mt. 8.3 with Mk 1.41, and Mt. 19.14 with
Mk 10.14) and by eliminating offensive reports about Jesus (Mk
3.21, and cf. Mt. 13.58 with Mk 6.5). But Matthew's real aim in
writing his Gospel becomes recognizable when we consider his
extensive expansion of Mark. Approximately half of Matthew
has no parallel in Mark, and of this half about five-ninths is also
found in Luke, and this common material, we assume, reflects the
Q tradition. But what is the origin of the remainder, that special
material which amounts to about two-ninths of the entire Gospel?
Those who do not derive Matthew and Mark from a common
'proto-Matthew' and who therefore do not seek to derive the
special material from that source usually explain its origin in one
of two ways which we now outline.

The Special Material

According to one hypothesis, Matthew derived all or most of this
special material from the version of the Q material which he
employed and which was fuller than that used by Luke (so Bacon;
J. P. Brown, *NTS*, VIII, 1961–2, pp. 27–42; and Strecker, pp. 12f.).
It is quite possible that some texts found only in Matthew were in
the Q material, but there must be some doubt as to whether
material so extensive and so distinctive as Matthew's special
material formed part of Q at any stage of its development, if Q
(even as a layer of tradition) is to be considered as having any
character of its own. Indeed, the case for the origin of Matthew's
special material in Q is weakened by the fact that its defenders are
forced to derive parts of that material (in the case of Brown, the
parables, and, in the case of Strecker, the formula-quotations)
from additional sources, because Q seems to be unable to contain
them.

The second and more widespread view is that Matthew used as
further source(s)—in addition to Mark and the Q material—

material symbolized by 'M'. This material is usually divided into
two sections: special discourse (or sayings) material, and special
narrative material.

The discourse material was regarded by Streeter (*The Four
Gospels*, 1930, pp. 261ff., 512f.) as a written source, compiled about
A.D. 65 (after Mark and Q) and located in Jerusalem, largely
because of its predominantly Jewish tone. Its contents were
tentatively suggested to be, in the main, anti-Pharisaical discourse
material incorporated in the Sermon on the Mount and in
chapter 23, and a collection of parables of the Kingdom. Although
some parts of this special discourse material reveal a definite
structure (for example, what is left when we take Q material out of
the Sermon on the Mount seems to be five or six Beatitudes, three
contrasts between the Law and the new ethic of Jesus (5.21–24,
27–30, 33–37), and three contrasts between ostentation and the
new piety (6.1–4, 5–8, 16–18); cf. A. M. Perry, *JBL*, LIV, 1935,
pp. 103–15), this is not sufficient to carry the theory that the
special sayings material as a whole was a written document. The
lack of homogeneity and of connected thought which the special
discourse material shows, in any of its proposed forms, does not
warrant the postulation of a written source. It is probably better
to regard it as due to editorial work by Matthew and to oral
tradition. The Jewish character of this material in the Gospel is
surely attributable to the manner and method of the author's
selection.

The special narrative material in Matthew comprises the Birth
stories (chapters 1–2), Petrine stories (14.28–31; 16.17–19;
17.24–27; 18.15–22), Passion and Resurrection stories (26.52–54;
27.3–10, 19, 24f., 51–53, 62–66; 28.2–4, 9–20), miscellaneous
narratives (3.14f.; 4.23; 9.35; 15.22–24; 17.6f.; 21.10f., 14–16), to
which some add the formula-quotations. Many scholars have
detected some homogeneity in this material from its stylistic
features, references to angels and to prophecy, enhancements of
the miraculous, and explanations or justifications of the primitive
Christian tradition. Few however would be prepared to consider it
as having been a written document; rather, it would appear to
have been a cycle of tradition—mostly, if not entirely, oral—parts
of which probably grew up around Mark, but which was first put
into written form by the writer of Matthew. Much of this narrative
material—and in particular those sections which heighten the

miraculous or reveal a dogmatic interest (e.g. 3.14f. and 17.24–27)
—is regarded as the least valuable of the Gospel traditions. This
may be a true assessment of them in terms of their historical
worth, but they do possess value in that they reveal a good deal
about the influences upon and the manner of the development of
Gospel material.

This point may be explained by reference to Grant's description
of the material (*Gospels*, pp. 146ff.). He claims that the cycle of
tradition derives from a North Palestinian or Syrian church, and
he isolates the following elements in it:

(a) *Christian Midrashic haggadah*, i.e. edifying religious stories
    based on free exegesis of Old Testament texts and earlier
    traditions: of this examples are the Birth narratives, the
    Petrine stories, and 27.3–10. In the case of the Birth narra-
    tives, it should be pointed out that Matthew's interest is
    really in Jesus' names and place of origin, rather than in
    the description of the birth-event itself (cf. K. Stendahl,
    ZNW, Beihefte 26, 1960, pp. 94–105): nevertheless, the
    whole section seems to contain much haggadic material.

(b) *Christian exegesis and homiletics*, e.g. John's hesitation to
    baptize Jesus (3.14f., 12.5–7), and the interpretation of the
    Weeds (13.36–43).

(c) Material of a *codal* type, like the Didachē: e.g. parts of the
    Sermon on the Mount (10.41; 18.18; 19.10ff. and 23.2f.,
    8–10).

(d) *Early liturgical material* probably underlies 6.7–13 (the
    Matthean form of the Lord's Prayer (11.25–30; 18.19–20;
    28.18–20).

(e) *Apocalyptic material*, found in 13.24–30; 20.1–16; 22.1–14; 25.

(f) *Apocryphal material*—for example, the Passion and Resur-
    rection additions in chapters 27 and 28—in which the
    emphasis on the miraculous is comparable with the super-
    natural embellishment of Apocryphal Gospels.

(g) A collection of *Old Testament passages, or testimonia*, used in
    the explanation of events, and probably also affecting
    directly the tradition itself.

We have suggested that much, if not all, of this cycle of tradition
was first put into written form by the author of Matthew himself,
but the importance of Grant's list lies in the fact that it highlights

B

the widely accepted view that (i) liturgical elements have strongly influenced Matthew's Gospel, and (ii) a Christian tradition of exegesis lies behind the author's work. It is the special Matthean material which reveals the operation of these factors.

BIBLICAL QUOTATIONS: THE WORK OF KILPATRICK AND STENDAHL

The mention of liturgical and exegetical factors provides a convenient place at which to introduce discussion of two important studies of Matthew: *The Origin of the Gospel according to St Matthew* by G. D. Kilpatrick, 1946, and *The School of St Matthew and its use of the Old Testament* by Krister Stendahl, 1954.

According to Kilpatrick, the Gospel is a revision of a lectionary which grew up in answer to the liturgical needs of a Christian community in Syria or probably in Phoenicia. The liturgical use of the Scriptures, he maintains, was the focus of the Church's use of the Gospel material, and for this use he finds supporting parallels in the liturgical background of Judaism in both its Palestinian and Hellenistic forms: in the former, the making of Targums breaks down the sharp distinction between the sacred texts and the interpretations (haggadic and halachic); and in the latter, expository material becomes the literature admitted to liturgical use. According to this view, Mark and Q (which Kilpatrick accepts) were read and expounded in services, with the needs of the Church in mind; as this exposition was repeated time and time again, the tradition became more or less fixed and was admitted to liturgical use. At this stage traditions of the Matthean church (discourse and narrative) were combined into a revised edition of the Gospel (i.e. our Matthew). Kilpatrick argues that the lucidity, conciseness, parallelism, and balanced language of the Gospel point to its liturgical use. But are these characteristics possessed by liturgies alone? On this hypothesis, the Gospel of Matthew—though actually compiled or edited by one person—virtually becomes a community product.

A view similar to Kilpatrick's has been advanced by P. Carrington (*The Primitive Christian Calendar*, 1952) who considers Matthew to be an enlarged lectionary based on Mark which itself is a lectionary (see Carrington, *According to Mark*, 1960). The whole lectionary theory concerning the Synoptic Gospels has been criticized by W. D. Davies (*BNTE*, pp. 124–52; reprinted in

COJ, pp. 67–96). We need not go into detailed criticism here, but
it must be pointed out that, although Matthew was used and
apparently lent itself to liturgical purposes in the early Church,
this does not mean that it is itself a liturgically-created work. The
liturgical recitation of Gospel material in the second half of the
first century (*c.* A.D. 65–95) cannot be assumed without question.
Was the practice of Scripture reading in the synagogue followed so
early, and at *all* early Christian services? Even if it was, the
recitation of Mark cannot be taken for granted. There is certainly
no clear evidence that books of the New Testament were *expounded*
homiletically at an early date. Moreover, the indications given by
Kilpatrick of liturgical-homiletical usage in Matthew (conciseness,
grouping of similar subject-matter, repetition of formulae, etc.)
could equally well point to catechetical usage, if they are not
simply due to a careful and conscious literary style.

Whereas Kilpatrick defended his liturgical approach to the
Gospel against a catechetical one, Stendahl brings forward
another alternative. In form and compass the Gospel of Matthew
is similar to the Qumran *Manual of Discipline* and to parts of the
Didachē (1–6 and 7–15), which was a real 'manual of discipline' for
Church leaders and teachers, not for beginners on the Christian
way. The Gospel cannot be explained (Stendahl maintains) as
merely catechetical, even if that term is extended to cover post-
baptismal instruction and is freed from the common limitation of
definition in terms of ethical instruction. The degree of systematization (which gives the Gospel the form of a hand-book), the
adaptation towards casuistry instead of broad statements of
principle (cf. 5.31f. and 19.9 on divorce), the reflection on the
position of Church leaders and their duties (e.g. chapter 18)—
these and other features point to a milieu of study and instruction.
In this way Stendahl brings forward his hypothesis of a Matthean
school in which the Gospel originated as a manual of instruction
and administration: its final form was due to the work of a member of the school, regarded as a Christian rabbi. According to
Stendahl, the 'almost decisive argument' for the view that
Matthew is the product of a school is derived from the Old Testament quotations in the Gospel. Detailed study of these reveals that
the 'author's' Bible was the LXX, as it was of Mark and the other
New Testament writers: but the distinctive feature of Matthew is
the quotations introduced by the words 'this was to fulfil what

was spoken by the prophet(s)', which, as is well-known, follow neither the M.T., nor the LXX, nor any known Targum or version, but (as Stendahl suggests) incorporate elements from all of these, together with some features which are peculiar. The view that these quotations were derived from a special source, perhaps a Testimony-book (J. R. Harris, F. C. Burkitt) is rejected because (i) subsequent collections of *testimonia* (in Justin and Cyprian) do not follow Matthew's model in order or in language; and (ii) when a quotation in Matthew is found in other New Testament writings change is always apparent. Although the discovery of the Qumran *testimonia* document (4Qtest.), which contains biblical quotations of Messianic expectations, now gives fresh support to the idea of testimony-collections, Stendahl regards the formula-quotations as too much part of their contexts and too striking a feature of the Gospel as a whole to be explicable in terms of a special source. They are, he maintains, closely analogous to the lemmata in the Qumran Habakkuk commentary which show similar textual abnormalities, due (so the theory argues), not to the writer's familiarity with some non-standard text, but to the interaction between the *ipsissima verba* of prophecy and the factual details of its fulfilment. Matthew's formula-quotations belong to the same *pesher* milieu as does the Habakkuk commentary: 'just as Matthew's formula quotations are expressly interpreted as fulfilled by the words or deeds of Jesus, so DSH applies chapters 1 and 2 of Habakkuk verse by verse to the Teacher of Righteousness and the events which surround him' (Stendahl, p. 183). The formula-quotations are, like the Habakkuk text, the product of a school and exclusive to it, the Matthean school of scriptural study, and the form of the other quotations in the Gospel is mainly that of the LXX, i.e. the Greek text common to the church and synagogue.

The importance of Stendahl's theory justifies some further comment on it, in the course of which we may approach a more satisfactory view of the special character of Matthew's Gospel. The exegetical method employed in the Habakkuk commentary and that illustrated by Matthew's formula-quotations are not so similar as Stendahl suggests: in 1QpHab the words of prophecy are primary and serve as 'pegs' on which the *pesher* interpretation depends, but in the Gospel they seem to be secondary and only to 'point' the evangelist's words. Again, the lemmata in 1QpHab are not nearly so abnormal in the form of their text as the formula-quotations in Matthew. Even if it were certain (and it is not) that the *pesher*-izing method of a Qumran school created the mixed text found in the Habakkuk commentary, it would not necessarily follow that the Matthean text-forms were due to the work of a similar school: in fact, the Matthean exegesis of the Old Testament may show a likeness to the Habakkuk commentator's, simply because both used a mixed text, the only kind of text then in existence (cf. Gundry, p. 159). Moreover, it is doubtful if the formula-quotations are so closely integrated with their contexts as Stendahl's argument requires: some of them are (in chapters 1–2 and 27.9–10), but others (8.17; 12.18; 13.35) are no more than appendages to the Marcan material taken over by the author, and therefore they are—when they appear without accompanying peculiar Matthean material—quotations, and nothing more. It could be argued that if the quotations integrated with their contexts require the activity of a school of interpretation to explain them, those not so integrated require the postulation of some other source to account for them. In fact, Stendahl's study of the quotations is not nearly so decisive for his 'Matthean school' hypothesis as he appears to think. Although the finished book, in its present form, does look like the product or compilation of a single individual, the view that there lies behind the Gospel a group or school of Scripture study, possibly even familiar with rabbinic methods, is very plausible, but the formula-quotations do not unambiguously point in this direction. Bertil Gärtner (*ST*, VIII, 1954, pp. 1–24) argues that the formula-quotations owe their origin to the missionary preaching tradition which employed scriptural proofs against opponents, mainly Jews: they do not point to a written or even to a continuous oral source. Lindars argues that the text-form of Matthew's formula-citations reflects the lengthy process of reworking Old Testament texts engaged in by the Church at large as it sought to answer Jewish objections against Jesus' Messiahship by showing how the Old Testament was applicable to the various phases of Jesus' career, beginning with the resurrection, and then, successively, the crucifixion, the ministry, the baptism, and pre-existence. Although he is sympathetic to the idea of a Matthean school of exegesis, he claims that the Gospel was written not by one of the exegetes but by one to whom the fruits of the school's work was known, and that the quotations employed represent the school's stock of biblical citations used orally *in its work of catechizing and apologetic* and developing textually in that work (p. 265). Catechesis and apologetic not only provide the probable origin of the Matthean quotations, but may also indicate the purpose behind the production of the Gospel as a whole.

3. THE CHARACTER AND PURPOSE OF THE GOSPEL

ORDER AND CONCISENESS

Among the characteristic features of Matthew's Gospel which may be dealt with briefly are its conciseness in narration (cf. Mt. 14.3–12 with Mk 6.17–29, and Mt. 17.14–21 with Mk 9.14–29), and its orderly arrangement. These features may have led the Gospel to be widely used for liturgical purposes in the early Church, but they do not require a liturgical (or lectionary) origin for the work. The most obvious feature of Matthew's structure is the alternation of large blocks of teaching or discourse material with the narrative sections. This is not altogether an accidental pattern. A similar formula concludes the five discourse sections (7.28; 11.1; 13.53; 19.1 and 26.1) and acts as a literary link giving continuity to the whole. It has been suggested that this five-fold structure was based on the five books of the Law, the idea being that Matthew was seeking to provide a new Pentateuch (or new Law) for the community of the Church, the new Israel (so Bacon, Kilpatrick and Benoit). Despite its popularity, this pentateuchal approach to Matthew remains questionable for the following reasons:

(i) It leaves chapter 23 out of account, and treats chapters 1–2 and 26–8 as merely prologue and epilogue respectively, and this cannot be regarded as satisfactory.

(ii) Do the five formulae really form anything more than connecting links? The author does not make obvious allusions to them; they may be quite insignificant and unable to bear the symbolic and structural strain placed on them by this theory.

(iii) There is no correlation between the five divisions of the Gospel (each consisting of narrative with discourse) and the corresponding five books of Moses; and it is not at all

certain that the narratives in Matthew are intended to be
paired with the discourses which follow.

(iv) The idea of Jesus as 'new Moses' is not so obvious as
Bacon thinks: in fact the motifs of 'new Exodus' and 'new
Moses' are used with such noticeable restraint (see Davies,
SSM, pp. 25–93) as to add no significant support to the
pentateuchal hypothesis. 'The fivefold structure cannot
certainly be held to have any theological significance, that
is, it does not necessarily point to a deliberate interpretation of the Gospel in terms of a new Pentateuch as, in its
totality, a counterpart to the five books of Moses' (Davies,
p. 107).

ECCLESIASTICAL ELEMENTS

Matthew is the only Gospel which records any specific teaching
about the Church, and it is the only one which attributes the use
of the word *ekklēsia* to Jesus. It is easy to over-emphasize the
ecclesiasticism of the Gospel: it is found mainly in chapter 18 and
16.17–19, with traces in 9.35–10.45. The Church is represented as
having developed a discipline and organization: both of these
factors suggest that one of the influences to which the Matthean
church was open was that of sectarianism, similar to that evidenced
in the Qumran literature. Rabbinic or synagogue influence is
present also. 'To claim that there was anything like a capture of
the Matthean church by Qumran so that it thereby became
institutionalized under the peculiarly potent impact of the Essenes
after A.D. 68 is to outrun the evidence' (Davies, *SSM*, p. 255).

JEWISH CHARACTER

The most immediately striking characteristic of Matthew's Gospel
is what may be loosely termed its 'Jewishness'. The formula-
quotations clearly emphasize the fulfilment of scriptural prophecies in the person and work of Jesus, and are therefore
obviously intended to prove that Jesus is the goal of the Old
Testament revelation of God.

Although the Gospel contains attacks on Jewish attitudes and
practices (e.g. chapter 23), the validity of the Law is emphasized
(5.18f.) and the instructions (if not the behaviour) of the scribes
and Pharisees are to be followed (23.2f.) and the commandments
are to be kept (19.17f.): the disciples are expected to keep the

Sabbath, to fast, and to bring their offerings in accordance with Jewish tradition (6.16ff.; 24.20; 5.23f.) and also are obliged to pay Temple tax (17.24ff.). Jewish usages, ordinances and expressions are employed without explanation; e.g. 'tradition of the elders' (15.2), hand-washing scruples, phylacteries (23.5), 'whitewashed tombs' (23.27); cf. also *raca* (5.22) and *korbanas* (27.6). The Gospel sometimes recasts reports as a specifically rabbinic formulation of a question: the general question, 'Is it lawful for a man to divorce his wife?' (Mk 10.2) is given as, 'Is it lawful to divorce one's wife *for any cause?*' (Mt. 19.3), and this brings the question into the realm of the casuistical discussion on the permissible grounds for divorce.

In this connection, Matthew also adds the 'except for unchastity' clause (19.9) to the unconditional statement of Jesus in Mk 10.11, and this appears to have the effect of making Jesus advocate the position of the school of Shammai. Matthew puts on Jesus' lips sayings which expressly limit his activity to Israel (10.5, 6; 15.24). Jewish speech-formulae ('the Kingdom of heaven', 'your Father in heaven') are often found in Matthew, and the use of *dikaiosunē* to describe the conduct required of disciples is found only in this Gospel. The form of the Lord's Prayer in Matthew also suggests Jewish liturgical usage (in the address, the seven-fold petition, and in the use of the word 'debts').

It is on the basis of considerations of this kind that it is argued by many scholars that Matthew's Gospel is written from a Jewish Christian standpoint, in order to defend Christianity, to make it acceptable to Jewish-Christian readers, and to prove that Jesus is the Messiah of the Jews. The writer is regarded as being a Jewish Christian who also had at his disposal rabbinic knowledge. For instance, Kilpatrick claims that the Gospel 'came into being in an essentially Jewish Christian community, where the building up of a church life in independence of contemporary Judaism was in progress. It is significant that the attitude to Judaism displayed by the book enabled this community to take over so much from Judaism and at the same time it radically distinguished the Church from the Synagogue' (p. 123.).

Bornkamm and Barth (*TIM*, pp. 31, 63) go even further in linking the Gospel with Judaism. They maintain that the church whose views Matthew represented was still connected with

Judaism, and interpreted the Law in a Jewish manner: the
validity of the Sabbath commandment is maintained in 12.1–8
(note the addition 'they were hungry' and the omission of Mk
2.27): the lasting validity of the Law is indicated by the Matthean
transformation of 'the law and the prophets were until John'
(Lk. 16.16a) to 'all the prophets and the law prophesied until
John' (Mt. 11.13). But that the Church Matthew knows was in
real sense separated from, if not actually opposed to, Judaism is
indicated by the fact that the author again and again refers to
'their scribes', 'their synagogues' and 'your synagogues', when
speaking to Jews: see 7.29; 9.35; 23.34; cf. Kilpatrick, pp. 110f.
Indeed Kilpatrick thinks that these phrases imply a radical
separation of church and synagogue such as was intended in the
Birkath ha-Minim, the liturgical addition introduced into the
Tefillah (as the Twelfth benediction) around A.D. 85 and which
effectively formed a ban against heretics, including Jewish
Christians, or against heretics and specifically Jewish Christians.
Not all scholars are convinced of this (cf. Hummel, pp. 28–33, and
Lohmeyer, p. 335) mainly on the basis of 23.2; but, in our opinion,
the evidence is such as to suggest that the engagement of Matthew
with Judaism did not take place *intra muros* (i.e. as a dialogue,
however critical, within Judaism), but *extra muros*, as an appeal or
apologetic to the synagogue from a church that was already outside it. That situation does not preclude an acceptance by the
Church of some of the dominant modes of thought in Judaism,
such as the importance of the Law as precept and guide in action.
In short, the Jewish Christianity evidenced by the Gospel is a
Christianity which has just severed connection with the Jewish
communities, but which expresses itself in forms and categories
borrowed from Judaism. Cf. Daniélou, *Theology of Jewish Christianity*, pp. 7–11, and Goppelt, pp. 23–30.

GENTILE OR UNIVERSALIST EMPHASIS

In emphasizing (rightly, we think) the Jewish Christian character
of Matthew's Gospel, we must not forget features which, if they do
not point in the opposite direction altogether, at least force us to
wrestle with the ambiguity of the work. It has been maintained
(for example, by K. W. Clark, *JBL*, LXVI, 1947, pp. 165–172 and
Strecker, pp. 15–35) that the author (or final redactor) is a Gentile,
and that he addresses himself to the Gentile Christian Church.

The arguments for Gentile authorship do not seem to be strong: that Matthew does not reproduce some Semitic words from Mark (Mk 3.17; 5.41; 7.11, 34; 10.46, 51; 14.36) does not prove that he did not understand them, for he generally abbreviates texts, and in fact does take over some Semitic words (6.24; 10.4, 25; 27.33) as well as introducing others (1.23; 5.22; 27.6): that he uses the Greek form *Iskariōtēs* (10.4; 26.14) instead of the Semitic *Iskariōth* (Mk 3.9; 14.10) does no more than prove that he was writing in a society which spoke Greek. Clark maintains that only a Gentile Christian who confused the *tefillin* (the phylacteries of the Jews) with amulets could have written 'they make their phylacteries broad'; this is a weak argument, for it may be that here Jesus was actually attacking the show of wearing amulets, since it is not certain that the *tefillin* were called 'phylacteries' in the time of Jesus (see J. Bowman, in *Stud. Evan.*, 1959, 523ff.), and even if they were the 'making broad' could refer to the straps binding them around the head and arm. Most important of all, the hypothesis that Matthew was written by a Gentile fails entirely to explain the intense anti-Pharisaism of the Gospel, an emphasis which is especially noticeable in the redactional elements.

The arguments offered for the Gentile Christian authorship of Matthew are weak; but, on the other hand, the evidence pointing to a Gentile destination is more significant. Despite the 'Jewishness' of the book and sayings which limit Jesus' activity to Israel, there is a strain of universalism which must be taken into account. The final commission to the apostles is to 'make disciples of all nations' (28.19) and some scholars (Trilling, Blair) consider these words as normative for the understanding of the entire Gospel in terms of the lordship of Christ over the Church (the new Israel) whose mission is to all the world. The general universalist position is further deduced from significant phrases—'the field is the world' (13.38); 'this gospel . . . will be preached throughout the whole world as a testimony to all nations' (24.14, cf. Mk 13.10); and 'Go therefore to the thoroughfares and invite to the marriage feast as many as you find' (22.9). Matthew, it is argued, does not advocate the view that the gospel was exclusively intended for the Jew, as one might deduce from 10.5, 23 and 15.24: see Trilling and Nepper-Christensen. Indeed, attention has been drawn to verses which are supposed to prove that the Jews have been entirely supplanted by the Gentiles: 'the sons of the kingdom will

be thrown into the outer darkness' (8.12); 'the kingdom of God
will be taken away from you and given to a nation producing the
fruits of it' (21.43; cf. 28.15). But surely this goes too far. Does not
'all nations' (in 28.19, as in 25.32) include both Jews and Gentiles?
And the phrase 'a nation producing the fruits (of the kingdom)'
refers, not to Gentiles exclusively, but to the true and believing
people of God, without the distinction of Jew and Gentile playing
any part in it: the new 'nation' or people of God is the Church
(cf. Hare, pp. 153f.) And the puzzling words of 23.39, 'You will
not see me again until you say, "Blessed is he who comes in the
name of the Lord" ', if they do not promise the ultimate conversion of Israel, at least presuppose that there will be some Jews who
will welcome the appearance of Christ in the Parousia. It seems
clear, therefore, that the Jews are not finally supplanted and
rejected in the view of Matthew, though their specially privileged
role as 'chosen people' may be regarded as ended. The rather
stricter Jewish formulation of material taken over, the use of the
formula-quotations, and the texts which advocate the continuing
validity of the Law certainly show that the author of this book
comes from a Jewish Christian *milieu*, but the universalist strain
shows that it is not a Jewish Christianity which called in question
the Gentile Church and opposed a Gentile Christian (antinomian?) view of the Law, but a Jewish Christianity which, while
retaining the very old (perhaps authentic) tradition of Jesus'
mission to the Jews alone (see Jeremias, *Promise*, pp. 19ff.), has
transcended that viewpoint by seeing this Jesus as the living
Lord of the worshipping Church, the people of God which
includes both Gentiles and Jews, and which at the same time
opposes the narrow pharisaical (i.e. casuistical) interpretation of
the Law (cf. *FBK*, pp. 82f.).

Matthew's purpose is to provide a church with a distinctly Jewish Christian ethos a work from which to teach and preach, which
declares that Jesus is Messiah and Son of Man and supremely
Lord of the Church, in relation to whom, as the fulfilment of the
purpose of Judaism, the believer's understanding of and attitude to Law, ethics, mission and service must be formed. That
it makes its appeal to Jews is certain, but in doing so it has to
defend itself against Jewish antagonists, especially Pharisees, who
deny the very things the Church proclaims. 'Here is a body of
Christians "explaining" themselves as true Israel, *vis-à-vis* near

neighbours who spit out their name as unclean.' (Moule, *BNT*, p. 88.) The Gospel seeks to convince, to instruct and to refute.

If we view Matthew as a collection of traditions by a Christian group who may have had a definite view-point of their own and a definite defence to maintain against Jewish antagonists, but who yet were more anxious to preserve the traditions than to observe consistency everywhere, we shall perhaps be seeing it in its true light. It need hardly be added that its careful arrangement in topical sections makes plausible the idea that it was planned for the instruction of believers in their faith and its vindication. This is a manual . . ., a catechist's book: but it is for instruction in apologetic quite as much as in religion and morals (Moule, p. 91).

4. AN ANALYSIS OF THE GOSPEL

5. THE HISTORICAL ORIGINS OF THE GOSPEL

DATE AND PLACE OF COMPOSITION

The assumption that Matthew's Gospel depends on Mark requires us to postulate a date after A.D. 65, the date at which Mark is usually placed. The *terminus ad quem* is provided in the fact that the epistles of Ignatius strongly suggest acquaintance with, even the use of, our Greek Matthew, and these belong to *c*. A.D. 110–15.

Among the most important internal guides to date are the following:

(i) The words in the parable of the Marriage Feast 'The king was angry, and he sent his troops and destroyed those murderers and burned their city' (22.7) point to a date after A.D. 70, because they seem to contain an allusion to the Fall of Jerusalem. Even if it is claimed that the words reflect a fixed description of ancient expeditions of a punitive kind, Matthew could hardly have inserted them (they are absent from Lk. 14.16ff.) without thinking of the destruction of the city of Jerusalem. Verses such as 11.12; 27.8 and 28.15 suggest a considerable lapse of time from the days of Jesus.

(ii) Ecclesiastical conditions reflected in the Gospel—with a developed church order and interest (16.19; 18.17f.),

increased reverence paid to apostles (8.26; 13.16; 14.33;
16.9; 17.4, 9, 23), the existence of persecution (24.9), of
dissension (24.16), and of false prophets (24.11)—point
to a time between A.D. 80 and A.D. 100. It must be added,
however, that the nature of the Qumran community and
its organization has caused some (e.g. Stendahl, in *Peake*,
673k) to question the necessity for this relatively late
date.

(iii) The theological reflection found in the Gospel suggests that a
considerable period of time had elapsed since the appearance
of Mark: the emphasis on eschatology in Matthew has led
some scholars to connect the work with the beginning of the
second century, when there was a heightened apocalyptic
Messianism culminating in the Bar-Cochba revolt (cf. Grant,
Gospels, p. 138). This date is too late: the likely dependence of
Ignatius on the Gospel precludes a date after *c.* A.D. 100.

As mentioned above, G. D. Kilpatrick traces the influence on
the Gospel of the Birkath ha-Minim which excluded heretics (and
so Christians) from the synagogues. This would date the work
after A.D. 85. But further considerations adduced by Kilpatrick
led him to propose a date in the last decade of the first century.
These considerations are: (a) that the Pharisees appear to have
emerged as the dominant party in Judaism, (b) that the Sadducees
and other groups are entirely overshadowed, and (c) that the
discussions of legal questions in the Gospel recall those of the
Mishnah, since the niceties of the schools are introduced into
them (e.g. on divorce, and on the Sabbath). These points enable
Kilpatrick to relate the Gospel to Jamnia, where the foundations
were laid for the rabbinic Judaism of later history. But the points
made in favour of this date in the last decade of the first century
are not all convincing. For instance, Kilpatrick's claim that the
Sadducees had virtually ceased to be a party when Matthew's
Gospel was written, and that the name had become an inclusive
title for all non-Christian, non-Pharisaic Jews is doubtful: the
influence of the party and its identity did not disappear 'overnight'
after its eclipse in the period A.D. 70–85. Again, it must be borne
in mind that discussions of divorce such as are recorded in
Matthew took place before the Fall of Jerusalem in the schools of
Shammai and Hillel, and they need not be taken to reflect

Jamnia. Indeed, Allen (pp. lxxxiv, lxxxv) regarded it as impossible to date the Gospel much after A.D. 70. He claimed that the consummation of all things which takes place 'immediately after the tribulation of those days' (24.29) implies a date very shortly after the Fall of Jerusalem, and he thought it probable that the author saw in the apostolic preaching in the West, culminating in Paul's arrival at Rome, an ample fulfilment of the 'preaching of the gospel of the kingdom throughout the whole world as a testimony to all nations' (24.14). But this date has seemed to many rather early: ecclesiastical developments and the theological reflection in the Gospel have caused many to suggest the period A.D. 80–90 as the most probable date of composition (so Bonnard, p. 10). Streeter was more precise in declaring for A.D. 85, but he did not claim that that date could be mathematically demonstrated (cf. Fuller, *Introduction*, p. 114).

The place of origin of Matthew's Gospel is likely to have been either Palestine or Syria. We cannot seriously infer from the story of the flight into Egypt that the Gospel was produced in Alexandria (so Brandon, *The Fall of Jerusalem and the Christian Church*, 1957, pp. 217ff.) The majority of scholars—among them Schniewind, Schlatter, Allen and Bultmann—favour a Palestinian Jewish-Christian *milieu*. The main arguments in support of this view are as follows: (i) the Gospel is concerned to carry on an *Auseinandersetzung* with Judaism and this suggests a Palestinian setting: (ii) the Greek of the Gospel has a strongly Semitic cast: (iii) the Gospel has indications of a Palestinian circle of readers, the most noteworthy of which are the ways in which the writer takes for granted knowledge of Jewish customs (the allusion to 'whitewashed tombs' in 23.27, the Jewish garment worn by Jesus, 9.20, and to the practice of Jewish (Christian) piety, 5.23; 23.3; 24.20). These allusions would not, of course, have been unintelligible to Jews of the Diaspora, but they would have been more meaningful to Palestinian Jews. The Anti-Marcionite Prologue to Luke's Gospel affirms that Matthew was produced in Judaea and the Papias tradition that Matthew (or, at least, some part of it) was written in Hebrew (Aramaic) would point in the direction of a Palestinian milieu.

On the other hand, some of the points raised in the earlier discussion of Gentile features in the Gospel suggest that the author was at home in a Greek-speaking community. Such a community

is not an impossibility in first-century Palestine, but it may more
probably locate the writing in Syria. Streeter (*The Four Gospels*,
pp. 500ff.) chose Antioch, because he claimed that the Gospel was
compiled for the use of one of the great churches, and Rome and
Ephesus were ruled out by external evidence. Moreover, Streeter
argued that such an origin would explain the author's interest in
Peter, because Antioch had followed Peter in adopting a *via
media* between the Christianity of James (Jerusalem) and that of
Paul. (The absence from Matthew of the Pauline theological
themes is to be noted.) In addition Antioch could well be the
home of the Gospel's intermingling of Jewish and Gentile Christianity and of its haggadic expansions of Mark.

The external evidence also might point to Antioch, for Ignatius,
who was bishop of Antioch, shows early familiarity with Matthew,
as does the *Didachē*, which Streeter located in Syria *c.* A.D. 100.
There is an interesting detail offered to confirm this suggested
place of origin, namely that the *statēr* was equal to two didrachmas
only in Antioch and Damascus, and this fact seems to be implied
in Mt. 17.24–7. B. W. Bacon was equally convinced that the
author of Matthew was remote from Palestine: the use of 'their' in
describing Jewish scribes, synagogues and cities (7.29; 9.35; 11.1;
and 13.54), the use of 'that' in 9.26, 31 and 14.35 ('that region',
'that district', referring to the area in which Jesus ministered)
point away from Palestine, as do the vagueness of the geographical
references in 5.1; 8.28; 14.35; 15.29, 39; and 28.16, and the
reference to the Jews in 28.15: and the use of the term 'Canaanite'
in 15.22 suggests Syria. But Bacon went on to reject Streeter's
reasons for locating the Gospel at Antioch in particular. He
claimed that the *Didachē* is later than Streeter suggested, and that
the use of Matthew by Ignatius is not so certain as he wanted
to maintain, since the quotations made by Ignatius are chiefly
from the birth-narratives. According to Bacon, Antioch was not
the place of the Gospel's composition, but the place of its dis-
semination: the Gospel came to Antioch from some eastern
locality of mixed Aramaic and Greek speech, possibly Edessa, and
was given the title 'according to Matthew' to distinguish it from
other Gospels which were circulating in that city: later, it was
'sponsored' not only by Antioch, but by Phrygia, Asia and Rome
as well; but it was not the Gospel of the Antiochene church in the
particular sense that it originated there.

The attack on Antioch as the place of origin has been taken up by Kilpatrick (pp. 130ff.). He does admit the strength of the case made by Streeter and others for that city and, in fact, introduces further points in its favour—viz. that it was near enough to Palestine to feel the effect of any measures taken by Judaism against Christianity, and this state of affairs seems to have obtained in the Matthean church; and, as the rival of Alexandria, Antioch always displayed an independence in thought which would account for the absence from Matthew of the similarities to Philo which we find in John's Gospel. But against the claims of Antioch Kilpatrick brings significant considerations. The works of Ignatius (who, it is argued, was bishop of Antioch when Matthew was written) show no trace of that Jewish influence which is so strong in the Gospel. The pre-eminence of Peter in Antioch does not mean that he was not influential throughout Syria. (In fact, Kilpatrick argues that Peter's importance at Antioch may be over-emphasized: Ac. 11.19–26 suggests that Antioch was the centre of the Gentile mission, but according to Gal. 2.8 Peter was called to the ministry of the 'circumcision'. This, says Kilpatrick (p. 134) would bring Peter and Matthew together and separate both from Antioch.) The fact that Kilpatrick believes that our Gospel originated in a community in close contact with the Judaism of Jamnia, and because this would be truer of the Christian community in Tyre, for instance, than in Antioch, makes him propose one of the southern Phoenician cities as the place of origin. In favour of a Mediterranean coastal city, Kilpatrick suggests that since Matthew describes the Sea of Galilee as *ta hudata* he may have reserved *thalassa* for the Mediterranean. This is not a strong argument; nor is the evidence adduced from the word 'Canaanite' in 15.22 decisive for a Phoenician location.

It seems impossible, on internal or external evidence, to name the precise city of origin of the Gospel: we may be content to say, with many scholars (e.g. Bonnard, Davies, Goppelt, Filson, Kümmel), that it was compiled somewhere in Syria.

AUTHORSHIP

Early tradition is unanimous in naming the apostle Matthew as the author of the Gospel. The key-witness is Papias, whose important statement has already been discussed. He declares that

'Matthew compiled the *logia* in the Hebrew dialect, and each one
translated them as he was able.' Although it is possible that
Papias meant our present Gospel, it would be extremely hard to
argue that our Matthew is a translation from any Semitic tongue:
as it stands, it was written in Greek by one who could, when left to
himself, compose good grammatical Greek; there are very few
solecisms in Matthew. Nevertheless, as Moule points out (*BNT*,
p. 89), 'it is difficult to see how the tradition of a Semitic and
apostolic original sprang up at all if there is absolutely nothing
behind it'.

We have put forward again the view that this tradition can
be adequately accounted for if we postulate a Semitic sayings-
source, identifiable, at least partially, with the material designated Q, and compiled by the apostle Matthew, the former tax-
collector. Such a person would undoubtedly have been literate
and, as a provincial employee in Galilee, would have known
Greek, as well as Hebrew and Aramaic, and probably also a few
words of Latin—and a Latinism like *milion* (5.42) could just have
slipped into his record of Jesus' words and have been retained
when the sayings were translated. Moule (*Stud. Evan.*, II, 1963,
pp. 91–9) relates Matthew's occupation to the famous saying
(13.52) about the scribe (*grammateus*) who is trained (or 'discipled': the Greek word *mathēteutheis* occurs three times in this
Gospel, but elsewhere in the *NT* only once, and it is easily
translated into a good Semitic word for a disciple–master relationship) for the Kingdom and brings out of his treasure things new
and old. These words, often regarded as the author's signature,
are usually interpreted as of a rabbinic scribe, but Moule would
have us understand *grammateus* as a 'secular scribe' or 'clerk'. 'Is it
not conceivable that the Lord really did say to that tax-collector
Matthew: "You have been a 'writer' (as the Navy would put it):
you have had plenty to do with the commercial side of just the
topics alluded to in the parables—farmer's stock, fields, treasure-
trove, fishing revenues; now that you have become a disciple,
you can bring all this out again—but with a difference." And is
it not conceivable that this was a saying actually recorded in
Aramaic by the tax-collector turned disciple? It shows clearer
signs of a Semitic base than some other parts of the Gospel.'
However this may be—and Moule admits that it is speculative
(to which we might add 'romantic')—there is no straining of

evidence in supposing that a tax-collector like Matthew could have recorded sayings of Jesus in Aramaic. Knowledge and use of this material—composed by an apostle—caused the Gospel to be called *kata Matthaion* (cf. Allen, pp. lxxx, lxxxi).

Recently Gundry (pp. 178–185) has offered a hypothesis similar to but more developed than Moule's to account for the apostolic connection of Matthew's Gospel. Noting that the mixture of LXX, Hebrew and Aramaic elements in the Synoptic *OT* quotations harmonizes satisfactorily with the tri-lingual *milieu* which is now known to have existed in first-century Palestine, and having argued for a common tradition (in the case of some quotations) behind all three Gospels which is not identifiable with Q or an Aramaic 'proto-Matthew', Gundry puts forward as the one view which will adequately meet the requirements that 'the Apostle Matthew was a note-taker during the earthly ministry of Jesus, and that his notes provided the basis for the bulk of the apostolic gospel tradition' (p. 182). The wide use of shorthand and the employment of note-books in the Graeco-Roman world, the ancient school practice of circulating lecture notes which could be used later in published works, and the later transmission of rabbinic tradition through shorthand notes support the suggestion. 'As an ex-publican, whose employment and post near Capernaum on the Great West Road would have required and given a good command of Greek and instilled the habit of jotting down information, and perhaps as a Levite, whose background would have given him acquaintance with the *OT* in its Semitic as well as Greek forms, Matthew the Apostle was admirably fitted for such a function among the unlettered disciples' (p. 183). This hypothesis is not entirely convincing—and, when Gundry goes on to suggest that the Apostle might be considered as the author of our Greek Matthew, he is obliged to regard the ancient tradition about a Semitic work by the Apostle as irrelevant or as referring to the Gospel's literary style—but it does indicate, yet again, the seriousness with which the connection of the tax-collector and apostle Matthew with the Gospel which bears his name is being taken.

To sum up the discussion: the Gospel in its present form took shape in a predominantly Jewish-Christian community which lived so close to antagonistic Judaism that it needed to understand the relation of its faith and Gospel to Judaism and the best way to

6. FORM-CRITICISM AND MATTHEAN THEOLOGY

FORM-CRITICISM AND THE GOSPEL TRADITION

A very considerable part of this Introduction has been taken up
with source-criticism in relation to Matthew's Gospel. That this
should be the first concern of the commentator is right, both from
the critical and from the historical points of view. We must first
raise questions of literary criticism about the interrelations of the
Synoptics and about the possible sources behind our Gospels
before we discuss the development of the material used in these
sources; and source-criticism was in fact practised long before the
rise of Form Criticism (German *Formgeschichte*, 'form-history'),
that discipline which is concerned with the history of the oral
tradition of the Gospel material. This method of study was first
applied by German philologists to the folk literature of primitive
peoples, and then by H. Gunkel and H. Gressmann to the Old
Testament in order to classify materials according to literary
category (*Gattung*)—fairy-tale, saga, historical narrative, song etc.
Later, Rudolf Bultmann (*HST*) and Martin Dibelius applied the
method to the study of the Gospels.

The process involves three main steps:

(i) The single, small units of tradition (*pericopai*) out of which the
     Gospels or their literary predecessors were formed must be
     separated again from the framework in which they now
     appear, and be classified according to form—sayings of Jesus,
     parables, pronouncement-stories ('paradigms' in Dibelius'

terminology), tales or miracle-stories, cult and personal legends (or rather 'stories about Christ'). Only the Passion narrative, it is agreed, took shape early as a connected account.

(ii) These forms are assigned to the *Sitz im Leben* ('life-situation') to which they relate, since 'the literature in which the life of a given community . . . has taken shape springs out of quite definite conditions and wants of life from which grows up a quite definite style and quite specific forms and categories' (Bultmann, *HST*, p. 4). According to the exponents of Form Criticism, the conditions and needs which led to the preservation and shaping of the Gospel materials (and indeed to the creation of some of it) were the requirements of the primitive Christian preaching, and not interest in or faithfulness to the biography of Jesus. The practical needs of the Christian community—catechetical, instructional, liturgical, apologetic, controversial, and so on—governed the selection and shaping of the material, and the patterns of development or modification it underwent are common to other kinds of popular literature: viz. frequent repetition imparts brevity and pointedness to pronouncement-stories, rhythm and roundedness to didactic sayings, dramatic unity to parables, and fulness of details to stories of the marvellous.

(iii) The historical value of the individual pericope is assessed on the basis of its form and the creative *milieu*. Certain forms are assigned to particular 'life-situations', as, for instance, the paradigm (or pronouncement-story) to the Church's preaching, and certain of these 'life-situations' are such as to guarantee the reliability of what is preserved in the form: for example, Dibelius assumes that, because the primitive preaching was a central activity of the early community, it was under the control of original eye-witnesses, and so the relative antiquity and reliability of the paradigms is assured.

It is in relation to this third stage in the approach of Form Criticism that the most serious limitations of the method are to be seen. The assigning of a specific form to a particular *Sitz im Leben* is not always successful, and often not agreed on by the Form Critics themselves. Frequently the *content* offers a more certain clue to the 'life-situation' than the form. Furthermore, it is

extremely difficult to see how the form in which material is
presented (save, perhaps, in the case of the parabolic form) can
be the ground on which the authenticity (or origin) of that
material can be gauged. The problem of the historicity of the
miracle-stories, for instance, is not raised by their form (i.e. by
their conformity to the style of the Hellenistic wonder-tales) but
by their substance. And in practice, the historical verdict on these
and other stories is pronounced by the Form Critics themselves on
the grounds of substance or content, that is, by traditio-historical
criticism. The quest for the 'historical' in the Gospels, being a
part of and the goal of the study of the entire history of the Gospel
tradition, involves the scholar in an attempt to assign the various
strata to their proper place in the history of the tradition:

(i)   the redaction (i.e. the material which links units) which is
      usually the creation of the evangelist (but see Dodd, *Studies*,
      pp. 1–11), and which can be detected by source criticism;
(ii) primary sources, again established by source criticism;
(iii) the oral tradition, in the discovery of which the presence of
      Aramaic traits and forms, as well as the insights of Form
      Criticism, are vitally important;
(iv) the authentic Jesus tradition, in the establishment of which
      certain criteria are employed. According to the terminology
      of Perrin (pp. 39ff.) these are: (a) the 'criterion of dissimi-
      larity'—that is, if a saying attributed to Jesus is strikingly
      different both from the Judaism out of which Jesus came and
      also from the environment out of which the early Church
      spoke, this two-fold difference will give a strong indication
      that it is genuine material; (b) the 'criterion of coherence',
      which affirms that material from the earliest strata of the
      tradition may be accepted as authentic if it can be shown to
      cohere, or 'fit in with', material established as genuine by the
      first criterion; and (c) the 'criterion of multiple attestation',
      which must be employed with great reservation, allows the
      acceptance of material (and especially motifs, like Jesus'
      concern for outcasts) which is attested in all or most of the
      sources detected behind the Gospels (e.g. Mark and Q).
      The most important of these criteria is obviously that of dis-
      similarity, but it is in itself an oddly stringent test, in that it
      would rule out as spurious any genuine insight that Jesus may

have taken over from the *OT* and also any insight of his that the early Church accepted and perpetuated. (It is interesting to observe that Perrin himself does not apply this criterion rigidly, since he freely considers that the use of the word *Abba* (Father) must be original to Jesus, even though its presence in Rom. and Gal. proves that it was also used in the early Church.) Unless it is used with very great caution, and only after other tests (e.g. the linguistic) have been applied, this criterion tends to lead to minimal results and in the direction of the undue scepticism of the Bultmann school.

In a sense, the quest for the 'authentic' in the Gospel tradition has passed the stage at which the method of Form Criticism was assumed to have produced all the answers. And necessarily so, for its answers tended to be so thoroughly negative. By and large, it was the faith of the early Church, not facts about Jesus, which emerged from the Gospels: the early Church had no interest in the biography of Jesus. And so the Gospels come to be seen as thoroughly kerygmatic in intention, and, although the *kerygma* is acknowledged to rest on historical events, the substance of these events in history is either unknowable or, even if it could be known with certainty, quite unimportant for the proper understanding of Christianity.

In repudiating the kind of historical judgments which were characteristic of the work of the more extreme Form Critics, H. Riesenfeld and B. Gerhardsson have argued that the words of Jesus (and even the narratives of his actions) have been preserved intact in the New Testament along the channels of a fixed Christian tradition (inaugurated by Jesus himself in a kind of rabbinic teacher–pupil relationship which emphasized the memorization of material) which treated them as 'holy word'. But is there any indication in the Gospels that Jesus conducted his ministry along the lines adopted in the rabbinic schools? Moreover, if there had been such a rigidly fixed tradition, the divergencies which exist in the various strata of the tradition would be impossible to explain. 'There was no degree of fixation sufficient to interfere with the editorial activity of the evangelists and their predecessors, and this activity was not confined to the exposition and application of given material' (Barrett, *JGT*, p. 10). The 'Scandinavian approach' to Gospel criticism, for all its value in compelling the recognition of the structural parallelism between much in primitive Christianity and Pharisaic Judaism, tends to over-simplify the problem of disentangling the 'authentic' from inter-pretation. (See the critiques of the theory by Fuller, *Introduction*, p. 103, and Davies, *SSM*, pp. 464–80.) Form Criticism has established its claim that the tradition of the words and works of Jesus has been elaborated, re-interpreted, even modified in the course of its transmission by the needs of the Christian community. But this is not to admit that the tradition owes its origin to the Church: the tradition about Jesus has its source in his life and work—it is not created *ex nihilo* by the community, however much it may be coloured by its needs.

The New Testament scholar must be engaged in the continuing task of isolating the original deposit of tradition from its increasing modification, and he may engage in this with hope of arriving, by way of the most serious and critical analysis, at a residue of authentic tradition. Nor is this other than we would expect. It is impossible to rule out entirely the influence upon the community and on developing tradition of eye-witnesses of the historical events: and it cannot be assumed that the early Church was totally uninterested in the facts of Jesus' life. The Gospels are evangelistic and apologetic in purpose, but do they not also suggest (so Moule, *NTE*, pp. 175ff.) that 'a vital element in evangelism is the plain story of what happened in the ministry of Jesus'? How else can we explain many of the features of the tradition? Though written more than a quarter of a century ago, the words of William Manson retain their forcefulness.

> If the tradition had unfolded itself smoothly out of the mind or theology of the Church, how do we explain the presence in it of enigmatic words such as the saying in Mt. 11. 12 about the King-dom of heaven suffering violence, which the Church probably did not understand, . . . or of utterances like Mk 10. 18, which by seeming to limit the perfect goodness of Jesus must have been offensive to its Christology, or of ethical principles like 'Resist not evil' and 'Love your enemies', which certainly were not any mere overflow of the Church's moral life? To these features may be added the frank revelations which the tradition offers on such points as the denial of Christ by Peter or the rebukes administered by Jesus to self-seeking and worldly apostles. Such things do not look like inventions of the Church in the interest of warning its

> members against infidelity, but suggest the presence to the
> Church's mind of a tradition which was not of its own making,
> but which was objectively given to it.   (*Jesus*, pp. 28–9)

In the era of the 'new' or 'resumed' quest for the historical Jesus
most if not all the points mentioned by Manson, and a very great
deal more, would be adjudged as belonging to the authentic Jesus
tradition. The amount so acknowledged by Fuller (*Introduction*,
pp. 99–102) is striking, and is largely based on traditio-historical
criticism rather than on the sceptical assumptions of the form-
critical method. Such criticism involves the application of the
main criteria already mentioned—literary, linguistic, historical
(and this includes the immensely valuable insights provided by
DSS into the state of sectarian Judaism), together with the search
for evidences of theological editing of tradition by the evangelists.
Of these, the one which has been receiving most attention
recently and which is of very great interest in connection with
Matthew's Gospel, is the last mentioned—the investigation of the
theological presuppositions and interests of the authors of the
various Gospels. To this we now turn in the last part of our
Introduction.

MATTHEAN THEOLOGY

The Evangelists as Authors

The study of the editing of traditional material, which is a development of the approach of Form Criticism, and which, incidentally,
lends strong support to the hypotheses of Mark's priority and the
existence of a sayings source Q, is called *Redaktionsgeschichte*: it has
been demonstrated in H. Conzelmann's work on Luke (*The
Theology of St Luke*, 1960), in W. Marxsen's commentary on Mark
(*Der Evangelist Markus*, 2nd ed. 1959), and in the important
composite work of G. Bornkamm, G. Barth and H. J. Held,
Tradition and Interpretation in Matthew, 1963.

Words by Bornkamm from the introduction to the last-mentioned book indicate clearly the importance of this development
of the form-critical method.

> It belongs to the established conclusions of Synoptic research that
> the first three evangelists were, in the first place, collectors and
> editors of traditions handed on to them. . . . This is true in spite
> of the fact that the first three Gospels are documents expressing

a definite, though in each case very different, theology, which
gives to each of them, without detriment to what they have in
common, a more or less consistently and systematically developed
theme, which makes it possible to recognize as their background,
different communities with their particular problems and views.
. . . The Synoptic writers show—all three, and each in his own
special way—by their editing and construction, by their selection,
inclusion and omission, and not least by what at first sight appears
an insignificant, but on closer examination is seen to be a characteristic treatment of the traditional material, that they are by no
means mere collectors and handers-on of the tradition, but are
also interpreters of it (p. 11).

Thus we must think of 'Matthew' as, in a real sense, an author,
leaving his own impress on the material with which he worked,
partly by direct modification, and partly by the way in which he
arranged or combined different pieces of tradition.

This can be seen from his handling of some of the stories he
found in Mark. When Mark relates the story of Jesus walking on
the lake (Mk 6.45–52), he probably intends this to be an illustration of Jesus' authority and glory, demonstrating the eschatological
power of God and the fulfilment of the Old Testament. Matthew
(14.22–33) adds that Peter also walks on the water, but is overcome with fear and is in danger of sinking, and that Jesus rebukes
him for his 'little faith'. This addition not only focuses attention on
Peter (a characteristic of Matthew's Gospel) but gives to the
story a parenetical character: when in distress, a man must look to
Jesus. Again, in the story of the storm on the lake (Mk 4.35–41)
Jesus, as cosmic Lord, displays his power over elemental forces;
but Matthew (8.23–7) modifies this meaning by placing the event
after his sayings about discipleship. The word 'follow' (*akoloutheō*)
links the miracle and the preceding sayings, cf. verses 19, 22 and
23. 'He (Matthew) is the first to interpret the journey of the
disciples with Jesus in the storm and the stilling of the storm with
reference to discipleship, and that means with reference to the
little ship of the Church' (*TIM*, p. 55). The prayer of the disciples
is to the 'Lord', a divine predicate of majesty (not 'teacher', as in
Mark, or 'master', as in Luke); and the fearful group is accused of
having 'little faith' (a favourite theme of Matthew's) before the
miracle occurs. The story becomes, in Matthew's hand, a description of the risks awaiting thoughtless discipleship and of the

reward given to absolute trust and confidence in Christ, whose authority subdues demonic powers. 'The story becomes a kerygmatic paradigm of the danger and glory of discipleship' (Bornkamm, *TIM*, p. 57).

Form as the Vehicle of Theology

The use made by Matthew of the healing miracle stories in Mark's Gospel is also instructive. The stylistic traits (as the Form Critics, especially Bultmann, list them) are found much less frequently in Matthew. The amount of introductory and concluding descriptive material is strikingly compressed: secondary people and secondary actions are omitted: the conversation between Jesus and the person seeking healing tends to become the focus of meaning, and so gives prominence to the rôle of faith: formal expressions and catch-word connections within the story appear to a greater extent than in Mark. H. J. Held discovers these characteristics in the healing of the leper (Mt. 8.2–4), in the healing of the woman who suffered from a haemorrhage (9.20–2) and in the healing of the blind men (9.27–31); see *TIM*, pp. 213–25. He also argues that they are present in the other miracle stories of the Gospel as well. His assessment of their significance is that 'the form of the healing miracle in Matthew's Gospel corresponds most closely therefore to the paradigm . . .' (*TIM*, p. 242). The emphasis falls on instruction rather than on wonder-working, and Held goes on to suggest that the omission of Mk 7.31–7 and 8.22–6 by Matthew is due to the fact that these two stories are simply wonders, without points of departure for a theological interpretation.

'The miracles', says Held (*TIM*, p. 210), 'are not important for their own sakes, but by reason of the message they contain.' And that instruction for the Church is concerned with three main themes.

(i) Most obviously, there is a message conveyed on the nature of faith; cf. Mt. 8.13; 9.22; and 15.28.

(ii) In the case of the healing of the paralytic (9.2–7) and the exorcism of the Gadarene demoniac (8.28–34)—and perhaps in the case of the healing of Peter's mother-in-law, where, in relation to the words of 8.16–17, Jesus is presented as fulfilling prophetic prediction—the miracle story is concerned with Christology. In the former, the usual elements of a miracle narrative are omitted or made ancillary to the saying about the sin-forgiving power of the Son of Man. That this is what the writer is really concerned about is shown by the conclusion of the story (9.8) in which the catchword 'authority' (*exousia*) is taken up from verse 6: the conclusion (the words of which in Mark are not connected with the controversy which forms the central part of the story) is made to serve the theme of the central section; and the glorifying of God no longer refers so much to the miracle as to the power of Jesus to forgive sins. In the case of the expulsion of the demons from the Gadarene, Matthew (unlike Mark) attaches little or no importance to the person healed, and shows little interest in the actual healing and the man's desire to follow Jesus: it is the person and mission of Jesus on which attention is focussed. Matthew passes by the words of adjuration (Mk 5.7), and puts a Christological statement on the lips of the demons to the effect that Jesus has come to deliver them to the judgment of torment before the 'time', i.e. before the final inbursting of the rule of God. That a Christological interest in Jesus—as subduer of demons—is found in Mark too is undeniable, but in Matthew there seems to be an almost exclusive concentration on the Christological element in this particular narrative.

(iii) The feedings, the healing of the epileptic, and the calming of the storm and the walking on the water (see above, p. 61) are determined by the theme of discipleship: abiding illustrative instruction is derived from the reported events of the past in which the rôle of the disciples as mediating between Jesus and his actions and the crowds is important.

If the miracle stories are re-narrated by Matthew for the instruction of the Church in the nature of faith and discipleship and on the person of Christ, this theological re-forming of the narratives suggests that the evangelist's primary purpose in writing or compiling this Gospel was catechetical—a view at which we arrived earlier in this Introduction.

Christology in Matthew's Gospel

An interesting, though brief, attempt to illustrate the development
of the Matthean Christology over the Marcan was recently made
by G. M. Styler (*NTS*, x, 1963–4, pp. 398–409, esp. 404–6). He
finds evidence of a desire on the part of Matthew to make the
Christology clear and explicit in passages where the Marcan
parallels leave it veiled or ambiguous. In the narrative of the
triumphal entry, he argues, Matthew elicits what is already in
Mark, but thinly veiled—that Jesus *is* the king, but makes it
clearer and central. Again, in the controversy about plucking corn
on the Sabbath, Mark's Christology has an element of ambiguity,
but when Matthew gives more prominence to the argument that
Jesus has an authority overriding that of Sabbath rules, and when
he adds a reference to the dispensation given to priests for Temple
duties and then makes Jesus affirm that 'something greater than
the temple is here', he is making Christology more explicit. Styler
refers to the Passion narrative, and in particular to 26.2, 25, 50, 53,
for evidence of Matthew's tendency to surround the figure of
Christ 'with greater reverence, with a brighter halo, and to give
him a sort of Olympian calm' (loc. cit., p. 405).

The third development which Styler detects is the beginnings
of an interest in ontology—that is, in the divine nature of Christ.
He offers three examples of this. When Mark's 'Why do you call
me good? None is good but God alone' (10.17–8), becomes in
Matthew 'Why do you ask me about what is good? One there is
who is good' (19.16–7), 'Matthew seems to be running away from
the apparent implication that Jesus is repudiating the description
"good" and any claim to divine nature', because in fact he does
believe Jesus to be divine. But even if Matthew's form does avoid
suggesting that Jesus was not 'good', there is no doubt that the
'one' who is good is God, whose commandments must be obeyed:
the commandments derive their goodness and their effectiveness
in leading to eternal life from God alone. The alteration implies
nothing about Jesus' status in relation to God. Styler's second
example is taken from the story of the paralytic (Mt. 9.1–8).
Because Matthew omits the Marcan words 'Who can forgive sins
but God alone?', it is argued that 'he wants to avoid even raising
any question that might conceivably throw doubt on Christ's
divinity' (p. 406). But is not the omission of the Marcan words due

to the fact that Matthew is concerned to affirm the presence of forgiveness 'on earth' in the Son of Man and also in the Church (cf. 18.15–20)? The conclusion of the story 'they glorified God who had given such authority to men' is admitting that the power to practise forgiveness is *not* an exclusively divine prerogative.

The third example given of Matthew's advance into ontological thought is the fact that in his special material he lays stress on the presence of Christ among his own, and especially noticeable in this connection are 18.20 ('where two or three are gathered in my name . . .') and 28.20 ('Lo, I am with you always'). Even if Styler's other examples were accepted as proving Matthew's developing interest in Jesus' divine nature—and I do not think that they can be accepted—this last example cannot be treated so simply as Styler proposes. In fact, his entire discussion seems to over-simplify the Matthean Christology. 'The continuing presence of Christ with his own' is not a pointer to the evangelist's interests in ontology—is the New Testament anywhere interested in ontology?—but evidence of his assumption of Christ's divine *function* with reference to his people. And that position is not reached by Matthew simply on the basis of developing Marcan material: it is the outcome of his distinctive view of *NT* time as divided into three epochs: the historical ministry of Jesus, the post-Easter period, and the end-time. To the first epoch belongs the appearance of Jesus in lowliness and humiliation as the obedient servant of God, acting with God's full authority, ministering in humility, and interpreting the Law according to the will of God. He is demonstrated to be the expected Messiah by his teaching and mighty deeds, and his mission on earth is to Israel. (To this period, as Matthew portrays it, belong Styler's first two examples of the evangelist's interest in ontology. But do hints at Jesus' divine nature belong here at all?) In the second epoch, Jesus is the exalted Lord of the community (*ekklēsia*) and Lord-designate of the world. In this epoch the Church lives as a community organized under the new righteousness, 'which exceeds the righteousness of the scribes and Pharisees': it is aware of and sustained by the continuing presence and help of its Lord (Styler's third example belongs here), and its life and mission is a preparation for the third epoch when, by judgment, the Kingdom will be established. But in the time before the end—and this is not just a brief interim filled out by the Messianic woes—

the Church is called to discipleship, obedience to the Law as
interpreted by Jesus, and to allegiance to the person and way
(i.e. suffering service) of the Messiah. This discipleship must
determine conduct now, and will be the basis for judgment at the
end.

It is indeed significant that the final judgment (with which
Matthew is so preoccupied) is passed not on Jews who reject
Jesus' message but on the Church, according as its members have
lived in obedience to the law of the righteousness of the Kingdom.
The great discourses are laying down, at one and the same time,
conditions for entry into the community of Christ and for entry
to the eschatological Kingdom of God. In presenting Jesus as
Lord of the Church—which is in the world to stay for some time,
and must therefore settle to organize its life—Matthew is struggling towards a conception of Jesus as the inaugurator of a new
(and continuing) phase of redemptive history. To the period of
promise and fulfilment (i.e. the Old Testament prophecy and the
actual ministry of Jesus), and before the end-time, there is added
the period of the Church's life and mission, over which Christ is
Lord. (Cf. *TIM*, pp. 38–51.)

Matthew's Christology is inextricably woven with his doctrine
of the Church and his eschatology. It is not discerned adequately
in terms of the simple developments which Styler suggests, and
the description of it is further complicated by the fact that from
time to time Matthew makes the narratives concerning the words
and actions of the ministry of Jesus (e.g. in the miracles) the
vehicles of teaching on the risen and living Lord's relation to the
community.

Law and Discipleship

Matthew's teaching on the Law to which all disciples are to be
obedient is striking and significant. The enduring validity of the
Law is affirmed. Because Lk. 11.16 (possibly the more original
version of the saying) suggests, if it does not explicitly maintain,
that the Law and the Prophets were valid only until John the
Baptist appeared, Matthew alters the saying to avoid misunderstanding, and the usual order 'law and prophets' is reversed. The
addition to the Golden Rule of the words 'for this is the law and
the prophets' (7.12), and to Jesus' two-fold pronouncement, 'on
these two commandments depend all the law and the prophets'

(22.40), make it quite clear that through these commandments the abiding validity of the Law and the Prophets is confirmed (cf. also 5.18).

Why this assertion of the lasting validity of the Law? Is it directed against some group within the Matthean community? Some have suggested that Matthew is opposing a Pauline group, or some ultra-Paulinists, whose *credo* was Rom. 10.4, 'Christ is the end of the law'. But I can find no convincing evidence that the Matthean church was in any way touched by the Pauline problems. Indeed, we may often be guilty—with the book of Acts!—of over-emphasizing Paul's part in the development of the early Church. His impact and influence may have been more limited than we sometimes imagine, and limited by the absence of the kind of problem he answered. The Matthean church may have been a church in which the issues confronting Paul were not being faced (where the transition from Judaism to Christianity was easier), and where the Pauline injunctions had no relevance. This may also be the situation of those to whom the Epistle of James is addressed, a group not involved with Paul's problem and answer. If so, the attempt to see Matthew's opponents as 'libertines' of the kind opposed in Jas 2 (behind whom it is maintained —wrongly, I imagine—stands the shadow of Paul) is not any more convincing. Admittedly, the 'false prophets' (the assumed 'libertine' opposition in Matthew's church) are called 'evil doers' (lit. 'workers of lawlessness (*anomia*)', and that suggests to many their antinomian character: cf. *TIM*, pp. 74f.). But the other features of this group—they confess Jesus, effect their prophecies and miracles 'in his name', and call him 'Lord, Lord'—do not necessarily, or obviously, point in that direction: rather, these features suggest a group of enthusiasts or charismatics. (It is of interest to note that the words of Mk 9.38f. on exorcisms by those outside the recognized band of disciples are not taken up in Matthew's Gospel; cf. Lk. 9.49f.) It is not against a group of 'libertines' or antinomians that Matthew directs his assertion of the lasting validity of the Law, any more than it is against such people that he writes his whole Gospel: the validity of the Law is being stressed against those who are depicted as the real opponents of Jesus throughout this Gospel—namely, the Pharisees (and Pharisaic Judaism). Were the Pharisees not in fact under-mining the validity of the Law and the Law's real intention by their emphasis on 'tradition', the scribal interpretation and application? The sect of Qumran was bitterly critical of those whom it called 'the expounders of smooth things' (CD i.18; 1QpHab ii.15 and iv.2), and these are rightly identified with the Pharisees. (In the Scrolls, 'smooth things', *halaqôt*, may be a deliberate alteration of, or play on, *halakôt*, the 'legal customs' which were the special interest of the Pharisees.) The Qumran characterization of the Pharisees is exactly right: 'as expounders of the Law, they (the Pharisees) sought those interpretations which were the easiest for themselves and offered them ways of circumventing or evading the full rigour of its provisions' (G. R. Driver, *The Judean Scrolls*, p. 94): their interest in making the Law practicable and 'livable' allowed its lasting radicalness to be lessened. It is against this Pharisaic tendency that the Matthean teaching on the abiding validity of the Law is addressed. The Sermon on the Mount, therefore, sharpens the Law, emphasizing the ethical over against the ritual (food, calendars, etc.). When the Law is thus read in an ethical key, it is clear that Jesus, in his person and teaching, is really establishing the Law as the will of God for those who seek to enter the Kingdom (5.17) and himself obediently fulfils it.

The demand for righteousness—which is obedience to the Law in its radically ethical intensity—is laid upon disciples: there can be no discrepancy between doctrine and deed. Christian obedience will be better than Pharisaism and more profound than scribalism, which failed to enquire about the original meaning of the divine demand and refused to perceive the essentials of the Law. For Matthew the essence of the Law is the commandment of love in its two-fold direction, towards God and towards one's neighbour. This becomes the principle for the interpretation of the whole. It determines the conduct demanded of the disciple (e.g. it limits the application of the Sabbath law in 12.12), and it affects the disciples' conception of God as merciful, gracious and loving (9.13; 12.7): the obligation to show love is motivated by the love which has been received (18.12ff.).

It is sometimes suggested, e.g. by Bacon (*JBL*, XLVII, 1928, p. 223) and Kilpatrick (pp. 107f.), that in Matthew's Gospel Jesus is depicted as the giver of a new Law. If by this is meant that the activity of Jesus included the proclamation of a new Law, that his preaching (and particularly the Sermon on the Mount)

becomes parallel to or antithetical to the giving of the Law through
Moses on Sinai, then it must be pointed out that the teaching
of Jesus for Matthew was *not* radically 'new'. It is significant that
Matthew omits the incident described in Mk 1.21-8, in which
Jesus' teaching is characterized as *kainē didachē* ('a new teaching'):
and as far as the Law is concerned Jesus presented no antithesis
to the Mosaic law, but rather his attitude to the Law was one of
intensifying its demand, reinterpreting it in a higher and ethical
key (see Davies, *SSM*, pp. 93-108).

If by the 'new Law' is meant that the gospel itself is understood
by Matthew as 'law', i.e. in terms of legal prescriptions, then two
things must be said to correct the imbalance suggested by this
terminology. First, the law of Jesus, his moral demand (especially
in the Sermon on the Mount) cannot be read in isolation from its
context: it is preceded (4.23-5) and followed (in chapters 8 and 9)
in the Gospel by an emphasis on the mercy of his acts. As Davies
says (*SSM*, p. 433), 'the infinite demand is embedded in infinite
succour', and that succour reaches its climax in the saving deeds
of Jesus' death and resurrection. The ultimate mercy and the
ultimate demand are inseparable in the first Gospel. In the second
place, the note of demand and regulation which results from
Matthew's codifying and applying of Jesus' teaching was not a
new thing with the evangelist: he was accenting a note already
struck in the proclamation of the Christian message, and one
found in the words of Jesus himself.

> Nowhere in the New Testament is the Gospel set forth without
> moral demand, and nowhere is morality understood apart from
> the Gospel. . . . Emphasis on the act and person of Christ in life,
> death and resurrection, central and essential though it be, is
> never wholly free from the danger of abstraction from life. The
> meaning of the kerygma for life has to become concrete. And it is
> the penetrating precepts of Jesus as they encounter us in the
> Sermon on the Mount, and elsewhere, that are the astringent
> protection against any interpretation of that person, life, death
> and resurrection in other than moral terms (Davies, *SSM*, p. 435).

Israel and the Church

Although the Gospel of Matthew is sternly anti-Pharisaic, it is
an over-simplification to say that it is an anti-Jewish writing.
Matthew, like the other Synoptists, uses the two noble words

'Israel' and 'the people' to designate his own people, the former eleven times and the latter nine. The term 'the Jews'—which in Palestinian-Jewish writings is used only on the lips of pagans—is found on five occasions, of which four (2.2; 27.11, 29, 37) occur in utterances by pagans, while the fifth is in Matthew's own reference to a tale concerning the resurrection current 'among the Jews to this day' (28.15). Twice 'Israel' is a geographical expression (2.20; 10.23), but of the nine remaining instances of the term six are found in Matthew alone (2.6; 9.33; 10.6; 15.24, 31 and 27.9) and are concerned with the mission of Jesus to Israel. Almost all of the uses of 'the people' (eight out of nine) are peculiar to Matthew and appear in the Old Testament citations and allusions or in the phrase 'the chief priests and elders of the people'. The once unique place of Israel in God's purpose is underlined by the fact that Jesus' ministry is limited (at least primarily) to Israel. Only Matthew contains the instructions to the disciples, 'Go nowhere among the Gentiles and enter no town of the Samaritans, but go rather to the lost sheep of the house of Israel' (10.5f.)—words which are taken up again in Jesus' saying to the Canaanite woman, 'I was sent only to the lost sheep of the house of Israel' (15.24). The authenticity of these words (and one *logion* may lie behind both sayings) is of the highest probability: the language has a strongly Semitic character, and the Church which since pre-Pauline times had been engaged on mission (Ac. 11.20ff.) would not have created such a particularistic saying: 'Matthew's only reason for preserving the *logion* in spite of its repellent implication was that it bore the stamp of the Lord's authority' (Jeremias, *Promise*, p. 27).

The first Gospel records the unique honour which belongs to Israel in being the recipient of God's favour: it therefore underlines all the more tragically the rejection by Israel of this visitation. When compared with Luke, in his handling of the common tradition Q, Matthew shows signs of sterner condemnation. In the healing of the centurion's servant Matthew adds 'the sons of the kingdom will be thrown into the outer darkness' (8.12): when Jesus upbraids the cities of Bethsaida and Chorazin, Matthew adds the reason for their ruin: they have seen the mighty works, but have not believed and repented, and therefore they are worse than Sodom (11.20ff.). To the words on the return of the unclean spirit Matthew alone makes an addition to draw the explicit conclusion, 'So shall it be also with this evil generation' (12.45). The explanation by Jesus of his use of parables is recorded by Matthew in such a way as to suggest that judgment has already fallen on the hearers: they are *already* rejected, and their resistance to repentance is presented by Matthew as being almost a pre-condition of Jesus' ministry (13.10–5, 34–5). The parables of the Wicked Husbandmen and the Wedding Feast make a common affirmation: the Kingdom is withdrawn from Israel and is given to 'a nation producing the fruits of it' (21.43). 'What was still in the future during Jesus' ministry has become a reality in the time of the evangelist' (Rigaux, p. 197). The discourse against the Pharisees—Jesus' last address to the people and to his enemies— draws the inevitable conclusion, 'Your house is forsaken and desolate' (23.37).

The clarity with which the first Gospel witnesses to Israel's once privileged position and her 'self-inflicted' condemnation may be explained in three ways, all of which must be considered as complementary to each other. There is, first of all, a literary consideration. Matthew wishes to present the full content of the traditions known to him, especially those which transmit words of Jesus (for example, 10.6 and 15.24): even materials which seem to have a contradictory emphasis must be presented. Secondly, there is a historical consideration. The Matthean church was concerned to know about the history out of which it came, and the evangelist offers this. The story of the events, however tragic, must be told. Nothing was more certain than that Jesus was crucified. To answer the questions 'Why?' and 'By whom?' meant that the sad tale of Israel's rejection (and especially the attitude of her religious leaders) had to be told, and, in the telling, attitudes towards the Jews which had been created by the first half-century of the Church's life found expression. In the third place, a theological factor is of great significance. The Matthean church was intensely aware of being the heir of God's promises and purposes. This is unmistakably clear in its understanding of the Law and of Scripture. The refusal of Israel, the chosen race, to receive her Messiah becomes the decisive reason for the Kingdom passing to the Church: it is the new creation built upon the foundations which un-believing Jews were unwilling to accept, but it is not an exclusive community. The apostles are to make disciples 'of all nations' (28.19), and the Jews are included in the scope of that command. This interpretation is shared by Trilling (pp. 12–14), but is rejected by Hare (p. 148, n. 3) on the grounds that, because of the following clause 'baptizing them' (*autous*, masc.), the word 'nations' (*ethnē*, neut.) must, in this instance, refer to individuals, not nations, and can therefore refer only to non-Jews. The first of these two points is based on a strict deduction from grammatical features, and, even if it is correct and inevitable, it does not lead to Hare's conclusion. Were *Jewish* individuals, on conversion, not baptised 'in the name of the Father, the Son and the Holy Spirit'? And, in any case, were not Jews (like Matthew himself) who had accepted Jesus already members of the Church? It cannot fairly be said that the rejection by the Jews of Jesus and even their rejection of the early mission of the Church means, for Matthew, that God has rejected his people permanently and completely: he has created a 'new people' of which Jews may and will form part, but *without special rôle or significance*. It is Paul who gives to the old Israel a positive significance in the history of the 'new Israel' (cf. Rom. 11.25ff.): Matthew does not accord it such a place, but, by putting on the lips of Jesus as he leaves Jerusalem for the last time the words, 'You will not see me again until you say, "Blessed be he who comes in the name of the Lord" ', he may be giving expression to the poignant hope that some at least of his people will yet recognize and acknowledge their Messiah. It is unwise to build too much on the appearance of these words: both Trilling (pp. 67ff.) and Hare (p. 154) regard this verse as evidence of Matthew's desire to show that the abandonment of Israel by God is final: 'from now on' Israel will know the Messiah only as judge. Hare is of course concerned to emphasize the ending of the 'special relationship' between Israel, as chosen race, and God, and that insight is true to Matthean theology: but, in interpreting 23.39, it does seem right to allow for the possibility that the author is implying his hope that members of Israel (as distinct from the nation as a whole) would turn to Christ and admit his lordship. Writing as he did from within a Jewish Christian Church, Matthew had grounds for this hope, and part, at least, of the purpose of his Gospel was to bring it to realization.

THE GOSPEL ACCORDING TO
MATTHEW

The genealogy of Jesus in the Gospel of Matthew is arranged in three sections (verses 2-6a, 6b-11 and 12-16), each avowedly containing fourteen names, although the third in fact contains only thirteen generations. It is possible that this artificial arrangement is to be connected with the name David, the three Hebrew consonants, of which (D, w, d) have a numerical value (by *gematria*) of fourteen $(d = 4, w = 6)$. As well as providing an aid to memory, this schematization would strengthen the already clear emphasis on the Davidic character of Jesus. In Matthew the descent is traced from Abraham through the direct royal line (David and Solomon), whereas in the Lucan genealogy (Lk. 3.23-38) the line goes back through David's son Nathan (cf. 2 Sam. 5.14) to Adam, 'the son of God'. The considerable differences between the two genealogies may be accounted for by the view that Luke provides a pedigree of actual descent, while Matthew gives the throne succession. Matthew's list of names reflects the LXX form of 1 Chr. 1-3 (and cf. Ru. 4): from Zerubbabel onwards, the names are derived from a non-biblical source, probably a family genealogy (cf. Josephus, *Vita* i.6). The naming of women (Tamar, Rahab, Ruth and Bathsheba) in a Jewish genealogy is contrary to custom: their presence may be intended to suggest the lack of convention in the processes of divine providence, and so to lead up to the strange event, the 'holy irregularity' (Stendahl; *Peake* 674d), of the Virgin Birth. The genealogy, as a whole, is an impressive witness to Matthew's conviction that the coming of Jesus was no unpremeditated accident, but occurred in the fullness of time and in the providence of God, who overruled the generations to inaugurate in Jesus the time of fulfilment, a new beginning.

1. The book of the genealogy of Jesus Christ: usually interpreted as the title to the genealogical table which follows in verses 2-16; but something more may be implied. On the only two occasions in the LXX where the phrase *biblos geneseōs* appears (Gen. 2.4a; 5.1) it does not merely introduce a genealogy, but also

mentions the process of the creation of the universe or of man.
It is therefore possible that the use of this phrase at the beginning
of the Gospel deliberately suggests that the advent of Jesus inaugurates a 'new creation', or, at least, a new era for humanity
and the world. This view would make the first words the title of
the whole Gospel and would require 'of Jesus Christ' to be understood as a subjective genitive: this, though difficult, is not impossible (cf. Mk 1.1; for consideration of the view, see Davies, *SSM*,
pp. 67ff.) **Jesus Christ:** a formula in which the title Christ
(= Messiah, the Anointed One) has become almost a proper name.
the son of David, the son of Abraham: these phrases take up
the two most important names in the following lists. The former
emphasizes the royal Messiahship (cf. Ps. Sol. 17.21), the latter
Jesus' origin within the Jewish nation and faith: he is the true
seed of Abraham in whom the promises of God are fulfilled. Luke
takes the ancestry of Jesus back to Adam, thus stressing his descent
from the universal father of mankind: Matthew goes no further
than the father of the Israelites. 'Son of Abraham' may also be a
Messianic title: the descent of Messiah from Abraham is expressed
in Test. Levi 8.15.

2. and his brothers: an addition which indicates that of the
several possible ancestors of the royal line Judah alone was chosen
(Gen. 49.10).

3. Perez and Zerah: cf. Gen. 38. Jewish tradition traced the
royal line of Judah to Perez (Ru. 4.12, 18ff.) and 'son of Perez' is
a rabbinic name for the Messiah.

5. Salmon the father of Boaz by Rahab: cf. Ru. 4.20f. and
1 Chr. 2.11. It is not stated in the Old Testament that the mother
of Boaz was the harlot Rahab, but she was a woman who figured
prominently in Jewish legend and tradition; cf. Heb. 11.35 and
Jas 2.25.

6. David the king: the addition 'the king' emphasizes the
importance of David in the table of descent. 'The royal dignity
acquired by David, and lost by his descendants at the exile, was
regained in Jesus the Messiah' (Box, p. 68).
David was the father of Solomon: Luke's genealogy passes
through Nathan, another of David's sons. A Jewish tradition
(Targ. Zech. xii.12) seems to have recognized a double line, but
Matthew is concerned to stress the royal succession.

7. Abijah the father of Asa: the better reading is 'Asaph', although king Asa is undoubtedly meant. In verse 10 'Amos' is read where we would expect 'Amon'. Schniewind (p. 10) thinks that the changes are deliberate and designed to recall the Psalmist (Ps. 73.1; 75.1) and the prophet: thus the genealogy contains, in a cryptic form, the idea of the fulfilment of prophecy and of the hopes of the Psalmist. This view, however, is based on very uncertain premises: the LXX rendering of the names varies.

16. Jacob the father of Joseph: according to Lk. 3.23, Joseph's father was Heli. If this is correct, the Matthean statement may indicate the evangelist's concern to trace the royal succession through a relative or ancestor to whom Joseph was legal heir.

This third section of the genealogy, from the exile to Jesus, has only thirteen generations. It is possible that the name Asir (1 Chr. 3.17(LXX) has dropped out between Jechoniah and Shealtiel (see McNeile, p. 3) or that the first reference to Jechoniah (verse 11) should be 'Jehoiakim', who was the son of Josiah and father of Jechoniah (1 Chr. 3.15–16).

Joseph the husband of Mary, of whom Jesus was born, who is called Christ: a reading which is supported by the best Greek texts: it presupposes the virgin birth of Jesus which will be recounted in verses 18–25. Some Greek manuscripts and the Old Latin version read, 'Joseph, to whom was betrothed the virgin Mary who begat Jesus', and the Syr. Sin. has, 'Joseph, to whom was betrothed Mary the virgin, begat Jesus'. The former reading is an attempt to make the doctrine of the Virgin Birth more precise, while the latter could be used to deny it, but only if 'begat' (= was the father of) was interpreted as referring to actual physical paternity and not, as elsewhere in the genealogy, to descent which was *legally* recognized.

17. The artificiality of the arrangement is indicated by the fact that in the second series the writer omits the names of three kings between Joram and Uzziah: viz. Ahaziah, Joash, and Amaziah, descendants of the infamous Athaliah who attempted to destroy the Davidic royal line (2 Kg. 11).

THE BIRTH OF JESUS **1.18–25**

The Matthean nativity narrative has few points in common with the Lucan account. The circumstances attending the actual birth of Jesus, the activities of Joseph and Mary, the point of view from

which the narratives are related, are all so different that most
scholars assume their independent origin and many doubt the
historical accuracy of both. A number of factors support a sceptical judgment on the historical worth of Mt. 1–2: the obvious
artificiality of the genealogy; the improbability attaching to the
visit of the Magi and to Herod's failure to discover Jesus' birthplace; the delay in mentioning the place of birth, Bethlehem.
Moreover, the emphasis on the fulfilment of prophecy suggests the
possibility that the story was being manipulated to suit, if not
created from, scriptural quotations.

It is unlikely that the origin and explanation of these narratives
should be sought in the mythological ideas of the first-century
Hellenistic world: the unmistakably Jewish atmosphere of the
Prologue suggests that its contents should be treated as examples
of Christian or Jewish-Christian midrashic activity; the literary
genre to which they belong is *haggadah*, homiletical interpretation or illustration which, by emphasizing the marvellous and
supernatural, underlines the theological significance of historical
events. The formation and use of such materials in Mt. 1–2 (and
the style, vocabulary and contents suggest the unity of the chapters
as part of the Gospel from the first) are unlikely to have been
designed to combat Jewish calumny of Jesus' origins, since those
calumnies belong to a date later than Matthew's gospel; nor were
they aimed at producing an impression on the pagan world: they
were, like all such material, products of piety and devotion within
communities of faith, either Jewish or Christian. 'They are neither
simply history, although they deal with a historic fact, the birth
of Jesus, nor apologetic or polemic, but rather confessions of a
faith, proclamations of the truth about the person of Jesus adorned
in tales about his birth. This means—to use a familiar distinction
—that they are not primarily didactic but kerygmatic' (Davies,
SSM, pp. 66–7).

18. the birth of Jesus Christ: the Greek word rendered
'birth' is that translated 'genealogy' in verse 1. The reading 'of
Jesus Christ' is well attested, but it is possible that 'of the Christ',
i.e. of the Messiah (Syr., Vulg.), is the original and correct text:
it would strengthen the author's emphasis on the Messianic motif.
When his mother Mary had been betrothed to Joseph: in
Jewish law betrothal constituted a relationship of binding obligation between the parties which conferred the status of marriage:

the marriage proper took place when the bridegroom took the bride to his home and consummated the union. If the man died before the marriage, the betrothed girl was treated as a widow. During the period of betrothal the fiancé was legally called 'husband' (verse 19) and the bond could be cancelled only by formal repudiation or divorce, i.e. the giving to the woman of a writ and the payment of a fine.

before they came together: i.e. before they began living together and before the marriage was consummated.

she was found to be with child of the Holy Spirit: the unexpected character of the conception is due to the action of the Holy Spirit (cf. verse 22). The fact that the Holy Spirit is not often referred to in the Synoptic Gospels makes its prominence here (and its even greater prominence in Luke's birth narrative) very significant. The association of the divine Spirit with the work of creation is declared in Gen. 1.1–2. Although emphasis on this theme was less characteristic of Palestinian-Jewish teaching than of Hellenistic-Jewish, rabbinic thought appears to have retained the notion of the Spirit's activity as the *re*-creating, *re*-vivifying power of the Messianic era (Exod. R. 48.102d). Just as the Spirit of God was active at the foundation of the world, so that Spirit was expected to be active at its renewal. With this background of thought, Christians could regard the entry of the Messiah upon the stage of history (an event closely associated with the renewal of the world) as having been brought about by the work of the Spirit: therefore Matthew implies that the creative power and activity of God ('Holy Spirit') is inaugurating the New Creation by the conception of the Messianic redeemer (cf. Barrett, *The Holy Spirit*, pp. 23ff.).

19. Joseph being a just man . . . resolved to divorce her quietly: Joseph was a righteous Jew: in taking action to end his partnership with Mary, he was 'in the right' before the Law (Dt. 22.13ff.): but he did not want to involve his fiancée in public disgrace, and therefore he decided to avail himself of the less strict judicial procedure whereby divorce could be effected privately and 'quietly' before two witnesses (Mish. Sotah 1.5; see D. Hill, *ET*, LXXVI, 1965, pp. 133f.).

20. an angel of the Lord appeared to him in a dream: characteristic of Mt. 1–2 are the terms 'angel of the Lord' (1.20,24; 2.13, 19) and 'dream' (1.20; 2.12,13,19,22). These features belong, not to sensational apocalyptic revelations, but to *OT* piety within which dreams were regarded as a medium of divine communication, and the 'angel of the Lord' was considered as representing the divine will (Gen. 16.7ff.; 22.11; Exod. 3.2; etc.). God intervenes discreetly, but with absolute effectiveness, in the life of a family in order to fulfil his purpose for his people.

to take Mary your wife: i.e. to take her to his home and enter into full marriage relationship.

21. you shall call his name Jesus: this verse preserves *OT* language (cf. Gen. 16.11; 17.19, etc.). The name was given at the time of circumcision, eight days after birth. 'Jesus' is the Greek form of the Hebrew *Yᵉhôšuaᵉ*, 'Yahweh is salvation'.

for he will save his people from their sins: cf. Ps. 130.8(LXX). The play on words 'Jesus' and 'shall save' (*yōšîᵉa*) points to a Hebrew original for the verses. Ps. Sol. 17 expresses the late Jewish expectation (first century B.C.) of a Davidic Messiah who would deliver his people and also purify them for judgment, but the simplicity and directness of 'save them from their sins' is missing there.

22. All this took place to fulfil . . .: this type of formula is very frequent in Matthew (2.15, 17, 23; 4.14; 8.17; 13.35; 21.4; 26.56; 27.9). Whether we regard the form and use of these citations as indicative of early collections of *testimonia* or Messianic proof texts, or of the application of primitive Christian bible study and interpretation to apologetic and catechetical needs (see Introduction pp. 35–8), it is clear that the allusions to fulfilment in the birth narratives are designed to underline the fact that the coming of Jesus is continuous with Jewish hopes: it attests the continuity of the divine purpose within history. The advent of Jesus the Messiah might be a new creation by the Spirit, but, at the same time, it represented the last stage in, and the expected fulfilment of, a long process of development.

23. Behold . . . God with us. The citation from Isa. 7.14 agrees in the main with the LXX, where Greek *parthenos* ('virgin') represents Hebrew *ᶜalmāh* ('a young woman [of marriageable age] whether married or not'). The LXX rendering does not necessarily witness to a Jewish expectation of a Messianic virgin birth: *parthenos* could be used for one who had lost her virginity (Gen. 34.3). What Isaiah meant was that the approaching deliverance of Israel would be so notable that a young woman would give to her child (an ideal king?) the name Emmanuel as a tribute to the active and succouring presence of God with his people. This name, given to Jesus, signifies his rôle in history: in him, God will be present in the midst of his people to succour, judge and save. See, further, W. C. van Unnik, 'Dominus Vobiscum', *NTE*, pp. 270–305.

24. Throughout this chapter, the divine initiative is described first, and is followed by human action and obedience.

25. Syr. Sin. has '. . . he took unto him his wife and she brought forth a son', a reading which lessens the emphasis on the supernatural element. Possibly the words **knew her not until** were omitted because they seemed to suggest that Joseph later had other children by Mary. As the text stands, however, the words reiterate the miracle (which was Matthew's concern here), and do not lend support to the idea of the subsequent virginity of Mary, although they do not absolutely deny it. But it must be admitted that, if the notion of Mary's perpetual virginity had been familiar to the evangelist or to the milieu for which he wrote, he would surely have been more explicit.

THE VISIT OF THE MAGI **2.1–12**

Unlike Luke, Matthew offers no description of the birth of Jesus: he simply affirms the fact, with a brief and general indication of the time ('in the days of Herod the king'), and passes on to clarify its meaning and significance with the help of interpretative stories. These stories are constructed around a series of testimonies (Num. 24.17; Mic. 5.1,2; Hos. 11.1), and are, despite their sobriety of tone, primarily instruments of theological statement rather than examples of historical description.

The legend of the Magi is the means of affirming (a) that the place of Messianic origin is Bethlehem, and (b) that the appearance of the Messiah (of the Davidic tribe of Judah) on the stage of history provoked hostility on the part of the leaders of his own people, but was acknowledged by representatives of the non-Jewish world; their search for and worship of Jesus prefigure the conversion of the pagan nations to Christ (cf. 8.11). Many parallels to this story and its astrological features have been noticed, e.g. the visit of Parthian Magi to Nero in A.D. 66, the astronomical phenomena associated with the birth of great men (cf. Cicero, *De Divin.* i.47, concerning Alexander), and Suetonius' report

(*Aug.* 94) on the oracle about the birth of Augustus which led the
Senate to decide that no one born that year should be allowed to
live. But a more significant parallel to this thoroughly Jewish
narrative is found in the midrashic traditions concerning the birth
of Moses. In the Midr. Rabbah to Exod. 1 we are told that
Pharaoh's astrologers were aware that the mother of the future
saviour of Israel was with child, and that they had foreseen that
this redeemer (Moses) would endure suffering through water. Not
knowing whether this saviour-figure was to be an Israelite or an
Egyptian, Pharaoh ordered that for nine months all children
should be drowned. Although Exod. R. is not itself earlier than
the eighth century A.D., the tradition embodies older material: in
its main outline it was known to Josephus (cf. *Ant.* II.ix.). It may
also be noted that the Rabbinic tradition records that at the birth
of Moses the whole house was filled with a great light, like that of
a star, the sun or the moon: see R. Bloch, *Moïse: L'Homme de
l'Alliance*, pp. 115–16. It is therefore plausible that by means of
these allusions to traditions referring to Moses (and other veiled
hints, see Davies, *SSM*, pp. 78–82) the evangelist intends to suggest a parallel between the career of Moses and that of the Messianic redeemer: Jesus is the new or second Moses, and greater
than he (Dt. 18.15). Almost certainly, the story which forms the
main part of this chapter emerged from Jewish-Christian circles
in which the use of *midrashim* was common and their purpose well
understood (cf. McNeile, p. 23).

   1. when Jesus was born in Bethlehem of Judea: there was
a Bethlehem in Galilee, 7 miles NW. of Nazareth, but the town
indicated here is a few miles south of Jerusalem, the 'city of
David' and his birthplace.

in the days of Herod the king: i.e. Herod the Great (born 73
B.C.), who became governor of Galilee in 47 B.C. and was named
'King of Judea' in 40 B.C. by the Roman Senate. Among the
building works which were a feature of his reign (and which
demonstrate his Greek sympathies), the most notable was his
commencement of the construction of the Temple in 20 B.C. He
died in 4 B.C. (For an account of his reign, see S. Perowne, *The
Life and Times of Herod the Great*, 1956.) The Lucan birth-narrative
gives more details about the exact date of Jesus' birth; see Ellis,
Luke, pp. 78–9, and G. Ogg in *Peake*, 635b–g.

wise men from the East: the magi (Greek *magoi*) were originally

a priestly class among the Persians (Herodotus, *Hist.*, I. 101, 132),
as were the Chaldeans in Babylon (Dan. 1.4; 2.2). Later the word
was used to refer to all kinds of magicians, sorcerers and charla-
tans (cf. Ac. 8.9; 13.6, 8). Here the term designates astrologers
from E. of Jordan (probably from Babylonia, or possibly from
Egypt or Arabia). There is nothing to indicate that they were
kings, but under the influence of such passages as Ps. 72.11 and
Isa. 49.7; 60.1–6 (of which verse 3 reads, 'And nations shall come
to your light, and kings to the brightness of your rising') later
Christian tradition pictured the wise men as kings—three in
number, to correspond to the triple gift. The Armenian Infancy
Gospel (from the late sixth century A.D.) names the royal magi as
Melkon (Melchior), Balthasar and Gaspar.

   2. for we have seen his star in the East: the last three
words of this phrase (*en tē anatolē*) should probably be rendered 'at
its rising'. The occurrence of the star or constellation (a common
association in the ancient world with the birth of a notable person)
has been used as a means of fixing the date of Jesus' birth, most
notably (by Kepler) with reference to the combination of the
planets Jupiter and Saturn in the zodiacal sign Pisces during
7 B.C.

   Although the evangelist does not cite the passage, it seems certain that the words of Num. 24.17 have influenced his thought:
'a star shall come forth (*anatelei astron*) out of Jacob, and a sceptre
shall rise out of Israel'. This forms part of an oracle of Balaam
(called 'from the eastern mountains', Num. 23.7) to Balak, king
of Moab, who attempted to bar the route taken by God's people
as they journeyed from Egypt. Its Messianic interpretation is
attested from an early date (in the Qumran community CD 7.19f;
1QM 11.6; 1QSb 5.27; 4Qtest 12–13 (cf. Test. Levi 18.3f., Test.
Jud. 24.1), the text probably underlies a significant Christian
testimonium; cf. Rev. 22.16; 2 Pet. 1.19; Justin, *Dial.* 106.4; 126.1;
Irenaeus, *Haer.* 3.9.2). At Num. 24.7 the LXX rendering already
implies the Messianic motif: the opening Hebrew words ('water
shall flow from his buckets'), which are manifestly corrupt, are
replaced in Greek by 'a man shall come forth from his seed', and
that enables the beginning of verse 8 ('God brought him out of
Egypt') to be understood of Messiah rather than of Jacob; see
J. Daniélou, *Theology of Jewish Christianity*, pp. 218ff. To argue
(with Box, p. 81, and McNeile, p. 22) that a star which heralds

Messiah's birth could not be derived from a star which would be
Messiah himself, is to apply a too rigid logic to the poetical
haggadic story.

to worship him: the verb *proskuneō* ('worship') is frequently
found in Matthew to describe the attitude of men before Jesus
(2.8, 11; 8.2; 9.18; 14.33; etc.) cf. also Ps. 72.11 (LXX) 'all kings
shall worship him and all nations (Gentiles) serve him'. The
evangelist is clearly hinting at the submission of the Gentiles to
Christ.

3. and all Jerusalem with him: the city is here personified,
as often in the *OT*, and this bears witness to the traditional Jewish
style of writing employed by the author (cf. 3.5; 8.34; 21.10b).
The meaning is that the entire population of the city was disturbed along with Herod.

4. the chief priests and scribes of the people: the priestly
aristocracy and the scribes (in the time of Matthew, mostly
Pharisaic) comprised the great Sanhedrin, together with the
'elders'. The latter, mostly 'lay', were not consulted because the
issue was of a theological nature.

5. in Bethlehem of Judea: the orthodox Jewish answer to the
question of Messiah's place of origin. Cf. Jn 7.42; Targ. Mic. 5.1.

6. This quotation is a typical example of Matthean adaptation
of prophetic scripture for catechetical (paedagogical) reasons in
the light of its fulfilment. The text combines Mic. 5.1(2) with
words from 2 Sam. 5.2, but differs from both M.T. and LXX.
The variations are designed to emphasize the proper credentials
for Messiahship: they stress Bethlehem as the place of the Messiah's origin to the exclusion of any other Judean city like Jerusalem: the strong negative **by no means** (*oudamōs*) has been added
for the sake of this interpretation, since it throws into relief the
choice of the **least among the rulers of Judah** to be the birthplace of the Messiah who will take upon himself the rôle of
shepherd (or prince) over Israel (2 Sam. 5.2). This last clause
establishes the association of the ruler with David's family.

9. the star . . . went before them: the patently miraculous
character of the star in the narrative makes it gratuitous to seek
a material explanation of it from astronomical science.

11. they offered him gifts . . . : the giving of gifts in the
ancient East indicated submission and allegiance (Ps. 72.10f., 15;
Isa. 60.6). The Church Fathers and Luther saw in the three gifts

given the symbols of Jesus' royalty (gold), divinity (incense), and his Passion and burial (myrrh); but it is probable that the evangelist was simply naming the most common offerings in the ancient East. All the gifts were products of Arabia, but not exclusively so.

12. This verse may reflect the structuring of the story in the interests of catechetical instruction within the church.

THE ESCAPE TO EGYPT AND THE SETTLEMENT AT NAZARETH
2.13–23

The style and structure of the three short narratives which make up this section—the flight into Egypt (verses 13–15); the massacre of the children at Bethlehem (verses 16–18); and the settlement at Nazareth (verses 19–23)—suggest that they form a literary unit. The words 'an angel of the Lord appeared to Joseph in a dream' are found in verses 13 and 19: the same verb 'fulfil' (*plēroō*) occurs in verses 15, 17 and 23; the three stories begin with sober and solemn narrative, from which anecdotal additions (for which see *Protevangelium of James*, 22ff., and *Gospel of Pseudo-Matthew*, 18ff., in *NT Apocrypha*, 1) are absent: and they end with a reflection on the theme of *OT* fulfilment in the events of Jesus' early life. The whole gives the impression of a stylized narrative, shorn of inessentials and adapted for the purposes of instruction. The episodes recalled, however, contain nothing which is historically impossible: escapes to Egypt on the part of suspect Jewish families, the violence of Herod, a settlement in Galilee to avoid the ruthless terrors which marked the nine years of Archelaus' reign over Judea, Samaria and Idumea—these are all features which agree with what is known of the period. Nevertheless, it must be said that, even if actual events are narrated here, the evangelist's real concern is not with historical exactitudes and details, but with theological reflection on the theme of *OT* fulfilment.

13. an angel of the Lord appeared: as at verse 20 and elsewhere in the Nativity stories, this intervention underlines the divine initiative in events and the necessity for obedient response. **flee into Egypt:** Egypt was always a natural asylum for Jews, especially from the time of the Maccabean struggle. The era of Herod was remembered as one in which Messianic tendencies were not welcome in Judea. (It was only after Herod's death in 4 B.C. that the Qumran community returned to its centre, which

had been destroyed in 31 B.C.) An early attested tradition in the
Talmud (Abodah Zarah 16b–17a) that Jesus brought magical
powers from Egypt and used them in his miracles hardly corrobo-
rates the historicity of this story (*pace* Box, p. 85); the tradition
was probably built upon this story, in a distorted version. See
Daube, pp. 189–92, on the haggadic tradition concerning the
sending of Jacob into Egypt.

to search for the child, to destroy him: this recalls Pharaoh's
attempt on the life of Moses (Exod. 2.15).

15. and remained there until the death of Herod. Herod
died shortly before Passover, in March–April 4 B.C. According
to apocryphal tradition, the sojourn in Egypt lasted from one to
seven years.

This was to fulfil . . . 'Out of Egypt I called my son'. The
Matthean citation of Hos. 11.1 does not reproduce the LXX
('Out of Egypt I called his children') because that would not suit
the evangelist's purpose. The form given follows the Hebrew
text, and agrees with Aquila's translation: either Matthew translated the Hebrew text, or he was dependent on a (Palestinian)
recension of the Greek text which brought it into closer accord
with the Hebrew (i.e. a precursor of the versions of Aquila and
Theodotion). The application of the text in Matthew may presuppose a tradition about an actual flight to Egypt which is being
here interpreted as a 'recapitulation' of the Exodus deliverance
of God's people in the early experience of the Messiah. It is also
possible that the evangelist is dependent for his interpretation of
Hos. 11.1 on Num. 24: Num. 24.7–8 (LXX) could be understood
to mean that God led Messiah (rather than Jacob) out of Egypt;
see on verse 2 above. The original application of the Hosea prophecy within the Church however may not have been to a Messianic exile, but to 'the deliverance of God's people from bondage,
"in Christ" (for the place where the Lord was crucified is "spiritually called Egypt", Rev. 11.8)' Dodd, *Acc. Scrip.*, p. 103. The words
could have been transferred later from the redemptive significance
of Jesus' death to the story of his early life.

16. he sent and killed all the male children: though no
such occurrence as is here described is referred to in Josephus, it
is in accordance with what we know of Herod's character (cf.
Jos. *Ant.* XVI.xi.7; XVII.ii.4). The parallelism with Pharaoh's
attempt to destroy Israel's saviour Moses (Exod. 1.15–2.10) is

obvious, and especially with that story as expanded and elaborated in Midr. Rabbah (see p. 81 above).

17–18. The quotation of Jeremiah 31.15 follows, in its entirety, neither the LXX nor the Hebrew text. Stendahl (pp. 102f.) claims that it is an independent translation from the Hebrew, but without intentional changes. The use of the quotation by Matthew does not seem to agree with its original context: the passage in Jeremiah introduces a prophecy of hope; lamentation could give place to joy, because Rachel's children will return. The application of the oracle may have been suggested to the evangelist by a tradition which identified Ephrath (cf. M.T. of verse 6), the place of Rachel's sepulchre according to Gen. 35.19, with Bethlehem; in which case, the citation is meant to stress the rôle of Bethlehem as 'the place of revealed history' (Stendahl). On the other hand, it is possible that the verse from Jeremiah was used in order to point forward to the hopeful note expressed in the following verses: the sorrow of the bereaved mothers (like the sorrow of Rachel for the Babylonian exile) was destined in the divine providence to result in great reward, the preservation of Jesus for his saving ministry (see Tasker, p. 44).

19–20. The stylized form in which the three narratives are cast is noteworthy (cf. 13–14a above).

20. those who sought the child's life are dead: cf. Exod. 4.19 (of Moses), 'all the men who were seeking your life are dead'. Just as Moses was able to return from Midian to Egypt and save his people, so Jesus returns from Egypt (after Herod's death) to Israel where he will save his people. The new Moses motif is strongly felt throughout the nativity stories (see Davies, *SSM*, pp. 78ff.) but less so elsewhere.

22. Archelaus inherited from Herod Judea, Samaria and Idumaea, with the title 'king' (this being subject to Augustus' confirmation). Ruthlessness and misgovernment led to his banishment in 6 A.D. His brother Herod Antipas ruled Galilee and Peraea. The fact that this area became a refuge and assembly-place for patriots and agitators against Rome suggests that its ruler would not have been a threat to the life of the child Jesus. **a city called Nazareth:** apart from the Gospel history, Nazareth was unknown; it cannot have been an important place (cf. Jn 1.46).

23. He shall be called a Nazarene: this 'quotation' has long been an enigma, for no such words occur in the *OT*. However, the fact that Matthew introduces the saying as having been **spoken by the prophets** may indicate intentional vagueness; what took place was entirely in accordance with prophecy. The adjective *nazōraios* is not found in the *OT*, but is used several times of Jesus in the Gospels and Acts (once, Ac. 24.5, denoting the Christian sect), as is the form (Latinized) *nazarēnos*, which is almost completely confined to Mark's Gospel. Benoit (p. 46) and Bonnard (p. 30), claim that both words have the same meaning, 'a man from Nazareth' (a designation which came to be used contemptuously), and are derived from the name of the town, in spite of the long 'o' in the first: they were transcriptions of a Galilean-Aramaic adjective *naṣᵉraya* from *Naṣᵉrath* (Nazareth). This is probably the most straightforward explanation (see Gundry, pp. 97–104). The suggestion that because Epiphanius (*Haer.* xxix.6) speaks of a pre-Christian Jewish sect named *nasaraioi* who were descendants of John the Baptist's group, and, because the Mandaeans (again associated with the Baptist) called themselves *naṣorayya* (= the 'guardians' or 'keepers' of traditions and rites, from Hebrew *naṣar*), the adjective originally designated a strict pre-Christian sect out of which Jesus and the Church emerged, is a matter of discussion (see Gärtner, *Die rätselhaften Termini*); the Mandaean term was probably derived from the Syriac word for 'Christians'. This in itself, however, may increase the possibility that the adjective indicates an early name given to Christians because of their popular identification with the Baptist's movement, itself part of a much wider baptizing movement: its contemporaries may have seen in the Christian movement 'only a widespread sect of Judaism, associated with the name of the Baptist and called *nazōraioi* on account of its peculiar tenets and customs' (Black, *Aramaic Approach*, pp. 198–200).

The name here used and that of the pre-Christian sect (*nasaraioi*) may have a connection with the ancient Nazirites. Black (*Scrolls*, pp. 70–2) suggests that Epiphanius' ascetic 'Nasaraeans' were a sectarian survival of the ancient Nazirate: and since it is probable that Mt. 2.23 contains an intentional allusion to Samson's life-long vocation as a Nazir (Jg. 13.5, 7, and 16.17 (LXX *Naziraios*); cf. also Lk. 1.35) as prefiguring that of Christ (see Stendahl, pp. 103, 198 ff., and E. Lohmeyer, *Galiläa und Jerusalem*, p. 60), there may be a reference to the original Nazirite character of the earliest Christian movement in Galilee—and it is Jesus' Galilean background which Matthew is concerned to establish.

The vague reference to the source of this statement ('spoken by the prophets') permits us to see in it also a punning allusion to Isa. 11.1, 'There shall come forth a shoot from the stump of Jesse, and a branch (*neṣer*) shall grow out of his roots': *neṣer* was a name applied to Messiah in the Targum and rabbinic literature to emphasize his obscurity and lowliness, but the noun does not easily provide the adjectival form *nazōraios*. Another explanation of the form (Box, p. 89; Lindars, pp. 195f.) sees in it a reference to Isa. 49.6, from one of the Servant Songs applied to Jesus in early Jewish Christian circles. There the word rendered 'the preserved' (usually vocalized as a passive participle, *neṣīrē* [Q're *neṣōrē*] from *nṣr* = guard; see Isa. 42.6) could be interpreted (with different pointing) as an adjective from *neṣer* of Isa. 11.1, or even as an adjective 'Nazorean' (*naṣorai*), and applied by Jewish Christian exegetes (employing legitimate Jewish exegetical methods) to Jesus. In the latter case the verse would read, 'It is too light a thing that you should be my servant to raise up the tribes of Judah and a (the) Nazorean to restore Israel.' Some support for this view is provided by the word *klēthēsetai* which, though not in the Hebrew text of Isa. 49.6, is found in the LXX (*klēthēnai*). If one adopts this view, then, already in the second chapter of Matthew's Gospel, Jesus is represented as the servant of the Lord, guarded or kept by God (cf. Isa. 42.6), but rejected by his people: and these are certainly themes set forth in this chapter concerning the Messianic child.

THE FOUNDATIONS OF THE KINGDOM 3–7

THE MINISTRY OF JOHN THE BAPTIST 3.1–12

The three Synoptic Gospels (cf. Jn 1.6ff.) begin their accounts of Jesus' ministry by describing the ministry of the Baptist (Mt. 3.1–17; Mk 1.1–11; Lk. 3.1–22), whose appearance (as Mk 1.1 says) indicates 'the beginning of the gospel of Jesus Christ'. The problem of the relation between John's work and that of Jesus is an important one in the Fourth Gospel (Jn 1.19–51; 3.22–4.3), but, of the Synoptics, Matthew seems the most concerned to give John his proper place in the plan of God (3.13ff.; 11.7–19; 14.1–2;

17.9–13; etc.). That the relation between the early Church and
John's followers remained something of a problem is clear from
Ac. 19.1–8. The activity of John is referred to in Josephus, *Ant.*
xviii.5.2, and the short account there agrees on the whole with
the information given in the Gospels: he was called 'the Baptist'
(Mark calls him 'the Baptizer'); he taught baptism and required
of his followers an ethical life: he was put to death by Herod
Antipas, who feared that his movement could lead to a rebellion,
probably of a Messianic nature. Whether John originally belonged
to an Essene community or to the Qumran sect is a controverted
issue: both were baptizing groups, and Qumran baptism was
practised in relation to a movement of repentance, of entry into
a new covenant in preparation for an impending divine (eschatological) judgment, but the baptisms were repeated, ritual
acts. Johannine baptism (like Christian baptism) was a single
unrepeatable act, and had no ritual, purificatory significance in
the *NT* (cf. Black, *Scrolls*, pp. 97f.).

   1. In those days: such a vague time reference is characteristic
of Matthew, but the words are more than a connecting link. They
appear often in the *OT* drawing attention to a period of historic interest (Gen. 38.1; Exod. 2.11; Dan. 10.2; etc. Cf. Mt. 24.19, 38; Mk
1.9; 8.1; 13.17, 24; etc.) rather than to chronological sequence: they
are equivalent to 'in those crucial days' or 'in that critical time'.
John the Baptist: the Baptist is introduced without explanation.
Luke prepares for his activity by describing, in strictly *OT* terms,
his miraculous birth, his probable entering upon the great line of
the 'Nazirs' of God (Lk. 1.15) and his dwelling in the wilderness
'till the day of his manifestation to Israel' (1.80).
in the wilderness of Judea: the regions which slope down from
the highlands of Judea to the Dead Sea. It was in this area (according to Pliny, v.15) that the Essenes, 'a solitary people', lived:
'through thousands of ages . . . a people lives on for ever, though
among them no one is born (because of celibacy), so prolific for
them is the repentance which others feel for their lives'. With this
region (slightly inland from the west side of the Dead Sea) the
Qumran site is usually identified (Burrows, p. 280).
   2. 'Repent for the kingdom of heaven is at hand': the
content of John's preaching is summarized in exactly the same
words as the initial message of Jesus (4.17). The theme of repentance is repeated in John's proclamation (verses 8 and 11), and

is obviously significant within Matthew's gospel (cf. 4.17; 11.20, 21; 12.41). In the *NT* and in eschatological contexts, 'repentance' means more than a change of mind, more than remorse. From the time of Jeremiah, the root *šûb*, which best represents the meaning of 'repent' in the *NT*, is closely connected with the covenant, and indicates a deliberate turning or returning: the term designates the return of Israel to Yahweh, i.e. to the covenant established between God and his people (see W. L. Holladay, *The Root* šubh *in the Old Testament*, 1958). 'Repentance' is the radical conversion to God of those who have broken faith with him. The Qumran baptismal rites also demanded repentance on entering into the New Covenant (1QS iii.4-6; v.13).

To the demand for repentance, John adds the apocalyptic announcement of the imminence of the Kingdom. The 'kingdom of heaven'—the Matthean equivalent for the 'kingdom of God' (indicating faithfulness to the Aramaic and avoiding the name of God)—means the establishment on earth (not in the heavens) of the sovereign rule and authority of God. It refers primarily to divine sovereignty (*malkût* in Hebrew, Aramaic *malkûta*), and only secondarily to the sphere over which the sovereignty is exercised, although it does imply a community of subjects who accept the lordship. In the *OT* the Kingdom, or rule, of God is interpreted in eschatological terms: it is almost synonymous with 'the age to come', the time of perfect righteousness and bliss. But this eschatological reference in no way implies that Yahweh is not already and always king; his present rule is accepted, the final manifestation of his rule is expected. It is this aspect of *OT* thought which is emphasized here rather than that of rabbinic Judaism within which, by the time of Jesus, the 'kingdom of God' had become something spiritualized and even planted in the hearts of men (cf. B. Berak, 4a). To declare that the Kingdom 'is at hand' means that the decisive establishment or manifestation of the divine sovereignty has drawn so near to men that they are now confronted with the possibility and the ineluctable necessity of repentance and conversion. See, further, on 4.17.

3. The quotation is from Isa. 40.3, and it is cited at this point by all the Synoptists. While Luke and Mark (who adds Mal. 3.1) refer the quotation to the whole activity of John, Matthew uses it as a description of his person, and for this purpose, the LXX text is suitable (with the simplification **his paths** for 'the paths of

our God'). With this modification and in the light of Messianic
fulfilment, the text can be made to refer to the announcement
of Christ (*kuriou*), not of Yahweh. The original Hebrew text must
be read with punctuation after 'crying',—'a voice crying: "In
the wilderness . . ." '—and in that form it was used in the
Qumran community (1QS viii.14; ix.19) to show the eschatological importance of the study of the Law by the sectarians at their
spiritual centre in the wilderness: their return to the Law prepares for the definitive revelation of God. The evangelists cite
Isaiah to announce that this revelation has taken place in Christ.

4. The description of John's dress points to the picture of a
prophet (cf. Zech. 13.4), and in particular Elijah (2 Kg. 1.8: cf.
Sir. 48.10–11 for the eschatological function of Elijah). The food
mentioned would be found in the wilderness, and it may indicate
(if abstention from flesh is implied) Nazirite asceticism.

5. The regions are personified (cf. on 2.3), and are represented
as coming to John and accepting his preaching. All the Synoptics
agree in suggesting that the Baptist's preaching aroused widespread interest and response (Mk. 1.5; Lk. 3.7, 10).

6. The baptism was administered by John or under his super-
vision and was accompanied by confession or acknowledgement
of sins, although it is not clear whether confession preceded or
followed the baptism. Baptismal rites were practised as a sign of
purification and renewal by most Jewish sects of the time, and even
by 'official' Judaism, if proselyte baptism existed as early as this time.
Even if it did, John's baptism differs from it in two ways: (a) it
was administered to Jews, and did not confer membership of the
chosen people; and (b) it was an eschatological rite anticipatory
of the coming of the Kingdom in the Messiah. The baptism practised by the Qumran sect is a closer parallel to (or preparation
for) Johannine baptism. The rites of the sect (Essene) were practised in relation to a movement of repentance characterized by
confession of sins (1QS i.24ff., v.13), on entering into a new
covenant (the sect itself being the covenanted people) in preparation for an impending divine judgment.

Although the Qumran rites were eschatologically oriented, they
differ significantly from John's baptism in that they were frequently repeated and dealt with ceremonial or ritual uncleanness
only (though they may have been popularly construed as removing sins), and they were the means of entry to an exclusive sect

which required an obedience to the Law more strict than even the Pharisees prescribed. John's baptism, as the Gospels represent it, was a single, unrepeatable act, with no ritual significance. (Josephus, *Ant.* XVIII.v.2, represents John's baptism as a rite of purification, but it seems more probable that this account has been assimilated to Jewish or Essene practice, rather than that it is to be preferred to the New Testament versions.) The scrolls of the Qumran sect add to our knowledge of the wider background of John's movement, but there is no evidence that John himself belonged to such a group: he emerged from such a *milieu*, and that is the most that can be claimed. In its unique character, its availability (as moral purification) to all, and its preparing for an imminent eschatological baptism in spirit and fire, the Johannine rite demonstrates a profound originality which may be due to reflection on the prophetic demand for purity and righteousness of life before the judgment of God (Isa. 1.16).

7. many of the Pharisees and Sadducees coming for baptism: *lit.* 'coming to the baptism' (perhaps out of curiosity). Luke makes John address his rebuke to the multitudes, but Matthew confines the address to the Pharisees and Sadducees. Throughout Matthew's Gospel the Pharisees are cast in the rôle of Jesus' main opponents, and this may reflect the situation of the community at the time he wrote when Pharisaic opposition to the Church was strong (see Hummel, pp. 12–17). The 'Sadducees' as a title may mean, for Matthew, all non-Pharisaic Jews (Kilpatrick, pp. 120f., and Hummel, pp. 18ff.), but there is evidence of the evangelist's interest in the distinctive features of Sadducean doctrine. The likelihood of members of the two parties being associated in a common desire for John's baptism is small: the combination is a literary device used to denote representatives of Israel (cf. Walker, pp. 11–16).

You brood of vipers! Who warned you to flee from the wrath to come? The words of rebuke are exactly the same in Luke (3.7), and, according to Mt. 12.34, the opening words were used later by Jesus of the Pharisees. The 'wrath' from which they try to flee is that of the final judgment (cf. Rom. 5.9; 1 Th. 1.10; 2.16; etc.), the anger of 'the day of Yahweh' announced by the prophets and now made imminent by the coming of Messiah.

8. In the coming judgment what counts is the fruit (i.e. the deeds and the character) which emerges from a total reorientation

of life through baptism. The whole disposition of life must be
consonant with taking baptism seriously.

**9. Do not presume to say to yourselves, 'We have
Abraham as our father':** neither pride in the fact of descent
from Abraham (i.e. in belonging to the true people of God) nor
reliance on religious privilege is of any avail. According to Jewish
teaching, the merits of Abraham were counted to Israel's advan-
tage: 'it is by the merits of Abraham their father that I walled up
the sea for them' (Mek. Exod. 14.15; see Schechter, chapter 12).
The uselessness of dependence on forebears and of trust in membership of the chosen race is declared again at Jn 8.39 (cf. Rom.
2.17–29).

from these stones to raise up children to Abraham: the
words for 'stones' and 'children' in Aramaic (and Hebrew) are
similar in sound and would provide a striking assonance. The
Semitic expression 'to raise up . . . from' means 'to cause to be
born from' (Dt. 18.15, 18). God may at any time raise up authentic members of Israel: it is not linked to the privilege of descent
from Abraham. Bonnard thinks that the word 'stone' here does not
simply refer to the useless objects lying about on the ground, but
contains an allusion to the 'rock-Abraham' from which Israel
had been drawn by the sovereign will of God (Isa. 51.1–2).

10. The judgment is already beginning with the appearance of
John the Baptist and the imminent coming of the Messiah. (For
the metaphor of the axe and the tree, see Isa. 10.34 and Jer. 46.22.)
The 'good fruit' brought forth (note the repetition of the saying in
7.19) is the life of sincere repentance. There may be an Aramaic
word-play within the verse on 'the root' (*'iḳḳar*) and 'hewn down
(*"aḳār*). See Black, *Aramaic Approach*, pp. 144f. for the poetical
characteristics of the Baptist's sayings.

11. I baptize you with water for repentance: at this point
in his narrative, Luke (3.15, also Jn 1.20) sharpens the distinction
between John and Jesus by mentioning that some people supposed
that John himself was the Messiah. In Mark, the Baptist simply
announces Christ and the baptism with the Holy Spirit, but
Matthew insists more on the subordination of John with reference
to Jesus: John is the preparer, the baptizer *for repentance*. This variation in the narrative within the Gospels probably reflects the
debates which must have taken place between the Christian interpretation of John's ministry and the Messianic view of John taken

by certain of his followers. The literal rendering of the words is, 'I baptized you . . .', probably an instance of the Greek aorist being used for the Semitic perfect (of general truth, or acts immediately completed). The 'you' must refer to the large circle of baptized people, not to the group of religious leaders present. The intention of the evangelist here is to compare the Johannine baptism (not the recipients of it) with Jesus' baptism.

He who is coming after me is mightier than I: 'The coming One' (a rather vague expression signifying 'Messiah') is on his way, but his appearance after John does not indicate here (as it usually does) dependence on, or subordination to, a predecessor in terms of discipleship (cf. 16.24 and Jn 1.15). He who comes after John is stronger than him. The adjective 'mighty' is used of God (Dan. 9.4 (LXX); Jer. 32.18); the noun formed from it occurs, in Ps. Sol. 17 with reference to the Messiah, the Son of David; but the emphasis there is on 'force' rather than on 'authority'.

whose sandals I am not worthy to carry: the variation between 'carry the sandals' and 'untie the thongs of sandals' (Mark and Luke) may reflect two translations of the Aramaic *šķl*; cf. McNeile, p. 29. The idea is that of the menial service given by a slave to his master.

he will baptize you with the Holy Spirit and with fire: the Messianic baptism—unlike that of John—is not a preparation, not even for the Spirit; but itself will give the Spirit. The expectation of a 'baptism' with the Spirit appears at Jl 2.28 (Hebrew 3.1) ('I will pour out my spirit on all flesh'), and at Ezek. 36.25–7; 39.29. The view that the original form of this saying was either 'He will baptize you with fire' ('with the Holy Spirit' being a Christian insertion) or 'He will baptize you with wind and fire' rests on the assumption that a reference to 'Spirit' is unsuitable to a context concerned with destroying judgment. Although it is likely that the text we have was interpreted in the light of the Pentecost understanding of 'spirit' as gracious endowment, there is no strong objection to taking the words as an accurate expression or summary of the Baptist's teaching, for neither 'spirit' nor 'fire' need be the agents of destroying judgment: both may refer to *redemptive* judgment, to refining, and to cleansing, while verse 12 refers to destruction; cf. Zech. 13.9; Mal. 3.2f. An important and close parallel to this refining and cleansing is provided

in Qumran expectation that in the final visitation of God, the
season of decreed judgment, 'God will cleanse by his truth all the
deeds of a man [i.e. either man in general or a special representative individual, the messiah], and will refine him some of the
children of men in order to abolish every wicked spirit out of the
midst of their flesh: and to cleanse them by a holy spirit from all
evil deeds: and he will sprinkle upon him a spirit of truth like
purifying water [to cleanse him] from all lying abominations and
from defilement by the spirit of impurity', 1QS iv.20, 21: cf.
J. A. T. Robinson in *HTR*, L, 1957, pp. 175–91. The baptism
'with the Holy Spirit and with fire' means the cleansing and
purification of the true Israel in the time of God's great and final
visitation.

12. The Baptist predicts that Messiah's coming will also involve
destructive judgment. The winnowing fork lifts corn and chaff into
the air, where the wind separates them; and thus the threshing-
floor is cleansed. So will Messiah separate the repentant from the
unrepentant: the former will be gathered into his Kingdom, and
the latter will be destroyed by the 'unquenchable fire' of judgment (Isa. 34.10; 66.24; Jer. 7.20; etc.). The vocabulary is Palestinian, found in Josephus and in the rabbis (cf. Gen. R.83;
B. Niddah 31a). According to Mt. 12.41; 24.31, the eschatological
sifting is carried out by angels.

THE BAPTISM OF JESUS 3.13–17

This event is recorded by all four evangelists (cf. Mk 1.9–11;
Lk. 3.21ff.; Jn 1.32–34). In Mark, John is the agent, and Jesus'
baptism does not embarrass him; according to Luke, it was an
epiphany while all the people were being baptized, and John is not
explicitly mentioned as agent; the Johannine account (which
expresses the official view of the Baptist as 'witness' to Christ) does
not affirm that the Baptist actually baptized Jesus. But Matthew
stresses this, and also emphasizes the intention of Jesus to be
baptized by John. The place of John the Baptist in relation to
Jesus must have been one of the most discussed topics in the
church of the 1st century.

13. The time reference is vague, and the location is the banks
of Jordan (not the baptistries of Qumran!). The clear statement
of Jesus' intention prepares for the dialogue which follows.

14. This verse, and the following one are peculiar to Matthew and characteristic of his interests. The words **would have prevented him** represent an imperfect of attempted action (Moule, *Idiom Book*, p. 9, Turner, p. 65)—'tried to prevent'. Apparently John somehow recognized Jesus as Messiah, and his words imply that such a one ought to baptize him with the spirit. The problem is essentially one of inferiority-superiority, not of the sinless Son of God accepting a baptism of repentance, as it is expressed in the mid-second century *Gospel of the Nazaraeans*, frag. 2: 'Wherein have I sinned that I should go and be baptized by him?' (*NT Apocrypha*, 1, pp. 146f.).

15. The answer of Jesus expresses his own and John's obligation to 'fulfil all righteousness'. This problematical phrase is sometimes interpreted as 'to fulfil (through obedience) every divine ordinance', John's baptism being one such regulation: but the word *dikaiosunē* in Matthew (3.15; 5.6, 10, 20; 6.1, 33; 21, 32) does not bear this sense, which belongs to *dikaiōma*: furthermore, this view would make of baptism a purely formal act submitted to because it was commanded. Cullmann (*Baptism*, pp. 18–19) interprets the words as meaning that Jesus, by undergoing this baptism which anticipates his own baptism of death, acquires 'righteousness' (i.e. pardon) for all. This theory involves a Pauline understanding of *dikaiosunē* and of *pasan* ('for all'), an unusual and non-Matthean interpretation of the verb *plēroō*, and it is governed by the assumed presence of the suffering Servant motif (cf. Isa. 42.1). In the context of Jesus' baptism, the word 'righteousness' refers to the righteousness of life which was demanded of those who accepted that baptism (cf. Mt. 21.32): by submitting to John's baptism, Jesus acknowledged this standard of righteousness as valid both for himself and for others, and affirms that he will realize and establish it ('fulfil') as the will of God in the Kingdom. To interpret *dikaiosunē* as righteousness of life through obedience to God is consonant with Matthean usage. See further *TIM*, pp. 140–1, and Benoit, pp. 49–50.

16. the heavens were opened: the addition in some manuscripts of 'to him' would emphasize what is already implicit—that the vision was seen by Jesus, but not necessarily by others present. **he saw the Spirit of God descending like a dove:** cf. Lk. 3.22 'in bodily form, as a dove'. Gen. 1.2 may be the source of the comparison of the Spirit to a bird brooding; cf. B. Hagig, 15a. In late Jewish literature the dove is a symbol of the Holy Spirit

(Targ. Ca. 2.12) and of the community of Israel; Philo used it as
a symbol of the Divine Wisdom. The coming of the Spirit of God—
whose activity in the present time was denied by the rabbis,
though they expected a great outpouring of Spirit in the eschatological Messianic age—upon Jesus indicates his endowment with
power, wisdom and holiness for the fulfilment of the Messianic
ministry (cf. Ps. Sol. 17.37; 1 Enoch 49.3; Test. Levi 18.6ff.).

17. a voice from heaven: this is the *baṭ-ḳôl* (lit. 'the daughter
of the voice') which was the substitute or 'echo' of the Spirit in an
age when it was not available to the people, as it had been directly
for the prophets. It was, in a sense, an agent of revelation, and
often recited Scripture for the guidance of men (see Marmorstein,
Studies, pp. 135ff.): its authority was not equivalent to that of the
Spirit because, on occasion, its guidance could be set aside. The
'voice' was heard at the Baptism and the Transfiguration (Mt. 17.5
and parallels), and before the Passion (Jn. 12.28).

This is my beloved Son, with whom I am well pleased: the
words of the 'voice' indicate the Messianic character of the event
and narrative. The form of the text here agrees with that given
in the Transfiguration narrative, but the Western text, supported
by the Latin and Syriac versions, reads, 'Thou art my Son, the
beloved . . .' (as Mk and Lk.). The variations are probably due to
the mutual influence of the parallel passages. If Matthew was
responsible for the alteration of 'Thou art' to 'This is', he may
have intended to make clear that the proclamation was a public
one, and this would illustrate the growing tendency towards
objectivity. The quotation is composite (as in similar sayings of
the *baṭ-ḳôl*): basically, the allusion is to Isa. 42.1, 'Behold my
Servant, whom I uphold, my chosen in whom my soul delights;
I have put my spirit upon him'; but the language is different,
and the *'ebeḏ(pais)* ('servant', or 'child') has been changed to
huios ('son'), perhaps under the influence of Ps. 2.7, 'You are my
son: today I have begotten you', the LXX of which the Western
text of Lk. 3.22 quotes exactly.

The source of the quotation is important for the understanding
of Jesus' baptism. If there is an echo of Ps. 2.7 (and, although the
LXX order of words is not reproduced, it is noteworthy that there
is reference to presumed Sonship in the following Temptation
story) then the point is 'Messianic (royal and Davidic) enthronement', for Ps. 2.7 is the coronation formula of Israel's Messianic

king. (There is now firm evidence from Qumran that 'Son of God' was used as a Messianic title in pre-Christian Palestinian Judaism (4QFlor 10–14): it did not refer to divine nature, but to authority given). If the words of the voice are a conscious reference to Isa. 42.1, then it suggests the 'ordination to ministry' of the Isaianic Servant of the Lord, and the whole quotation declares that the vocation of Messiah is being interpreted in such terms: the King Messiah, the vicegerent in God's kingdom, fulfils his destiny in the mission of the Servant. Lindars (pp. 139–52) suggests that Ps. 2.7 originally was applied to the Resurrection and was later linked to Isa. 42.1 in the baptismal saying because it expressed, poetically, the moment when Messiah is revealed; but is it necessary (or illuminating) to go on to conjecture a more primitive use of the composite quotation than that which stands in the three Synoptics?

The word **beloved** may signify 'only' or 'only-begotten' (C. H. Turner, *JTS*, xxvii, 1926, pp. 113ff.: cf. also Gen. 22.2 and the whole Isaac episode), in which case the uniqueness of Jesus' relationship to God is being defined (cf. Jn 1.18). It is probably best understood here as a separate designation echoing *beḥîrî* in Isa. 42.1; a 'chosen' one is the special object of love (cf. Mt. 12.18). This word and the remainder of the *OT* allusion in the saying primarily indicate that Jesus is the elect one of God.

There is little or no indication that the evangelist is aware of Jesus' baptism as a prototype for the Church's rite. The emphasis is on Jesus' manifestation as Messiah-Servant, and therefore as the one supremely endowed with the gift of the Spirit as equipment for his ministry. For the view that the essential element in the Messiahship of Jesus as seen by the early Christians was simply that he was 'the person possessed of the Spirit', see W. C. van Unnik, *NTS*, viii, 1961–2, pp. 101–16.

Since it is hard to imagine that the earliest evangelist Mark himself conflated Isa. 42.1 and Ps. 2.7 to supply the meaning of the Baptism, the presumption is that it was instinctive or traditional in the early Christian community to think of Jesus the Messiah at the same time as the Servant in whom the Lord had pleasure; for the view that the association should be traced to Jesus himself, see Manson, *Jesus*, pp. 110–13.

THE TEMPTATION OF JESUS 4.I–II

The Gospels contain two accounts of Jesus' temptation: a short
narrative in Mark (1.12–13) and a fuller form represented by
Mt. and by Lk. (4.1–13). Although most scholars argue that the
longer narrative represents a combination of Mark's information
with details drawn from the Q tradition, it is possible that the
brevity of Mark's account (and especially the enigmatic phrase
'among the wild beasts') presumes that its readers are familiar
with the longer narrative, in which case the Marcan version would
not be the point of departure for the Matthew–Luke expansion,
but itself the abbreviated form of a developed oral tradition
('abbreviated' because, perhaps, Mark was not interested in the
scriptural-rabbinic dialogue between Jesus and the devil). See on
this point, and on the whole narrative, J. Dupont, NTS, III,
1956–7, pp. 287–304.

The narrative of the Temptation derives from three Biblical
themes: (i) the temptations of Israel in the wilderness to which the
quotations Dt. 8.3; 6.16, 13 belong: (ii) the parallelism between
Jesus and Moses (Dt. 9.9–18), and (iii) the protection of God
given to the hero of Ps. 91, a figure apparently interpreted by the
evangelist as Messianic in character. The strict LXX form of the
OT quotations suggests that the narrative has been influenced
by a Greek-speaking milieu; the structure of a rabbinic controversy
in the conversation between Jesus and the tempter (with its
biblical proof-texts) may reflect an apologetic interest on the part
of the early Church in clarifying its understanding of Jesus'
Messiahship. In his confrontation with Satan, Jesus triumphs over
the temptations to which Israel succumbed in the desert, and
takes upon himself the destiny of Israel to carry it to its fulfilment;
in so doing, he proves himself to be the Messiah, the Son of God,
as declared at the Baptism: despite the attractiveness of other
methods of carrying out his mission (recognized as Satanic suggestions), the true Messiah remains faithful to the task assigned
to him by God. Although the narrative is thus theological (strictly,
Christological) rather than biographical, it certainly implies the
reality and historicity of Jesus' temptation and spiritual struggle,
else it could hardly have been composed: the form and content of
the temptations, as here given, possibly represent imaginative
dramatization, although it is not improbable that hints of Jesus'

real and continuing struggle against temporal and political ideas
of Messiahship were given at some time by him to the disciples,
from whose memory they would enter the tradition.

1. It is after the Baptism, when he was endowed with the
Spirit for his Messianic ministry (3.16), that Jesus is brought by
the same Spirit into **the wilderness**—probably the desert of
Judah, though the passage recalls that it was in the wilderness that
Israel experienced temptation, succumbed and was succoured by
God. (Lk. 4.1 expresses a rather different idea of the relation of the
Spirit to Jesus at this juncture; 'full of the Holy Spirit'.) Jesus is
brought 'to be tempted'. This is more than a proving; it is an
attempt by the Satan to make him renounce his vocation to be
the obedient Son.

2. And he fasted forty days and forty nights: Israel was
tested in the wilderness for forty years (Dt. 8.2), and Moses engaged in a fast of forty days and nights as a preparation for writing
down the words of the Law on Mount Sinai (Exod. 34.28; cf.
also I Kg. 19.8). The fast is the natural preliminary to a great
spiritual struggle.
and afterward he was hungry: or 'latterly, he was hungry'.
Lk. 4.2 clearly implies that Jesus' hunger was not experienced till
the days of the fast were ended: but Matthew suggests that the
experience of privation occurred during, or towards the end of,
the fast. The physical desire to break the vow of fasting before it
was completely fulfilled prepares the ground for the first temptation.

3. And the tempter came: the 'tempter' (here the participle
of the verb 'tempt' is used) is called 'Satan' in what are given as
the actual words of Jesus (verse 10; cf. 12.26; 16.23), whereas 'the
devil' (verses 1, 5, 8, 11) appears in passages where the influence
of the Church's vocabulary may be surmised (cf. 13.39; 25.41).
If you are the Son of God: the 'if' expresses assumption, rather
than doubt: since Jesus is 'Son of God' (3.17), let him prove his
superiority over others by breaking the vow of fasting.
command these stones to become loaves of bread: i.e. let
Jesus use spectacular magic or employ his power for the selfish
gratification of his physical needs.

4. Jesus does not reply in an autonomous fashion, but cites
the Jewish scriptures. The text employed (Dt. 8.3b) is quoted
from the LXX (which renders, as do the Targums, the Hebrew

'everything' by 'every word': see on this Stendahl, pp. 88f.) and the passage affirms that Israel's trials, even their hunger in the wilderness, were designed to teach them dependence on and obedience to God. Jesus' use of the words implies that bread, even when miraculously produced, is not his means of sustenance, but rather perfect obedience to God. Thus he triumphs as Messiah and Son of God where the old Israel (also God's 'son', and *ho anthrōpos*, Exod. 4.22; Dt. 14.1; Ps. 80.17) failed (Exod. 16; Num. 11).

5. the holy city: Matthew's equivalent for 'Jerusalem' (thus named by Luke, who makes this the third temptation). The **pinnacle** suggests some projecting turret or buttress of the Temple buildings.

6. This temptation is more subtle, for the appeal is no longer to the satisfaction of physical need, but to a testing of the divine providence in the place consecrated by the divine presence (so Box, p. 100): and the devil makes his appeal to Scripture. The quotation is from Ps. 91.11–12 (LXX), which affirms God's special protecting care of those who trust in him. In giving these words to the devil, the evangelist probably intended them to be understood as a prophetic oracle concerning the Messiah. The temptation is for Jesus to engage in miraculous self-vindication by means of a compelling proof, such as was expected of a claimant to Messiahship.

7. The force of **again** is probably explicative rather than adversative: the protection of God is assumed on the basis of Ps. 91, but that confidence is not a ground for testing God. The answer is from Dt. 6.16 (LXX)—'You shall not tempt the Lord your God', as you did at Massah, where the children of Israel put the Lord to proof and almost compelled him to provide the miraculous sign of water from the rock (Exod. 17.1–7; cf. Num. 20.1–13). As it was wrong for Israel to demand miraculous confirmation of God's presence and providence, so it is wrong for the Son of God to seek proof of his care: trusting obedience was the right attitude for Israel (Dt. 6.17) and for Jesus: but where Israel failed, the Son remains faithful.

8–9. Luke does not mention a mountain in his narrative, and seems to imply that this temptation experience was wholly mystical. Matthew gives concreteness to his description by introducing under Old Testament influence the **very high mountain.** The

Jesus–Moses theme is here taken up again. Dt. 34.1–4 describes the panoramic view over the promised land shown to Moses by God on Mount Nebo (see the LXX version for language parallels, and J. Dupont, *NTS*, III, pp. 296f. for comments: cf. 2 Bar. 76.3–4). As the Lord showed and promised to give all Canaan to Moses, so the devil shows and promises the entire world to Jesus if he will fall down in worship and submission to him. Earthly power and glory for Messiah (cf. Ps. Sol. 17) is a Satanic suggestion; the ideal of world political domination is rejected by the one who will serve God and mankind by his humble obedience and suffering.

10. The command to Satan to depart is accompanied by the quotation of Dt. 6.13 (probably from LXX, Codex A), a verse which demands of Israel the worship of Yaweh alone, and condemns (verse 14) the recognition and adoration of any other gods. Thus Jesus relives, in a sense, the experience of Israel's temptation to idolatry. Though confronted by Satan himself, whose power lies behind all idolatry, Jesus remains loyal to God: the Messiah is the faithful Son and Servant.

11. Less explicitly than Luke, Matthew, by using the historic present tense which usually implies punctiliar action, suggests that Satan has only left provisionally. Jesus experienced temptation, trial, and testing throughout his ministry, but at the outset of his mission (according to the evangelist) he firmly rejected false understandings of Messiahship based on power and compromise. **angels came and ministered:** this detail is omitted by Luke, but is found in the account by Mark (who either provided it to Matthew, or conserved it from a more developed tradition). Angelic service was probably intended to mean the provision of food (cf. the story of Elijah (1 Kg. 19.5–8)), as well as of strength and help (Heb. 1.14); in the Qumran War Scroll the angels form an army fighting on the side of God against the forces of evil (1QM 1.10, 12.8–9, 13.10).

THE BEGINNING OF THE GALILEAN MINISTRY **4.12–25**

Although the Synoptic accounts do not definitely exclude the possibility of an earlier unrecorded Judean ministry (cf. Jn 4.13, 43f.), they present Jesus' Galilean ministry as the real and effective beginning. Both Matthew and Mark state that the imprisonment of John the Baptist marks the commencement of Jesus' teaching. They agree on the place of ministry (Galilee), and on the content

of the proclamation (Mk. 1.15)—viz. repentance and the nearness
of the Kingdom. They both see as characteristic of the ministry
the calling of disciples and the activity of healing (cf. Mk. 1.16ff.);
but, whereas Mark takes time to describe his so-called 'day in
Capernaum' (Mk. 1.21ff.), Matthew is content to summarize
Jesus' activity (verse 23), and to describe the impact of this
ministry over a wide area. This sets the stage for the first discourse
towards which his narrative is hastening.

12. when he heard that John had been arrested: the
arrest and imprisonment of John (which is not described till
14.3–12) is here the reason for Jesus' departure to Galilee; in
Mark's gospel it is given as the date. Luke's account (4.14) might
imply that Jesus' work had commenced before John was arrested
(cf. McNeile, p. 43).

he withdrew into Galilee: the word for 'withdraw' (*anachōreō*)
is characteristically Matthean (2.14, 22; 12.15; 14.13; 15.21). It
may mean here no more than 'returned' to his own country, but
it may suggest (as elsewhere in Matthew) that the rejection of
God's word in one place leads to the proclamation of it in another,
and, in particular, that the rejection of John by Jews occasioned
the offer of the message to the Gentiles (note verse 15, 'Galilee of
the Gentiles'); cf. Fenton, p. 66. The population of Galilee was
exceedingly mixed (as a result of the importing of colonists and
others during the Maccabean conquest) and its acceptance of
Judaism varied, but there was a strong Jewish nucleus and a
tradition going back to the time of the destruction of the Northern
kingdom which was sufficiently rigid in outlook, and indeed so
'orthodox' and legalistic, that it could give birth to the nationalistic
Zealot movement. Admittedly there were differences between the
Judaism of Galilee and that of Jerusalem, and these differences
may have had their effects on early Christianity (though not so
significantly, perhaps, as Lohmeyer assumes, *Galiläa und Jerusalem*,
1936, pp. 5ff.), but the contrast ought not to be overdrawn (cf.
Guthrie, p. 77).

13. and leaving Nazareth: the arrival at Nazareth is not
recorded here; but there may be an allusion to a record of activity
there, such as is given in Lk. 4.16–30 (Q?), since it is only here
and at Lk. 4.16 that the name of the town is given as *Nazara* (in
Greek); elsewhere it is *Nazaret(h)*, and Souter, *Novum Testamentum
Graece*, gives this longer form at this point.

he dwelt in Capernaum by the sea . . . Capernaum is probably to be identified with the modern Tell Hum, on the north-west shore of the Sea of Galilee. The details 'by the sea' and 'in the territory of Zebulon and Naphtali' are inserted to make the connection with the prophecy which follows.

14–16. The text of Isa. 8.23–9.1 (LXX 9.1–2) is specially adapted to prove that Galilee was to be the place where Messiah should first appear. The form of the citation shows some contact (especially in vocabulary) with the LXX, but in the main it is an independent rendering of the Hebrew. The words **who sat in darkness** may have been introduced by the evangelist (from Ps. 107.10, cf. Lk. 1.69) to allude to the spiritual condition of contemporary Judaism in the region; but it is more likely that they depend on the use of the same verb in the following phrase; see Stendahl, pp. 104ff. The change from a verb meaning 'shine' to one meaning 'rise', or 'dawn' (*RSV*), is intended to suggest that Messiah *begins* his work (or even originates) in the region of Galilee. 'It is not as if the light were already shining, and then turned its beam on the dark north, but the sun actually arose there, as the prophecy foretold' (Lindars, p. 198). Therefore Matthew makes the ministry of preaching, teaching and healing commence there.

17. From that time Jesus began to preach: Matthew uses the expression 'from that time' again at 16.21 (elsewhere only in 26.16) to introduce private instruction to disciples: here it marks the beginning of a new stage in his narrative, the public preaching of Jesus.

Repent . . . at hand: Matthew concentrates on what was for him the nucleus of Jesus' message, which he has already given as the content of John the Baptist's preaching (3.2). He omits Mark's reference (Mk. 1.15) to the fulfilment of time and acceptance of the good news: the former is, in any case, presupposed in the approach of the Kingdom; but Matthew's understanding of evangelism is different from Mark's: (to the latter the term really stands for the person of Jesus, its content is Christ: for Matthew the gospel is a synonym for Jesus' teaching; see Marxsen, pp. 95–8). For the interpretation of 'repent' as involving radical conversion, a turning about, see on 3.2.

The Kingdom of Heaven—God's sovereignty exercised over and acknowledged by his people, and therefore an age of bliss

and righteousness—'is at hand'. It has been argued by C. H.
Dodd (*Parables*, pp. 43ff.) that the verb *ēngiken* here means 'has
come, has arrived and is here', and that it is equivalent to
ephthasen (*humas*) in 12.28 (on the assumption that the same
Aramaic expression lies behind the two). But on lexicographical
and exegetical grounds this view is open to criticism (see J. Y.
Campbell, *ET*, XLVIII, 1936–7, pp. 9f., K. W. Clark, *JBL*, LIX,
1940, pp. 367ff., and Kümmel, pp. 23ff., 105ff.) 'It would be misleading to move beyond the meaning that its [the Kingdom's]
powers are in operation in, with and around Jesus' (Stendahl, in
Peake, 677k). The decisive manifestation of the divine sovereignty
has drawn so near to men in the words and deeds of Jesus that they
are now confronted with the possibility and ineluctable necessity
of repentance. Yet the consummation of divine sovereignty in an
age of bliss is yet to come: the eschatology of the Kingdom is
inaugurated, not wholly realized.

18–22. *The call of the first disciples* follows immediately on the
beginning of Jesus' ministry in Galilee, though there may well
have been some lapse of time so that Jesus might get to know the
men he called. Although it is likely that the form of the story here
depends on a long period of pedagogical use, it is hard to deny
to it all value as history, as Bultmann (*HST*, p. 28) does when he
claims that it is 'a description of an ideal scene', perhaps spun
out of the metaphor of 'fishers of men'. The Synoptic Gospels
are unanimous in declaring that Jesus called his disciples: that
they would be ordinary Galilean fisherfolk seems inherently likely.

18. the sea of Galilee: i.e. the lake of Gennesaret. This name
occurs again only in 15.29; elsewhere Matthew and Mark call it
'the sea'.

two brothers: Matthew gives both the names 'Simon' and 'Peter'
at this point, indicating that Peter was a name given to Simon
later (*legomenos* = 'called'; cf. 16.18). The name 'Peter' represents
the masculine Greek word *petros*, which corresponds to the Aramaic
kēpā = 'rock', 'stone'. Both Peter and Andrew were natives of
Bethsaida (Jn 1.44), and Mk. 1.29 (cf. Lk. 4.38) suggests that
they were living at Capernaum.

19. 'Follow after . . .' is a technical description of discipleship.
'It was by following his master in a quite physical sense that a
Jewish student was trained and his life under the "yoke" was
shaped', Stendahl, in *Peake*, 677m. But Jesus' disciples were not

simply *auditors* (as at Qumran and in the Rabbinic schools); they were *collaborators* as 'fishers of men'. This image is probably drawn from the men's professional occupation (though it is found in Jer. 16.16 with reference to searching out men for judgment, and this could account for the urgency in Jesus' call for radical obedience), and indicates that the disciples will be preachers and active witnesses of the Kingdom: they will be as effective in seeking men as they have been in catching fish.

21. Together with Simon Peter and Andrew, James and John formed the group closest to Jesus (cf. 17.1–8).

he called them: the emphasis is on Jesus' action, not on the men's future vocation. The formal phrase is probably based on Christian tradition and the theme of the revival of prophetic calling; cf. Elijah's call of Elisha in 1 Kg. 19.19–21, where Elisha is taken from his work, and leaves it and his father. It is doubtful if there is any point to Fenton's suggestion (pp. 73–4) to link the Greek verb here used of 'mending' (*katartizō*) with its occurrences elsewhere in the *NT* (1 C. 1.10; 2 C. 13.11; etc.) in connection with the perfecting of the Church, and so to see an allusion here to the pastoral ministry.

23–5. *A summary of Jesus' activity* (cf. Mk 1.21ff.), made up of sentences from Mk 1–6. Jesus' ministry throughout Galilee consists in teaching, preaching and healing. The content of verse 23 reappears, in almost the same words, in 9.35—i.e. at the end of the first section of the Gospel, which includes instruction in chapters 5–7 and healing activity in 8–9. Bonnard (p. 51) claims that the literary 'summary' goes far back into the history of Israel (1 Kg. 10.27; 2 Chr. 1.15; 1 Esd. 2.1; 1 Mac. 9.14; 15.13–14), and derives from oral teaching which required material to be simplified and synthesized as an aid to memory. But their origin does not take away from summaries all their documentary value: the main activities mentioned and the general impression created are historically accurate.

23. teaching in their synagogues: cf. Mk 1.39 and Lk. 4.44 (B, sin., D). A visiting Jew was often asked to teach in the synagogue (cf. Lk. 4.16), where scriptural interpretation was a feature of the worship. The term 'teaching' commends itself to Matthew when he mentions the synagogue.

preaching the gospel of the kingdom: the message of Jesus (both in and outside the synagogue) was that concerning the

nearness of the Kingdom. Mark prefers to speak of the 'gospel',
the 'gospel of Christ', or the 'gospel of God' (Mk. 1.1, 14.15;
8.35; 10.29; 13.10), but for Matthew the content of the good
news is the proclamation of the Kingdom and its demands, cf.
9.35; 24.14.

healing . . . among the people: the healing ministry is a sign
that the Kingdom is inaugurated (cf. 11.2–6). The precision of
'every disease . . . every infirmity' ought not to be generalized:
Jesus did not heal everyone (according to the Gospels) as if he
wished to display the wonder of his power to the greatest possible
extent; rather he performed certain cures indicative of the Kingdom's presence and of his personal authority. 'The people' among
whom the healing occurs is the people of God, Israel (cf. 1.21;
2.6; 4.26). The healing of Gentiles was relatively rare (cf. 8.5–13;
15.21–8).

24. his fame spread throughout all Syria: the public report (14.1) about Jesus was the result of his healings. In the *NT*
'Syria' usually denotes the Roman province of that name, which
included Palestine (Lk. 2.2; Ac. 15.23, 41; Gal. 1.21; etc.), but it
probably means here the area to the north of and bordering on
Galilee, i.e. 'Syria' according to Jewish usage: to the Jew, this
'true Syria' did not include Phoenicia. The mention of Syria in
first place may not be accidental: it may be the place of provenance
of the Gospel of Matthew (see Introduction, pp. 50–2, and
Goppelt, pp. 178ff.).

all the sick: this general phrase (in which the 'all' ought to be
interpreted in a non-quantitative way: it refers to 'all kinds') is
defined by three specific kinds of illness, demon-possession, epilepsy
(lit. 'moon-struck', cf. 17.15), and paralysis. According to the
rabbis, sickness atoned for sin; in fact it was a sign of sin, and often
a punishment for it; cf. Sir. 38.15. 'He who sins in the eyes of his
Maker, let him fall into the hands of a physician'.

25. The crowds who follow Jesus come from all over Palestine
(cf. Mk 3.7–8; Lk. 6.17). Decapolis was a confederacy of Hellenis-
tic cities incorporated in the kingdom of Judaea by Alexander
Jannaeus and later in the Roman province of Syria by Pompey.
Although Jews would have been present there, the population
would have been very mixed (Greeks and Syrians), as it was in
Galilee. Yet there is no apparent awareness of the problem here.
Jesus' contacts with Gentiles are treated as rare exceptions later

in the Gospel; but, at this point, Matthew may be assuming that those who followed Jesus were all Jews, or he may be reflecting the Church's belief in Jesus' universal appeal.

The Sermon on the Mount 5.1–7.29

This is the first of the five great blocks of teaching which are a most striking feature of the structure of Matthew's gospel (see Introduction, pp. 38–9): the idea that this arrangement is meant to represent a 'new Pentateuch' remains questionable. The section ends with a formula (7.28, 29; cf. Jos. 4.11, LXX) which also concludes the other four blocks of discourses (11.1; 13.53; 19.1; 26.1). This suggests that Matthew regarded the chapters as an essential unity. Some of the material of the Sermon is found in Luke, notably in Lk. 6.20–49 (which begins with the Beatitudes and ends with the parable of the Builders), but also is scattered throughout the Lucan travel-narrative (9.57–18.14). In the cases where parallels to Matthew exist, the Matthean forms of the material display more the characteristics of structure, systematization, and catechetical codification, but this does not always mean that Luke is providing the original version of the saying(s). The Lucan discourse in chapter 6 has its own point of view and its own features of composition, centred around the theme of humility. Although the compilation of the Sermon here is clearly Matthean, the contents (or much of them) may reach back to very early tradition, and in places the language reflects those Aramaic poetical forms which may allow us to posit authenticity in Jesus' own teaching.

Among recent studies of the Sermon available in English may be mentioned H. Windisch, *The Meaning of the Sermon on the Mount*, 1941; A. M. Hunter, *Design for Life*, new edn, 1962; and H. K. McArthur, *Understanding the Sermon on the Mount*, 1961. The most thorough, discerning and illuminating discussion of the background to the Sermon is W. D. Davies, *The Setting of the Sermon on the Mount*, 1964: this volume investigates the place of the Sermon in Matthew's Gospel, in Jewish Messianic expectation, in contemporary Judaism, in the early Church, and in the ministry of Jesus.

1. Matthew gives the impression that Jesus left the crowds to teach his disciples (cf. Lk. 6.20), but at the end of his Sermon

'the crowds' express astonishment at Jesus' teaching (cf. Mk 1.22).
The word 'disciples' (first used here) may be more comprehensive
in its meaning than the Twelve (the call of whom is not mentioned
by Matthew till chapter 10: cf. Lk. 6.13), and may denote all
those who wished to hear the teacher's instruction. 'The mountain'
(cf. Mk 3.13; Lk. 6.12) probably refers to the hill country rising
from the W. shore of the Sea of Galilee, a region of quietness and
privacy. The suggestion that the mountain indicates a 'new Sinai',
and that Jesus is here presented as a 'New Moses' ('the prophet
like unto Moses', Dt. 18.15; cf. 1 Mac. 14.41, 2 Mac. 8.1–8) may
be implicit; but no features from the account of the giving of the
Law in Exod. 19, as they are developed for instance in Heb.
12.18ff., appear here. The reserve and tentativeness of Matthew's
use of the Exodus Moses theme causes Davies to ask (*SSM*,
p. 93) 'whether Matthew could not have been somewhat bolder
in his "Mosaism" had the idea of a New Moses played a great
part in his purpose in writing the Gospel', and to give the answer
that, 'the strictly Mosaic traits in the figure of the Matthean
Christ . . . have been taken up into a deeper and higher context:
he is not Moses come as Messiah . . . so much as Messiah . . . who
has absorbed the Mosaic function'.

when he sat down: Jewish teachers in synagogue (Lk. 4.20) and
schools sat to teach (cf. 13.2; 24.3 and 23.2).

2. he opened his mouth: a traditional formula (Ac. 8.35;
10.34) and a Semitic idiom (Dan. 10.16; Job 3.1; 33.2).

THE BEATITUDES 5.3–12

The form 'Blessed are . . .' (which gives to the sayings the name
'Beatitudes') is familiar from the Wisdom literature and especially
the book of Psalms: in the *OT* 'blessedness' is made up of personal
trust in God and of obedience to his will. (In classical Greek
literature, the 'happy' or 'blessed' man is one who takes cognizance
of the essential harmony which binds him to society and to the
world. There are only rare examples of Beatitudes in the DSS,
from Cave 4; see *RB*, LXIII, 1956, pp. 64ff.). Bonnard (p. 55)
examines the Beatitudes of the Gospels (outside the Sermon they
are found at Mt. 11.6; 13.16; 26.46, and parallels; 16.17; Lk. 1.45;
11.27–8; 14.14, 15), and discovers four characteristics: (i) they are
Christocentric: the blessedness described has its source in the
presence and activity of Jesus; (ii) blessedness is eschatological,

but not apocalyptic; (iii) it is not derived from mere resignation, but is a blessedness declared, promised and given by Christ to those who obey him with faith in spite of their present hardships and sorrow; (iv) this happiness has a 'worldly' character: it is in the midst of life and within creation—a creation restored through Christ—that happiness is found.

Luke gives four Beatitudes with four corresponding Woes, and since he gives them in the second person, which is more natural for blessings and cursings (though utterances of this type in the third person are more common in the *OT*), it may be that his version is more primitive. Matthew has Luke's four Beatitudes, but the Woes have disappeared; and he has added five more to the list: the problems created by this are discussed in the comments below. It has been suggested that verse 5 (quoting Ps. 37 (LXX 36).11) may be a gloss, and that verse 11 (the last Beatitude) may have originally belonged elsewhere: that would bring the number to seven, which is a favourite number for grouping in Matthew's gospel (cf. seven clauses in the Lord's Prayer, seven parables in ch. 13, and seven Woes in ch. 23). The first three Beatitudes recall Isa. 61.1–2, which Jesus sets out to fulfil, according to his opening declaration at Nazareth (Lk. 4.16ff.); it is not inconceivable that the Beatitudes represent part of the sermon Jesus then proceeded to preach. Dodd has shown (*Mélanges bibliques*, pp. 404ff.) that Matthew describes in his Beatitudes 'types of character which have God's approval'. It is essentially in what they are now that the blessedness of men lies, even though aspects of the divine approval are represented in terms of the 'eschatological' blessings of the Kingdom of Heaven. The promised life of the Kingdom is actualized in those who are 'blessed'.

3. Blessed are the poor in spirit: 'Blessed' (*makarioi*) corresponds to the Hebrew *'ašrê*, used as an interjection, and meaning 'O, the blessedness(es) of . . .'. The 'poor in spirit' are neither the 'poor in courage' (i.e. in 'spiritedness'), nor 'in the Holy Spirit', nor 'in spiritual awareness'; they are the *ʿanāwîm* of the *OT* (LXX *ptōchoi*)—those who, because of long economic and social distress, have confidence only in God (cf. Ps. 69 (LXX 68).28f., 32, 33; Ps. 37(36).14; Ps. 40(39).18; Isa. 61.1). The term had a clear religious connotation: the poor and afflicted saints of God (cf. Ps. Sol. 10.7). *ʿanî*, *ʿanāw* and *'ebyôn* are synonyms for this attitude of heart and mind, and the Greek *ptōchos* and *praüs* (which trans-

lates ʿānî, ʿānāw at Zech. 9.9 and Ps. 25(24).9) cannot easily be
distinguished. The phrase 'the poor in spirit' is the exact equivalent of ʿnwy rwh in 1QM xiv.7 (cf. rwh ʿnwh in 1QS iv.3), which
denotes 'the humble poor who trust in God's help'; this proves
the Palestinian origin of the phrase, but the parallelism does not
indicate a confrontation with the Qumran sect, whether in terms
of opposition or of confirmation. The 'poor' of Lk. 6.20 probably
denotes the same trusting, though afflicted, poor people; but
Matthew has made the sense explicit by adding 'in spirit'. Cf.
Hill, pp. 234, 251.

for theirs is the kingdom of heaven: the poor saints will obtain
what throughout life they desire, the establishment (? on earth)
of God's reign, when they will be vindicated. 'The Kingdom of
God belongs to these simple devoted souls, because they belong
to it, having accepted God's will as the only rule in their lives.
As they submit themselves to the obligations of the Kingdom, so
they become heirs of its privileges' (Manson, *Sayings*, p. 47).

4. Blessed are those who mourn: cf. Isa. 61.2-3. Luke has
'Blessed are you that weep now, for you shall laugh' (6.21): while
this may have been softened in the Matthean (and therefore
secondary) version, the fact that Matthew has *pentheō* (derived
from LXX of Isa. 61.2-3), which Luke also uses in his corresponding Woe (6.25), could argue in favour of Matthew's originality.
The Matthean and Lucan Beatitudes, when taken together, would
form a *parallelismus membrorum* (cf. Black, *Aramaic Approach*, p. 157).
'Those who mourn' are the oppressed, the afflicted because of the
humiliation of Israel.

for they shall be comforted: in the *OT* and later Judaism,
affliction and consolation go together; cf. Isa. 61.2, where the LXX
uses the same verb, *parakaleō*. God promises his succour to those
who are oppressed and 'look for the consolation of Israel' (Lk.
2.25).

5. The 'meek' (*praeis*) are the same as the 'poor' (*ptōchoi*), the
humble oppressed saints of God. Since the verb *klēronomeō* (Hebrew
yrš) appears in Dt. 4.1; 16.20; Ps. 68.36 (LXX) with reference to
possessing the land of Israel, it would be better to translate here
'shall inherit (or possess) the land', i.e. the new promised land.
Just as obedience and righteousness (for the Deuteronomist) are
the conditions of entrance into the land of promise, so is humble
obedience to the pattern of life approved in the Beatitudes the

means of entering the new land of God's Kingdom. The spatial reference in 'land' ought not to be pressed; it is those who do the will of God that matter, not the place where it is done. Because he does not think that Jesus envisaged a Messianic kingdom *on earth*, and because the saying seems to have been derived from Ps. 37 (LXX 36).11, Manson (*Sayings*, p. 152) regards this verse as a Jewish Christian interpolation. It is of interest to note that Ps. 37 (the themes of which are close to the entire series of Beatitudes) was interpreted in the Qumran sect as a prophecy in process of fulfilment through the establishment of their Messianic community (4QpPs 37). There is strong support in Western texts (especially the versions) for the transposition of verses 5 and 4. If this is done, the first and third Beatitudes form synonymously parallel couplets of a four-line stanza, and 'inheriting the land' becomes equivalent to 'receiving the Kingdom', the realization of Israel's hopes in a new community of obedience and righteousness.

6. Blessed are those who hunger and thirst after righteousness: Luke omits 'and thirst after righteousness', but this does not necessarily mean that he understands the 'hunger' as purely physical (see Cross, p. 67, on Lk. 6.21 as a reference to the Messianic banquet which is associated with words about the poor in 4QpPs 37). Matthew expands the shorter form in the interests of clarification. The 'hunger and thirst' denote ardent desire for something spiritual: and 'righteousness' is usually interpreted here as the vindication of the cause of the afflicted, the fulfilment of Isa. 61.3, and therefore as tantamount to 'salvation'. But 'righteousness'—which is a crucial term for Matthew—does not seem to bear that meaning elsewhere in the Gospel. It is therefore better to understand *dikaiosunē* here (as at verses 10 and 20) in terms of righteousness of life in conformity to God's will; cf. Hill, pp. 127f.; Descamps, p. 172; Strecker, pp. 156–8; Schrenk, p. 35. The desire for this rightousness is not passive waiting but active obedience, and its full realization is in the gift of God (see *TIM*, pp. 123–4).

7. That those who show mercy will experience mercy from God (for it is divine mercy which is in view here) was a commonplace of Rabbinic ethical teaching (Schechter, p. 202). But that does not mean that Matthew is just inventing the Beatitude, possibly on the basis of his own training. The theme of conditioned mercy is expressed by Jesus in the Lord's Prayer, 'forgive . . . as we forgive', 6.12–15 (cf. also 9.13; 12.7; 18.33). 'Show mercy and mercy will be shown to you [by God]' circulated as an unwritten saying of Jesus outside the Gospels (1 Clem. 13.2; Polyc. 2.3). It is noteworthy that, when taken together, verses 7 and 9 form a four-line stanza in parallel couplets.

8. In Ps. 24.3f. access to God's presence during Temple worship is for him who has 'clean hands and a pure heart'. These are the spiritually 'pure', not the ritually or ceremonially clean. To 'see God' is a pictorial expression indicating the bliss of fellowship with God in the Kingdom (cf. Ps. 17.15; 42.3; 4 Ezra 7.98— 'for they hasten to behold the face of him whom they served in life and from whom they are to receive their reward when glorified'.) Black, *Aramaic Approach*, p. 158, n.2, has noted that the rendering of 'pure in heart' into Aramaic gives *dakē leḇ*, an expression which is consonantally very close to *dakîkê leḇ* which is an Aramaic equivalent of Isaiah's *niśbᵉrē leḇ* the 'broken-hearted' (Isa. 61.1). If this is a mistranslation, then the original meaning would be that the 'contrite' will 'see God'.

9. peacemakers: a word rare in Greek and usually applied to emperors, this does not mean people who live in peace, practising non-resistance, but those who actually bring about peace, overcoming evil with good. Parallels are not infrequent in the rabbinic literature, e.g. Aboth i.12; and cf. 1 Enoch 52.11. 'Blessed is he who brings peace and love'.

sons of God: a distinction bestowed by God Himself, and acknowledged and adopted by Him. This is Israel's destiny and title (Dt. 14.1; Hos. 1.10; Ps. Sol. 17.30; Wis. 2.13, 18). 'The peacemakers are the true Israel and acknowledged by God as his children' (Manson, *Sayings*, p. 151).

10. persecuted: the participle is in the perfect tense. This suggests that, when the text assumed its present shape, persecution had already been experienced in the church. The cause of persecution is devotion to 'righteousness', i.e. faithfulness to God's law. Those who so suffered would include both Jewish and Christian martyrs. The reward for such faithfulness is (or 'will be', since the tense would not be espressed in Aramaic) a share in the Kingdom of Heaven; cf. 1 Pet. 3.14.

11. Here and in the next verse there is a specific application of verse 10 to the persecuted disciples and the Church. The verses resume contact with the Beatitudes in Lk. 6.22–3. Luke mentions

four kinds of attack; Matthew's three are included, the additional
one being the general introductory term 'hate'. The expression 'cast
out your name as evil' in Luke represents a Hebrew or Aramaic
phrase which can be translated as 'send out an evil name upon',
i.e. 'issue an evil report concerning' (cf. Dt. 22.14, 19), and of
this Matthew gives the correct sense, 'speak evil against' (see
Black, *Aramaic Approach*, pp. 135f.); **all kinds of** and **falsely** are
editorial additions. Matthew has 'on my account', whereas Luke
has 'on account of the Son of Man'. The fact that Matthew elsewhere (16.21) alters the 'Son of Man' to a personal pronoun
suggests that Luke has retained the more original wording.

12. Matthew's word for 'be glad' (*agalliasthe*) does not contain
the idea of the physical expression of joy, such as is contained in
Luke's 'leap for joy'. The Hebrew and Aramaic *dus* has a range of
meanings which would cover both expressions, and Matthew's
rendering would be more correct in the context, whereas Luke's
would be the more individual interpretation (see Black, *Aramaic
Approach*, pp. 158, 193). Matthew's word is something of a technical term for joy in persecution and martyrdom (cf. 1 Pet. 1.6, 8;
4.13; Rev. 19.7). The promise of reward is a not insignificant
element in the teaching of Jesus (5.19, 46; 6.1; 19.29; 20.8); it
was prominent in the teaching of the rabbis (see Marmorstein,
Doctrine of Merits), but there reward was understood as being
proportionate to merit. It is possible that **reward** here denotes
'good repute' or 'glory', i.e. the opposite of 'slander'. The difference between Luke's 'for so their fathers did to the prophets' and
Matthew's 'for so men persecuted the prophets who were before
you' may be explained by a slight confusion (or mistranslation) of
the original Aramaic (Black, op. cit., p. 192), but the attempt to
make a four-line stanza out of verses 11 and 12 is rather precari-
ous. Stendahl (in *Peake*, 678k) draws attention to the possibility
that Jesus may be referring to his disciples as 'prophets', as some
of the Essenes considered themselves, and were so considered by
Josephus; cf. K. Schubert, 'The Sermon on the Mount and the
Qumran Texts', *SNT*, pp. 118-28.

SALT AND LIGHT **5.13-16**

Comparison with separate logia where the metaphors of salt and
light are used (Mk 9.50; 4.21; Lk. 8.16; 11.33; 14.34f.) shows
that early tradition had preserved these words of Jesus in other

contexts and with different meanings. The double parable here is
linked to the preceding sayings by the use of the second person
plural, which in itself suggests Matthew's concern to direct the
teaching to the Christian community. Another Matthean emphasis finds expression here—namely, the importance of good works
(16b). It is by their good works that disciples will be 'salt' and
'light'. The use of the light-image here is quite different from its
use in the Qumran texts (especially 1QS) in the contrast between
darkness and light which corresponds to the distinction between
the good and the evil.

13. You are the salt of the earth: in Mk 9.50 the disciples
are bidden to have salt in themselves: here they are themselves
the salt. In the ancient world salt symbolized that which purifies
and gives flavour; cf. Allen p. 43: 'The disciples are the element
in the work which keeps it wholesome.' In rabbinic metaphorical
language 'salt' mainly connotes 'wisdom', and this idea may be
indicated by the next clause. It is possible that Jesus is warning
his disciples that they must not go the way of Israel, which ought
to have been the salt of mankind, but has lost all its savour and
usefulness. See W. Nauck, 'Salt as a Metaphor in Instructions
for Discipleship', *ST*, VI, 1952, pp. 165–78.

but if salt has lost its taste . . .: the fact that, strictly speaking,
salt cannot lose its saline qualities has led some to suggest that
Jesus means that, just as salt cannot lose its taste, so the disciples
will serve as the salt of the world by inner necessity. It is more
probable that the *logion* is a warning: salt can become adulterated
and therefore 'good for nothing'; unless disciples serve in the world
by their good deeds, they will become useless—even dangerous—
and rejected. The word *mōranthē* (cp. Hebrew *tāpēl*) could mean
'become foolish' as well as 'become unsavoury': the insipid salt
may refer to *foolish* disciples. A further confirmation that *tāpēl* was
the original word is that it provides a word-play with the Aramaic
for 'seasoned', 'salted' *tabēl*. Taken together with Lk. 14.35, the
Matthean saying would form a four-line verse, two synthetic lines
followed by two synonymous lines (Black, *Aramaic Approach*,
pp. 166f.). 'Thrown out and trodden underfoot by men' indicates
that the worthless salt's destination is the street, the common
refuse-tip in the East.

14. You are the light of the world: as the new community
of disciples (the church) has taken over the role of the 'savour' of

the world from Judaism, so have they taken over the mission of the Servant, to be 'a light to the nations' (Isa. 42.6; 49.6). In Rom. 2.19 the Jews are represented as thinking of themselves as 'a light to those who are in darkness', and in Phil. 2.15 Christians are described as 'lights in the world'.

A city set on a hill cannot be hid: the connection of this saying with the context is neither obvious nor close. It may represent a piece of common worldly wisdom, used here to suggest that the Church is the city (Jerusalem?). The saying in Pap. Oxy. i.37–42 seems to be an expansion of this text: 'A city which is erected on the top of a high mountain and firmly established can neither fall nor remain hidden' (*NT Apocrypha*, 1, pp. 109–10). The emphasis there lies on the invincibility of the Church, whereas in Matthew the stress is on its being seen and recognized.

15. Cf. Mk 4.21; Lk. 8.16; 11.33. In this context, the disciples (church) are the lamp which gives light to 'all in the house'. For Matthew this may mean a reformation of Judaism from within, whereas Luke's 'that those who enter may see the light' may imply conversions from outside (Manson, *Sayings*, p. 93). The 'bushel' would be the wooden measure in which the day's bread would be measured. The impersonal plural ('*men* light . . .'), which is infrequent in Greek (save in the special *legousi* ('men say') phrase) but common in Aramaic, and the use of the definite article ('under *the* measure . . . upon *the* lampstand') to denote a single person or thing as being present to the mind under given circumstances (an acknowledged Semitism) suggest the Aramaic origin and authenticity of the saying. On the possibility that there is a reference to the special Hanukkah lamp which was hidden so that its light might not be desecrated, see J. D. M. Derrett, *ET*, LXXVIII, 1966–7, p. 18.

16. By the shining of the disciples' light—which evidences itself in good works—others will be led to pay attention and give glory to God. Thus the disciples inherit the task of Yahweh's Servant in that they are 'lights to the nations' and therefore help to bring to fulfilment the hope of God's glorification in the messianic era: cf. 2 C. 4.6; 1 Pet. 2.12. The expression—'my (your, our) Father who is in heaven'—is common in early Rabbinic literature, and occurs twenty times in Matthew's gospel, but only once in Mark (11.25), and in Luke it does not appear at all.

JESUS AND THE LAW 5.17–20

Apart from a parallel to verse 18 in Lk. 16.17 and Mk 13.31, this pericope is peculiar to Matthew. Its purpose in the structure of the Gospel is probably to prevent misunderstanding of the contrasts which follow. To the devout Jew, the Law was something given directly by God, and therefore perfect and irreformable. Conservative Palestinian Christians would have been sympathetic to this high view of Torah, and would have been under pressure, not only to define the relation between Jesus' teaching (and their own attitudes) and orthodox Jewish doctrine, but also to defend their position against those (of the Hellenistic wing, perhaps) who were less concerned about the abiding validity of the Law. The *Sitz im Leben* of the passage in the Matthean church is therefore the different attitudes adopted towards the Law in early Christianity: but this setting does not require us to deny that at least part of the section reflects the spirit and teaching of Jesus. On this important passage, see *TIM*, pp. 64–73; Davies, *SSM*, pp. 334–6; Manson, *Sayings*, pp. 153–5; H. Ljungmann, *Das Gesetz erfüllen* (who sees the section as a unit), and E. Schweizer, *TLZ*, LXXVII, 1952, pp. 479ff.

17. The formula 'Think not that I have come to . . .', which recurs in Mt. 10.34, alludes to an error which was circulating about Jesus' teaching either among the Jews, the disciples, or in the Matthean church, though these possibilities are not mutually exclusive. The purpose of Jesus' mission is not to overthrow the validity and authority of the Law and the Prophets, but to fulfil them. The meaning of *plērōsai* is variously interpreted—'confirm', 'validate', 'bring to actuality by doing', 'set forth in its true meaning', and therefore 'complete'. The interpretation must be guided by the context (especially verses 21–48), and by Matthew's use of the verb elsewhere in the Gospel, and these factors suggest that it be understood as 'establish': Jesus establishes the Law and the Prophets by realizing (or actualizing) them completely in his teaching and in his life (see *TIM*, p. 69).

18. truly I say to you: the use of *amēn* in this way may be unique and original to Jesus (see Jeremias, *Prayers*, pp. 112–15; also Daube, pp. 388–93). The 'I say unto you' (cf. 22, 28, 32, 34, 39, 44) indicates a solemn and authoritative pronouncement. Between this verse (which comes to Matthew out of tradition, perhaps Q: cf. Lk. 16.17) and verse 17 (which forms an interpretation of it) there is a seam (cf. McNeile, p. 58, Kilpatrick, p. 18 and *TIM*, pp. 66–7).

till heaven and earth pass away: i.e. for ever, until the end of the world. The eternity of the Law is constantly asserted in Jewish writings, cf. 4 Ezra 9.36f. and Exod. R.i.6: 'Not a tittle shall be abolished from the Law for ever.'

not an iota, not a dot: the Greek *iota*, the smallest letter in the Greek alphabet, substituted here for the Hebrew *yôḏ*, the smallest letter of the Hebrew alphabet.

dot: the Greek word is usually explained as meaning 'horn', a tiny mark used to distinguish similar letters (*śîn* and *šîn*). Burkitt suggested that it might mean 'hook (letter)', i.e. the Hebrew *wāw*, 'not one *yôḏ*, not a *wāw*', two very similar letters which were often omitted in Hebrew and Aramaic texts; see McNeile, p. 59.

until all is accomplished: the phrase may refer to the eschatological events; 'till all that must happen has happened' (*NEB*): but this is tautologous with 18a. Davies (*Mélanges bibliques*, pp. 428ff.) understands it as 'till all things come to pass'—i.e. only until the death of Jesus inaugurates finally the New Covenant within which Law is 'completed'. It has also been tentatively suggested that the meaning is 'till the New Age comes', i.e. the Messianic age in which there would be a New Law, the old being abrogated; see Davies, *Torah*, and *SSM*, p. 184. The **all** could possibly denote 'the law' itself or 'what the law demands'; this would oblige us to see the verse as the creation of the unadulterated legalism of the Jewish Christian church (cf. Bultmann, *HST*, pp. 138, 405). These interpretations may have viewed the meaning too much in terms of an assumed limitation of the law's validity ('until'): the sentence however is concerned with an aim and goal—the complete accomplishment of God's will: it is for this that the Law stands and the validity of the Law serves this comprehensive goal. (Note the *NEB* alternative rendering: 'before all that it stands for is achieved'.)

19. The absence of any expressed antecedent for the term 'these' raises the question whether the commandments referred to are those of the Law (verse 18), or those of Jesus which follow. Kilpatrick (pp. 25f.) has suggested that originally verse 19 followed verse 41, and that 'these' referred to Jesus' own revised commandments; the first interpretation is more likely. The Jewish

Christians for whom Matthew was writing would have been upholders of the validity of the Law, and in any case the subsequent
teaching of Jesus in the Sermon on the Mount does not represent
annulment of the Law, but rather its completion, its intensification. Many have found in this verse an attack on the work and
teaching of Paul, and it is claimed that the term 'least in the Kingdom' recalls Paul's description of himself (1 C. 15.9) as the 'least
of the apostles'. This interpretation would assume Matthew's
knowledge, not only of Paul's significance, but also of his letters,
and of 1 C. 15.9 in particular: furthermore, 'least', which is probably derived from the immediately preceding phrase, may not be
superlative: the Aramaic could as easily mean 'little'. The possibility of anti-Paulinism in the verse must be left open: it could
only be claimed as definite if there was substantial evidence
throughout the gospel for this tendency. The distinction between
'heavy' and 'light' commandments is recognized in later rabbinic
literature (Sifre Dt. 187, 108b); but the rigid Shammaite school
refused to draw the distinction. Cf. also Jas 2.10. The verb 'to
relax' would mean 'to show by example and teaching that a
commandment was obsolete'.

20. Here, as in verse 10, **righteousness** means faithfulness
and obedience to the law of God. The quality of obedience from
disciples and the nature of the demand laid upon them must
surpass that displayed and accepted by the scribes and Pharisees.
The **scribes** (who were not all Pharisees) were a group who
expounded, developed and applied (in courts) the Law. The
Pharisees were the body of orthodox priests, the 'separatists'
who professed to live in strict accordance with the Law. Matthew,
here and elsewhere, represents the Pharisees much as did the
Qumran sectaries when they called them the 'seekers of smooth
things'—those who made the Law practicable for themselves, and
by so doing broke its ultimate and radical demand by their
casuistry. Jesus' criticism of the Pharisees, according to Matthew,
is not that they were not good, but that they were not good enough!

THE SUPERIOR RIGHTEOUSNESS **5.21-48**

In the light of what precedes, we must understand this section—
the so-called 'antitheses' passage—as setting forth the radical intensification of the demands of the Law. This is not an antithesis
to the Mosaic Law set forth by a New Moses: it is 'a messianic

intensification, producing the true righteousness which belongs to
the Kingdom' (Stendahl, in *Peake*, 679a). The attitudes which
illustrate this 'true righteousness', unfortunately, have been interpreted often in a lower, even romantic, key. 'The point is not
inner motivation compared with pharisaic casuistry, or warm
concern for human values as opposed to hair-splitting legalism.
We are faced with Matthew's collection of statements concerning
the superior righteousness and its root in Jesus' messianic restoration of the Law' (Stendahl, loc. cit.). On the sharpening of the
Law to its ultimate implication of holiness in the time of the
Messiah, cf. Davies, *Torah*. On this passage as a whole, see Daube,
pp. 55-62 and Davies, *SSM*, pp. 101ff.

The form in which the antitheses are couched by and large
follows the same pattern: (a) 'You have heard . . .'; (b) 'But I
say to you . . .' In the light of rabbinic texts and formulae adduced
by Daube, (a) is to be interpreted in verses 21, 27f., 33, 34a, 37
(where the antithesis deepens the demand of the Law) as meaning
'You have understood the meaning of the Law to have been',
and in verses 31f., 38f., 43 (where there *seems* to be a contravention
of the Law) as meaning, 'You have understood literally'. Simi-
larly, behind (b) lies a rabbinic formula which expresses a contrast between 'hearing' (i.e. the literal understanding of a rule)
and what we must 'say' it actually signifies. The main point is
that in none of these passages is there an intention to annul the
demands of the Law, but only to carry them to their ultimate
meaning, to intensify them, or to reinterpret them in a higher key.
This is the true fulfilment of Law, not its destruction.

On Anger 21-6

21. the men of old: both those who received the Law and its
first interpreters. In the commandment 'You shall not kill' Exod.
20.15(LXX); Dt. 5.18), both the Hebrew and Greek verbs indicate
murder (or assassination), not just any kind of taking of life.
whoever kills shall be liable to judgment: the word *krisis*
refers to legal proceedings, indicating either the tribunal dealing
with criminal affairs, or the *Beṭ-din*, the council of twenty-three
members.
22. The Messianic radicalizing of the Law applies it to the
underlying cause of murder—namely, anger. The words 'without
cause', though supported by good manuscript authority, are

probably a later addition to the text. The fact that Jewish legal
proceedings did not deal with (or punish) such things as anger and
unseemly speech makes it possible that the point here is simply
that matters which were taken so lightly in Judaism as to have
no part in their legal system are now raised by Jesus to a new
significance (cf. E. Percy, *Die Botschaft Jesu*, 1953). But the emphasis on 'brother' here and throughout the Sermon on the Mount
may point in another direction: they recall the provisions of the
Qumran *Manual of Discipline* regarding personal relations within
the sect (1QS vi.24–6) where the punishments are meted out in
the 'communal investigation' (*mdrš yḥd*). The tone of the passage,
with its gradations of anger and speech, suggests that the ethical
concern of Matthew is with relations between disciples as members
of a religious community (for Matthew, the Church) rather than
with rules for general human behaviour (see Stendahl, in *Peake*,
679c, and Davies, *SSM*, pp. 236–8).

whoever insults . . . council: lit. 'whoever says to his brother
Raka'. The origin of this word is the Aramaic *rêḳā* = 'imbecile',
'fool', a gross term of abuse, and used sometimes of the excommunication of one rabbi by another (cf. Neh. 5.13). (An Aramaic
papyrus from Qumran, dated A.D. 133, uses the root *ryḳ* with the
meaning 'worthless, invalid'.) The use of such a phrase renders
a man liable to disciplinary action, perhaps by the Sanhedrin or
in a local court of discipline meeting in the synagogue, but, in
the light of what was suggested above, the reference may be to
some investigating body within the community.

whoever says 'You fool' . . . the hell of fire: the word *mōros*
'fool' may be the Greek equivalent of the Aramaic *rêḳā*'. In addition to its common reference to senselessness, the word may have
suggested (to a Jew) the charge of religious impiety (Hebrew
mōreh = 'rebellious', 'apostate', Jer. 5.23; Ps. 78(LXX 77).8). The
hell or Gehenna (Hebrew *Gê-Hinnōm*), of fire belongs to the
realm of apocalyptic ideas. The original Valley of Hinnom was a
ravine S. of Jerusalem, where the refuse of the city was burnt. It
was once associated with the fire-worship of Moloch, and later
became the symbolic designation of the place of future punishment (1 Enoch 54.1–2; 2 Bar. 85.13). The introduction of final
divine judgment represents the climax of the scale of punishments,
although McNeile (p. 62) interprets 22a and 22c as Jesus' antitheses to the current Jewish teaching reflected in 21 and 22b.

23–6. Matthew uses these verses to provide two illustrations of the necessity of subduing anger by engaging in reconciliation. Although the first illustration is quite apposite in the context here, it may, if original, belong elsewhere, since it is really closer to the problem of attitude to enemies. On the other hand, it may be an independent saying emerging from the primitive Church at Jerusalem, while the disciples were still participating in the offices of the Temple (cf. Bonnard, p. 64). The second illustration is found in the context of eschatological urgency in Lk. 12.57–9, which preserves the primitive meaning of the *logion*. From being an appeal to impenitent Israel to be reconciled with its divine Adversary before it is too late, Matthew makes it a moral exhortation directed towards believers.

23. that your brother has something against you: i.e. 'has a just claim against you'. The implication is that the person fulfilling his Temple duties is himself at fault. This spoils the connection with the preceding antithesis, which is concerned with feelings of hostility towards a brother (a fellow member of the Christian community).

24. The duty of seeking reconciliation with him whom one has offended takes precedence over Temple sacrifice. The idea of reconciliation existed in contemporary Judaism (M. Yoma viii.9), but was overshadowed by the desire to avoid desecrating the Temple or defiling one's self (cf. CD vi.14–vii.4), and not, as here, by the idea of respect for an offended brother.

25. Make friends quickly with your accuser: lit. 'be favourably minded'. Luke has 'make an effort to settle with him'. Matthew may have introduced the change to make the exhortation more suitable to his context, or the alteration may have arisen from a mistaken rendering of *slm* ('pay back a debt'), as though it meant 'make peace' (McNeile, p. 63). The 'accuser' is the injured party in a legal action. Some exegetes (both ancient and modern) understand the verses as an allegory indicating the necessity of being reconciled, while there is still time in life, before the accuser (Law, or Satan) arraigns you before God the judge.

26. the last penny: *quadrans*, the fourth part of an *as* (10.29), equal to 'two mites' (Mk 12.42). A sum of infinitesimal value.

On Adultery 27-30

The intensification or Messianic sharpening of the sixth commandment (concerning adultery) is presented in terms of the tenth (concerning covetousness, and desire for what is not one's own). The theme of adultery is treated, not in terms of asceticism or personal purity, but in terms of one's relation with another person. It is not to preserve himself from impurity that the disciple must avoid adultery, but in order not to break into another man's marriage. The commandment itself (Exod. 20.13; Dt. 5.17) and Jewish interpretations of it (see M. Ketuboth and M. Kiddushin) condemn adultery, not because it involves a man's infidelity to his own wife, but because it means his taking of another man's wife (i.e. theft). Verses 29-30 do not follow easily on 28. The 'eye' in verse 29 could take up the 'looking' in 28, but the 'hand' has no clear reference to the theme of the verse. In a fuller form the passage is found again at Mt. 18.8-9 (= Mk 9.43-8), where three members (hand, foot and eye) are listed as causes of sin. Here Matthew found reason to use the passage in abbreviated form, and later to give it in full in its context in Mark.

27. The formula introducing the commandment makes no mention of 'the men of old' (verses 21, 33), but the sense is the same.

28. Jesus speaks as the Messianic restorer of Law in its ultimate fundamentals. He identifies the lustful look at a married woman with the actual act of adultery. 'To interpret on the side of stringency is not to annul the Law, but to change it in accordance with its own intention' (Davies, *SSM*, p. 102). The verse ought not to be interpreted as a condemnation of the natural desire of a man for a woman: the lustful desire is for the wife who belongs to another man.

29. If the eye, which ought to preserve a man from stumbling, becomes a cause of sinning (*skandalizō*), then it should be torn out: thus will the disciple be rid of the instrument or means of action *against* another person. In this and the following verses, it is not the destiny of the soul or of the heart which concerns Matthew, but that of the *body*, i.e. of the actual person (concrete and historical) in relation to others.

30. The same lesson—that security in the future may involve suffering and deprivation in life—is made with reference to the right hand, the more active of the two, but not specifically associated with lust, except in so far as it involves theft.

On Divorce 31–2

Jesus' intensification of the Law on divorce appears again, with somewhat different wording, at 19.9. It is arguable that here Matthew is following his own special source (M), and at chapter 19 is dependent on Mk 10.11–12: but it is more probable that Matthew, while leaving the teaching on divorce in its later context, introduced it here as well, in a formal style, within the framework of his series of antitheses, because it suited the theme so well. Matthew is concerned with the Messianic radicalizing of the Law: and here Jesus is presented as going beyond the Mosaic permission—an example of his intensification of the Law's demand; see further on 19.1–9. The introduction of the exceptive clause suggests that Matthew is making Jesus' total prohibition of divorce (so Mk and Lk.) a principle to be applied in a regulatory fashion: he makes the absolute practicable and therefore a matter of legality. But see comments on verse 32.

31. The reference is to Dt. 24.1ff. which allows a man to divorce his wife 'if she finds no favour in his eyes, because he has found some indecency (*'erwaṯ dāḇār, aschēmon pragma*) in her'. Chapter 19.7–8 claims that this allowance was made by Moses because men were unable to live according to God's will.

32. But I say to you: Jesus goes beyond the Mosaic position and points out that divorce leads to remarriage, and therefore to adultery, on the part of one or both parties.

except on the ground of unchastity: the exceptive clause is absent from Mk and Lk., as also in 1 C.7.10ff. The word 'unchastity' (*porneia*) could refer to any sexual irregularity, either before or after marriage. In the latter case, the qualifying phrase could represent agreement with the view of the Shammaite school which admitted divorce only on the grounds of a wife's unchastity. This view was based on the inversion of the words *'erwaṯ dāḇār* ('something unseemly') in Dt. 24.1 to *dᵉḇar 'erwāṯ*, 'a matter of unchastity' on a married woman's part, short of actual adultery which was strictly punishable by death (Dt. 22.22).

It is usually assumed that the exceptive clause represents an element of later Christian legislation accommodating the original absolute prohibition of divorce to the situation of the Church to-

wards the end of the first century. This may well be a correct
assumption, but it is not absolutely necessary. A man was not just
allowed, but was *compelled*, by Jewish law (in New Testament
times) to divorce his wife when fornication before marriage was
discovered (cf. Mt. 1.19; Dt. 22.13ff.) or adultery detected, and
this fact may have been taken for granted, without statement, by
the other Gospels when they recorded the total prohibition of
divorce. Matthew's clause may be making the matter explicit:
divorce is denied, except in the case of unchastity—which case in
fact requires it, since unchastity destroys the unity between man
and wife, the creation of which was God's design in instituting
marriage.

H. Baltensweiler (*TZ*, XV, 1959, pp. 340–56) argues that
porneia indicates a marriage contracted within prohibited degrees of kinship (Lev. 18.16–8; cf. Ac. 15.28–9). In this he is
followed by Bonnard (pp. 69f.) and Benoit (pp. 121f.). Such
marriages were contracted among pagans and tolerated by Jews
in the case of proselytes: they would have become a problem for
legalist Jewish Christian circles, and Matthew might have been
prepared to permit divorce in such cases. In doing so, he would
not be far from the absolute prohibition; in fact he would be
maintaining the sanctity of marriage by condemning illicit
unions.

On Swearing 33–7

The Mosaic Law forbade only false and irreverent oaths which
were regarded as profaning the name of God. Jesus would abolish
oaths altogether as being quite unnecessary for those who habit-
ually speak the truth, as his disciples (and believers) are expected
to do.

33. you have heard that it was said: on this formula, see the
introductory note to verses 21–48. Barth (*TIM*, p. 93) draws
attention to the fact that the words 'hear' and 'say' (Hebrew
šmr and *'mr*) are frequently used of belief in the tradition: 'you
have heard' means 'you have received as tradition', and 'it was
said' means 'it was taught as tradition'; cf. Daube's 'You have
understood the meaning of the Law to have been . . .'
'You shall . . . sworn': this is not an exact quotation of any
passage in the *OT*, but is a summary of the substance of Exod.
20.7; Lev. 19.12; Num. 30.2; and Dt. 23.21–4. The word *epiorkeō*

means both 'commit perjury' and 'break an oath'; the latter
rendering fits more satisfactorily with what follows. The law was
designed to safeguard the sanctity of oaths against the 'often in-
discriminate and frivolous' use of them by Jews (McNeile, p. 67).
Casuistical discussion on the validity of oaths occupies the entire
Mishnah tractate Shebuoth.

34. Do not swear at all: Jesus goes behind the current
prescriptions against breaking oaths to establish the supreme righteousness which does not require any oaths to emphasize truthful-
ness and sincerity. Josephus (*BJ* ii.viii.6) speaks of the Essene
aversion to oaths, and gives to their attitude the same significance
as is found here: truthful words need no support from oaths. But
he also indicates that an oath had a significant rôle in the rules
of Essene initiation (*BJ* ii.viii.7); see CD xv.5, and especially
1QS v.7-11, on the oaths of admission to the Qumran sect.
either by heaven ... footstool: 'heaven' here means the
heavenly world; it is not the Jewish periphrasis for the divine
name. In M. Shebuoth iv.13 it is said that swearing by the
heavens and by the earth is not an oath which is binding upon
witnesses. The words here contain an allusion to Isa. 66.1:
'Heaven is my throne and the earth is my footstool'.

35. or by Jerusalem: the preposition denotes 'towards'
Jerusalem. This may reflect the Rabbinic view (Tos. Nedarim 1)
that a vow made 'by Jerusalem' is nothing unless it is sworn 'towards Jerusalem' (i.e. while facing in the direction of Jerusalem).
The rest of the phrase is a reference to Ps. 48.2.

36. Cf. 6. 27. An oath 'by the life of thy head' is referred to in
M. San.3.2. Although it might be thought that a man has absolute power over his head (i.e. over the colour of his hair), it is
not so: that is determined by God.

37. Let what you say be simply 'Yes' or 'No': (lit. 'Let
your speech be "Yes, Yes", or "No, No" '). The second 'yes' and
'no' might be understood as adding emphasis to the first, but unnecessary emphasis is just what Jesus is condemning. According to
B. Sanhed. 36a, a double 'yes' or 'no' actually formed an oath.
The interpretation implied by *RSV* is more literally: 'let your "yes"
be (i.e. really mean) "yes" and your "no" "no" '. This is supported
by Jas 5.12, which may be an earlier (and more original) form of
this verse: In James there is no suggestion that the words are a
logion of Jesus, but it is likely that at this point, as in others, James

drew upon a tradition of the sayings of Jesus for his paraenetic purposes (cf. Davies, *SSM*, pp. 402ff.).

from evil: masc. and neut. forms of *ponēros* coincide here. Therefore it is very difficult to decide whether 'evil' or the 'Evil One' (Satan) is meant. The same uncertainty exists at 5.39, 6.13, and 13.38.

On Retaliation 38-42

In keeping with the piety expressed in the Beatitudes, the well-known and generally applied view of retaliation is set aside in favour of the attitude of self-restraint. Four illustrations of this new principle follow; they are not to be understood as actual juridical prescriptions, but rather as examples of the general principle enunciated. Luke adds part of this section to his discussion on loving enemies (6.29-30), but in Matthew's Gospel (which has probably preserved the correct arrangement of the words) the issue is not the principle here presupposed, of love over against that of justice, but (as in Rom. 12.18-21) the principle of awaiting divine vindication over against that of vindictive, exacting behaviour (cf. 1QS 10.18: 'I shall repay no man with evil: I shall pursue man with good, for with God is the judgment of all the living'; also Test. Benj. 4.1-5.5, and the repudiation of vengeance in CD viii.5-6).

38. The well-known principle is found in Exod. 21.24, Dt. 19.21; and Lev. 24.20; and also in the ancient Code of Hammurabi. In its original intention, the old Hebrew law was restrictive rather than permissive: it was designed to limit revenge and retaliation by fixing an exact compensation for an injury. By this humane measure, the law of blood-revenge (which could involve the destruction of a whole family in a feud) was greatly limited.

39. The verb *anthistēmi* ('resist') can mean also 'oppose' or 'take action against'. But the context here (and the parallels found in the rabbinic comments on the *ius talionis*) suggest that it has a juridical meaning—'resist' in a court of law, or 'oppose' before a judge. On this interpretation 'the evil' must be understood as 'one who wishes to do injury' (**one who is evil** *RSV*) rather than as 'the Devil' or 'evil' in the abstract. The doctrine of absolute non-resistance to evil is not enunciated here: the issue is one of individual conduct in specific circumstances. Disciples of Jesus (and members of the Christian community) must not behave according to the principle of strict retaliation in asserting legal rights. This attitude surpasses the spirit of the legal codes, but does not supersede them.

if any one strikes you . . . also: an example of the kind of behaviour by which a disciple may avoid going to law and thereby witness to the new righteousness of the Kingdom. The Greek verb *rhapizō* refers to striking another on the face with the back of the hand, an action which was regarded as a very great insult meriting punishment. It is therefore not an act of violence that is being referred to in the Matthean context, but insulting behaviour: the version at Lk. 6.29 uses the verb *tuptein* ('beat'), and is dealing with a violent act. The example (for Matthew) amounts to this: If a man insults you, let him insult you again, rather than seek reparation at law.

40. This second illustration of non-retaliation is also concerned with law-courts. Matthew's version is dealing with a case in which the plaintiff is claiming the defendant's *chitōn* (a long close-fitting undergarment). The action (says the Gospel) should not be taken into court; the disciple will surrender his outer garment (**cloak**)—which, according to Exod. 22.26; Dt. 24.12 and in the spirit of Hebrew humanitarianism, was an inalienable possession. Luke omits the verb *krithēnai* ('sue') and uses only 'take', thus indicating that he has in mind robbery (with violence).

41. forces: the word (*angareuō*) is of Persian origin, and had to do with commandeering service or property for public use (cf. McNeile, p. 70). It refers to the right of the government or the army to demand services: a civilian could be compelled to carry a soldier's luggage (cf. Mt. 27.32; Mk 15.21, where the word is used of the Roman soldiers forcing Simon of Cyrene to carry Jesus' cross).

The **mile** is a roman measurement (*mille passuum* = 1 mile), and is presumably the distance a Roman soldier could require a non-Roman to carry his equipment. The reading 'go with him two miles' has strong support in early versions, and may be genuine. The behaviour here suggested as appropriate to disciples may have anti-Zealot overtones.

42. Cf. Exod. 22.25, which relates to loans to fellow-Israelites. It seems likely that the two clauses are parallel, and that *aiteō* (Aramaic *šeʼal*) means 'ask for a loan', rather than **beg** (RSV).

From the person who wishes to borrow, the disciple is not to 'turn away' (lit.); indeed, he is to *give* (instead of lend?). (One wonders if, in the light of Luke's version, **do not refuse,** or 'turn away from', represents a mistranslation of Aramaic which originally meant 'do not require back from'.) Matthew, by using the aorist of the verbs 'give' and 'refuse', pictures single scenes: Luke has nothing about 'borrowing', and makes a general and universal principle: **give to him who begs** (lit. 'Make a habit of giving (present tense) to everyone who asks of you'). He adds a clause against reclaiming property of which one has been robbed. Matthew preserves the right understanding of the teaching: it is concerned with the matter of borrowing and lending, in which members of Christ's Kingdom will be neither selfish nor exacting, but generous beyond what could be normally expected of them.

On Loving Enemies 43-8

This antithesis is presented as the conclusion of the series which opened with verse 21. It is founded on Lev. 19.18, 'You shall not take vengeance or bear any grudge against the sons of your own people, but you shall love your neighbour as yourself: I am the Lord.'

While this principle lies at the very core of Jewish ethics, one will search the *OT* in vain for an explicit order to 'hate your enemy'. There is no ground for suggesting that the words are a late interpolation, but they are not found as a quotation; nor are they a fair interpretation of Jewish ethics at the time, not even if the Semitic 'hate' can mean 'love less' or 'esteem less'. However, the terminology of 'love' and 'hate' is characteristic of that Jewish teaching which is dominated by the notion of the eschatological division of men into two opposing camps. The Qumran *Manual of Discipline* advises the sectaries (themselves members of the eschatological community) 'to love everyone whom God has elected, and to hate everyone whom he has rejected . . . to hate all the sons of darkness' (1QS i.4, 10). In view of this parallel and because the original Levitical commandment referred to love of a fellow member of the community of Israel, it is possible that by 'enemy' here is meant, not a personal or political foe, but a persecutor of the faith, the enemy of the Messianic community formed by the first Christians. In the LXX, *echthros* often designates the enemy of the people of God (Ps. 31(30).8; 139(138).21). In this case, 'neighbour' will refer here to a member of the same religious community (the Church), and the evangelist may be regarded as having underlined the ecclesiastical aspect of the teaching, whereas Luke (by omitting the reference to persecution) keeps the teaching more general, and concerned with personal relations. For linguistic arguments which suggest that the version of this teaching in Lk. 6.27-36 preserves more of the original form which Matthew abridged and telescoped, see Black, *Aramaic Approach*, p. 179ff. The poetical character of the language when it is turned into Palestinian Aramaic shows that the teaching derives from ancient tradition; this fact, together with the nature of the exhortation itself, suggests that much of the section (especially in Luke's form) may well go back to Jesus himself. The behaviour of disciples must demonstrate love in action, reflecting the generous and loving concern of God.

43. You shall love your neighbour: Lev. 19.18 is cited without the words 'as yourself' (reproduced later at 19.19 and 22.37). For a full discussion of the clause 'hate thine enemy' and of its possible relation to the sectarian Judaism, see M. Smith, *HTR*, XLV, 1952, pp. 71ff., and Davies, *SSM*, pp. 245ff.

44. The love which is inculcated is not a matter of sentiment and emotion, but, as always in the *OT* and *NT*, of concrete action. Its meaning is found in the Lucan parallel where 'love' is defined as 'do good to', i.e. practical concern for another's well-being. Prayer on behalf of those who persecute (the same verb is used in 5.10, 11, 12; 10,23; 23.34, and usually indicates religious persecution) is one manifestation of such love. In distinguishing this from the Qumran rules which demanded hatred of those outside the community, Davies says 'Jesus too demanded obedience to the will or Law of God, but as he understood it this was not an iron discipline equally applicable to all in a closed community, but an all-inclusive love of the brethren and of those outside. . . . The difference between them lies in their interpretation of the will of God which demands this total obedience' (*SSM*, p. 427).

45. The motive for the disciple's love is the desire to be (lit. 'become') sons of the heavenly Father, who himself acts in this way. The actions of God's loving concern are not calculated according to worth or merit, but are generously given to all. For

parallels to the illustrations, cf. Seneca, *De benef.* iv. 26, and B.
Taanith 7b.

46. What reward have you? On the idea of reward in the
Matthean version of Jesus' teaching (5.12; 6.1f., 5, 16; 10.41f.;
20.8), see above on 5.12, and M. Smith, *Tannaitic Parallels to the
Gospels*, 1951, pp. 54–73. The notion of 'merit' may explicate the
saying here, and perhaps Lk. 6.32 is using *charis* as a mistranslation
of the Aramaic *ṭebu*. On the other hand it is possible that Luke has
the right idea with *charis* ('grace'), and that Matthew's *misthos*
('pay') denotes the grace by which the recipient becomes a son
of God (Smith, p. 57); cf. Lk. 6.35. Customs officers ('tax-
collectors') were a despised class by reason of their rapaciousness
and their being in the pay of the Romans.

47. The salutation is more than a gesture of greeting: it is an
expression of a desire for the peace and welfare of the other. The
word **brethren** means fellow members of a religious community
(the Church); cf. above on 'enemies', verses 43–4.

48. This verse could form the conclusion to the whole series of
antitheses, as well as to verses 43–7 in particular. It is based on
Dt. 18.13 ('be blameless'—Greek *teleios*, Hebrew *tāmîm*) and
Lev. 19.2 ('be holy as I . . . am holy'). The emphasis is not on
flawless moral character, but on whole-hearted devotion to the
imitation of God—not in the perfection of his being, but of his
ways—(cf. B. Rigaux, *NTS*, iv, 1958, pp. 237–62). In their acts
of love, reconciliation and faithfulness, the disciples are to show
God's attitude to men, that 'perfection in love which seeks the
good of all' (Allen, p. 56); 'the perfection of the disciples is shown
in their undifferentiating observance of the commandment of love
towards friend and foe', (*TIM*, p. 80). On the connection between
the idea of 'perfection' in Matthew and among the Qumran
sectaries to whom it denotes obedience to a revealed interpretation
of the Law, see Rigaux, *loc. cit.*; Davies, *SSM*, pp. 209–15; and
TIM, 97ff. The version of the saying in Lk. 6.36 has 'merciful';
this is suitable both to the context and to the picture of Jesus drawn
in the third Gospel; but Matthew's *teleioi* (Aram. *šᵉlîm*) plays on
the Aramaic word for 'salute', 'ask for the peace of' (Greek
aspazō, Aramaic *šᵉlam*), and that probably assures the originality
of the Matthean version. The Targ. Ps.-Jon. to Lev. 22.28 has the
same word as Luke ('merciful'), and this may have influenced the
Lucan variant.

THE PRACTICE OF PIETY **6.1-18**

With chapter 6 there begins a new section of the Sermon on the Mount: concern with the practical moral life of disciples (presented in the six antitheses of chapter 5) gives way to instruction on religious practice, beginning with the three fundamental acts of Jewish piety—almsgiving (2–4), prayer (5–8) and fasting (16–8). The teaching is presented in the form of a warning against hypocritical behaviour, such as characterized degenerate Phariseeism. The Lord's Prayer (9–15) probably did not originally belong to the context in which it appears here.

The literary structure of the three sections of teaching in 1–8, 16–8 has common elements: a polemical description of the ostentatious piety of hypocrites; an ironic affirmation of the results they will achieve; and thirdly, a description of the true way of practising piety. Bonnard (p. 77) suggests that this type of literary rhythm may reflect traditional didactic methods which helped the teaching to be firmly fixed in the memory. On the frequent word-play in verses 1–7, see Black, *Aramaic Approach*, pp. 176–8.

1. Beware of practising your piety before men: this verse states the theme and supplies the introduction to the section. Some MSS. start the verse with a connecting 'but' (*de*), thus balancing the preceding demand for more intensive righteousness with the warnings which follow as that righteousness is described. The word **piety** (lit. 'righteousness') denotes the totality of religious duties, summed up under alms, prayer and fasting. Because the Hebrew word for 'righteousness' was often translated by *eleēmosunē* ('alms') in the LXX, and in the terminology of the synagogue 'righteousness' could have the specific meaning of 'alms', the word *eleēmosunē* appears in some MSS. at this point; but this makes the appearance of the word 'alms' in verse 2 redundant, and it implies that verse 1 is not a general introduction to the section.
you will have no reward: the reward of unostentatious piety remains in the hands of God, and he himself will give it. It is probable that the idea of 'merit' is involved here, for the chief means of acquiring merit was, in the eyes of Jews, the practice of almsgiving, prayer and fasting.
2. when you give alms: it is not the practice of almsgiving that Jesus criticizes, but the degradation of the practice among hypocrites. He assumes that his disciples will continue to perform what had always been a sacred duty (cf. Dt. 15.11).

sound no trumpet before you as the hypocrites do: this clause may be a metaphorical way of describing vanity, but it could contain an oblique reference to the practice of blowing trumpets at the time of collecting alms in the Temple for the relief of some signal need (see Bonnard, p. 78). The Greek word *hypocritēs* means 'actor'; Matthew uses the term for those who consciously play at being pious (15.7; 22.18), and, more particularly, of those who are actually unaware of their religious vanity and 'play-acting', among whom at least some of the Pharisees could rightly be numbered.

they have their reward: the reward which the ostentatious receive (the word *apechō* is used in commercial transactions to mean 'sign a receipt for') is recognition and good repute among men: the reward for the truly pious is from God in heaven.

3. This verse advises disregard of self in the action of alms-giving: alms are given for the sake of the poor, not for personal satisfaction, or the glory of the giver: cf. B. Bab. Bath. 10b: 'The giver ought not to know to whom he is giving, and the receiver ought not to know from whom he receives.'

4. Almsgiving without ostentation, and motivated only by the desire to glorify and obey God in the relief of poverty, will be rewarded by God. The word 'openly', added in some texts here and at verse 6, is a gloss, but it agrees with the thought of the passage: the reward will be given in the coming age.

5. In the time of Jesus, prayer at the synagogue services was led by a member of the congregation who stood in front of the Ark of the Law for this purpose. At times of public fasting (and perhaps in response to the call to prayer at the time of the afternoon Temple sacrifice) prayers could be offered in the streets (cf. M. Taanith ii. 1f). There is no criticism here (by Matthew, or by Jesus) of public worship as such, only a warning against succumbing to the temptation to 'showiness' in performing it.

6. go into your room . . . and pray: reminiscent of Isa. 26.20, with 'pray' instead of 'hide': 'entering your room' is a metaphorical way of denoting privacy and the absence of pious admirers.

7. do not heap up empty phrases as the Gentiles do: it is not hypocrites who are criticized here, but Gentiles, whom Matthew does not specifically identify. Verses 7 and 8 and the Lord's Prayer break the strict pattern of verses 1-18 and its concentration on the avoidance of hypocritical behaviour. To **heap up empty phrases** (*battalogeō*) is probably connected with the Aramaic *baṭṭāl* ('idle, useless'): the word is used in an Aramaic papyrus from Qumran meaning 'without effect'. The Sinaitic Syriac MS. renders 'do not be saying idle things'. The idea behind the verse is that of the long prayers made by heathen people who believe that, in order to be sure of addressing the right god by the right name, all the gods and their titles have to be named. In place of **Gentiles** here Luke 11.2 (D) has 'the rest of men': this when rendered into Aramaic (*šarka deᵉnaša* = all others who were not disciples) would maintain the remarkable series of paronomasiae in this section (Black, *Aramaic Approach*, p. 177). Matthew's 'Gentiles' may be a Jewish interpretation of what is more correctly preserved in the Lucan variant.

8. The disciple has to address only one God, the Father in heaven, who does not require to be informed of a worshipper's need; as a father knows the needs of his family, yet teaches them to ask in confidence and trust, so does God treat his children.

The Lord's Prayer 9–13

It is not likely that the Lord's Prayer was originally (or in Matthew's sources) part of the context within which it here appears. The Lucan setting (11.2–4) is more natural (i.e. within the context of Jesus' private prayer and in response to a request), whereas in Matthew the prayer interrupts the succession of warnings against hypocritical piety.

Between the Matthean version of the prayer (with which the form in *Didachē* 8.2 is almost identical) and the Lucan there are considerable differences. Comparison of the best manuscripts demonstrates this clearly (see *RSV*), although the tendency to allow the Matthean version to influence the Lucan text has minimized the divergences in a large number of manuscripts (see *AV*). The shorter and less formal Lucan prayer is usually regarded as being nearer to the original. This view is supported by the following points:

(i) The introductory words in the Matthean version, 'Pray then like this', suggest a fixed or standardized form of prayer, and the emphatic 'you' in the Greek sets off the new Christian community from the synagogue (and Gentile usage) whose

piety is being contrasted with Christian worship in the
surrounding context.

(ii) Matthew's liturgical formulation of the prayer may reflect
      a desire to provide a counterpart to the main prayer of the
      Synagogue, the *Shemoneh Esreh* (to which it is noticeably
      similar in structure and form; cf. Kuhn, *Achtzehngebet*), or
      to an abbreviated Eighteen Benedictions (see Davies, *SSM*,
      pp. 310–13).
(iii) Luke would not have omitted clauses if the longer form
      had been known to him.
(iv) The shorter Lucan form is completely contained in the
      longer form of Matthew.

Not all scholars, however, are convinced that the problem can
be disposed of so easily. For instance, Lohmeyer (*Der Vater Unser*,
new edn, 1952) suggests that the Matthean and Lucan forms of the
prayer represent two separate traditions, each echoing Jesus' own
teaching and each with its own theological perspective; the
Matthean form emphasizes the eschatological outlook, while the
Lucan is concerned more with daily life. This is an important
insight, but Lohmeyer's attempt to demonstrate that the Matthean
form is the prayer of the Galilean community and the Lucan the
prayer of the Jerusalem church is not conclusive. Bonnard (p. 81)
appears to think that the Lucan form is a simplified version of a
fuller prayer like Matthew's. Our view is that the prayer in Matthew is an elaboration (for liturgical purposes) of a simpler form
of prayer (for private use) taught by Jesus himself to his disciples
and more truly preserved in Lk. 11.2–4.

Nowadays the 'Our Father' is regarded as a common property
of all people, but, in early times, the prayer and the privilege of
using it were reserved for full members of the Church. The connection of the prayer with baptism goes back to the first century:
the arrangement of the contents of the *Didachē* suggests that the
Lord's Prayer, as well as the Eucharist, was reserved for those who
had been baptized. (In addition to books already mentioned, the
reader is referred for further discussion to J. Jeremias, 'The Lord's
Prayer in Modern Research', *ET*, LXXI, 1960, pp. 141ff., and
Prayers, pp. 82–107; T. W. Manson, 'The Lord's Prayer', *BJRL*,
XXXVIII, 1955, pp. 99–113 and 436–48; Bornkamm, pp. 128f.; and
H. Schürmann, *Das Gebet des Herrn*, 1957.

9. Pray then like this: an introductory redactional formula linking the prayer to the preceding instruction on the avoidance of hypocrisy in devotion. Matthew does not discuss who is to say the Lord's Prayer or when: but according to *Didachē* 8.3 Christians were to say it three times a day, which corresponds perhaps to the Jewish practice of praying the Tefillah (*Shemoneh Esreh*) in the morning, afternoon and evening; cf. M. Berak iv.1.

Our Father who art in heaven: the address to God as 'Our Father' ('*abînû*) was employed in Jewish prayers (cf. Tob. 13.4; *Shem. Esreh*, petitions 5 and 6; B. Taanith 25b, '*Ahabâh rabâh*, and in graces after meals), but, out of reverence, the form 'Our (your, their) Father which is in heaven' was sometimes used. Luke has 'Father', and this is probably original. The Aramaic equivalent to it is '*abba* ('my father'), the address used by Jesus in his own prayer (e.g. Mk 14.36). It seems to be established that *abba* was a homely, family word, the tender and intimate address of a child to his father ('Daddy'). It was not used as the address of a Jewish worshipper to God, but the more formal termination of the same root, '*abînû* was employed; cf. Jeremias, *Prayers*, pp. 29–65, 108–112. From Rom. 8.15 and Gal. 4.6 we learn that this address of daring intimacy, originating with Jesus, became the Christian form of address to God; the actual Aramaic *abba* used by Jesus was retained in the prayer vocabulary of the early Greek-speaking Church. Matthew's version of the invocation here is his own expansion for liturgical purposes, and in accordance with customary Palestinian piety, of *Abba, ho patēr* (Mk 14.36; Rom. 8.15). **Hallowed be thy name:** the verb *hagiazō*, almost unknown in extra-biblical Greek, is frequently found in the LXX, where it translates the root *qds*, always in texts relating to the cult (Exod. 29.21; Dt. 22.9; Ezek. 29.23). It appears only here (= Lk. 11.2) and at Mt. 23.17, 19 in the Synoptic Gospels. To 'hallow' the name (i.e. the nature of God as known through his self-revelation in history) means, not only to reverence and honour God, but also to glorify him by obedience to his commands, and thus prepare the coming of the Kingdom.

10. Thy Kingdom come: this petition, along with the previous clause, recalls the *Qaddish* ('sanctification'), an Aramaic prayer which formed the conclusion of every synagogue service. In its oldest form this probably ran: 'Hallowed be his great name in the world which he created according to his will: may he establish his

Kingdom during your life, even speedily and soon. So say Amen.'
The petition desires the final establishment of God's sovereignty
(*malkûṯ* = *basileia*), the definitive consummation of the divine rule
over the lives of men which had been inaugurated in the coming
of Jesus: cf. the Aramaic prayer in 1 C. 16.22: *Maranatha* ('Our
Lord, come'), and Rev. 22.20. For the Marcionite variant of this
clause found in some late manuscripts of Luke, see Leaney, pp.
6of., 68; and Ellis, p. 163.

Thy will be done. On earth as it is in heaven: a petition not
found in Luke. Its content is parallel to the preceding clause, and
it may have been introduced by Matthew to give a three-fold
liturgical parallelism. If the meaning of 'will' (*thelēma*) here is
something like 'God's purpose in history' (or his 'goodwill', in the
sense of 'election', since the Aramaic *rᵉʿûṯa* (= Hebrew *rāṣôn*) is
translated *thelēma* in Ps. 40.9, but often by *eudokia*), then the link
with the preceding clause is closer—the will of God being the
manifestation of his reign—and the thought has a striking similarity
with the angels' song in Lk. 2.14. This interpretation is strengthened
by the Qumran parallels; see E. Vogt, *SNT*, pp. 114–17. However, it is likely that for Matthew the word 'will' had ethical
connotations as well—the will of God which men must obey—
for this is an outlook characteristic of Matthean catechesis (cf.
7.21; 12.50; 18.14; 21.31). 'There is a sense in which the Kingdom
comes whenever and wherever God's will is acknowledged and
obeyed on earth' (Manson, *Sayings*, p. 169). The phrase 'on earth
as in heaven' probably qualifies only the preceding petition, not
all three, for it would rob them of much of their eschatological
character: it means either 'both on heaven and on earth', i.e.
everywhere, or 'on the earth (at the end) as in heaven (now)'. But
see G. H. P. Thompson, *ET*, LXX, 1959, pp. 379–81.

11. Give us this day our daily bread: this form of the petition is probably more original than the Lucan, 'Give us (Greek
present imperative) each day our daily bread'. The meaning of
epiousios ('daily') has been much discussed; it is not attested with
certainty outside the Lord's Prayer in Matthew and Luke (cf.
B. M. Metzger, *ET*, LXIX, 1957, pp. 52–4.) The suggestion that the
term means 'for our essential need (*epi tēn ousian*) is as unlikely as
Jerome's Eucharistic interpretation, *panem superstantialem* (*ousia* =
substans)—'bread of a superstantial, spiritual kind'—and Debrunner's 'for the present (day)', i.e. *epi tēn ousan* (*hēmeran*) (Blass-

Debrunner, *Greek Grammar*, p. 66). Black (*Aramaic Approach*, pp. 203–7) offers the suggestion that an Aramaic idiom for 'this day and tomorrow' (= 'day by day') has been mistranslated in Matthew, but correctly rendered by Luke's addition *to kath' hēmeran*. Perhaps the most probable explanation of the word is that which is based on the derivation *ep-iousa*, 'that which is coming'—i.e. bread for the coming (day). Jerome attests the Aramaic reading of the *Gospel according to the Hebrews* (*Nazareans*) as *maḥar* ('of tomorrow'). If this is correct, the 'coming day' would mean the day then in progress if the prayer was said in the morning, or the following day if the prayer was said in the evening; but the futuristic reference in the word would permit of an eschatological understanding as well, and this would be in keeping with the tone of the prayer as a whole. 'Bread for the morrow' would include the nourishment of the Messianic banquet, and perhaps also that required by the disciples for the final testing days of the Messianic community (cf. Bonnard, p. 86). 'The petition does not sever everyday life and the Kingdom of God from one another, but it encompasses the totality of life. It embraces everything that Jesus' disciples need for body and soul' (Jeremias, *Prayers*, p. 102).

12. And forgive us our debts: the Greek *opheilēma* means a literal 'debt' in the LXX and *NT*, except at this point: but the Aramaic word *ḥôbā* ('debt') was often used (e.g. in the Targums) for 'sin' and 'transgression'. Matthew gives a literal translation of the original Aramaic word, whereas Luke has reproduced its meaning. **as we also have forgiven our debtors:** this translation suggests that disciples' forgiveness precedes God's forgiveness, and that it must do so. The aorist is found in the best texts, and must be retained (Luke has the present tense); but it should probably be understood as an Aramaic *perfectum praesens*, indicating an action which takes place here and now ('as we herewith forgive our debtors' (so Jeremias). He who prays for God's forgiveness must himself be prepared to forgive; cf. Mk 11.25; Col. 3.13. We have an anticipation of this petition in Sir. 28.2: 'Forgive thy neighbour the injury [done to thee] and, when thou prayest, thy sins will be forgiven.' There are also rabbinic parallels (*SB* I, pp. 424ff.).

13. and lead us not into temptation: the original Aramaic was probably 'and cause us not to enter', the causative having a permissive force ('allow us not to enter'); and the question whether God directs toward temptation is hardly involved. The idea may be of not being allowed to be overwhelmed by the temptation, and therefore of not succumbing; cf. the old Jewish evening prayer: 'Do not bring me *into the power of* a sin, a temptation, a shame' (B. Berak. 60b). The word 'temptation' can mean 'trial' or 'test', in the sense of suffering, persecution, martyrdom (cf. *NEB*, 'do not bring us to the test'), and, in the eschatological context of this prayer, it may well include reference to the final testing of God's people, the sufferings which precede the consummation of the Kingdom (cf. Matt. 24; Rev. 3.10).

but deliver us from evil: the verb 'deliver' (*rhuesthai*) may mean, 'rescue from' or 'protect against'. Whether 'evil' (*tou ponērou*) is 'evil' in the general or abstract sense, or the 'Evil One' (the Devil) is not clear from the Greek; but since neither Hebrew nor Aramaic uses 'the evil (one)' to denote Satan, it is probably better to regard the word as neuter and the 'evil' as being that evil, either spiritual or moral, which may befall men in this present time (so Gaechter, p. 220) or (stressing again the eschatological note, as in verse 13a) the evil of apostasy that threatens the disciples at the end; cf. the seventh petition of the Eighteen Benedictions: 'Look upon our affliction . . . and redeem us speedily for thy name's sake.'

Doxology. At this point in some manuscripts, but not the best or most important authorities, there follows the doxology ('For thine is the kingdom, the power and the glory, for ever, Amen'). It is omitted by Luke, by most of the early Fathers, and in most modern texts and translations. It is probably a fixed liturgical addition giving a private prayer a form suitable for use in worship: if so, it is not an original part of the prayer, nor of Matthew's version. Based probably on 1 Chr. 29.11, it was added not later than the early second century. The *Didachē* adds a shorter doxology: 'for thine is the power and the glory for ever'. On the possibility that the doxology does belong to the original prayer, see Davies, *SSM*, pp. 451–3, and C. F. D. Moule, *JTS*, x, 1959, pp. 253f. Even in the time of Jesus it would have been very unusual for a Jewish prayer to have ended without a doxology, expressed or assumed, but the form of words may have remained the choice of the person praying until this prayer became increasingly used as a common prayer in worship when a fixed form of doxology was established.

14–15. These two verses, which are absent from Luke, emphatically restate, in positive and negative forms, the substance of verse 12. They do not belong to this context. The form and setting of verse 14 in Mk 11.25 looks more original, and there is a doublet of verse 15 at Mt. 18.35. The verses should be understood in the sense of the Parable of the Unforgiving Servant (18.23–35); the community that prays with power must be a forgiving community. As in Mk 11.25, the word for 'sin' is no longer 'debt' but 'trespass' (*paraptōma*), lit. 'a falling from the right way'.

16–18. After the insertion of the extra teaching on prayer (verses 7(9)–15) Matthew returns to the warnings against hypocritical piety, and gives instruction on fasting.

16. When you fast: the practice of fasting is here taken for granted, although in 9.14–17 Jesus defends its disuse by his disciples as long as he was with them. In addition to the solemn fasts of the Day of Atonement, the New Year, and the anniversaries of notable calamities in Jewish history, public fasts were also occasioned by special circumstances, e.g. if the autumn rains failed. In such an event, stricter Jews would fast on Mondays and Thursdays (M. Taanith i.4–7); these 'fasts of the hypocrites' (i.e. the Jews, or perhaps the Pharisees) are referred to in *Didachē* 8.1, and Christian fasting on Wednesdays and Fridays is enjoined. Private fasts were also undertaken by individuals as a means of moral and religious self-discipline (cf. Lk. 18.12; Mk 2.18), and these offered an opportunity for winning a reputation for piety. Jesus is not opposed to the practice in principle, only to its hypocritical use. **do not look dismal:** lit. 'do not be gloomy'. The word translated 'dismal' (*skuthrōpos*) is used in Dan. 1.10 (Theod.) in connection with fasting, and also at Lk. 24.17. The point is not that the 'hypocrites' look gloomy and are in fact not so, but that they can draw attention to themselves by their moroseness.

for they disfigure their faces: by not washing the face, by not tending the hair, and by strewing ashes on the head. These outward signs advertise the fact that fasting is taking place, and the only reward for this kind of exercise is the popular admiration won (cf. Abrahams 1, pp. 121–8). In later Jewish teaching such ostentatious piety is condemned. The word for 'disfigure' (*aphanizō*) is literally 'make invisible', and probably is a play on *phanōsin* ('that they may be seen'). The same verb occurs in verse 19 with the stronger meaning 'destroy'.

17. This saying probably means that disciples are not to change their daily behaviour during a voluntary fast: they are to appear as they normally do. 'Anointing', as a symbol of joy, has suggested to some writers that disciples, when fasting, are to appear as if prepared for a feast; this practice, however, would draw just as much attention to itself as the actions of the hypocrites. Normal behaviour is what is enjoined; and the Father, who knows the inward attitude that is expressed by a disciple's unpretentious fasting, will reward his sincerity of purpose.

WEALTH AND WORRY 6.19-34

This section brings together in the Matthean sermon material which originally had other settings: verses 19-21 = Lk. 12.33f.; verses 22f. = Lk. 11.34ff.; verses 24 = Lk. 16.13; verses 25-34 = Lk. 12.22-31. The theme which unites the passages for the evangelist is that of an obedient loyalty to God which excludes wordly concerns.

Treasure 19-21

The emphasis on reward (from men and from God) in verses 1-18 leads naturally to this saying. The poetical character of these verses is demonstrated by Black, *Aramaic Approach*, pp. 178f. A short strophe of three three-stress lines (verse 19) indicates the wrong way: a second such strophe describes the right way (verse 20), and a four-stress line, stating a general truth, rounds off the piece. Such rhythm and balance suggests that these verses contain original dominical teaching.

19. The treasures gathered on earth include (in true ancient oriental style) costly clothing which moths may 'corrupt' or 'consume' (*aphanizō*). The word translated 'rust' is *brōsis*, which denotes any act of eating or corrosion: 'rust' suggests the destruction of something made of metal, but the alternative rendering 'worm' (*RSV*n) again suggests the corruption of garments and woven articles. Older commentaries suggest that the picture is of farm produce being devoured by mice and other vermin (McNeile, p. 84). A further danger to accumulated goods is the activity of thieves, who 'break through' (*lit.* 'dig through') house walls made of mud-brick and steal property.

20. Treasures in heaven are exempt from corrosions and decay, and are beyond the reach of thieves. The Lucan form of the saying, 'where no thief approaches and no moth destroys' (11.33), gives a striking example of paronomasia when translated into Aramaic. The idea of 'treasures in heaven' (i.e. what wins divine approval and reward in the coming Kingdom) is thoroughly Jewish; cf. M. Peah i.1; Test. Levi 13.5; Ps. Sol. 9.9.

21. Cf. Justin, *Apol*. i.15: 'Where his treasure is, there also is the mind of man.' Each individual sets his heart on what he counts important, and this allegiance determines the direction and content of his life.

The Sound Eye **22–3**

In Lk. 11.34–36 this saying is attached to words on the theme of 'light' (=Mt. 5.15) but its connection with the immediate context here is not clear. Depending on the interpretation put on the word for 'sound', the meaning may be either 'Give undivided attention to heavenly treasure', or 'Be generous with earthly possessions'.

22. The eye is the lamp of the body: i.e. the eye is the light which enables the body to find its way. In the *OT* the 'eye', as well as the 'heart', may indicate the total direction of a person's will and life (cf. 'the hostile eye', Dt. 15.9).
if your eye is sound: the Greek word is *haplous*. Since this term is obviously opposite to 'evil' (*ponēros*), and since in Jewish parlance 'the evil eye' denotes a jealous or niggardly attitude, it can be argued that *haplous* means here (as its cognates in Hellenistic Greek) 'generous', 'liberal' (cf. Rom. 12.8; Jas 1.5). In this case, Matthew intends the saying to refer to the generous giving away of possessions (Allen, p. 62). But *haplous* and cognate words in the LXX represent the Hebrew root *tām*, meaning 'singleness of purpose', or 'undivided loyalty', especially to God (e.g. 1 Chr. 29.17; Ps. 101.2), and the Aramaic *šᵉlîm* (= Hebrew *tām*) can mean both 'undivided commitment' and 'health'. This interpretation is to be preferred. 'If man divides his interest and tries to focus on both God and possessions, he has no clear vision, and will live without clear orientation or direction' (Filson, p. 100). The theme of undivided loyalty to God is continued in verse 24.
your whole body will be full of light: 'your whole body' is a literal rendering of an Aramaic expression which means 'you yourself'. 'Full of light' (*phōteinos*) includes the idea of giving light.
23. not sound: Greek *ponēros*, which could mean 'miserly', but which here probably denotes the eye that is 'focussed on evil' and draws a man into evil ways. The last part of the verse simply

reiterates what has been affirmed: the man whose eye (=direction
of life) is not fixed on obedience to God will be plunged into darkness. The contrast between 'light' and 'darkness' (spiritually understood) is found in John's Gospel and in the Qumran literature.

Singleness of Service 24

In Lk. 16.13 this saying appears at the end of the parable of the
Unjust Steward and its application (cf. *Gospel of Thomas* 47). The
reference to 'mammon' may have caused Luke to assume that the
verse belonged to a series of instructions on money. In Matthew's
placing, the saying sums up clearly the intention of the two preceding paragraphs (verses 19–23). Loyalty to God must be undivided.
No one can serve two masters: 'serve' is used in the sense of 'be
a slave to'; 'men can work for two employers, but no slave can be
the property of two owners' (McNeile, p. 85).
hate the one . . . love the other: the verbs here have a comparative force: 'to hate' means 'to be indifferent to, or unconcerned
for'.
be devoted to: Greek *antechesthai* (cf. 1 Th. 5.14, Tit. 1.9),
which means here 'hold firmly to', or 'stick by', and therefore
'support'. Some versions have 'endure', which presupposes
anexetai rather than *anthexetai*. These clauses have the balance and
rhythm of Semitic poetry.
mammon: the word (properly spelt, *mamōn*) is probably derived
from the Hebrew root *'mn*, used to denote that in which one has
confidence. Its use is well attested in rabbinic literature with the
meaning 'money', 'profit', 'wealth' (not necessarily with any bad
connotation) (J. Peah 1.1; B. Berak. 61b). The term is found
frequently in 1 Enoch to denote the illusory security of this
world as contrasted with the single-minded trust in God on the part
of the poor saints of Israel. It is impossible to combine devotion to
God with devotion to wealth.

On Worry 25–34

This section carries forward the main theme of the preceding
paragraphs, viz. the necessity for exclusive engagement to the
service of God. 'To seek God's kingdom and righteousness' (verse
33) is to serve God, to be concerned with his will alone (verses
22–3), and to be detached from transient treasures (verses 19–21).
Although Luke breaks up the material gathered together in verses

19-24, he has a block corresponding to verses 25-33 in 12.22-31 (part of his discourse on earthly and heavenly riches): but he has nothing parallel to verse 34, nor to 'righteousness' in verse 33, a term which is undoubtedly important to Matthew. The literary structure of the passage—general instruction; two illustrations (birds, flowers); more precise statement of the instruction on the three basic kinds of worry; and a conclusion (verse 33) which elucidates the meaning of the injunction—suggests that it may have belonged to primitive catechesis.

25. The connection in thought with what precedes seems to be that single-minded devotion to God dispels anxiety about ordinary material needs. 'Do not be anxious' (better than 'take no thought', *AV*) forbids agitated worry (cf. Lk. 10.41). The word *psychē* could be rendered 'soul', and the parallelism between 'soul' and 'body' in the verse would be very suitable; but 'soul' would have to be understood in the Jewish sense, as the essential element in a man's vitality or aliveness (obviously sustained by food), and that is not far from the meaning of 'life'. The form of argument in the second half of the verse, *a minori ad maius* (cf. 7.11) is very common in rabbinic usage.

26. The illustration from the birds teaches freedom from worry, not idleness. Lk. 12.24 has 'the ravens', and this may be original, since in Palestinian Syriac the word for 'ravens' provides a paronomasia with the word for 'feed'. In its Lucan context this discourse is preceded by the parable of the Rich Fool, who decided to pull down his barns and build larger ones. This suggests that the Lucan setting of the teaching is correct, but it should be pointed out that 'gather into barns' is a suitable sequel in any context to the mention of sowing and reaping.

27. one cubit to his span of life: The cubit is a small unit of length (about 18 inches). *RSV*n gives the alternative 'to his stature' (cf. Lk. 19.3); 'span of life' is the more normal meaning of *hēlikia*. The point is that a man cannot add to the length of his life by worrying.

28. Consider: the Greek word *katamanthanō* occurs only here in the *NT*; it implies careful study with a view to learning.
lilies: possibly wild flowers in general; 'flowers of the field' would then balance 'birds of the air'.
toil, spin: probably the words represent a play on the Aramaic, *ʿāmal* and *ʾazal*.

30. the grass of the field: this either includes or is equivalent to 'lilies', which must therefore indicate wild flowers.

O men of little faith: cf. 8.26; 14.31; 16.8, where the word refers to lack of trust in Jesus' power. Here it means 'lacking confidence in God's care and provision'.

32. the Gentiles: possibly the meaning underlying *ethnikoi* here (as in 5.47 and 6.7) is 'the rest of men'—i.e. the rest of the world, as contrasted with the inner circle of disciples. If this is not so, the point is that anxiety about food, drink and clothes is *pagan*, as well as being an affront to God, who will not overlook the legitimate needs of his people.

33. The primary object of the disciples' unceasing quest (the present imperative in Greek indicates continuing action) is to be **his kingdom** (some manuscripts, not the best, add 'of God'), which means God's sovereign rule or kingship. While this is not established by man, a man's undivided loyalty and obedience to God shows his purposeful desire to make the divine will and reign (already present in Jesus) his real objective. If this is a man's dominant concern, then all other necessary requirements will be satisfied in the generosity of God. The words **his righteousness** are a Matthean addition (cf. Lk. 12.31); the term could be used here, as in Deutero-Isaiah, to denote the vindicating action of God which saves those who seek him (so Filson, p. 102). This interpretation would necessitate understanding the Kingdom as wholly eschatological, but for Matthew the Kingdom is a present reality in those who believe and acknowledge God's sovereign demand. Therefore it is more probable that 'righteousness' here means (as elsewhere in Matthew) righteousness of life in agreement with the will of God, at the heart of which lies obedience and trust.

34. This verse (absent from Luke) is added by Matthew because it is consistent with the theme of the section (i.e. 'do not be anxious'); the implication is that only by faith in God and by seeking first his Kingdom will men be delivered from worry about tomorrow; cf. B. San. 100b: 'Be not anxious for the morrow, for thou knowest not what a day may bring forth.' The second clause also has a rabbinic parallel in B. Berak. 9a: 'There is enough trouble in its hour.' The word *kakia* is used to denote what is evil from the human point of view; it is a frequent translation in the LXX of *rā'āh* = 'trouble'.

On Judging Others 1-5

These verses, which contain warnings addressed to disciples, have
no connection in thought with what immediately precedes. Their
context in Luke (6.37f., 41f.) indicates that they logically follow
from 5.48, the point at which Matthew departed from his source
to introduce the material gathered in chapter 6. The structure of
the section is simple, and typical of rabbinical methods of teaching:
the instruction is first stated (verse 1), and followed by its theological justification (verse 2); then come two illustrations of the
main point, one of which is elaborated (verse 5) in order to re-
affirm, in an ironic way, the inappropriateness of judging others.
The longer form of verses 1-2 in Luke shows a poetic structure (cf.
Burney, pp. 114, 123), and may be the more original. Rabbinic
tradition provides numerous parallels to this passage; cf. B. Shab.
127b; M. Sotah i.7; and B. Bab. Metzia 59b.

1. Disciples must not be censorious and condemning in their
attitude to others; cf. Jas 4.11f. To sit in judgment on others is to
invite condemnation by God, and that condemnation may operate
through judgment by others. It is possible, but not necessary, to
understand the second clause as referring to God's final judgment.
The word **that** (*hina*) probably represents a forceful rendering of
the Aramaic *de*, which Lk. 6.27 translate by 'and'.

2. **For with the judgment you pronounce you will be
judged:** this is not simply a recommendation to be moderate in
judgment on others. The meaning is that, if you condemn, you
exclude yourself from God's pardon. 'Nothing more surely shuts
out a man from love than a censorious and unforgiving disposition.
He who will not forgive closes his own heart against God's forgiveness', Manson, *Sayings*, p. 56. Cf. 18.23-35.

the measure you give will be the measure you get: this saying, which may be proverbial (cf. M. Sotah i.7), is found in Mk
4.24b referring to the spirit in which a man receives teaching.
According to the rabbis, God judged the world by two 'measures'
—mercy and justice (Lev. R. xxix.3). If this idea lies behind the
saying, then the meaning is: 'If you want to be mercifully dealt
with, show mercy now', and that is parallel to the meaning suggested for the preceding clause.

3-4. These sayings about the 'speck' (the Greek word denotes a little piece of dried wood or straw) and the 'log'—a piece of Oriental hyperbole—are not intended to set forth conditions for legitimate judging: they are meant to exclude all condemnation of others. The words many have become proverbial; cf. B. Arachin 16b: R. Tarphon said, 'If one said to another, "Cast the mote out of thine eye", he would answer, "Cast the beam out of thine eye".'

5. This verse would seem to contradict what precedes by allowing judgment of others after self-judgment has taken place. It is probably correct, therefore, to regard the verse as an ironic statement with the meaning: 'Since you will never be able to get rid of all your own hindrances and see absolutely clearly, do not condemn your brother's fault.' The sentiment is the same as in Jn 8.7: 'Let him who is without sin among you be the first to throw a stone at her.'

On Discrimination 6

This enigmatic saying, which is peculiar to Matthew, does not seem to be linked either to what precedes or to what follows. The best suggestion is that it is intended to limit the range of application of the command 'Do not judge'. The disciple must not act without some discrimination and discernment and give 'what is holy' to those who are irresponsible and unappreciative. The words are quoted in *Didachē* 9.5 in forbidding the admission of unbaptized persons to the Eucharist: cf. also the liturgical form used before the distribution of Eucharistic elements, 'Holy things (*ta hagia*) to the holy'.

Do not give . . . swine: 'what is holy' forms a strange parallelism with 'pearls'. There is much to be said for the suggestion (made by A. Meyer and F. Perles) that *to hagion* is a mistranslation of the Aramaic *qᵉdaša* (Hebrew *nezem*) 'a ring' usually of gold; see further Black, *Aramaic Approach*, pp. 200ff. Prov.11.22 describes a beautiful woman without discretion as 'a gold ring in a swine's snout'. Black suggests that *to hagion* may just not represent a mistranslation, but may be an intentional interpretation of the Aramaic, just as the *Didachē* further interprets the words of the Eucharist. A less satisfactory suggestion is that *to hagion* refers to holy foods or meals which had been offered in the Temple (cf. Lev. 22.14 and for the opposite regulation, Exod. 22.31). The theory has been put forward that in this verse 'dogs' and 'swine' symbolize heathens or Gentiles, *and* that the meaning is a directive against mission to the Gentiles (cf. 10.5): even if this idea can be taken legitimately from the words, it is unlikely to have been part of the meaning of the original Aramaic saying, which simply warned against lack of discrimination (in teaching?), for God gives forgiveness only to the forgiving and mercy to the merciful. The last two clauses may be a chiastic arrangement, the 'trampling' referring to the swine and the 'turning to attack' being the action of the dogs.

On Praying 7–11

In Luke (11.9–13) this passage suitably follows the parable of the Friend at Midnight and the Lord's Prayer, and it is applied to the gift of the Holy Spirit; here the verses seem to have no connection in thought with the passages which precede and follow. The structure of verses 7–8 reveals an almost perfect symmetry: each verse has three lines in synonymous parallelism, as are the two verses themselves. There follow two illustrations from everyday life and the passage ends with an *a fortiori* argument, characteristic of rabbinic and of Matthean teaching. Rabbinic tradition laid great stress on God's willingness to answer prayer.

7–8. The imperatives **Ask ... seek ... knock ...** are emphatic, and express a confident attitude towards the Father in heaven. No limitations or conditions are attached to the statement, though presumably sincerity is required; cf. Jer. 29.13 (LXX 36.13): 'You will seek me and find me, when you seek me with all your heart.'
Knock: cf. B. Meg. 12b: 'Mordecai knocked at the doors of mercy, and they were opened to him'; also Pesik. 176a (with reference to studying the Mishnah), 'If a man knocks, it will be opened to him'. At this point in Matthew, the knocking does not mean seeking to enter the Kingdom (13f.); the situation presupposed is that described in Lk. 11.5–8.

9–10. These two verses indicate that prayer takes place in a father–son relationship. Both in Judaism and Christianity, this natural relationship was used to clarify the relationship of the believer to God. Bread and fish represent the foods that would be most common around the Sea of Galilee.

11. The *a fortiori* type of argument ('how much more') is typical of rabbinic methods of teaching. 'You ... who are evil' is a comparative statement; cf. Mk 10.18. When compared with God, all men, even kind parents, are evil. The meaning of the word **evil** need not be confined entirely to 'grudging', 'niggardly'. Instead of **good things** Luke has 'the Holy Spirit'; but, although the Lucan setting of this passage is more natural, Matthew's version is likely to be nearer to the original.

The Golden Rule 12

In Matthew the Golden Rule appears as a separate *logion*, which sums up the good works demanded of Christians in 5.20–7.11. In Luke, it has a more natural setting among sayings on love of enemies (6.31), following the verse parallel to Mt. 5.42. The negative form of the Rule was known in Judaism before the time of Jesus (cf. Tob. 4.15), and Hillel enunciated it again in the negative: 'What is hateful to you, do not do to your fellow-creature. That is the whole law; all else is explanation' (B. Shab. 31a). Only in the teaching of Jesus is the rule given in the positive form (but see Isocrates, *Nikoclēs*, 49; 2 Enoch 61.1); yet it is surprising to find that this positive note was not retained when early Christians referred to the rule. The Western text of Ac. 15.29 has the negative form, as has the *Didachē* (1.2) and the *Apostolic Constitutions*: Theophilus (*ad Autol.* i.35) and Irenaeus III.xii.14 give both forms, while Tertullian (*adv. Marc.* 4.16) remarks that the positive form must imply the negative. Matthew's concluding remark 'for this is the law and the prophets' means that for him (cf. 22.40), as for Hillel, the Rule was an acceptable summary of God's revelation. 'It must therefore appear quite odd', says Stendahl (*Peake*, 681m), 'when the Golden Rule is used as an epitome of what was new with Jesus.' Those who regard it thus overemphasize the fact that the positive form seems peculiar to Jesus' teaching. The actual substance of the Rule was not new.

12. The Matthean form stresses not only the quality of the action (**do so** (*houtōs kai*)) as does Luke, but also the quantity (lit. 'everything that you wish men to do'). The second part of the verse is absent in Luke, and probably does not belong to the primitive tradition.

THE TWO WAYS 7.13–29

The four concluding paragraphs of the Sermon on the Mount (verses 13–14, 15–20, 21–3 and 24–7) contain sayings which in Luke have different contexts. The theme which binds them together here seems to be the warning note expressed in a series of contrasts. The emphasis in these verses is both eschatological and ethical. The catachetical use of this material in the Matthean church is indicated by the distinctive form in which it is presented.

Two Gates, Two Ways 13–14

What is found in Luke (13.23f.) in a definitely eschatological context (answering the question, 'Will those who are saved be few?') appears in Matthew in the form of instruction on the Two Ways. The idea of the Two Ways is found in Dt. 30.19 and Jer. 21.8, and had wide currency in Jewish and Christian writings (*Didachē* 1.1; Barn. 18.1; 4 Ezra 7.7ff.; Test. Asher 1.3, 5, P. Aboth ii.12–13). It may have been employed originally as a Jewish catechetical form and have been taken over as a pattern for Christian instruction (see P. Carrington, *The Primitive Christian Catechism*). The same theme is found in the writings of the Qumran sect: cf. the way of light and the way of darkness, 1QS 3.20ff.

13. Enter by the narrow gate: the gate leads to the Kingdom (for which 'life' in verse 14 is a synonym). In Matthew the Kingdom is not wholly futuristic: therefore this saying need not be entirely eschatological in orientation. Those who find and follow Jesus enter the life of the Kingdom, which is inaugurated at his coming.

the gate is wide and the way is easy: some manuscripts omit 'the gate' and read 'for the way is wide and easy': but the word preserves the balance of the clauses. The *RSV* rendering suggests that the path to destruction is easy to walk: but the Greek word *eurychōros* means 'spacious, roomy'—the kind of road in which 'many' are found.

14. hard: the translation is rather misleading. The Greek *tethlimmenē* means 'pressed together', i.e. not spacious and roomy: it is not the road for everybody; only the few (cf. the antithesis in 22.14) will find and follow this path.

On False Prophets 15–20

The first verse of this section is probably the work of the evangelist himself. The verses following have parallels in Lk. 6.43–5, where they are concerned with genuineness in personal religion.

Matthew has used them, with reference to the ecclesiastical situation, to suggest criteria for judging false prophets.

15. This is not a reference to the Pharisees or to some other 'false' Jewish teachers, but to false Christian prophets, as in 24.11, 24, where their coming is predicted (cf. also 1 Jn 4.1). The discernment of true and false prophets was to be one of the chief interests of the *Didachē* (11.7–12). The 'false prophets' could easily be taken for good teachers: they are like lambs, and 'this deception more befits a false Christian than either a Pharisee or any other kind of Jewish "false prophet" who could not so easily deceive' (Davies, *SSM*, p. 200). For 'wolves' used in this sense, see Ezek. 22.27; Zeph. 3.3; Jn 10.12; Ac. 20.29. Since the verse envisages the situation in the early Church, it is unlikely that it is a genuine utterance of Jesus.

16. You will know them by their fruits: i.e. 'by their conduct'. *Didachē* 11.3 says 'By their behaviour shall the false and the true prophets be known'. The Lucan saying (6.44), 'each tree is known by its fruits', is more clearly echoed in Mt. 12.33. It is probable that Matthew has transformed that saying in order to provide a connection between the false prophets and the simile of the trees. The theme of the verses is that before God a man is what he *does*, not what he pretends to be.

17, 18. These verses illustrate a Semitic way of emphasizing a point: the statement is made positively (17), and then negatively (18).

19. This saying appears in the preaching of the Baptist (Mt. 3.10; Lk. 3.9). Matthew has added it here from its earlier occurrence, but Luke does not employ it in 6.43ff.

On True and False Service 21–3

Those who cry 'Lord, Lord', are the false prophets of verses 15f. This identification is suggested by the context as a whole and by the use of the word 'prophesy' in verse 22.

21. Not every one who says to me, 'Lord Lord' . . .: Luke's form ('Why do you call me Lord, Lord and not do what I tell you?', 6.46) is more direct and personal, and is likely to be more original (Bultmann, *HST*, p. 116). Matthew gives the saying an eschatological reference. The title 'Lord' occurs as a form of polite address to Jesus (= 'Sir'), but most scholars think that more than that is meant here. Some would see Jesus here assuming the name and authority of him who will judge at the last day ('Lord' was the later title of worship); others think that the verse reflects the constant use of the name 'Lord' by disciples in order to authorize their miracles (so Bonnard, p. 106). Such interpretations presuppose the influence on Matthew of the post-Resurrection thought of the Church, which makes of this address more than it could have meant to Jesus' hearers—if it is an original utterance. That original sense could only be something like 'master, teacher' (i.e. the one with right to lead and to teach), which is the meaning implied by Luke's saying.

the will of my Father: the divine guidance for daily conduct has been revealed by Christ in his interpretation of the Law (chapters 5–7), and entry into the Kingdom depends on obedience to that. The Matthean church seems to have been unaware of or uninfluenced by Pauline Christianity (cf. Rom. 10.9), probably because the problems posed to it were of a different kind.

22. On that day: an allusion to the Last Judgment. The words are derived from the *OT* and prophetic literature originating in the period between the *OT* and *NT* (cf. Mal. 3.17–18 and Enoch 45.3), and form a technical eschatological expression.

many will say to me . . .: the reference to prophecy, to mighty works, and to exorcisms in the name of the Lord (i.e., claiming to act for and with the authority of Jesus) reflects the situation of the early Church when the claim to charismatic endowment was widespread (Ac. 19.13; Jas 5.14f.). The early Church soon discovered that not all the enthusiasts who made such claims were genuine.

23. It is not denied that deeds of power and prophecy have taken place, but they do not prove that those who performed them are true disciples. The criterion for genuine discipleship is obedience to the will of God. Cf. *Didachē* 11.8: 'But not everyone who speaks in a spirit is a prophet, except he have the behaviour of the Lord.' The rejection 'I never knew you' corresponds to the mildest form of ban pronounced by the rabbis (*SB* IV, p. 293): it means 'I have nothing to do with you', or 'You mean nothing to me.' The reference to Ps. 6.9 in the last clause is interesting; the Lucan version (13.27) follows the LXX in having *apostēte* ('depart'): Matthew has *apochōreite*, a verb which does not appear again in his Gospel. But Matthew has retained the LXX's 'workers of *anomia*', whereas Luke has 'workers of *adikia*'. Mat-

thew's 'lawlessness' is behaviour contrary to the law of God as
reinterpreted by the Sermon on the Mount; the emphasis on the
importance of conduct persists. The form of the saying in 2 Clem.
4.5 has *anomia*, but in other respect it is nearer to the Lucan
version. Stendahl (pp. 89f.) points out that a certain freedom in
quoting *OT* texts is characteristic of apocalyptic passages such as
this.

The Parable of the Two House-Builders 24-7

In verses 15-20 the emphasis was on 'bearing fruit', and in verses
21ff. on 'doing the will of the Father': in both cases the Greek verb
is *poiein*, and this is again the central word in verses 24ff. The
parable marks the conclusion of the Sermon on the Mount, and it
ends the Sermon on the Plain in Luke (6.47-9). The important
material of the passage is common to both Gospels, but there are
slight differences in presentation. Matthew's builder has security
because he chose solid rock rather than sandy soil as his foundation; Luke's because he dug deep and laid foundations instead of
building on the surface. An interesting parallel to the main idea of
the parable is found in Dt. 28.15, 30, 'If you will not obey the
voice of the Lord your God, or be careful to do all his commandments and his statutes . . . you shall build a house, and you shall
not dwell in it.' In Matthew's context the threat is predominantly
eschatological, although the testing of the foundations may take
place at any time throughout life as well.

24. these words of mine: these are the words which appear
in chapters 5-7: 'mine' is emphatic, and the translation might be
'everyone who hears me, in respect of these saying' (so Davies,
SSM, p. 94, who goes on to point out that 'in this sense, the
ethical teaching is not detached from the life of him who uttered it
and with whom it is congruous').
a wise man: the adjective *phronimos* is characteristic of Matthew's
vocabulary (10.16; 24.46; 25.2, 4, 8, 9). The prudence or wisdom
of a man is shown in his putting into practice the teaching of Jesus.
25. rain . . . floods . . . winds: the image of the tempest in the
OT often indicates the divine wrath and condemnation (Ezek.
13.10ff.). Luke speaks of an inundation without winds; and
Bonnard (p. 109) suggests that the evangelists adapted the parable
to the geological and climatic conditions known to their hearers or
readers.

Editorial Conclusion **28–9**

This is the first of five times a formula appears in Matthew (the other places are 11.1; 15.53; 19.1; 26.1), which, on each occasion, marks the transition between a long discourse and the continuation of the narrative. That this is important for the structure of the Gospel is undeniable, but it does not necessarily mean that Matthew intended the five blocks of teaching material to correspond to the five books of Moses: see Introduction, pp. 38–9.

28. when Jesus finished . . .: this is the repeated formula and it is only when Matthew uses it that he employs the expression *egeneto*, lit. 'it came to pass' (a Semitic expression characteristic of Mark's Greek).

the crowds were astonished at his teaching: this is the only one of the five editorial conclusions which mentions the surprise of the crowds. It seems very probable that Matthew is now returning to the Marcan material at 1.22, the point at which he introduced his first block of teaching (i.e. after the first reference to Jesus' teaching in Mk 1.21). The astonishment of the crowds (who were not actually present at the Sermon!—cf. 5.1) is a mixture of admiration and religious shock.

29. as one who had authority, and not as their scribes: Mark's 'the scribes' is changed by Matthew to 'their scribes' probably to distinguish Jewish scribes from the class of Christian scribes which by the time of writing of this Gospel had grown up in the Church (cf. 13.52; 23.34). The scribes argued from scripture and tradition, quoting older authorities to support their teaching. Jesus had spoken with freshness, directness, and in his own name: 'I say unto you'. (Daube, pp. 205–16, suggests that ordained rabbis, with full rabbinic authority to promulgate new decisions, were not often heard in Galilee, and that therefore the people would be surprised to hear authoritative teaching of this kind. But was Jesus an ordained rabbi?) 'The scribes' were the men devoted to the study of the Law and to the task of drawing out its implications for daily living: their teaching was of necessity derivative and repetitive. They figure frequently in Matthew's gospel, and this fact may indicate that, at the time of the composition of this Gospel, the Christian communities (or Matthew's at least) still retained some contact and discussion with Rabbinic Judaism; and this would locate the work, at the latest, soon after

A.D.85, when Jewish Christians were expelled from the synagogue. Davies is prepared to suggest that the Sermon on the Mount is a kind of Christian counterpart to the formulation of the way for the Old Israel by 'Jamnia' (*SSM*, pp. 256–315).

THE PROCLAMATION OF THE KINGDOM 8–10

With chapter 8 there begins the second main section of the Gospel which contains narrative material on Jesus' ministry (ten miracles are recorded in chapters 8–9), followed by the discourse on mission and martyrdom (9.35–10.42). Matthew seems deliberately to have gathered most of the miracle stories which demonstrate the power of the Kingdom in action into one block: probably Mk 1.40–2.22 provided the basic frame, but earlier Marcan material (used in 8.14–17) as well as later (in 8.23–27 and 9.18–31) have been added to give a fuller account of the miraculous ministry.

THE HEALING OF A LEPER 8.1–4

In this story (as in the other accounts taken over from Mark) Matthew omits what is not essential; in particular, the end of Mark's story (1.45) is not given (cf. Lk. 5.15–16), and the emotion of Jesus is not mentioned (cf. Mk 1.41–3). This does not mean that Matthew is independent of Mark here (so Lohmeyer, Schlatter), but that he utilized the Marcan account, while abbreviating it in terms of his own point of view. We must also allow (as Bonnard, p. 112, points out) for the influence of the oral tradition, not only on Mark, but throughout the process of literary fixation.

1. The whole of this verse is editorial, linking with what precedes (cf. 17.9). The 'great crowds' are those of 4.25.

2. The attitude, as well as the words, of the leper indicate that he recognized the power and authority of Jesus: one knelt before gods and kings. In the community of Israel, leprosy was regarded as a pollution from which society had to be preserved by means of strict rules which denied freedom of movement to a person with the disease. The ritual purification of the leper was performed only by the priests (Lev. 13): to Moses and Elisha was attributed the power to treat the disease (Num. 12.10ff.; 2 Kg. 5.9ff.). The cleansing of leprosy was expected as one of the signs of the Messianic time (11.5). It is not certain that the leprosy of which the Bible speaks is exactly the same as the paralysing disease known by that name today: it may have been some kind of skin disease (see *IDB* and *HDB*, s.v. 'Leprosy').

3. Matthew has no reference to Jesus' feelings: Mark (1.41) refers to his compassion (or, according to the Western text, his anger). Jesus' authoritative word follows his healing touch (cf. 8.15; 9.20f., 29; 14.36) in order to render it efficacious: both word and action are agents of power. To touch a leper was considered a violation of the ceremonial law of uncleanness (Lev. 5.3). The cure is immediate and complete: there could be no doubt concerning the effectiveness of Jesus' power.

4. See that you say nothing to any one: commands to silence are numerous in Mark's Gospel. Matthew omits many of them, but retains a few (cf. also 9.30; 12.16; 16.20; 17.9). These injunctions have been considered historical by many scholars and interpreted as attempts by Jesus to prevent the growth of false understanding of his power and of his Messiahship. Others, such as Wrede and Bultmann, regard the commands to silence as creations of Mark himself and part of his attempt to reconcile the non-messianic character of his sources with his own post-Resurrection christology. It is doubtful if this view really does justice to the implicit messianic character of Jesus' life, or to the Christological interests of the entire Gospel tradition, even in its earliest pre-Marcan stages, and it may be that the secrecy concept (in Mark) represents a theological presupposition which was necessary for the writing of any Gospel: he whom faith recognized and proclaimed as 'Lord' and 'Son of God' worked and taught: the full significance of this life was not, and indeed could not be known in and from isolated episodes, for these were only preliminary glimpses of, or 'pointers' to, what was completely manifested and understood about the life after the Resurrection. 'Miracle-worker' was not the whole truth about Jesus. In this sense the messianic secret (in Mark and Matthew) is 'historical'; it is precisely the meaning of the events of Jesus' ministry, seen in the light of Easter faith.

but go show yourself to the priest . . .: this is not intended to be a contradiction of the command to tell no one, for the latter is a characteristic feature of Gospel narration, and implies widespread proclamation of a miracle. The injunction to go to the priest (at Jerusalem) is probably the main point of the story: it proclaims Jesus as one who was prepared to encourage men to live within the prescriptions of the Law (Lev. 14.2), and to do so himself. The 'gift that Moses commanded' is the guilt-offering prescribed in Lev. 14.10ff., which could be offered only in Jerusalem.

for a proof to the people: lit. 'for a testimony to them'. The Greek could mean 'for a testimony to the priests' (and, for Matthew, to the Jewish religious authorities in general) that Jesus was not opposed to the Law, as they might have supposed: or it could be (as *RSV* implies) a 'witness to the people' in general, that he was now clean and could associate with them. (Some think that the 'witness' was to all and sundry that a power was active in their midst capable of healing leprosy, a task which was reputed to be as difficult as raising the dead. But this probably reads too much into the phrase.) Matthew omits Mark's reference to the man's disobedience to the injunction to silence which caused Jesus to withdraw into remote regions.

THE HEALING OF THE CENTURION'S SERVANT **8.5–13**

Matthew and Luke (7.1–10) are probably indebted to a special source for this story, and in particular for the tradition of the words of Jesus to the centurion. If this source is Q, then it cannot be argued that Q contained only short sayings of Jesus: it would have had to contain narrative and sayings, and in written form, unless one evangelist copied the words of Jesus in the story from the other. With the narrative Matthew has combined an eschatological saying from another context (Mt. 8.11, 12 = Lk. 13.28–9) which is concerned with the theme to which Matthew relates this story, viz. the lack of faith among the Jews. It is very interesting to compare the Johannine version of this miracle (4.46–53), in which the officer is not definitely characterized as a pagan (Gentile) and where the condemnation by Jesus is directed at the expectation of 'signs and wonders', when belief in the life-giving power of the word of Christ is what is necessary. Despite the changes, it is likely that this story (though used in the interests of Johannine theology) was drawn from a tradition similar to that which lies behind Matthew and Luke. Comparison of the narrative in Matthew, Luke, and John is instructive in showing how texts developed in the process of Gospel tradition.

5. As he entered Capernaum: Luke attaches the story directly to the Sermon on the Mount: Matthew could be following Mark who makes Jesus return to Capernaum after the healing of

the leper. The Johannine story is located at Capernaum as well.
a centurion: Herod Antipas, tetrarch of Galilee and Perea, had
the right to levy troops, whom he would have recruited from outside his own region. Capernaum was a garrison city and an important customs post, and a military official (cf. Jn 4.46) would
quite naturally be present there. The title 'centurion' (a company
commander within a Roman legion) need not be pressed: the man
was a pagan (verses 8 and 10, but not so in John), but not necessarily a Roman.

6. Lord: the title is probably used, as in verse 2, as an expression of respect (= 'Sir'), though for the evangelists it possessed
weightier christological overtones.

servant: the Greek word (*pais*) may also mean 'boy'; Matthew
may have understood it as 'son' (so John), but Luke has the un-
ambiguous 'slave' (*doulos*).

Here the officer approaches Jesus in person, but in Luke's
version the centurion himself never appears. His words and reputation are reported by friends who return to find the patient
cured; the centurion was at home to witness the marvellous
recovery.

7. Parallels such as 15.21–8, and the emphatic 'I' in the verse
suggest that Jesus' answer may be a question: 'Shall *I* come?', or
'Am *I*, a Jew, to come and heal him?' But the positive meaning is
suitable to the context. Often in Matthew Jesus' decision is immediate and sovereign (Bonnard, p. 115).

8. Lord I am not worthy . . .: in liturgical tradition, and
especially in the Eucharist, these words are used as a confession of
sinful man before God. Here they probably indicate an attitude of
respect on the centurion's part: he would probably have uttered
this kind of disclaimer to any person on whose action he was so
utterly dependent. But he knows the effectiveness of an authoritative word. Trust in the *word* of Jesus (and in Jesus as the Word)
is emphasized in the Johannine parallel passage.

9. I am a man under authority: the Old Syriac has 'a man
that has authority' (which may preserve a true translation of an
original Aramaic 'a man to whom there is authority'), and that
would provide a perfect synonymous parallel in the centurion's
reply. As it stands, however, the Greek can be interpreted satisfactorily: 'I, although I am a man under orders, can effect things
by my word.'

10. not even in Israel have I found such faith: other authorities have: 'in the case of no one in Israel have I found such faith', and this may be preferable. The faith is confidence in Jesus' power to perform a miraculous cure: the greatness of the faith (here and in the case of the Canaanite woman, 15.28) lies in the belief of Gentiles that a miracle could be performed, even at a distance. The allusion to Israel's lack of faith may provide the point of the story. It allows Matthew to introduce the following saying, which Luke preserves in a more suitable context.

11. The **many** from the east and west are the Gentile believers who will enjoy the Messianic banquet, which often symbolizes the joys of the future kingdom (cf. 22.1-14; 25.10; 26.19). The verse reveals an interest in the ultimate salvation of Gentiles, but it cannot be used to establish Matthew's insistence on a Gentile mission before the end. It refers to the eschatological pilgrimage of Gentiles to God's holy mountain (Isa. 25.6). See further Jeremias, *Promise*, pp. 62f.

12. sons of the kingdom: a Semitic idiom for those who should inherit the Kingdom, i.e. the Jewish nation. ('Sons of his covenant' (1QM xvii.3) denotes 'heirs' of the covenant.) Because of their unbelief, the privileged children of Abraham will be cast forth from bliss.

The phrases 'outer darkness' and 'weeping and gnashing of teeth' are favourite Matthean expressions associated with eschatological doom (cf. 22.13; 24.51; 25.30). The idea that darkness is the inheritance of the wicked is well-known (4 Ezra 7.93; Enoch 63.10; Ps. Sol. 14.9; 15.10; Wis. 17.21), and in the Rabbinic literature 'darkness' is one of the names given to Gehenna. There is no hint here of the final 'mercy' for Israel expressed in Rom. 9-11.

13. Be it done for you as you have believed: 'as' is not comparative, but causative: 'because you have believed'. Jesus does not accord help in proportion to faith, but by reason of faith. **at that very moment:** lit. 'in that hour' (cf. 9.22; 15.28; 17.18), and that agrees with John's conclusion to the story (Jn 4.52-3). Some such words probably belonged to the earliest tradition of the story on which the evangelists built.

THE HEALING OF PETER'S WIFE'S MOTHER **8.14-15**

This story is placed at different points in the Marcan and Lucan narratives: in Mark (1.29-31) it follows the healing of the demon-

possessed man in the synagogue, an event which Matthew omits.
Matthew has simplified the account, stripping it of its anecdotal
characteristics and stylizing it carefully. This may be evidence of a
Christian 'rabbinic' mind in action, making a narrative easily
remembered for the community.

14. Peter appears to have been a native of Bethsaida (Jn 1.44)
but, according to Mk 1.29, he had a home at Capernaum where,
married (cf. 1 C. 9.5), he traded as a fisherman with Andrew, his
brother (Mk 1.16). Perhaps Peter's wife was a native of Capernaum, and both families lived in one house and carried on the same
business.

fever: in the ancient world this was considered as a disease in
itself, and not merely as a symptom (cf. Jn 4.52; Ac. 28.8).

15. Without rebuking the fever (so Luke), Jesus touches the
woman's hand, an action which Jewish legalism banned (cf.
SB I, p. 299). The restored woman **served him** (Mark and Luke
have 'them')—i.e., she provided hospitality at the family table.

THE HEALING OF THE SICK AT EVENING 8.16–17

Here again Matthew presents a narrative which is simplified and
abbreviated from Mk 1.32–4. The alterations introduced are
significant: the mention of the restoring 'word' of Jesus; the healing
of 'all' the sick ('many' in Mark and Luke); the quotation of Isa.
53.4 in verse 17; and the omission of Jesus' refusal to allow the
demons to speak (cf. Lk. 4.41).

16. Matthew presupposes what was stated by Mark, that the
day was a sabbath; the bringing-out of sick people would be
permissible only after sunset on the sabbath. The special mention
of Jesus' **word** in healing activities is characteristic of Matthew's
accounts of healing (cf. 8.8), and is consistent with his avoidance
of details about healing processes. Demons and spirits were regarded as agents of illness; 'spirit' is frequently used with this
meaning in the intertestamental literature, but it is usually
qualified by an adjective such as 'evil' in the New Testament.

17. For Matthew the demons are not the proclaimers of Jesus'
Messiahship (as in Mark, and especially in Luke); scriptural
witness and fulfilment declare it. This formula quotation is from
Isa. 53.4, and is based on the Hebrew text. The LXX (like other
interpretations) spiritualized the passage as referring to sin and
hardships. It is probable that Matthew himself translated the

Hebrew literally (Stendahl, pp. 106f.). The verbs 'to take' and 'to bear' virtually mean 'to take away, to remove [from the sick]', and therefore 'heal'. Unless Matthew is quoting a verse which had already become detached from its literary context and from *OT* theology, it seems unlikely that the idea of substitution and the vicarious action of the Servant is entirely absent here. But it is primarily the taking away of illnesses through the healing ministry, not the taking away of sins, although it must be remembered that for the prophet and the evangelist sin was the root cause of disease (cf. Gundry, p. 230). By the time of Matthew, Isa. 53 was certainly interpreted messianically and applied to Jesus. Whether the messianic interpretation of the chapter was pre-Christian is still hotly debated (cf. Jeremias, *Servant*), as is the question whether Jesus saw his own ministry in terms of the mission of the suffering Servant (see Hooker, *Jesus*; and Manson, *SM*, pp. 57f., 73). In the rabbinic literature of the third century, the idea of the Messiah being rightfully found among the sick, and especially among lepers, is clearly attested (B. San. 98a–b).

ON FOLLOWING JESUS 8.18–22

The departure of Jesus from the Capernaum region to the other side of the Sea of Galilee provides Matthew with an opportunity to introduce sayings on discipleship ('following' being used with the double sense of 'following from place to place' and of 'being a disciple'). The location and the action of leaving the crowds adds to the significance of Jesus' answers: loneliness and hardship are involved in following him. Luke places this teaching at a later period, during the last journey to Jerusalem.

18. The command to cross the lake, which involves breaking away from the crowds at Capernaum, corresponds to Mk 4.35; but in Mark this event is the sequel to the second period at Capernaum (cf. Mk 2.1; 4.34), whereas Matthew makes it follow the first period there. This departure from the Marcan order may be due to Matthew's desire to insert at this point the two sayings on discipleship: Jesus' leaving Capernaum would explain the haste of his would-be disciples and give added point to the replies.

19. a scribe: in Matthew's gospel the scribes play a more important rôle than in the other Gospels: together with the Pharisees and elders, they constitute the opposition to Jesus. But here, as at 13.52; 23.34 (and cf. verse 21, 'another of the disciples'), they

F

are not cast in the rôle of opponents, but of potential (if not actual) disciples. This may reflect the presence of 'scribes' as teachers in the Jewish Christian community which Matthew knows: cf. Kilpatrick, pp. 110ff., 126; Strecker, pp. 37f.

I will follow you wherever you go: the man places himself in the position of a rabbi's disciple: the student literally followed his teacher around as a means of training and maturing in the knowledge of the Law. But the Gospels make it clear that Jesus' disciples were not primarily students: 'Discipleship as Jesus conceived it was not a theoretical discipline . . . , but a practical task to which men were called to give themselves and all their energies. Their work was not study but practice' (Manson, *Teaching*, p. 239).

20. It is unlikely that in this context **foxes** is an oblique reference to Herod (cf. Lk. 13.32) and the Herodians, and **birds of the air** to the Gentiles (cf. 13.32). On this interpretation, the whole saying becomes a way of pointing out that only the Son of Man has no place in Israel, and that would hardly provide an appropriate answer to the scribe's request. The saying refers to the continuing hardship and loneliness involved in *following* the Son of Man.

The Title 'Son of Man'

This is the first time that the title 'Son of Man' is used in Matthew, where (as in Mark and Luke) it appears only on the lips of Jesus. Of the many occurrences of the title in each of the Gospels, some refer to the coming of the Son of Man in glory at the end of the age, some are used in connection with his suffering and death, and some represent Jesus' self-designation during his ministry. The words *ho huios tou anthrōpou* are an over-literal rendering of the Aramaic *bar nāsh(ā)*, which means 'man'. The understanding of the term is helped by the use of the Hebrew phrase 'son of man' at Ps. 8.4; Ezek. 2.1; etc., and at Ps. 80.17 where it designates Israel as God's chosen 'man'. But the significant background is usually listed as: (i) Dan. 7.13ff., where we read of 'one like unto a son of man' coming with the clouds of heaven unto the Ancient of Days. This figure represents 'the saints of the Most High'—a righteous remnant of the Jewish people brought to glory and vindicated *through suffering* (cf. Dan. 7.21, 25): (ii) the Similitudes section of the Book of Enoch (chapters 37–71), where the Son of Man is a superhuman figure of great dignity and power, a mysterious apocalyptic personage (identified with Enoch himself in ch. 71):

(iii) 4 Ezra 13, which speaks of the Son of Man as a transcendental figure of the end-time.

Since the date (or dates) of 4 Ezra is not certain (though it is likely to be post-Christian), and since the Enoch passages may not be early enough to have influenced Jesus and the Gospel tradition (the absence of the Similitudes from the Qumran material raises serious questions about their date), the only certain background for interpretation is Dan. 7, which clearly suggests that 'Son of Man' is a title with collective (or corporate) overtones. (The probably pre-Pauline 'man' christology in Philippians and the Son of Man christology in Heb. 2 and Rev. 14.14 are based on Daniel and Ps. 8.) The title may therefore be used in the Gospels to refer to the elect and faithful Israel about to appear for judgment, of which community Jesus is both part and representative; and this means that the term could be used by Jesus both to refer to himself and away from himself. The authenticity of the use by Jesus of the 'Son of Man' title in eschatological sayings is admitted by even those who deny the genuineness of its use anywhere else (see Higgins and Tödt; and for the contrary see Perrin, pp. 164–199: but they regard the title as referring to a transcendent figure who will confirm the results of Jesus' ministry at the end). However, in these genuine futurist sayings Jesus must mean himself; his claim to its fulfilment in himself (Mk 14.62) excludes the possibility that the term refers to anyone else. As focus and centre of the loyal Israel Jesus will be vindicated. As far as the 'Son of Man' sayings relating to suffering are concerned, there is nothing in the Danielic background to hinder the application of the title to a suffering figure: it is clearly stated that the 'saints' (= 'son of man') will suffer and be martyred. It is not necessary to invoke Isa. 53 to provide the theme of suffering to the title, although the traditions of Dan. 12 have been influenced by the language of that passage. Therefore it is not improbable that some or parts of some of the second group of 'Son of Man' sayings are genuine *logia* (see Black, *BJRL*, XLV, 1962–3, pp. 305–18). Some of the 'Son of Man' sayings which relate to the ministry may employ the title as a circumlocution for 'I', just as the Aramaic idiom *hāhū gabrā* (= 'that man') could mean 'I, the speaker' in certain contexts and under certain circumstances (see G. Vermès, Appendix to Black, *Aramaic Approach*, 3rd edn, 1967, pp. 320–7; and cf. Mt's 'I' in 10.32 and 5.11 for Lk's 'Son of Man', and Mt's

'Son of Man' for Mk's 'I' in 16.13), but it is hard to think of even
these sayings as having been uttered by Jesus without any reference to the overtones possessed by the phrase in its titular use.
Schweizer, *LD*, and in *NTS*, IX, 1962–3, pp. 259ff., has argued
for the genuineness of the sayings relating to Jesus' earthly
ministry which fulfils the pattern of the humiliation of the suffering
righteous in Wis. 2–5.

The authenticity of Jesus' use of the title 'Son of Man' is
established by the virtual absence of the name from the early
Christian community's usage; it had become sacrosanct. Furthermore, all strata of Gospel tradition are unanimous that the title
was used in the third person. If it had not been so used, would they
have been so consistent? We would not wish to deny that some of
the 'Son of Man' sayings may have been modified, or even created,
by the Church: but we would maintain that a significant number
of the sayings are authentic, and that these relate to Jesus' present
activity, his sufferings and to the vindication beyond. (See Hooker,
SSM, and Black, *Aramaic Approach*, pp. 328–30, Moule, *PNT*, pp.
34–6.)

The thesis put forward by Bultmann, Vielhauer and Conzelmann that, because 'Kingdom of God' and 'Son of Man' are not
connected in the Gospel sayings, and because 'Kingdom of God'
is certainly genuine, 'Son of Man' must be unauthentic, is not so
significant as at first appears. There is in fact a parallel between
the two concepts, especially if 'Son of Man' has a corporate
reference: the hidden Kingdom to be revealed is aptly paralleled
by the secret (and misunderstood) 'Son of Man' and the revealed
'Son of Man' (in the end-time). The 'Kingdom' may have been
a concept used in Jesus' general teaching, and 'Son of Man' may
have been originally employed only in teaching the disciples
(cf. Lk. 17.20–3). When due attention is paid to the Danielic
background, the title 'Son of Man', as a self-designation, can be
seen to have been a uniquely valid indication of the meaning of
the ministry—i.e., representative, and in the tradition of the suffering martyr who will be vindicated by God. Despite its ambiguity,
perhaps even because of it, 'Son of Man' seems to have been the
only title Jesus wished to use of himself. It is used here (8.20) to
point to the humble, homeless, insecure lot which he and the
community of his loyal followers must accept.

21. Another of the disciples: presumably there were many sufficiently interested in Jesus to be called 'disciples', but not all of them were able to accept the demands of committed 'following'. It is just possible that the phrase denotes another interested scribe (cf. verse 19).

let me first go and bury my father: in Palestinian Judaism filial piety, based on the Fifth Commandment, imposed the duty on children of attending to the burial of parents; cf. Tob. 4.3; 6.13. M. Berak. iii.1, claims that attendance to this duty freed a man from the performance of even the most binding religious obligations which might delay its being carried out.

22. This strong metaphor should not be over-interpreted. The meaning probably is that those who have not found the life of the Kingdom of God in Jesus can attend to matters of burial: the urgency of following Jesus unreservedly is greater than burial duties. McNeile (pp. 109f.) suggests that the Greek may obscure an Aramaic proverb analogous to 'Let the dead past bury its own dead', but no such proverb has ever been discovered. Black (*Aramaic Approach*, pp. 207f.) suggests that the original Aramaic may have read, 'Let the waverers (*mᵉṭinin*) bury their dead (*miṭihûn*)', and that the first word was translated as if it were *miṭin (nekroi)*.

THE STILLING OF THE STORM 8.23-7

According to Mk 4.35-41, this incident followed the second stay at Capernaum. Matthew has abbreviated the Marcan narrative (as has Luke), but he has retained what is significant in emphasizing Jesus' authority. With the authority of the divine, this man Jesus, who radically reinterpreted the Law and cured the sick, now extends his rule to include natural phenomena. In contrast to the preceding passages in which the humiliation of the Son of Man places him below the beasts and birds (but note Ps. 8.7-8), here we have demonstrated an authority no less than that of master of Creation. The theological source of this theme is found in the *OT*; see Ps. 29(28)3f., 10f.; 89(88).9; 104(103).7; 107(106).23-32: as the divine King of creation ruled the raging seas (Job 38.8-11, Prov. 8.22ff.), so the messianic figure must exercise power over wind and wave. Whatever be the historical basis of the story—and the search for this is not much advanced by recent suggestions of sudden storms subsiding on this stretch of water—the re-telling of the tale has become the medium for expressing belief in Christ as the bearer of divine power for the protection of his own, both individuals and Church. In early Christianity the Church was pictured as a boat tossed by the sea and preserved by Christ: cf. Tertullian, *de Bapt*, xii, and E. Peterson, *TZ*, vi, 1950, pp. 77–9.

23. The incident forms part of the sequence initiated at verse 18 with the decision to leave Capernaum and cross the Sea of Galilee. Notice that even in the matter of entering the boat (either a fishing boat or a larger vessel) the disciples 'follow' Jesus: the story of the storm is concerned with discipleship.

24. The **great storm** (lit. 'an earthquake', emphasizing the catastrophic character of the event) is a threat to the boat, rather than to the disciples. Matthew's interest in the **boat** may indicate that he is concerned with the Church and, in particular, the Church facing the upheaval of persecution (perhaps under Domitian, A.D. 81–96). The fact that Jesus sleeps does not mean he is unconcerned, but is confident in his ability to control the situation.

25. Save Lord: cf. 14.30. Matthew alone gives these words which have a liturgical ring about them. It may be that the influence of the forms of worship of the Matthean church are to be detected at this point (so Bonnard, p. 120).

26. Why are you afraid, O men of little faith?: only in Matthew's account does Jesus address the disciples before he rebukes the storm. The unnaturalness of this sequence suggests that Matthew is primarily interested in the condition and needs of his church. The sterner words to the disciples (in Mark and Luke) are toned down by Matthew: 'little-believing' is a favourite expression of this evangelist (6.30; 8.26; 14.31; 16.8; 17.20: elsewhere only in Lk. 12.28) and is always applied by him to disciples (and therefore to the Christians for whom he writes). On the basis of the parallel between 6.30 and Lk. 12.28, Held (*TIM*, p. 293) suggests that Matthew found this term in the common sayings source, and then introduced the idea in other places in his Gospel to describe the character of the Christians in his community. **rebuked the winds and the sea:** the word 'rebuke' (*epitimaō*) suggests that the elements are treated as evil powers which must be subdued as a sign of the kingdom over which Christ is king.

27. Mark implies that only the disciples marvelled: Matthew's words **the men** probably include both the disciples in the boat and also all those who hear the story. The amazement evokes a

question which evidences a measure of doubt but, at the same
time, provides a stepping-stone to faith. The answer of faith to
'What sort of man is this?' (Mark and Luke have 'Who is
this?') is implied. He is a man with divine authority over creation,
a man in whom absolute confidence may be placed because he is
able to protect disciples in times of stress and danger. See further,
Bornkamm, in *TIM*, pp. 52–7.

THE HEALING OF TWO GADARENE DEMONIACS 8.28–34

Although the three Gospels agree in placing this incident after
the stilling of the storm, Matthew differs from Mark and Luke
in having two demoniacs instead of one, in omitting any reference
to names, and in saying nothing of their desire to follow Jesus.
Matthew's abbreviation leaves out nothing of importance for his
real purpose, which is to demonstrate, without literary adornment
or wordiness, the authority of Jesus over sickness and all that
signifies the power of evil: cf. Held, in *TIM*, pp. 172–5. The theme
is continued from the stilling of the storm. The influence of Ps.
65(64).7 and Isa. 65.1–4 (especially verse 4) may be significant
in the formation and theological thought of this section; see
Nineham, pp. 152–3, and Hoskyns and Davey, pp. 86ff. Concerning the factual basis for this story it is hard to be certain; some
of the statements reflect notions current in popular folk-tales. But
behind the embroidered version and the theological superstructure
there may be a kernel of truth about the cure of a deranged person
whose final paroxysm frightened a herd of swine and provoked a
stampede.

28. the country of the Gadarenes: the exact location is
uncertain. Three readings appear in the manuscripts of all three
Gospels: (i) Gadarenes (probably the best reading for Matthew);
but Gadara was six miles SE. of the lake, whereas the city mentioned in verses 33f. was presumably close to the sea. (ii) Ger-
gesenes (which has support in Matthew, and may be original in
Mark); this would suggest modern *Kersa* on the edge of the lake.
(iii) Gerasenes—which refers to Gerasa, 30 miles SE. of the sea—
an unlikely location, but the name may have been confused with
Kersa. Whatever the exact spot, we are in Gentile country; that
explains the presence of pigs (not kept by Jews), and the curious
reaction of the townspeople.

two demoniacs . . . coming out of the tombs: Mk 5.2 and

Lk. 8.27 mention only one, but Matthew has also two blind men healed (9.27–31) and two asses (20.29–34): it is possible that Matthew infers plurality from the Marcan name and its explanation, 'Legion, for we are many'. Sepulchres would provide some shelter for distressed people who occupied the little ante-chambers in front of the 'rooms' in which bodies were laid. The implication may be that men possessed by evil spirits would find the habitat of spirits congenial. Matthew's brief statement on the fierceness of the men summarizes three verses in Mark.

29. What have you to do with us ?: lit. 'What to us and to you?'. These words, which are found in all three accounts (cf. Jn 2.4; Mk 1.24) express fear and unwillingness to be interfered with. ('What do you want with us?' *NEB*).

O Son of God: the demons are endowed with mysterious knowledge which makes them fear, and at the same time acknowledge, the power of Jesus as the one who is their ultimate master (cf. Mk 3.11; 5.7; Lk. 4.41 and Ac. 16.17). 'Son of God' means one possessed of divine power, but it came to be used (though not often so in the *NT*) in a messianic sense: Jesus was charged by God with the decisive mission which inaugurates the last days. The triumph of God's kingdom and the vanquishing of evil powers are no longer distant hopes, but actually happening through the presence of Jesus. In a sense, this verse is the answer to 'What kind of man is this?' (verse 27).

Have you come here to torment us before the time ?: the words 'here' (i.e. into a pagan country) and 'before the time' are important for the understanding of this passage in Matthew. The intertestamental literature gives expression to the idea that demons were given permission to act against mankind until the day of judgment, when they would be destroyed (1 En. 15–16, Jub. 10.8–9; Test. Levi 18.12). Only in Matthew is there the christological affirmation that Jesus' action with these demoniacs is an anticipation of the overthrow of Satanic forces, and this probably reflects the period of the early Church when exorcism was considered as a continuing sign of the annihilation of demonic powers. The emphasis on 'here' (a pagan community) in the question suggests an interest in the Church's ministry to Gentiles; this is Jesus' first visit into Gentile territory, and the resentment provoked may reflect the difficulty of the Church's mission in those regions of Palestine.

30. Since swine were unclean to the Jews, their presence is a clear indication of a Gentile (or at least mixed) community. The words 'at some distance' (Mark and Luke have 'on the mountain') may be an attempt to reconcile the position of the swine with the location of the incident at Gadara, six miles from the sea.

31–2. The reason for the demons' desire to go into the swine is not stated: it may be that they could not face the prospect of being without a home. Their presumed entry into the pigs would be a confirmation that they had in fact left the men, although Matthew (unlike Mark) does not explicitly say that the men were restored to health. It was widely believed at this time that, when spirits were exorcised, they expressed their rage by doing some mischief, clearly visible to onlookers (see Philostratus, *Vit. Apoll.* iv.20, Jos. *Ant.* viii.48).

34. Matthew omits details about the cured demoniac and his part in the proclamation of Jesus in his own region. He is concerned only with the city's request—caused by loss of property and fear—that the disturber should leave the neighbourhood. This may be intended to anticipate the rejection of the Church in certain Gentile areas.

THE HEALING OF THE PARALYTIC **9.1–8**

This story continues the theme of the preceding sections of the Gospel—viz., the authority of Jesus, affirmed in 7.28. This authority is exercised over the law which Jesus radically reinterpreted (9.5–7), over demons and sicknesses (8.1–17, 28–34), over would-be followers (8.18–22), over the creation (8.23–27), and now over sin itself (9.1–8). This authority, evidenced in works which are signs of the Kingdom's presence, is received by Jesus from God, and will be delegated by Jesus to his apostles (chapter 10). The relation of the Matthean narrative to the Marcan has been much discussed, and some claim priority for the Matthean version. But the economy of description in the Matthean account (as elsewhere in these miracle stories) is such as to make it necessary to presuppose for its understanding a fuller version such as Mark preserves; it is possible that the abbreviation reflects the pedagogical use of the story. Many scholars follow Bultmann (*HST*, pp. 14–16) in regarding this passage (and the Marcan parallel) as composite, a miracle story into which has been inserted a controversy about forgiving sin which reflects the Church's attempt to make its own forgiving function a part of Jesus' own ministry. Whether or not this is a correct view of the Marcan original, it is clear that Matthew treats the story as a unity whose central theme is the authority of Jesus over sickness and sin, and it is most likely that the question of authority was one of the main issues in Jesus' conflict with the religious leaders of his time.

The problem is acutely presented in an action of the kind here recorded, which therefore may well have an historical foundation in the ministry of Jesus. The close relation between sickness and sin was a widely accepted hypothesis in the ancient world, and it is being rediscovered by modern psychological medicine.

1. The whole Sea of Galilee is traversed to bring Jesus from the Gadarene neighbourhood to his own city, which, for Matthew, is Capernaum (4.13), the basis for the mission in the Galilean area. In contrast to Mk 2.1ff. and Lk. 5.17, Matthew's account contains the minimum of introduction necessary for the setting of the story.

2. **they brought to him a paralytic, lying on his bed:** the imperfect tense of the verb *prosphero* ('bring') suggests that they came bringing the man—whose paralysis was of the legs—to Jesus as he arrived in Capernaum. Mark and Luke set the event in a house. The bed on which the paralysed man lay would be a mattress-type of bed or pallet—the poor man's bed! Matthew and Luke avoid the colloquial term *krabatos* Mark employs. There is no mention of the picturesque details of four carriers, the crowded house, the hole in the roof; Matthew is hastening to the main point of the story in the words of Jesus; on their substance the three evangelists are agreed, although they differ significantly in other parts of the story. This fact indicates the importance which oral tradition attached to the words and deeds of Jesus, although considerable liberties might be taken in describing the setting and other details.

their faith: the faith of those who brought the man and his own faith as well, since he was undoubtedly consenting to the helpers' action. The surmounting of such difficulties as are mentioned in the other Synoptics makes the extent of faith shown even greater. The Matthean account possibly presupposes the fuller account to be completely understood.

'Take heart, my son; your sins are forgiven': only Matthew has the words 'take heart' (cf. 9.22; 14.27). Because the Jews saw in illness a sign, if not a proof, of sin, Jesus goes to the root of the matter, and bestows on the man forgiveness with the authority of God. The idea of God's forgiveness found frequent expression in orthodox and sectarian Judaism of the time, but never was it actualized and personally communicated, as in this narrative.

3. Matthew and Mark mention the reaction of 'some of the scribes', Luke that of the 'scribes and Pharisees'; but the three are agreed on the charge—blasphemy, which Mark goes on to explain as the usurping of the divine prerogative in forgiving. Among the Jews of Jesus' time the definition of blasphemy was much discussed (see *SB* on Mt. 26.66). If a man was to be accused of blasphemy he had to have used the divine name (M. San. vii.5), but here the scribes extend the meaning of the offence to include the claim to be able to exercise what was considered to be a divine prerogative (i.e. acting in the name and with the authority of God). The punishment for blasphemy was stoning (M. San. vii.4).

4. Some MSS. read 'seeing their thoughts'. The difference in meaning is very small; Jesus was aware, intuitively, of what they were thinking. The three evangelists record that the reflections of the scribes were 'in their hearts', i.e. in their inner being, from which spring will and action.

5. From the point of view of a sceptic it would seem easier to say to someone that his sins had been forgiven, since the effectiveness of the word could not be objectively verified; but a command to walk could be tested by watching to see if it was effective. The question is asked by Jesus from the standpoint of his opponents: it does not imply that communicating the pardon of God to a man is less difficult and less serious than healing his body.

6. The cure is to be not only evidence of forgiveness but also proof of Jesus' authority to forgive on earth. It is precisely this authority which was questioned and which caused amazement (verse 8). From the passage we see that: (i) it is a divine authority, in the sense that Jesus holds and uses it in the name of God; (ii) it is delegated to him and exercised now *on the earth*; and (iii) it extends to the whole of a man.

Son of man: the title is enigmatic. It can hardly mean 'man' (i.e. 'any man' in general), for not anybody can communicate pardon; even in verse 8 the authority of men is a special one derived from Jesus. The title could be a means of referring to 'I' (the speaker); but, in view of the fact that the paragraph is concerned with Jesus' *exousia*, it seems likely that the name is an indication of dignity. There is no evidence in Jewish apocalyptic tradition that the Son of Man forgives sins, and this is the only passage in the Synoptics where 'Son of Man' and forgiveness are brought together. It may be a community formulation (see Bultmann and Tödt), but, on the other hand, as a self-designation, the title could here mean 'the Son of Man whom you expect as Judge only in the last days is active now *on earth*, acting with authority, even to the extent of forgiving sins'. See further, Hooker, *SMM*, pp. 81–93.

7. The account of the actual miracle is extraordinarily short in all the gospels. Jesus' order is immediately carried out; and in this again his authority is demonstrated.

8. The three evangelists use strong language to express the reaction of the people, and Matthew says **they were afraid,** an expression which occurs in relation to a divine manifestation (such as the Transfiguration (17.6) and the Resurrection (28.5,10)). The granting of such authority to 'men' reflects the fact that the Church claimed the right to forgive: it is an allusion to or justification of ecclesiastical practice in the Matthean period. The theme of forgiveness reappears in contexts which are clearly ecclesiastical (Mt. 16.19; 18.18); see Benoit, p. 72, and Held, in *TIM*, pp. 273f.

JESUS CALLS MATTHEW AND EATS WITH SINNERS **9.9–13**

If the Matthean text here depends on Mark (or on a primitive form of Mark), we notice immediately the improvements Matthew has introduced: (a) he omits Mk 2.13, which is awkward and inappropriate in the context; (b) he simplifies the name of the tax-collector to Matthew; (c) he has abbreviated and improved the description of Jesus eating with sinners (Mk 2.15b is suppressed); (d) he has made concise and direct the attack by the Pharisees on Jesus' behaviour ('your teacher' is a favourite Matthean title); and (e) he has supported Jesus' important word in verse 13 by a fitting quotation from the *OT*. Despite these alterations, Matthew accurately preserves the words of Jesus contained in the passage: he is in complete accord with Mark in 9b, 12, 13b. Matthew's redactional freedom does not apply to the

words of Christ. Within Matthew's gospel these verses form a
coherent unity: the call of a tax-collector is an illustration of the
call of sinners, and the calling of sinners follows appropriately the
story which illustrates Jesus' authority to forgive sins. In view of
the coming reign of God, the moral and religious distinctions
among men are broken down; this is shown in Jesus' own actions.
He eats with tax-collectors and sinners, and dares to announce to
men the forgiveness of sins. His authority must be acknowledged
or rejected.

9. a man called Matthew: the person whom Mark calls
'Levi, the son of Alphaeus' (and Luke 'Levi') is here named
'Matthew'. It is probable that he is the same person as Levi, but
there is no evidence that Matthew was the name he adopted as
one of the Twelve. In the lists of apostles, he holds the seventh
(Mk 3.18; Lk. 6.15) or eighth (Mt. 10.3; Ac. 1.13) place. Nothing
is known about his life. The association of the name Matthew with
the first gospel may suggest the possibility that there was some
connection between the apostle and the church from which the
Gospel was written. It is true that Matthew's work as a publican
would require him to know Greek in addition to his mother
tongue Aramaic, and would make for a person of order and precision (see Gundry, pp. 181–3), and these points touch on the
problem of authorship. But is it likely that the person responsible
for this gospel lived 'on the despised outskirts of Jewish religious
life'? (Stendahl, in *Peake*, 673j.). See Introduction, pp. 52–4, and
Moule, *Stud. Evan.*, II, p. 98.

sitting at the tax office: if, as seems likely, the encounter between Jesus and Matthew took place on the outskirts of Capernaum, then the general accuracy of the narrative is maintained.
Near the city was a customs post, where goods passed out of the
territory of Philip into that of Herod Antipas. Those who collected
taxes and customs charges were usually recruited from among the
native population, by whom in turn they were despised, not only
because they were often in collaboration with the occupying
power, but because they were in contact all the time with 'unclean' pagans and were often dishonest. By being involved in
tax-collecting in Capernaum, Matthew was in the direct service of
Herod Antipas, rather than that of the Romans. Presumably his
occupation made him comfortably well-off, for he could invite
Jesus and his disciples to his house.

Follow me: i.e. 'be my disciple', 'attach yourself to my person in order to hear and serve me'. The immediate response is a further illustration of the authority of Jesus' call to a sinner (cf. verse 13).

10. as he sat at table in the house: Luke makes it quite clear that it was the tax-collector's house, and this is probably what Matthew expects his readers to understand, although the words 'sat down with Jesus' (*synanekeinto tō Iēsou*) suggest that Jesus was the host; but this phrase could be understood simply as 'had their meal along with Jesus'. The word literally means 'reclined', which was the Graeco-Roman custom, followed also at banquets provided by wealthy Jews.

many tax collectors and sinners: the three evangelists stress the large numbers of sinners who joined Jesus in Matthew's house. The tax-collectors (or customs officers) were regarded with great disfavour by pious Jews, because their occupation involved them in breaking the laws on uncleanness and on the Sabbath. 'Sinners' means not only immoral people, but the *'am hā-'āreṣ* ('people of the land'), who were content to ignore many of the strictly interpreted requirements of the law. 'He is a sinner not because he violates the Law, but because he does not endorse the Pharisaic interpretation' (K. H. Rengstorf, in *TWNT*, I, p. 328).

11. The question asked by the Pharisees, the upholders of the Law, is an accusation. To eat with people who are outside the Law is to identify oneself with them and thereby defile oneself. The act of eating food was the subject of innumerable rabbinic regulations.

12. The answer of Jesus is in the form of a brief parable in which the tax-collectors and sinners are equated with the **sick**. Jesus has entered into fellowship with these people not because they were sympathetic or receptive to him, but because he knew they were sick—and that describes not simply a psychological or moral state, but their situation before God.

13. Go and learn what this means, 'I desire mercy and not sacrifice': an addition by Matthew. The introductory words (a rabbinic formula) are characteristic of his method. Jesus invites the Pharisees to study the Scriptures in order that they may discover their true meaning in the light of his action; in effect, Jesus is made to say: 'See what Hos. 6.6 means as you watch my association with sinners.' The actual quotation (following the Hebrew), which is found again at 12.7, is not wholly germane at this point, but was 'a handy and useful slogan in discussions with the Jews' (Stendahl, in *Peake*, 682m). It would be wrong to interpret this passage as a condemnation by Jesus of all Israelite sacrificial ritual. The word 'sacrifice' here includes all prescriptions relating to ritual purity; these are condemned, in so far as they are allowed to create distinctions between the righteous and sinners. 'Mercy' (and the Hebrew word *ḥesed* approaches the meaning of 'love') is vastly more important for Jesus, and should be more satisfying to the Jews who condemn than ceremonial correctness. **I came not to call the righteous but sinners:** Luke adds 'to repentance', but the Matthean and Marcan versions allow for the term 'call' to mean both 'invite (to table-fellowship)' and 'call into the Kingdom of God'. It is often argued that 'righteous' here is an *ironical* allusion to the Pharisees, who think they are righteous but in fact are not. This need not be the case. It seems likely that Jesus was prepared to admit that his Pharisaic opponents were in some sense acceptable to God: they were righteous in terms of obedience to the Law; what Jesus condemns is their exclusion of others from the sphere of acceptability: it is the despised people whom he came to call (see Hill, pp. 130f.).

In spite of the fact that Bultmann and others suggest its derivation from the primitive catechesis, this *logion* may well be original. It expresses what we know from other passages was characteristic of Jesus' attitude (Lk. 7.41–7; 15.7; Mk 10.19–21). Moreover, if one thing is certain about Jesus, it is that he was the friend of despised tax-collectors and sinners, and frequently was found in their company.

A CONFLICT OVER FASTING **9.14–17**

Since it is only at verse 19 of this chapter that Jesus rises from the meal (at Matthew's house), it is likely that the evangelist regards this piece of controversy as having arisen in connection with the meal taking place. The question is not now: 'Should Jesus eat with sinners?'; it has become: 'Should Jesus be eating at all?', and this issue is raised not by the Pharisees but by John's disciples. Bultmann sees verse 15 (=Mk 2.19a) as the heart of the passage, a saying of Jesus around which was constructed a story by means of which the early Church defended itself against attack by the Jewish baptizing sect of John's followers who took the matter of fasting with great seriousness. Verse 15b is regarded by many commentators as a product of the early Church (see below).

The answer of Jesus to his questioners is illustrated by two analogies or short parables. These do not fit neatly into the context for they introduce a fresh idea, viz. that of the newness which Jesus brings, and which cannot be contained within the conventions of traditional Jewish piety.

14. All three evangelists mention 'the disciples of John' at this point, though only in Matthew do they pose the question. The phrase denotes a community gathered around the figure of the Baptist, presumably after his death (Jn 4.1; Lk. 11.1). The verse then alludes to an issue which could have been raised, not only during Jesus' lifetime, but also after his death and up to the time of the editing of the Gospel traditions. The question could be understood as relating to the present: 'Why are not your disciples fasting now?', i.e. during the meal with Matthew, which may have coincided with a Jewish fast. It is probably better to interpret the words in a present continuous sense: 'Why do your disciples not fast in general?', i.e. why do they not observe Jewish regulations on fasting. (For these see M. Taanith and under Mt. 4.2; 6.16–18.) It is likely that Jesus himself observed the regulations of his time about fasting (cf. 6.16ff.; 17.21). The question here concerns the attitude of his disciples (and the Church) over against the practice of Pharisees and the disciples of the Baptist. Within first century Christianity fasting was practised (Ac. 13.3; 14.23; 27.9), but fasting as understood by the Jews was not compatible with faith in the Messiahship of Jesus.

15. Can the wedding guests mourn . . . ?: this saying suggests that the issue was not one about fasting in itself, but about fasting as an expression of sadness and affliction. Bultmann (*TNT*, 1, p. 16) claims that the answer 'does not reject fasting on principle, but means that in the dawning of the messianic joy the mourning custom of fasting . . . does not make sense'. It also indicates that the Pharisees and John's disciples have not seen in Jesus the Messianic bridegroom. By 'the wedding guests' Jesus means his disciples: the word 'bridegroom' is a covert allusion to himself. The relationship of God with his people is often referred to in the *OT* in terms of 'marriage' (Hos. 2.16–20; Isa. 54.5f.; 62.4f.), and the rabbis sometimes used the metaphor of a wedding in connection with the coming of the Messiah. The imagery belongs also to the theme of the Messianic banquet.

The days will come . . . then they will fast: this is a thinly

veiled allegory of the death of Jesus; cf. the use of *aparthē* in Isa.
53.8 (LXX). The authenticity of these words is doubted by many
on the following grounds: (i) they turn 'parable' into 'allegory';
(ii) they involve a reference to the Passion too early in Jesus'
ministry; (iii) they are inconsistent with 15a. But allegory is found
in the words and parables of Jesus (see M. Black, *BJRL*, XLII,
1959–60, pp. 273–87, and Brown, pp. 254–64); the words may
have been uttered later in the ministry than their position here
suggests; and 15a only rules out fasting while Jesus is with his
disciples. Moreover, as Taylor points out (p. 212), the verse as a
whole has a poetic character which renders the hypothesis of
redactional adjustment to a later situation in the Church rather
doubtful. The difficulty is created by reading too much into the
saying. Jesus may have meant no more than that he would not
always be with his disciples; when he is eventually taken from
them (by death) then they will express their sadness by fasting.

16–17. These two little 'parables' (as Luke calls them at 5.36)
may have been part of an independent sayings collection. They
may then have been added to the saying on fasting because the
radical message they contain was applicable in the case of this
particular Jewish form of piety. The piece of new, strong, un-
shrunk cloth damages the old garment, and the new fresh wine, as
it ferments, bursts the old wineskins. So the new spirit of the
Kingdom cannot be contained within the old forms of Judaism
and its piety; it must develop new forms, although Jesus does not
define what exactly these new forms will be—it is enough to say
that the whole of the Jewish religion will have to be renewed if it
is not to be destroyed. (The Johannine sign of the wine at Cana
of Galilee makes the same point.) The last words of the saying:
and so both are preserved are a Matthean addition, and
probably indicate his own point of view: he envisages, not the
abolition of Judaism (so Mark), but its renewal and preservation.

THE HEALING OF A CHILD AND OF THE WOMAN WITH HAEMORRHAGE 9.18–26

With this story Matthew returns to the theme of Jesus' authority
to heal, prior to the presentation of the third discourse. The three
miracles described (verses 18–34) make the background to the
apostolic commission more complete, and may have been introduced at this point in order to provide examples of the remaining

types of people to whom the messiah ministers (indicated by 11.5): namely, the blind, the deaf, and the dead. The first section records a miracle within a miracle, as does Mk 5.21ff., but Matthew's account has altered and abbreviated the Marcan story: the location is changed from the lakeside to a house (Matthew's), and the number of words used to tell the story is reduced by one third. This may be because Matthew is drawing upon an independent tradition (e.g. the Galilean tradition, proposed by Lohmeyer), or it may be an instance of Matthew's simplification of a story in the interests of catechetical use: only what is essential in Mark's fuller account is given. It is noteworthy that, in recounting the words of Jesus, the three evangelists agree almost word for word, save for the command in Aramaic addressed to the girl (Mk 5.41): this Matthew omits while Luke gives it in Greek.

18. The first clause is a Matthean editorial link. In Mark and Luke Jesus has returned across the lake to find a crowd awaiting him, but Matthew still thinks of Jesus as being 'in the house'. According to the other Synoptics, the man was a ruler of the synagogue called Jairus: Matthew gives no name and calls him 'a ruler' (*archōn*), a title which could be used of any prominent civil or religious person in the community, and which could therefore include a synagogue ruler—the person who presided over the synagogue worship. According to Mark, the girl was 'at the point of death', and a message came later that she had died. Matthew abbreviates the narrative. The situation and father's request emphasize the supreme authority and power of Jesus.

19. Jesus' reaction is immediate. He **rose** (which presupposes that he was still sitting at table), and followed the father, along with his disciples.

20–1. Compared with Mark and Luke, Matthew's description of the woman suffering from a haemorrhage is greatly abbreviated. The conciseness in narration may be due to the need for easily memorized material in catechetical instruction. The faith of the woman expresses itself in the categories of popular magic. This is even more noticeable in Mark's account, where Jesus is aware of power going forth from himself (Mk 5.30). The verb *sōzō* here (and in verse 22) means 'heal'; it is usually translated in the New Testament as 'save'. The fringe, or tassel, of the garment probably had some liturgical connection (Num. 15.38–41; Dt. 22.12): the Pharisees made theirs broad (23.5) to display their piety.

22. Jesus encourages the woman (cf. 9.2; 14.27; etc.) and then heals her. The faith that had made her well is the expectant admission, by reason of her presence and action, that only Jesus can deal with her condition. This confidence is the ground on which Jesus authoritatively banishes her illness. It is the word of Jesus which heals, not the woman's action or faith.

23. Returning to the story of the ruler's daughter, Matthew tells his tale with the minimum amount of details. There is no mention of the message not to trouble Jesus any further, nor of the fact that only Peter, James and John accompanied Jesus into the house. From his knowledge of the funeral customs of the Jewish people, only Matthew mentions the **flute players.** Music and songs of lamentation were part of the burial ceremonies (B. Ket. 7a), and even the poorest families were expected to provide two flute players and one wailing woman to mourn the deceased.

24. In the *OT* the word 'sleep' is figuratively used of death (cf. Dan. 12.2); but it is unlikely that Matthew or those who told the story before him believed that the girl was still alive, or that death for her was only sleep. The point is that God is about to show, in Jesus' ministry, that death is not that final and absolute end which men fear. The reaction to this suggestion is ridicule!

25. Jesus communicates to the girl the power of God by which she is made alive (lit. 'was raised'). For parallels, see the stories of Elijah (1 Kg. 17.17–24), Elisha (2 Kg. 4.17–37), and Peter (Ac. 9.36–42); in all three cases the men are alone when they act to bring back life.

26. Matthew records the inevitable result for Jesus' reputation, but he does not include the injunction to silence given in Mark and Luke.

THE HEALING OF TWO BLIND MEN **9.27–31**

The story here closely resembles 20.29–34 (to which Mk 10.46–52 and Lk. 18.35–43 are parallel), and it is possible to regard the accounts as partial doublets. There are two blind men in each account, and they approach Jesus with the same request; but the words and actions of Jesus are not the same, and, more important, there is a great difference in context and didactic purpose. In chapter 20 what matters is that the king, even on his way to Jerusalem to suffer, does not despise the call for help; in this passage, Jesus puts before the blind men the question of faith (28b), and this term links the account closely with what precedes. Another factor in explanation of the doublet scheme may be that Matthew's arrangement of material requires an illustration of the healing of the blind to be given before 11.5, even before the apostolic commission in 10.1.

Why two blind men? Probably because of the account in 20.29ff., but it could be due to duplication. Mark describes two separate healings of a single blind man (8.22–6 and 10.40–52): Matthew omits one of these, and doubles the number healed. Behind the Matthean presentation of Jesus as the restorer of sight and of speech (verses 32–3) may lie the words of Isa. 35.4ff. 'Behold, your God will come with vengeance, with the recompense of God. He will come and save you. Then the eyes of the blind [plural in Greek] shall be opened, and the ears of the deaf [or dumb: LXX *kōphos*] unstopped . . . and the tongue of the dumb sing for joy.'

27. '**Have mercy on us, Son of David**': the cry of the blind men is not for pity or sympathy, but for that mercy which acts and helps. On the 'Son of David' as a royal Messiah title, see 1.1; 15.22; 20.30; 21.9.15. If Jesus is Messiah, then the promised time in which healing of the blind will take place has arrived. The use of the Davidic title in address to Jesus is less extraordinary than some think: in Palestine, in the time of Jesus, there was an intense Messianic expectation.

28. The brief interview focuses on the matter of faith (*pistis*)—faith in the person and power of Jesus.

29. The 'touch' of Jesus (cf. verse 21 and Mk 8.25) is not itself the means of healing; it is the introduction to the authoritative word. The formula **According to your faith** means the same as 'your faith has made you well' in verse 22; not 'according to the measure of your faith', but 'since you believe, your prayer is answered'.

30. **Jesus sternly charged them:** the word used expresses very strong feeling and deep emotion, even indignation or anger. Mark used it in his account of the cleansing of the leper (1.43), and John employs it (11.33) with reference to Jesus' reaction to the unbelief of Lazarus' friends. (It is used in classical texts of the snorting of horses and the howling of Cerberus: see McNeile, p. 127.) By using such a violent term, Matthew may be trying to indicate the intensity of Jesus' desire to avoid winning an inadequate or falsely-based loyalty. (On the secrecy concept, see above on 8.4.)

31. The account ends, as does the previous section, with the fame of Jesus spreading throughout the entire district around Capernaum.

JESUS HEALS A DUMB DEMONIAC 9.32-4

This short narrative is also peculiar to Matthew, and has a partial doublet in 12.22-24 (where the demoniac is both blind and dumb) leading to the discussion of blasphemy against the Holy Spirit raised by the Pharisaic attribution of Jesus' power to the prince of devils. This point is raised here, but it is less suitable to the general context, which is concerned, not with conflict and controversy, but with the illustration of Jesus' authority over the demons of illness. It seems likely that the story has been formed from 12.22-4 and inserted here in order to complete the cases of miraculous healing presupposed in 11.5 and 10.1.

32. The rapid succession of events is implied by making the dumb man arrive just as Jesus was leaving the house after the encounter with the blind men. The word *kōphos* means first 'deaf', then 'dumb', and then 'a deaf mute'; the three senses are found in classical, Hellenistic and Biblical Greek (cf. Exod. 4.11; Isa. 43.8). The man is called a 'demoniac' because illnesses and deficiencies were attributed to the power of evil spirits.

33. The story does not mention faith or any dialogue: the latter would be impossible for a man who was deaf and/or dumb. The cure is immediate and complete: for the evangelist to have mentioned the necessity for the man to learn how to speak would have seemed a limitation of Jesus' power. The crowds who witnessed the healing exclaim that such a demonstration of divine power is without parallel in their experience.

34. The reaction of the Pharisees is to attribute the power of Jesus to his being in league with the ruler of demons. The verse is probably an insertion from 12.24, and is not appropriate in the present context, which does not deal with the conflict between Jesus and the Pharisees. The verse is missing from some MSS.

INTRODUCTION TO THE MISSION OF THE TWELVE 9.35-10.4

Just as the first of the Matthean discourses was preceded by a statement about Jesus' general activities in the synagogues (4.23f.), so the final verses of this chapter form an editorial report stressing the extent of Jesus' ministry, the need for workers, and the urgency of the task—all as a prelude to the commissioning of the Twelve. The structure of the passage is complex: first it parallels Mk 6.6b, and follows with a repetition of 4.23; then it parallels Mk 6.34 and Lk. 10.2 (cf. Jn 4.35).

35. The elaboration of Mk 6.6b takes the form of a summary of Jesus' work. As in 4.23, it is a ministry of teaching, preaching and healing. For exegetical comments see on 4.23.

36. The compassion of Jesus is directed to the crowds because they were harassed and helpless (*erimmenoi* means 'cast down', 'thrown to the ground', and therefore 'helpless'). The image 'sheep without a shepherd' is closest to Num. 27.17, where Joshua is appointed as leader of Israel: but it may have been a more general figure of speech in the framework of *OT* language (1 Kg. 22.17; 2 Chr. 18.16; Isa. 53.6; Ezek. 34.5). The common people of Israel need guidance and help.

37-8. Lk. 10.2 associates this saying with the mission of the Seventy. It provides Matthew with another reason for the apostolic commissioning. In Christian and pre-Christian literature the figure of harvest was employed to denote final judgment (Jl 3.13; Isa. 17.11, and especially Mt. 13.30,39, 'the harvest is the close of the Age'). If 'harvest' here denotes judgment, then the task of the labourers must be to warn men of its approach and to call them to repentance: in Jesus' mission and that of his apostles Israel is being given a last chance to gather back in repentance to her true shepherd.

1. He called to him his twelve disciples: cf. Mk 6.7. The mention of the Twelve here is rather abrupt, since Matthew has not prepared the way (as Mark had done in 3.13f.) by listing their names; these follow in verses 2-4. In Matthew the group is referred to as 'the Twelve' (11.1; 20.17; 26.14, 20, 47), and it is clear that the number is meant to recall the twelve tribes of Israel (19.28): the disciples represent the new Israel, the new people of God, in its totality. Cf. the 'twelve' in the Council of the Qumran community, 1QS viii.1ff. The Jewish synagogue may have had councils of twelve men also.

gave them authority: the same term (*exousia*) as is used of Jesus' authority in 7.29 is here used of the disciples' power: it is a missionary authority to be used to advance the messianic ministry (verses 7–8), and it is authority delegated by Jesus himself, exercised in his name. 'Unclean spirits' are mentioned again by Matthew only at 12.43: they are spirits hostile to God's purpose and harmful to men's mental and physical wellbeing.

2–4. Only here are the Twelve called 'apostles' by Matthew. The title occurs more frequently in Luke, probably because of the continuation of his story of their works in Acts. The word **apostle** means 'a person sent, or commissioned', and is used only in this sense in the Fourth Gospel (13.16). It cannot be proved whether Jesus did or did not use the name 'apostles' for his disciples, but the tradition of this special commissioning is deeply rooted in the tradition. It is possible that the number and functions of the group have been influenced by the thought and experience of the primitive Church.

The lists of the names of the apostles found in the NT (Mk 3.16–19; Lk. 6.13–16; Ac. 1.13, besides these verses) do not entirely agree; it is probable that tradition contained variations of names. All the lists open with Peter's name (and Matthew emphasizes his position) and end with Judas. Although Matthew does not say that the Twelve were sent out two by two, he may reveal awareness of the tradition (cf. Mk 6.7) in his arrangement of the names in pairs. With Simon Peter (cf. Mt. 16.17ff.) is coupled Andrew, and with them the brothers James and John.

Andrew and Philip are Greek names, and Jn 1.43–4 makes them natives of Bethsaida, a Hellenistic town. Bartholomew is commonly identified with Nathanael (Jn 1.46). Thomas, a name meaning 'twin' (cf. Jn 11.16), is linked with Matthew, here referred to as the tax collector, and so linked with the Matthew mentioned in 9.9. James, the son of Alphaeus, is so designated to distinguish him from James, the son of Zebedee: Mk 2.14 claims that Levi, the tax-collector, was Alphaeus' son. Thaddaeus (for which some MSS. read 'Lebbaeus') is a name over which confusion existed in the early Church; the Syriac here has 'Judas of James' (cf. 'Judas, not Iscariot' in Jn 14.22). With 'Simon the Cananaean' the adjective can hardly indicate geographical origin, but is correctly interpreted by Luke as 'the zealot' (6.15): the Hebrew $ḳanā$' means 'zealous'. Whether this means that he had been a member of the Zealot party opposed to Roman rule, or that he was an energetic, zealous character, is a matter difficult to decide. The suggestion has been made that 'Iscariot' is not a geographical name ('man of Kerioth' in Judaea), but rather a description: 'man of falsehood, or betrayal' (Aramaic *šekarya*: cf. C. C. Torrey, *HTR*, xxxvi, 1943, pp. 51-62). The phrase would then mean 'Judas Iscariot who also (as his name declares) betrayed him'.

Little is known about many of these men. Their rôle may have been largely confined to the Jerusalem church and the Jewish Christianity which was separated from the main stream of Christian expansion after A.D. 68; if so, it is not surprising that their names were not clearly known in the Gentile centres in which the formation of the Gospel tradition took place. The legends about the apostles' activities and their claims to patronage in the various areas of primitive Christendom are considerably later; for some of these traditions see *NT Apocrypha*, II.

ON MISSION AND MARTYRDOM 10.5-42

This is the second of the five great discourses into which Matthew collects the sayings of Jesus. It takes the form of a mission charge to the Twelve, and may conveniently be divided into three sections: (i) verses 5-16, which deal with the immediate missionary task of the apostles (cf. Mk 6.8ff. and Lk. 9.1-5; 10.1-16); (ii) verses 17-25 which deal with the plight of disciples arraigned before tribunals and persecuted (cf. Mk 13.9-13; Lk. 21.12-19); and (iii) verses 26-42, which set out the conditions of discipleship in more general terms (cf. Mk 9; Lk. 12).

The arrangement of material in the discourse leads to some duplication (see 15.24; 16.24f.; 18.5; 24.9,13), but, with the exception of a few verses (5-6, 8, 16b), there is no material here peculiar to Matthew. The rôle of the evangelist is to arrange traditional material to serve the needs and situation of the church in which he lives. In this way the discourse became a kind of manual for the activities of leaders and teachers of the early Church.

THE MISSIONARY TASK 10.5-16

5-6. The sending forth (*apostellō*) of the Twelve is accompanied by a commission to go only to Jews, and especially to the 'lost' among the Jews. 'Go nowhere among the Gentiles' is more literally translated 'do not enter a road of Gentiles', and this should be understood as: 'do not go in the direction of (Aramaic *lᵉʾôrah*) Gentiles'; **Gentiles** here probably connotes (as in Romans)

'Gentile lands' or 'pagan peoples'; cf. Jeremias, *Promise*, pp. 19ff.
(Cf. *NEB*: 'Do not take the road to Gentile lands'.) The word
town (of Samaritans) should be rendered 'province'; the Aramaic
mᵉdînâ can mean both 'city' and 'province'.

Instead of going outside the borders of Judaism, the disciples
are to go to the **lost sheep of the house of Israel** (cf. 15.24).
Some have thought that this expression describes a section of the
Jews—viz. the despised *'am hā-'areṣ*, who did not take upon themselves the yoke of obedience to the Law, as the Pharisees did (so
Stendahl, in *Peake*, 683f.). However, the *OT* background of the
phrase (in Ezek. 34) suggests that it is all Israel which is scattered
like sheep on the mountains.

This passage, together with 10.23 and 15.24, has been interpreted as reflecting a current in primitive Christianity opposed
to the Gentile mission, whose chief champion was Paul. But the
Matthean church cannot be classed as particularistic: throughout
the Gospel (5.13; 10.18; 21.43; 24.14; and especially 28.16–20)
the universalist motif shines through and there is no justification
for considering this view as less representative of Matthew and his
church than the 'particularist' theme. Why then is the confine-
ment of Jesus' mission to the Jews retained here? It is impossible
to think that Matthew would have created sayings which contra-
dicted his own convictions on the Gentile mission. The only
acceptable reason for the preservation of these *logia* is that they
belonged to the tradition about Jesus which Matthew received
and passed on. The 'particularism' of Matthew is not a sign of a
Jewish Christian, anti-Pauline current, but of the evangelist's
faithfulness to the historical tradition about Jesus' own behaviour
and ministry.

7. The message to be proclaimed is the same as that of John
the Baptist (3.2) and of Jesus (4.17).

8. To the authority already given (in verse 1) there is added
the instruction to **raise the dead** (cf. 8.18ff.) and to **cleanse
lepers** (cf. 8.1ff.). These acts of power will be signs attesting the
reality of the Kingdom which has drawn near in the ministry of
Jesus.
You received without pay, give without pay: What is it that
the apostles received 'without pay'? Their commission, authority
and the good news of the Kingdom. This kind of saying was common in missionary circles (cf. 2 C. 11.7), although elsewhere

(1 C. 9.14) Paul argues for the right of an apostle to receive hospitality. The importance of the question of support for travelling teachers and preachers in the early Church is clear from the discussions of 1 C. 9 and *Didachē* xi–xiii ('if the prophet (apostle) demands money, he is a false prophet'). P. Aboth i.13 warns against utilizing the position of teacher for personal profit and glorification.

9. The meaning of the Greek (*ktaomai eis*) is: 'do not acquire, or procure . . . with a view to filling your belts', in the fold of which ancients hid their money. Whether this is a prohibition against accepting any payment for their ministry, or against providing money for themselves before starting is not certain, but the Marcan parallel suggests that it is the latter: 'take nothing for the journey' (Mk 6.9).

10. The prohibited **bag** would be a wallet for carrying food; presumably hospitality could be expected, and no stock of provisions was to be carried. To have two tunics was perhaps a sign of affluence, and certainly of a sedentary life. The denial of sandals and a staff (cf. Lk. 9.3; 10.4) to travelling men seems very strange. In allowing both (6.8, 9), Mark is probably original at this point. Schniewind suggests that the Matthean injunction means that apostles are to appear to men with the same attire as before God; those who fasted and prayed did so without a staff and barefoot. The purpose of all these prohibitions is not to advance ascetic poverty, but to ensure that apostles were unencumbered in their travelling mission and encouraged to trust in God's providence. Matthew alone adds **the labourer deserves his food** (cf. Lk. 10.7: 'worthy of his wages'). The necessities of life can be expected from those to whom the apostles minister (cf. Did. xiii.1 'every true prophet that sitteth among you is worthy of his food'; and also 1 C. 9.14 which states this right as resting on a command of the Lord).

11. The apostle is to lodge in one place during his stay, and not to change residences in search of greater comfort (cf. Lk. 10.7). A **worthy** person is one likely to receive an apostle and the message of the Kingdom (verse 14); the term is not used here to denote religious or moral worth, nor does it mean 'honourable'.

12–13. The salutation (to be given whether or not the house was worthy) would be a greeting, like: 'Peace be to this house' (Lk. 10.5). On the lips of the apostolic missionary the word 'peace'

(*šālōm*) would probably suggest the peace and blessing of the
Kingdom. On the worthiness or unworthiness of the house
(holder?) depends the effectiveness of the blessing. The Lucan
version, 'if a son of peace is there', preserves the original Semitic
idiom. The ancient blessing was thought of as having a kind of
objective existence of its own, once it had been uttered, and as
able to achieve its end or return void (cf. Isa. 55.11).

14. shake off the dust from your feet: a gesture of total
abandonment: no trace of association with the house or city is
to remain (cf. Ac. 13.51). Mk **6.11** and Lk. 9.5 add: 'for a testimony against them'. The apostles have discharged their responsibility; the community will suffer judgment for their rejection
of the Gospel.

15. Sodom and Gomorrah were examples of extreme wickedness and of the execution of the divine judgment (Gen. 19; cf.
Isa. 1.9; Jub. 36.10), and were often so used in the *NT* (Mt.
11.22, 24; Lk. 17.29; Rom. 9.29; 2 Pet. 2.6; Jude 7). The rejection
of the Gospel of the Kingdom will evoke a heavier judgment than
even the proverbial sinfulness of these cities.

**16. Behold, I send you out as sheep in the midst of
wolves:** Lk. 10.3 places this saying at the beginning of the charge
to the Seventy; Matthew uses it to link the preceding words of the
charge to the section on the hardships of disciples and of the
Church. The image on sheep here indicates the defenceless condition of apostles in a dangerous *milieu*. The figure of the wolf
is used to denote false prophets (Mt. 7.15; Ac. 20.29) or some
general menace (Jn 10.12); but in this context it probably indicates Jewish adversaries, especially Pharisees.

so be wise as serpents . . .: this proverbial saying is found
only in Matthew. **Serpents** represent the idea of prudence,
cleverness and shrewdness (perhaps recalling Gen. 3.1, where the
same word (*phronimos*) is used). The adjective **innocent** (*akeraios*;
cf. Rom. 16.19) indicates purity of intention, simplicity of purpose. The **dove** was used in Rabbinic literature as a symbol of
Israel—patient, submissive, faithful; cf. Midr. Ca. ii.14: 'God
saith of the Israelites: "Towards me they are as sincere as doves,
but towards the Gentiles they are prudent as serpents." '

THE SUFFERINGS OF APOSTLES **10.17–25**

The most important point in these verses (which are so different
from the preceding passage, where there is no hint of such suffering) is in verse 24: the consolation of disciples will be that of
knowing that their master has experienced the same troubles
before them.

The section has a clear theological unity, but its literary arrangement seems to have been due to Matthean editorial work.
Some parts of it are found in the context of the apocalyptic discourse (24.9,13) where Mark places them, and others are paralleled in Lk. 12.11–12; 6.40. In view of these factors, ought we to
treat this passage as a late collection of detached words designed
to warn and encourage the missionaries of the Church (A.D.
80–90), but having no connection with the prospects for a mission
of Jesus' apostles? That the passage was intended by Matthew to
relate to the persecution of the Church's missionaries is undoubtedly true (see Hare, pp. 96ff.); but is that the historical setting
of the *logia* which constitute it? It is difficult to deny that we have
in these verses any echo of Jesus' own teaching to his disciples.
The three Synoptics agree in putting upon the lips of Jesus similar
teaching on the fate of apostles. The vocabulary and ideas used
are strictly Palestinian, and it is likely that Jesus had some such
words to say to his disciples at some time during his ministry,
when hostility to his cause was growing. Their use in—even their
extension and reformulation by—the Church, in the light of its
own experience or expected experience, does not eliminate the
possibility that some of these words have a *Sitz im Leben* within the
teaching of Jesus.

17. These clauses show that for Matthew (though not necessarily for Mark) the men of whom apostles must be wary are Jews.
The **councils** (the only *NT* appearance of *synedrion* in the plural)
are the local assemblies of twenty-three influential members of the
synagogue whose duty was to preserve the peace. Ac. 22.19 and
2 C.11.24f. show that floggings for breaches of the peace could
take place in the synagogue itself, but no other evidence for this is
found. The word **their** draws attention to the rift between synagogue and Church.

18. and you will be dragged before governors and kings:
those who exercise executive power (including magistrates and

the Roman procurator, who is called 'governor' in 27.2,11,14) and
the Herodian princes will also be involved in persecuting Christian teachers. It is not certain that Matthew implies that Jews
are the instigators of this Gentile persecution, but such a view
would not be untrue to the anti-Jewish spirit of the passage.
for my sake: i.e. because you are apostles of Jesus. The Western
text has 'you will stand', as in Mk 13.9-10.

to bear testimony before them and the Gentiles: persecution offers to apostles the opportunity to witness to Christ and the
Kingdom before the authorities. The two groups could be the
Gentile judges and Gentiles generally (Hare, p. 108); or they
could be the Jewish accusers who bring charges against Christians
and the Gentile authorities.

19-20. Cf. Mk 13.11; Lk. 12.11-12 and 21.14f. Because they
witness to God, apostles ought not to be anxious about the words
of their defence; the Spirit of God will speak in and through them.
Luke refers to the 'Holy Spirit', but this title is not found in
Matthew. This is the only place, other than 3.11, where the gift
of the Spirit is said to be available to disciples; it is usually regarded as given only to Jesus as the endowment for the Messianic
ministry. It is promised now to disciples as they extend that
ministry, especially in times of distress and danger. The general
viewpoint here is very similar to that put forward by John in
relation to the Paraclete (14.16,26). See Hill, pp. 249f., 291f.

21. The tone of this passage is thoroughly apocalyptic, and is
reminiscent of Mic. 7.6—which is actually cited at verse 35. The
point is that members of their own families will denounce Christians to tribunals, thus bringing their lives into jeopardy. For
the same idea of family divisions as a sign of the End, see 4 Ezra
5.9; Jub. 23.19 and 2 Bar. 70.3.

22. for my name's sake: in accordance with the Semitic
idiom in which the name stands for the person, this may mean
'for me' (cf. verse 18), but it could also be 'because you bear the
name Christian' (cf. 1 Pet. 4.14). From earliest times in the
Church's history Christians faced unpopularity and constant
harrying because of the name they bore and the challenge presented by their faith to established religion. This reached a head in
the major persecutions, especially that under Trajan.

he who endures to the end will be saved: the verb 'endure'
does not mean 'resist', but 'suffer with patience' (cf. Mk 13.3;

Rom. 12.12; 1 Pet. 2.20 and Dan. 12.12). The phrase 'to the end' has no definite article, and could be simply adverbial: 'finally', i.e. 'without breaking down'. It is more probable, however, that it indicates the actual end of the persecution regarded as part of the Messianic woes. It does not mean 'the end of all things', nor does it seem likely that it refers to the 'end' of suffering—i.e. death in martyrdom. He who endures will be saved, not from his accusers, but into the joy of the Messianic salvation.

23. The first part of the verse (possibly based originally on the idea of eschatological flight) is a clear encouragement to apostles to persevere in missionary work in spite of persecution; in fact, through persecution the good tidings may spread from town to town more quickly. The second part has occasioned difficulty. It was made the focal point for Schweitzer's thorough-going eschat-ology (*Quest*, pp. 358ff.): Jesus does not expect to see the disciples back in the present age, and, because they did in fact return (Mk 6.30), 'the non-fulfilment of Mt. 10.23 is the first postpone-ment of the Parousia' (p. 360). Kummel (pp. 61ff.) has rightly criticized this view on the grounds that tacitly it combines, in an artificial way, the circumstances of Mt. 10 with those of Mk 6, in order to make the non-fulfilment of verse 23b an occasion of disappointment for Jesus which forced him to rethink his purpose and ministry.

The verse as it stands (even if 23b was originally an isolated *logion*) offers instruction and a promise to disciples who meet persecution during their missionary activity in Israel. Their task is not to be held up even by persecution; yet, even if they waste no time, the mission to Israel will not be *completed* before the Son of Man comes. That the disciples returned to Jesus *in the course of* their missionary activity (and Mk 6.30 probably does not refer to a final return) does not invalidate this assertion. Jesus promised the coming of the Son of Man before the *complete* discharge of their missionary commission.

This interpretation has the effect of bringing the expected coming of the Son of Man within the life-time of Jesus' disciples. The view that this coming is, not the Parousia, but a coming in judgment upon Israel, fulfilled in the destruction of Jerusalem in A.D. 70 (Benoit, p. 79) cannot be proved, and is improbable. The common assertion that this saying cannot go back to Jesus himself rests on one or other of two assumptions: either that Jesus

made no such temporal predictions, or that the experience and
expectation of the primitive Church is reflected here, and has
created the saying (Tödt, pp. 6off.). The first of these assumptions
runs counter to the widespread conviction that the Son of Man
sayings regarding the future are original (and, in the view of
many, the only original ones); the second assumption must come
to terms with the possibility that the eschatological enthusiasm
of the early Church was actually created by some such word as
this, which itself could not have been written by anyone who knew
the history of the Christian mission. The verse, it would appear,
suggests that Jesus expected not an imminent end, but an end not
long delayed, within perhaps 40–50 years.

24–5. These two verses form the conclusion to the section.
Luke gives the saying a more enigmatic setting and form (6.40).
The meaning is that the disciple cannot expect to suffer less
persecution than his teacher—an idea which is expressed often in
the *NT* (1 Pet. 4.1, and especially Jn 15.20, where the latter part
of verse 24 is quoted in connection with persecution). In B.
Berak. 58b similar words are cited in proverbial fashion: 'It is
enough for a slave if he is as his master (i.e. shares similar fortune).'
The Matthean form of 25a seems more original than Luke's
'everyone when he is fully taught will be as his master'. The view
that this saying seems to presuppose the destiny of Jesus (i.e.
suffering and crucifixion) has led many to deny that it could be a
dominical utterance: but surely Jesus encountered and expected
persecution before the final suffering took place.
If they have called the master of the house Beelzebul . . . :
this saying, peculiar to Matthew, probably alludes to, and may
have been uttered in connection with, the events of 12.22–32. In
both places, Beelzebul fills the role of Satan. The origin and significance of the name Beelzebul (the best attested form in the *NT*)
is debated; it may have been a Canaanite divinity, 'Baal the
prince'. The suggestion that *zeboul* is derived from a Hebrew word
meaning 'height', 'abode or dwelling', and that the name therefore means 'Lord of the dwelling' (i.e. of the nether world, perhaps) would suit the context here; it is more likely than the meaning
'Lord of dung'. The form Beelzebub (found in Vulg. and Pesh.)
is derived from 2 Kg. 1.2, and means 'Lord of flies'. The rejection
of Jesus and that of his disciples (the Christian missionaries
= **those of his household**) are brought together.

THE CONDITIONS OF DISCIPLESHIP 10.26–42

The general statement on the conditions of discipleship opens
with an exhortation to fearless confession (verses 26–33). This
section contains four *logia* (26–7, 28, 29–31, 32–3) which probably
circulated separately before being brought together in a thematic
unity (the word-link being 'fear not'). There is a significant parallel
to the verses in Lk. 12.2–9, although the context is different. But
the fact that some of the verses have partial parallels elsewhere in
the Synoptics (to verse 26 at Mk 4.22 and Lk. 8.17: to verse 30 in
Lk. 21.18: and to verses 32–3 at Mt. 8.38 and Lk. 9.26) indicates
that the literary connection between this section and Lk. 12.2ff
is more complex than is suggested by the affirmation that at this
point both evangelists are drawing on Q material. The parallel
to verses 34–6 (on division) in Lk. 12.51–3 raises this problem in an
even more acute form. The main theme is the same, but the style,
terminology and the reference to Mic. 7.6 are quite different. Such
differences are inexplicable in terms of a common source Q; it is
probably best to assume an oral original (which could be authentic
in substance, *contra* Bultmann, *HST*, pp. 152–6), of which the two
parallel traditions represent different literary states. Since verses
37–9 seem to be only distantly connected with the theme of
missionary witness, and verses 38–9 have a remarkable doublet in
16.24–5 (cf. Mk 8.34–5, which is addressed to 'the multitude with
his disciples'), it is possible that Matthew has included, at this
point in his instruction to apostles, words of Jesus given (on another
occasion) to his followers in general—which is the setting of the
parallel verses in Lk. 12.51–3. The last verses (10.40–11.1) represent the conclusion of the address by Jesus to his apostles (the title
'the Twelve' appears in 11.1). Having no parallel in Luke, they
may be a redactional arrangement including the characteristic
Matthean formula for the ending of a discourse.

26–7. The fear of men and of persecution ought not to menace
the apostles' work, which is to witness openly to that of which
knowledge is at present limited—i.e. the Kingdom of God. This
God will reveal to all men through the apostles. The words
what you have whispered are literally 'what you hear in the
ear'. The housetop was the traditional place from which public
announcements were made. In Lk. 12 the parallel verses form
part of a discourse to the disciples warning them against the hypo-

crisy of the Pharisees. That hypocrisy will be unmasked by the proclamation of the Gospel. A similar saying (to verse 26) is found in Mk 4.22 (= Lk. 8.17), with reference to the truth made known in parabolic teaching. It is possible that the word represents a popular saying or maxim, applicable in a variety of contexts. Here it is employed to emphasize the duty of apostles and teachers to proclaim to all what they have been told privately.

28. The apostles should have no fear of those who can kill only the body, but are unable to kill **the soul**. The word *psychē* in the *NT* is indebted for its meaning to the *OT nepeš*, and means (i) the vital principle common to all living things (Mk 3.4); (ii) the seat of thought and emotion (Mt. 22.27); and (iii) a man's real self (as here). Apostles should fear him who has power to destroy both soul and body in Gehenna, i.e. in the fiery hell of Jewish apocalyptic. Who has this power? Although Satan has great power in the time of ultimate trial (cf. 6.13 and 24.22), and the Son of Man has the power of condemnation (25.31–46), it is probably right to assume that God is meant here. It is more fearful to disobey God, who through Jesus commands apostles to proclaim the Gospel, than to be put to death as martyrs; cf. Wis. 16.13 and 4 Mac. 13.14f.

29–31. These verses form a unit, although verse 30 interrupts the simple *a fortiori* argument. **Sparrows** are common birds, sold very cheaply (an *assarion* is a small copper coin worth about a halfpenny) and used for food by the poor. Since they are the object of God's concern, how much more is the apostle's welfare his concern? The expression **fall to the ground** denotes the death of the sparrows, but this does not occur **without your Father's will.** The Greek has 'without your Father', and so some have suggested that the point is that the death of sparrows and the deaths of apostles are not deprived of the *presence* of God, although he may not have willed their end. The *RSV* rendering best preserves the sense: the expression 'without the gods' in the sense of 'without the will of the gods' is found in Hellenistic Greek (see Arndt, pp. 64–5).

32–3. These two verses sum up the general thought of endurance in mission. The parallel in Lk. 12.8f. retains the 'Son of Man' of Mk 8.38, whereas Matthew uses the 'I' of Jesus. It is likely that the Lucan form is original, and that the Matthean is a Christian interpretation (Kümmel, pp. 44f.): Jesus' veiled ascription of

G

sovereignty to himself (as Son of Man) has been made explicit in Matthew's version; a man's attitude to Jesus in the present time is decisive for the advocacy he will receive from the glorified Jesus at the final judgment. (That there is meant to be a sharp distinction between Jesus and the Son of Man in Lk. 12.8 and Mk 8.38 is unlikely if the concept of humiliation/vindication is kept central in the interpretation of the Son of Man sayings; see C. F. D. Moule, *Theology*, LXIX, 1966, pp. 175f.) To **acknowledge** Jesus means to 'affirm solidarity' with him (in action and even in death). Those who so acknowledge Jesus before men (and that may be before law courts) will be acknowledged by Jesus as his own before the Father, i.e. in the heavenly law court where God is judge. To **deny** means to 'declare that one does not know or have dealings' with someone (cf. 25.12). It should be noted that the confession required of men is christocentric in character: they must declare themselves apostles of Jesus. The final destiny of such depends on the word of Christ at the end, not on any transformation within themselves.

34. The peace which this verse denies is neither peace in Israel or between nations, nor peace between God and man. Jesus himself and the apostolic witness to him divides society into camps. The Lucan version (12.51) has 'division' instead of 'sword', and this correctly represents the thought. (The Old Syriac has 'division of minds and a sword'.) The mission and message of Jesus produces internal division; men are separated by reason of their response to him.

35–6. These verses refer back to Mic. 7.6 which had already been used by the Jews as a picture of the divisive effect of Messiah's coming. The passage is quoted in Lk. 12.52–3 in a different form (nearer to the LXX), and with a different context. Matthew's form of the passage represents neither the LXX nor the Hebrew M.T., and Stendahl (pp. 90f.) wonders if it represents a Greek version of the Micah passage already current in evangelical circles. The divisions of men caused by Jesus may be due to the obligations of discipleship (cf. verses 37–9)—or to their inability to agree on who Jesus is! Since the expected coming of Elijah (Mal. 4.5–6) was to issue in reconciliation, perhaps (so McNeile, p. 147) Jesus is hinting that he is not Elijah, the herald of Messiah.

37. The person whose affection for his family is so great that it will not allow him to break the ties (if that be necessary) in order to follow Jesus, is unworthy—i.e. behaves in a way that is unworthy—of him. The verse is not an attack on family relationships and natural attachments, but is a clear insistence that following Jesus is more important than family ties; if it is necessary to choose between the two loyalties, then a man ought to choose to follow Jesus. A somewhat similar sentiment finds expression in rabbinic literature with reference to the pre-eminence of the relationship of master and disciple: M. Bab. Metzia ii.11. Dt. 33.8–11, which includes a reference to Levi's disregard of family ties, is quoted in a series of testimonia at Qumran (4Qtest. 16f.).

38. This *logion* is paralleled in 16.24, where it suits the context better, and where it refers back to Jesus' own sufferings. To follow Jesus is to follow in a path which could lead to sufferings as terrible as he will himself endure, since it is marked by utter self-denial. The disciple must realize this, and accept the loneliness, opposition, and, if necessary, sacrifice of life. That martyrdom by crucifixion (at the hands of the Romans) is implied and predicted in the expression here is unlikely: the emphasis is on self-renunciation to the point of being a lonely outcast. The ideas expressed in verses 38–9 occur five times in the Synoptics.

39. Cf. Lk. 17.33; Mt. 16.25; Mk 8.35 and Lk. 9.24. In this type of context, to 'lose one's life' could mean to 'die a violent death' because of one's faithfulness in following Christ; but it seems more likely that it vividly denotes self-denial, without the suggestion of martyrdom. 'Finding one's life' means 'obtain, win, or preserve life'. Arndt (p. 326) notes that this meaning, already known in classical Greek, is found also in Hellenistic and Biblical Greek (Sir. 11.29, 22.13; Heb. 12.17; Ac. 7.46; Lk. 1.30; 2 Tim. 1.18). Those who remain faithful to Jesus at any cost will receive the life of the age to come.

40. The conclusion of the discourse returns to the earlier theme (verses 11–14) of receiving travelling missionaries into the house. The basic meaning of the verb *dechomai* here is 'receive hospitably', or 'in hospitality', though it may have added to it the idea of *accepting* the apostle's message. The verse has a clear Johannine ring about it (cf. Jn 11.44f., 13.20), but it expresses an idea familiar to Judaism: 'a man's emissary or agent is like the man himself' (M. Berak. v.5).

41. This verse is peculiar to Matthew. Although it is possible that **prophet** and **righteous man** are in apposition to 'apostle' (implied in verse 40), it is more likely that the saying belongs to the period of Jewish Christianity, when Christian prophets were a recognized class, distinct from apostles (cf. also 7.15f.). To receive a prophet **because he is a prophet** (lit. 'in the name of a prophet') means to receive him in his special capacity of prophet, i.e. as proclaimer of the good news. The righteous man is usually regarded as the faithful Christian who practises and exemplifies righteousness in his life (Manson, *Sayings*, p. 183, and Allen, p. 112), but the word *dikaios* could also refer to a semi-distinct class within the Church—namely, teachers (see the connection of prophets and righteous in Mt. 13.17 and 23.29); cf. D. Hill, *NTS*, xi, 1965, pp. 296–302. If so, then the **reward** of the prophet could be interpreted as the proclamation of God's message, and that of the righteous man as instruction in understanding the message. The genitive case after 'reward' is thus treated as a *gen. originis*, rather than as an objective genitive (the reward which the righteous man receives—namely, eternal life).

42. This verse is derived from Mk 9.41, which Matthew omits in his parallel narrative at 18.6. As in the Marcan context, the reference is to disciples (**little ones**). It may be that the setting of the verse here is meant to suggest that travelling and persecuted missionaries are dependent even on the hospitality and help of non-Christians.

Editorial Conclusion **11.1**

Cf. 7.28 and note. This formula brings to an end the preceding section. Jesus is represented as continuing his mission in Galilee on his own. There is no reference to the return of the Twelve (cf. Mk 6.30; Lk. 9.10), but they are found again with Jesus at 12.1. Perhaps chapter 11 is thought of as covering a period when they are absent, and during which Jesus receives the messengers from John and speaks to the people.

THE MYSTERY OF THE KINGDOM 11–13

At 11.2 begins the third section of Matthew's Gospel. The narratives of chapters 11 and 12 lead into the parabolic teaching of Jesus about the Kingdom (ch. 13); and the section ends at 13.53. Much of chapters 12 and 13 is dependent on the material found in Mk 2.23–3.12 and 3.20–4.34, but this Marcan material is prefaced

in Matthew by sections on John the Baptist (11.2–19), and on the
refusal of Jesus' own country to be converted, ending with the
thanksgiving to the Father and the invitation to the heavily laden
(20–30). This third section of the Gospel is held together by the
theme of response, or lack of response, to the Kingdom at work in
Jesus' ministry. It is in this setting that the parables of the Kingdom must be seen and interpreted.

JOHN THE BAPTIST'S QUESTION 11.2–6

This section is suitably placed at this point in the development of
Matthew's Gospel. The cures mentioned in Jesus' reply have been
illustrated in the preceding narratives: that 'the poor have good
news preached to them' is evidenced by the commission of the
Twelve (10.5ff.), which Luke records after the incident of John's
question.

The arrest of John was mentioned in 4.12, but for the reasons
for his imprisonment (and death) we have to wait till 14.3f. The
Lucan account, which is fuller at the beginning, does not mention
John's imprisonment, but only information given to him by his
disciples; this may mean that they had access to him while he was
under arrest. According to Josephus (*Ant.* XVIII.v.2), John was im-
prisoned by Herod in the fortress of Machaerus on the east side of
the Dead Sea. The phrase 'the deeds of the Christ' refers to all the
activity, but particularly the miracles of the preceding chapters.
The language here seems to be that of later Christianity. If *ho
Christos* was used to mean 'the Messiah', then the point of John's
question is lost, although it is possible that Matthew is expressing
his own knowledge in the light of later events, without caring for
the consistency of introduction and question in the section.

3. Are you he who is to come? In the mouth of the Baptist,
'the coming one' (*ho erchomenos*, cf. 3.11) must mean a messianic
figure, and probably *the* Messiah. It is not known as a title of the
Messiah in Jewish texts, but the verse 'he shall come to Zion as
Redeemer' (Isa. 59.20; cf. Ps. 118.26, LXX) was employed in the
synagogue services in a messianic sense, and is an ancient part of
the daily service. That 'the coming one' means Elijah, the precursor of the Kingdom (so Schweitzer) is very unlikely: the description of the coming one's actions in 3.11 (after the term is used
for the first time) does not correspond to the expected role of the
Elijah *redivivus*. John's question may have been prompted by a

current conception of an apocalyptic or political messiah: it might have been due to John's condition as a prisoner, for Messiah was expected to free the captives and especially the captives for faith (Lk.4.18; Isa.61.1). The word 'look for' (*prosdokaō*), in the sense of waiting for the expected messiah, belongs to the language of primitive Christianity (cf. Ac.3.5, 10.24; 2 Pet.3. 12–14).

4. The answer of Jesus does not directly deal with John's question; it focuses attention on what is already known, the interpretation of which remains withheld. The claim to messiahship is not openly made: a new basis for interpreting it may be suggested.

5. In this verse the themes of Isa. 35.5–6—a passage describing Yahweh's salvation of Israel—are represented, with the addition of the cleansing of lepers and the raising of the dead; **the poor have good news preached to them** recalls Isa. 61.1f. (the actions of the spirit-endowed prophet; cf. Lk. 4.18f.). The 'poor' here are, as in 5.3, those who are confident in God, though denied material riches—i.e. the pious who were despised and persecuted. The works described have been exemplified in the preceding chapters (except healing of the lame and deaf), and therefore Luke's reference to Jesus' actions 'in that hour' (Lk. 7.21) is not needed. 'The answer meant, in effect, "Ponder my works; they are not what you expect from the Messiah, but they show that the powers of evil are being undermined, and that the Messianic age is very close" ' (McNeile, p. 152).

6. These words, which must here be regarded as part of the message to John, crystallize the main theme of this entire section of the Gospel: the narratives and discourses of chapters 11–12 and the parabolic material of chapter 13 are all concerned with the theme of the coming of the Kingdom and the difficulties of outsiders in recognizing its presence in Jesus. The verb *skandalizesthai* (which *RSV* translates as 'take offence') may mean 'to be caused to stumble or fall (into sin or unbelief)'; cf. 16.23. John's disciples, though probably not John himself, might stumble from the way of righteousness through inability or unwillingness to recognize Jesus' mission and ministry as his Messianic claim.

JESUS' TESTIMONY TO JOHN **11.7–19**

That Jesus did take up a position with regard to the significance of John the Baptist and his ministry, and that he replied to questions asked him on this matter, is extremely likely; but that his judgment was made in the consecutive fashion represented here is unlikely. The composite character of this passage seems obvious from its studied literary form—the threefold question and answer (7–9); the theme of 'greater and least'—and from its anacolutha (12,13): the parable (16f.), with its unexpected application, is also separable. The section contains various declarations of Jesus (and perhaps of the early Church) on John and his relation to Jesus, put together in tradition but possessing a striking theological coherence. The Lucan version (7.24–35) is closely similar to Matthew (save at verses 13–14, which partially parallel Mk 9.11–13) and it is very likely that they are both in touch with an old common source.

7. As the messengers were leaving, Jesus 'took occasion' (so Knox's translation of *ērxato*, **began**) to speak about John's character and mission. **A reed shaken by the wind** may be a collective singular, referring to the cane-grass which grew on the banks of the Jordan. If so, then there is no suggestion of John's frailty or instability. People went to the wilderness, not to look at the grass, but to see a man. Variations of punctuation in this and the following verses have been suggested, but they do not affect the sense.

8. a man clothed in soft raiment: this may be intended as a contrast to John's actual dress in the wilderness (cf. 3.4–6), or as an ironic allusion to his presence at the court of Herod Antipas (cf. 14.1–12)—an interpretation which the second part of the verse could sustain. Stendahl suggests that the royal attire mentioned 'may refer to Davidic-messianic expectations' (*Peake*, 684d).

9, 10. The crowds had rightly recognized John as a prophet. Some even thought of him as Messiah (cf. Lk. 3.15; Jn 1.20; Ac. 13.25). This he disclaimed, but Jesus affirms that he was 'more than a prophet' in that he was the forerunner of the Kingdom, identifiable with Elijah. The quotation here (and in Lk. 7.27; Mk 1.2) is from the Hebrew of Mal. 3.1 and the LXX of Exod. 23.20 (the words 'before thy face' make more specific the application to the Baptist). The alteration of 'before me' in the original to **before thee** makes of the passage an announcement by God to the Messiah: it is no longer God whom the messenger precedes, but Jesus the Messiah. The method of quotation suggests the use in early Christian teaching of a collection of *OT* texts relating to the messianic beginnings and ministry (see Stendahl, pp. 49–54, especially p. 51). It is probable that the quotation has been inserted by the evangelist; it breaks the logical connection between verses 9 and 11, and anticipates the mysterious announcement in verse 14.

11. Couched in Hebraic expressions, the declaration means that no greater person has appeared (**risen** is a word used exclusively of prophets; cf. 24.11, 24) on the stage of human history than John the Baptist, because he has stood on the very threshold of the Kingdom. Yet the least disciple who, through following Jesus, already participates in the reality of the Kingdom (the **least in the kingdom**) is greater than John. Although this assessment of the Baptist could be attributed to the editor of the Gospel, it could also be understood on the lips of Jesus, for whom the greatness of any person is measured with reference to his participation in the Kingdom of God.

12. This enigmatic saying was probably handed down in the tradition in no definite context. It has been adapted here (with verse 13) to the context of sayings about John, but in Luke (16.16) it appears in a somewhat different form (with the order of the clauses reversed) in a context dealing with the Law. **From the days of John the Baptist until now** (and that 'now' may refer to both the moment at which Jesus speaks and the time of the editor's writing) indicates that the violence is a provisional occurrence which has an end. The description of the intermediate situation is difficult to interpret. Since Luke gives a simpler and much less strong version of the saying, it is likely that Matthew has preserved the more original form: **the Kingdom of heaven has suffered violence, and men of violence take it by force.** The parallelism of these clauses makes it clear that the verb *biazetai* denotes violence in a bad sense; therefore interpretations like 'the Kingdom forces its way through, or is striven after with violence' are incorrect; also unlikely is the rendering (*RSV* mg.) '**has been coming,** or manifesting itself, **violently** or powerfully'. The verse means that from the Baptist's time till the present the Kingdom is being violently assaulted, and violent men try to grab or rob it. The allusion may be to the opposition of Satan and evil spirits to the Kingdom, or to the violence of Herod Antipas to John; but a more likely explanation is that the reference is either to Zealots who try to bring in the Kingdom by employing force against the

Romans, or to Jewish antagonists of Jesus who continued to persecute Christians. While it is impossible to decide exactly who or
what is meant, it is clear that Jesus considers his ministry to be a
time when the Kingdom can be attacked as being present (see
Kümmel, pp. 121ff.). The Lucan form of the saying is open to the
interpretation that 'the enthusiastic (e.g. tax-collectors, etc.)
grasp the opportunity of entry into the Kingdom': Matthew's
language is too harsh to permit this view.

13. The shorter and stark form of the saying: 'the law and the
prophets were until John' (Lk. 16.16), may have been toned down
in the Matthean version; but the meaning is similar. The old
period of revelation came to an end with John the Baptist. His
was the last phase and predicted climax before the coming of the
Kingdom. Prediction has now given way to realization, in the
presence of Jesus. The Sinaitic Syriac MS. reads 'the prophets'
only, and this may be correct. Matthew's usual order is 'law and
prophets' (5.17; 7.12), and so the word 'law' might have been
introduced later. The meaning (for Matthew) of the saying is that
Prophets and Law pointed forwards up till the time of John who
heralded the arrival of the Kingdom. Thereafter Prophets and
Law are not exhausted of meaning and validity; rather they stand
as truly fulfilled.

14. The proof that John stands on the threshold of the new
order is that he is (i.e. takes upon himself the functions of)
'Elijah who is to come'; cf. Mal. 4.5. The expression 'if you are
willing to accept it' presupposes unwillingness or difficulty among
the Jews in making the identification (as verses 16-19 show): to
regard John, who was now lying in Herod's prison, as having come
'in the spirit and power of Elijah' was difficult for those who clung
to preconceived and apocalyptic notions.

16. to what shall I compare . . . ? It is like . . . this formula
represents the common Aramaic introduction to a parable in the
rabbinic literature; cf. Jeremias, *Parables*, p. 100.

this generation: this phrase occurs frequently in the Gospels, and
is usually found in contexts which show the failure of the Jews to
believe and obey Christ (cf. 12.39, 41; 17.17; 23.36). Here the
term corresponds to the 'crowds' of verse 7; they are the contemporaries of Jesus (and of the evangelist) who refuse to believe in the
Messiah.

It is like children . . . : the simile is drawn from the play of

children in the market-place: the 'piping and dancing' and the
'wailing and the mourning' represent either two types of game (a
wedding-game and a funeral game), or alternate cries within one
game. The point is clearly that some people will not respond to
any appeal. In the presence of John, the Jews should have
repented, but in fact they condemned John's stern asceticism and
rejected his appeal; in the presence of Jesus, they should have
rejoiced, since he inaugurated the reign of grace and glory, but in
fact they are rejecting Jesus and slandering his pleasure in life. In
short, the Jews would not 'enter the game'—they wouldn't play.
Neither the ascetic behaviour of John nor the ebullience of the
'Son of Man' (used ambiguously as messianic title *and* as 'a man'
denoting the speaker) could break through the conscious will to
resist on the part of the Jews; nothing pleases them! 'This parable
shows how differently John and Jesus lived, how widely rejected
both were, and how cleverly and wickedly people excused their
spiritual irresponsibility' (Filson, p. 139). On the poetical character of the language exhibited by the Syriac versions, see Black,
Aramaic Approach, p. 161.

19. wisdom is justified by her deeds: this *logion* is obscure;
it seems to have been so from early times, for the MSS. of Matthew
and Luke vary 'deeds' and 'children'. It is likely that 'deeds' is
the original reading at this point (with Peshitta): 'children' being
suspect on the grounds of harmonization with Lk.7.35. 'Wisdom'
(*sophia*) is not here identified with Jesus (but cf. Matthew's interpretation, at 23.24, of Lk. 12.49); it is the wisdom of God, God's
wise design or purpose for man (Wis. 8, cf. 1 C. 1.21,24). This is
vindicated (or proved right) by its works, the mighty acts or signs
which conclusively demonstrate that the Kingdom has been
manifested, that the decisive time has come. If the preposition *apo*
is given the sense of 'over against' (*min kodām*), then the reading
'children' is required. Wisdom is proved right, despite the rejection
by those who think that they are the true sons of Wisdom, i.e. the
Pharisees, who take offence at Jesus. But the preposition may be
interpreted as 'in view of', or simply 'by' (as above), and the
interpretation given here is suitable to Matthew. (Cf. Moule,
Idiom Book, p. 73 on the causal or instrumental use of *apo*, and note
the LXX of Isa. 45.25.)

THE WOES ON THE CITIES OF GALILEE 11.20–4

The true context of these sayings is unknown. In Luke they are incorporated in the instructions given by Jesus to the Seventy (Lk. 10.1–16). They are placed at this point in Matthew's work because they fit the theme of unresponsiveness which has been expressed in the preceding verses. If the word 'deeds' in verse 19 is understood in the way suggested, the opening words of this pericope are linked to it by the correspondence of 'deeds' and *dunameis* (= 'miracles' or 'mighty works') in verse 20.

20. The cities in which Jesus had done most of his mighty works (or a large number of them) have not repented and turned to God —i.e. they have not accepted the miracles as 'signs of the presence of the promised Kingdom': for this they are reproached and compared (unfavourably) with cities whose names were by-words for wickedness.

21. Chorazin: mentioned only here and in the Lucan parallel (10.13). Eusebius refers to it as a deserted town two miles from Capernaum. It may be identified with ruins found about two miles NNW. of Capernaum at Kirbet Keraze.
Bethsaida: ('house of fish'). Probably to be identified with Bethsaida Julias which stood near the point where Jordan flows into the Sea of Galilee.
Tyre and Sidon: two great Phoenician cities, near Galilee in the time of Jesus. They had been Philistine towns, denounced by the *OT* prophets as typical heathen cities doomed to disaster (Am. 1.9–10; Jl 3.4; Ezek. 26.28; Isa. 23; Zech. 9.2–4). Like Nineveh in response to the prophet (Jon. 3.5), those cities would have put on **sackcloth and ashes** (the outward signs of mourning and repentance) if they had heard John and Jesus.

22. it shall be more tolerable on the day of judgment: for the formula see 10.15. The lot of Tyre and Sidon would be more fortunate because their opportunity was less than that of Chorazin and Bethsaida.

23. Capernaum: the city (9.1) where Jesus lived regularly (Mk 2.1). The words **will you be exalted to heaven? You shall be brought down to Hades** echo Isaiah's prophecy on the pride of Babylon (Isa. 14.13, 15 in the Hebrew form). Capernaum's proud refusal to acknowledge Jesus' miracles as signs of God's reign will bring about her utter humiliation in judgment. Even

Sodom, proverbially notorious for its wickedness, if it had witnessed the mighty works of Jesus, would have repented and not been destroyed.

24. Cf. verse 22. The future tense in these verses implies a resurrection of both good and evil at the day of judgment.

THANKSGIVING, REVELATION, INVITATION 11.25-30

From the time of E. Norden (*Agnostos Theos*, 1913), many scholars have argued that these verses form a tripartite unity. Norden drew attention to a pattern of such 'self-revelations': (a) thanksgiving for revelation; (b) statement of its contents; and (c) invitation and appeal—the same sequence and structure as he found in Sir. 51. The presence of this pattern in Matthew suggested to Norden that this form is complete, and therefore prior to the Lucan form which contains only (a) and (b). Moreover, it is argued that there is an affinity of thought and meaning between 25-7 and 28-30; 'because Jesus is the revealer of God in his teaching, he holds the secret of life for all who turn to him' (W. Manson, *Jesus*, p. 73). But Sir. 51 did not originally form a unity; it is a thanksgiving-hymn to which an alphabetical acrostic was attached. And the omission of verses 28-30 in Luke would be extremely hard to account for if the three sections of Mt. 11.25-30 originally formed a unity: would they have been omitted only because it seemed inappropriate to the Lucan context (the return of the Seventy)? (Cf. Dibelius, *Tradition*, p. 279, n. 1.) The unity of Mt. 11.25-30 must therefore be considered doubtful.

The major issue in the study of these verses is that of authenticity; this has to be considered against the background of the strong Semitic character of the language, style, and structure (e.g. in verse 26); the Hellenistic parallels to the revelation-word; and the close similarity in style and content to Johannine sayings (Jn 3.35; 17.2; 7.29; 10.14,15) which has caused this passage to be called the 'Johannine thunderbolt'. These issues are considered in relation to the exegesis of the verses. (For a recent study of the passage as a whole, see A. M. Hunter, *NTS*, VIII, 1961-2, pp. 241-9; see also Jeremias, *Prayers*, pp. 45-52, and H. D. Betz, *JBL*, LXXXVI, 1967, pp. 10-24. Note also Manson, *Sayings*, p. 79: 'The passage is full of Semitic turns of phrase, and certainly Palestinian in origin.')

25-6. This saying has many marks of authenticity: the poetic structure; the formula of thanksgiving; the OT echoes (Isa. 29.16; Ps. 19.7); the word 'Father', which probably conceals the Aramaic *Abba*, Jesus' special form of address to God; the prayer formula, and the Semitic way of linking observed results with the providential purpose of God ('for such was thy gracious will'); the congruency of the content of the verses with the course of Jesus' ministry. The basic theme of chapters 11–13—the resistance to revelation on the part of the scribes and Pharisees—is continued here; **these things** probably refers back (in the Matthean setting) to the 'mighty works' of the previous paragraph, the events of eschatological significance witnessing to the appearance of the Kingdom. (The same kind of eschatological setting may be implied in the Lucan context also.) It is noteworthy that the juxtaposition of insight into the eschatological events and intimate knowledge of God has parallels in the DSS: see Davies, *COJ*, pp. 119–44.

The title **Lord of heaven and earth** recalls the opening of ben Sirach's prayer (Sir. 51.1) and Tob. 7.18. The meaning of the *logion* is clear: not to the **wise and understanding** (cf. Isa. 29.14)—the official custodians of Israel's wisdom, the scribes and Pharisees—but to the **babes** (cf. *nēpia* in Ps. 19.7; 116.6), the childlike disciples, has Jesus' teaching and activity come as the divine revelation it is.

27. This verse has been the subject of much discussion. The connection of the saying with the preceding verses seems natural enough. Verses 25–6 give thanks for the revelation and its recipients, and verse 27 declares the way by which the revelation comes —from the Father through the Son. The authenticity of the saying has been assailed on the grounds that it has a distinctly Johannine ring (cf. Jn 3.35; 10.15). But is it a legitimate canon of criticism that any Synoptic saying which has a parallel in John must *ipso facto* be spurious? In fact, it can be argued with Jeremias (*Prayers*, p. 48) that the saying is not precisely paralleled in John, but represents a stage on the way to Johannine thought; and that without such points of departure in the Synoptic tradition it would be an eternal puzzle how Johannine theology could have originated at all! It is not permissible to dismiss the saying as unauthentic by affirming that it is a Hellenistic 'revelation-word'. The Hellenistic parallels provided never were impressive, but recently the DSS have shown such an emphasis on knowledge that it is quite unnecessary to look outside a predominantly Jewish *milieu* to account for the passage; see Davies, *COJ*, p. 144. In any case, its Semitic language and style shows that the saying is not Hellenistic in origin (see Jeremias, *Prayers*, p. 46, for details). The formulation of the mutual relationship of Father and Son can be paralleled from Semitic sources as a type of expression necessary in languages which (unlike Greek) possess no reciprocal pronoun.

The greatest barrier to the acceptance of the genuineness of the verse is the supposition that Jesus could not have made such an absolute claim for himself. **All things have been delivered to me** looks like a reference to the kind of authority and power mentioned in Mt. 28.18; and it is commonly thought that the title 'Son' (or 'Son of God') was not used by Jesus of himself, but given to him by the early Church. On the first point Jeremias argues that the entire saying is governed by the thought of transmitting revelation rather than of possessing authority and power, and that the technical use of *paradidōmi* supports this understanding of the phrase, i.e. Jesus is supreme as *revealer*; God has given him a full revelation. With reference to the second point, Mk 13.32 has been advanced as a parallel to the absolute Father–Son relationship in this verse, but that particular verse is considered by many to be itself unauthentic (F. Hahn, *Christologische Hoheitstitel*, 1963, p. 327) or at least distorted (Kümmel, pp. 40–2, Jeremias, *Prayers*, pp. 36–7). Jesus' unique invocation of God as *Abba*, 'Father', might make it credible that he used the correlative term, 'Son' or 'the Son', for himself; but this is an assumption that not even Jeremias is prepared to make. In order to defend the saying as a whole, Jeremias claims that the words 'Father' and 'Son' have been given an absolute, titular sense in Greek, although in the original Aramaic saying they had a generic sense: 'All things have been transmitted to me by my Father, and as only a father (really) knows his son, so also only a son knows his father and he to whom the son wants to reveal this knowledge' (p. 50).

Thus the saying does not apply the title of 'Son' to Jesus, although it contains the seed from which the titular use developed. Jeremias adopts this view because: (i) he follows Dalman (*WJ*, pp. 193f.) in arguing that the use of the absolute form 'the Father' as a title for God is not found in Aramaic, and is attested only at a late stage in Christian sources. (But cf. its early use in Rom. 6.4 and Phil. 2.11.) (ii) because the title 'the Son' is never

used in Jewish sources or in pre-Hellenistic Christian sources as a
title for the messiah. But this is not strictly speaking accurate:
4Q Flor. 10–14 quotes 2 Sam. 7.14 'I will be his father and he shall
be my son', and applies it to the Branch of David. This shows that
Son of God *was just coming into use* as a Messianic title in pre-
Christian Judaism. . . . It meant not a metaphysical relationship,
but adoption as God's vice-regent in his kingdom' (Fuller,
Foundations, p. 32); but Fuller does not think it was a title used
by Jesus of himself. Given the availability of the title, that problem
still remains.

The arguments for the authenticity of the saying are strong (see
Hunter, *NTS*, VIII, pp. 245–7, and I. H. Marshall, *Interpretation*,
XXI, 1967, pp. 91–4), but it is difficult to affirm unhesitatingly that
it is a dominical word as it now stands: either it is a development
of some such word as Jeremias suggests (a statement of general experience, cf. also Jn 5.19–20a), or it is the expression—in the very
early (probably Palestinian) Church—of the Christology implicit
in Jesus' use of *Abba*. Jesus certainly called God his Father in a
unique sense, and he admitted others, through his eschatological
message, to the privilege of calling God '*Abba*'; that he took the
further step of referring to himself as God's son is debatable, but
that he laid the foundations for the Church's affirmation of faith is
certain. *Abba* is the point of departure in Jesus' own words for the
development of the Johannine theology of the Son: the words of
Matthew (and Luke) here represent the intermediate stage in the
process.

28–30. These verses, peculiar to Matthew, must be considered
with the preceding sayings. Even if they originally belonged to
another context in Jesus' ministry, they stand most appropriately
at this point in Matthew's gospel. Rejected by the cities of Galilee,
by the rabbinic schools of his native land, by the 'wise' of his time
—the scribes and Pharisees—Jesus turns to those who are weighed
down by the burden of Jewish legalism (a system central to the
controversies in 12.1–14). By reason of its form and content, this
logion is usually, and rightly, regarded as substantially genuine.
(On the Aramaic word-play detected by Meyer, see Black,
Aramaic Approach, pp. 183 f., 140–1.) The echoes of Sir. 51.23–7
have often been noted (e.g. T. Arvedson, *Das Mysterium Christi*,
Uppsala, 1937) but the view of R. Otto (*The Kingdom of God and
the Son of Man*, 1938, pp. 171ff.) that we have here a straight

quotation from Sir. 51 and that Jesus is speaking *in persona sapientiae* goes too far. What we have is an echo of Sir. 51 plus a sentence from Jer. 6.16 (Hebrew, not LXX): the words of ben Sirach are adapted by Jesus for his own purpose, which is quite different. Ben Sirach invites men to study the Law, saying: 'Put your necks under her (the Law's) yoke, and let your soul accept her burden. See, I have worked but little and found much rest.' In Jesus' saying, the contrast is between the yoke of the Kingdom (discipleship to Jesus) and the yoke of the religion of the Law.

Come unto me ... heavy laden: the invitation to come and attach themselves to Jesus goes to all who are tired and burdened, and the scribes received condemnation for loading men with burdens hard to bear (Lk. 11.46; Mt. 23.4). Jewish legalism could be very burdensome to many, though not to all.

I will give you rest: lit. 'I will refresh you'. The verb 'refresh' and its cognate noun belong to the terminology of Jewish apocalyptic (Rev. 6.11, 14.13; Mt. 12.43). It is in the Kingdom, and through attachment to Jesus, that the faithful will find their rest. The future tense indicates, not a distant prospect, or a rest in the beyond, but the rest which those who follow Jesus will immediately find.

29. Take my yoke ... from me: cf. Sir. 51.26. The 'yoke of the Law' (i.e. obedience to precepts and commandments) is a common expression in rabbinic teaching (e.g. P. Aboth 3.6). To 'take the yoke of Jesus' is to follow him and learn from him whose law (or *halakhah*) is not burdensome, but characterized by humility and concern for the despised.

for I am gentle and lowly in heart: could be translated as 'learn that I am gentle', or 'I who am gentle . . .' (a mistranslation of the Aramaic particle *de*). This self-description echoes the description of the Servant of the Lord in Isa. 42.2f. and 53.1ff., and especially of the messiah of Zech. 9.9: it is confirmed perhaps in 2 C. 10.4, where Paul appeals to the 'meekness and gentleness of Christ' as to something well known.

you will find rest for your souls: cf. M.T. of Jer. 6.16. The 'rest' is not that of inner contentment and inactivity: it comes from returning to God and faithfulness to the will of God (Jer. 6). The rest is identical with the yoke of discipleship, in bearing which the disciple learns to become himself 'gentle' and 'lowly'.

30. The kindliness and lightness of Jesus' yoke and burden do

not imply that he exacts less in obedience than the rabbis. He
exacts more (cf. 5.17–20), but in a different way. This is the yoke
of the Kingdom, in which 'Abba, Father' is sovereign and His
service is taken up: it is following Jesus and learning to serve
God and man in love.

THE SABBATH CONFLICT. I 12.1–8

The preceding chapter has shown how the presence of the Kingdom in Jesus was questioned by John the Baptist and rejected by
the cities of Galilee. Chapter 12 introduces material illustrating
the grounds on which Pharisaic opposition to Jesus developed.
The first issue is that of Sabbath observance (verses 1–13). At this
point Matthew comes back to Mark's outline (2.23) at the point
he left it in 9.18. In Mark and Matthew these are the only places
where Jesus' attitude to the Sabbath is dealt with explicitly (cf.
24.20; 28.1); Luke, on the other hand, gives fuller treatment
(13.15f. and 14.3).

Both this and the following incident are given in the form of the
typical 'pronouncement story', or 'paradigm': the narrative itself,
told with considerable restraint and economy of words, functions
as a means of giving prominence to a saying or pronouncement of
great significance. This does not mean that controversy on
Sabbath-observance during Jesus' ministry is unhistorical; it
must have been a real issue then, and, although the Matthean
presentation of the controversy reflects the conflict between the
Matthean church and contemporary rabbinism, the whole section
does not owe its origin to the early Church. The legalism and
fastidiousness of Judaism concerning the Sabbath can be seen
from M. Shabbath, but one ought not to forget the great religious
themes which formed the basis of Sabbath doctrine and made its
observance a joy (cf. Manson, *Sayings*, pp. 189f.). The Sabbath
was, like circumcision, a sign of the eternal covenant (Mek. Exod.
xxiii.15), a witness to the divine creation of the world in six days
(*ibid.* xx.16), and a means of adding sanctity to Israel through its
observance (*ibid.* xxvi.13); it was a special divine treasure given
to Moses (B. Shab. 10b). For an even more rigorous attitude to
Sabbath rest than that of orthodox Judaism, see CD x. 14–xi.8.

1. At that time: a Matthean editorial link (cf. 11.25)—Mark
and Luke have no note of time. It is possible that for Matthew the
thought is connected with what precedes: it is at the time when

Jesus sets his 'light burden' over against that of the Pharisees that
the Sabbath conflict arises.

his disciples were hungry: only the first evangelist adds this
detail. According to Kilpatrick (p. 116), its purpose is to show
that the disciples did not wantonly break the Law. This view may
be in danger of giving to the element of hunger a significance
in the narrative which it does not merit.

they began to pluck ears of grain: the right to pluck another
man's grain with the hand as one passed through his field was
established by Dt. 23.25.

2. The breach of the Law was not in the act of plucking, but in
what was regarded as reaping on the Sabbath (cf. Exod. 34.21):
this, with thirty-eight other different kinds of work, was forbidden
on the Sabbath (M. Shab. vii.2). Exceptions to Sabbath laws were
recognized in the case of Temple service and in situations where
life was at stake; if the disciples had been in imminent danger of
starvation, the act would have been permissible.

3, 4. The use of the counter-question with an appeal to the
Scriptures is characteristic of rabbinic arguments and is used
effectively in verse 5; and at 19.4; 21.16, 42; 22.31. The incident of
David and his companions eating the shewbread (on which see
Exod. 25.30 and Lev. 24.6–8) is described in 1 Sam. 21.1–6.
Although, according to the Midrash, this event took place on a
Sabbath, its relevance is limited; it merely shows that Scripture
witnesses to the infringement of the Law by no less a figure than
David and those who accompanied him. Human need or necessity
had a prior claim over ritual law; cf. Nineham, p. 105: 'The Law
was for man's good, and if the good of man was really furthered
by violating it, then a lower law was broken in order to keep a
higher law, here that of men's necessary bodily needs.' The attitude suggested by the argument of Jesus (which is not antithetical
to Law, but complementary) is akin to the rabbinic commonplace: 'The Sabbath is delivered unto you, you are not delivered
to the Sabbath' (Mek. Exod. xxvi.13).

5. Matthew adds another and stronger argument bearing more
directly on the Sabbath issue. Not only was a concession made in
the case of David, but the law itself commanded the priests in the
Temple to break the strict letter of Sabbath injunctions by doing
work, e.g. the changing of the shewbread (Lev. 24.8), the doubling
of the burnt-offering (Num. 28.9f.): yet they are guiltless. The

type of argument employed is the well-known rabbinic *qal wahomer* ('the light and the weighty', i.e. the *a fortiori* inference) which was one of the recognized hermeneutical norms for deriving a rule of *halakhah* from an actual Scriptural precept (see Daube, pp. 67ff.). The verse provides a precedent for the action of the disciples *within the Law itself*, and therefore places Jesus securely within the Law.

6. something greater than the temple is here: according to T. W. Manson (*BJRL*, XXXII, 1949–50, p. 191, n. 1) the 'something' is the community of disciples who with Jesus constitute the corporate Son of Man (verse 8): according to Lohmeyer (*Temple*, pp. 67, 69), it is the Kingdom of God effectively present in the eschatological community (or remnant) within the historical people of God. If this saying is interpreted as referring, not to the Messiah, but to the messianic community and its precedence over the Temple, then it may anticipate John's distinctive interpretation of the Temple of Christ's body, which replaces the old order of Temple worship (Jn 2.20–1). It should be noted that Matthew says 'greater than the Temple', not 'than the Law': verses 3–7 appeal *to* the Law as a witness for Jesus, and it validates the 'Son of Man' as Lord of the Sabbath (see *TIM*, p. 35).

7. The verse repeats Hos. 6.6, which already has been quoted in 9.13, where it suits the context better. The word **sacrifice** does not just mean those actually in the Temple, but the observance of religious prescriptions in general, and of Sabbath laws in particular. The opposition is between the practice of mercy (*hesed*) and the petty legalistic piety of the Pharisees, which was so ready to condemn those who did not obey the strict letter of the Law. The pre-eminence of mercy is grounded in the true will of God, which is characterized by kindness: God himself is the merciful and gracious one, and therefore the Sabbath commandment should be looked at from within the perspective of this kindness. The saying is very relevant to the Church situation in Matthew's time when Christians were in conflict with Pharisaic intransigence and casuistry.

8. All three Synoptic accounts of the incident have this verse, practically in identical form. The Marcan form is preceded by: 'The Sabbath was made for man, not man for the Sabbath.' This has led some exegetes to think that 'Son of Man' here and in Mark refers to 'man' in general; man is lord of the Sabbath, and can perform work on that day if needs arise (cf. McNeile, p. 170). But the context in all three Gospels clearly shows that **Son of Man** means Jesus himself (or Jesus and his disciples, if the corporate interpretation of the title is adopted). The words may be a veiled messianic claim, but many scholars have suggested that the voice of the Church is to be discerned in the saying rather than the voice of Jesus. Hooker (*SSM*, pp. 99–102, 193f.), however, can argue for its authenticity: in the presence of the Son of Man (Jesus and the community bound to him) the blessings of Sabbath—an occasion for man's restoration—are renewed.

THE SABBATH CONFLICT. II 12.9–14

The Matthean form of this healing narrative emphasizes the dialogue in which Jesus takes and holds the initiative and reveals the hypocrisy of his opponents. The incident follows naturally upon the preceding section; it shows what it means to put active pity ('mercy') before religious duties ('sacrifice'), since the will of God is concerned with the well-being of man rather than with pious scruples. The form of the narrative in Matthew is that of a 'pronouncement-story', not a miracle story; the healing is subordinate in interest to the religious question raised, although underneath the Marcan form there may lie an original tradition based on reminiscence (see Taylor, p. 220).

9. their synagogue: this strange expression (Mark and Luke have 'the synagogue') may reflect the time when the disciples of Jesus (in the early Church) were no longer able to go and discuss with Jews in the synagogue. This was prohibited by the Birkath ha-Minim, a liturgical innovation of *c*. A.D. 85 which resulted in the (self-) exclusion of heretics and Jewish Christians from the synagogues of the Pharisaic party. On the basis of this phrase and others like it, Kilpatrick (pp. 109–11) claims that the Gospel reflects the situation in the Church after A.D. 85: the synagogues are 'theirs' (i.e. the Pharisees), not 'ours' (Christian and Jew): but see Hummel, pp. 28ff., for a contrary view.

10. In Matthew the question is a general one concerning the legality of healing on the Sabbath, not about the healing of the particular case before Jesus. The principle admitted by the rabbis was that relief might be given to a sufferer on the Sabbath if his life was in danger (M. Yoma viii.6; Mek. Exod. xxii.2, xxiii.13). But this malady would not have entered into the category of mortal illness.

11, 12. The rescue of an animal which had fallen into a pit, or was otherwise in danger through accident, was permitted on a Sabbath or festival under certain circumstances (B. Shab. 128b and Bab. Metzia 32b); the general principle was that it was contrary to the Law to allow an animal to continue to suffer without help. The Qumran sectarians would have denied even such help on a Sabbath (CD 11.13–14). The argument used by Jesus is again *qal waḥomer*: if a sheep, then surely a man! The argument has the effect of placing Jesus firmly within the Law, rightly understood: he does good on the Sabbath, and so fulfils the will of God, who desires merciful action rather than ritualistic legalism.

14. This is the culminating point in the opposition of the Jewish religious authorities. This final breach with the Pharisees and its consequences seem to be located rather early in the ministry (cf. Mk 3.6.). If the reference is not to an early plot on Jesus' life, we must regard the verse as bringing forward in time the opposition which was evoked later by Jesus' persistence in the attitudes revealed in this passage. Mark says that the Pharisees acted with the Herodians; but for Matthew the Pharisees seem to represent the only real opposition to Jesus (see Hummel, pp. 12ff.).

JESUS, THE SERVANT OF GOD, HEALS **12.15–21**

In three short verses (15–17) Matthew summarizes the contents of Mk 3.7–12, and then adds a long citation from Isa. 42.1–4 which interprets Jesus' work in terms of the mission and character of the Suffering Servant of Yahweh.

15. Having become aware of the plot against him, Jesus withdraws to avoid publicity. He requires peace and quietness in his ministry (cf. Isa. 42.2), but it is not solitary inactivity; many followed him and he healed them all.

16. The authoritative injunction to silence may have been made to avoid further trouble from the Pharisees, to avoid creating a falsely-based messianic enthusiasm, or to direct attention away from Jesus himself to the mission and message of the Kingdom (Filson, p. 148); or it may represent the necessary theological presupposition (on the part of the evangelists) for the interpretation of Jesus' ministry in the light of the Easter faith (see comments on 8.4). What actually happened we cannot know for certain, but we know what Matthew thought of it from the citation he introduces.

17. The purpose of God which Jesus' ministry fulfils is discerned (for Matthew) in the Scriptures. The verses quoted from Isa. 42 show that, in refusing to quarrel with the Pharisees or to allow his Messiahship to be openly acknowledged, Jesus is the one who **will not wrangle or cry aloud.** We cannot be certain whether, in quoting this passage, Matthew was consciously identifying Jesus with the Servant or merely concerned to show that the methods employed by Jesus in his ministry fulfilled the Scriptures. Our judgment on this matter will depend on our understanding of the methods of Scriptural exegesis and application in this period (see Hooker, *Jesus*, p. 84). On the citation, see Stendahl, pp. 107ff.; Lindars, pp. 144–52; Gundry, pp. 110–16. The text does not correspond exactly to the M.T. or to the LXX. Stendahl finds close resemblance to the Syriac Old Testament (Peshitta), and suggests that we have here a form either used in Matthean circles or elaborated on the basis of Matthew's own exegetical reflection on the Hebrew text.

18. he shall proclaim justice: Hebrew *mišpaṭ* (LXX *krisis*), which may mean 'true religion' (*JB* 'the true faith'); but it is likely that in Matthew the term is correctly rendered 'justice' or 'judgment'. In the work of the Servant there is accomplished a work of righteousness, judgment, or justice for the Gentiles.

20. The quotation in the first part of the verse and the LXX correspond with M.T. The servant will help and comfort the weak-hearted and powerless.

till he brings justice to victory: the version is influenced at this point by Hab. 1.4, where justice is spoken of as not going forth *lāneṣaḥ*, 'for ever', or (in Aramaic) 'to victory'. The humble and discreet work of the Servant will ultimately achieve the victory for righteousness and judgment. The linguistic alteration suggests to Lindars the application of Isa. 42 to Jesus' resurrection.

21. and in his name will the Gentiles hope: Hebrew 'the coastlands wait for his law'; the LXX agrees with the quotation. The emphasis on the Gentiles in this citation (their 'justice' and their 'hope') echoes the Church's concern with the conversion of the pagan (i.e. non-Jewish) world to Christ. The appearance and use of the passage here witnesses to a universalist strain in Matthew's theology.

THE PHARISEES' ACCUSATION 12.22-4

Here and at Lk. 11.14ff. the accusation by the Pharisees is preceded by a healing miracle, and in Mark (3.20ff.) by an attempt on the part of Jesus' friends to take him away because he was (in their opinion) 'out of his mind'. The common source for Matthew and Luke is reproduced in the Matthean doublet (9.32-4) which mentions the Pharisees' accusation, but in a context which is not suitable.

22. The demon possession consists in being blind and dumb; it is not an affliction additional to the other two. Mt. 9.32ff. and Lk. 11.14ff. refer only to the dumbness of the man, and the emphasis in this story seems to lie there. Few healings are so quickly narrated; everything moves with haste to the accusation of the Pharisees.

23. were amazed: lit. 'were beside themselves' (the Greek word used of Jesus in Mk 3.21).
'Can this be the Son of David?': 'Son of David' was a popular messianic title in Judaism from the middle of the first century B.C. (cf. Ps. Sol. 17.21), and had ancient scriptural roots (2 Sam. 7.13ff.; Am. 9.11). Although miraculous healing was not associated in Judaism with the Davidic Messiah, in the Gospels Davidic sonship expresses Jesus' function as merciful healer (Mk 10.47f.). According to Fuller (*Foundations*, pp. 111, 189) the idea of miraculous help for the sick was at one time associated with the Mosaic prophet-servant: Matthew's Gospel (which has preserved more fully the 'Son of David' christology at 9.27; 15.22) quotes Isa. 53.4 (at 8.17) in connection with healing miracles, and therefore appears to associate 'Son of David' with the work of the Servant. That link may bind this narrative to verses 17-21, taken from the first Servant Song.

24. The Pharisees: Mark has 'the scribes who came down from Jerusalem'. Matthew seems always concerned to make the Pharisees the chief opponents, presumably because in his time Pharisaic opposition to the Christian mission was intense.
Beelzebul, the prince of demons: see note on 10.25. Jesus' power to cast out demons is attributed to his being in the service of and possessed by Satanic power.

JESUS' REPLY **12.25–37**

The structure of this section is that of the Marcan parallel (3.23–30), but its length is surprising in the work of Matthew, the master of conciseness. The additional material emphasizes the severity of the denunciation. It is probable that the section brings together into a single complex sayings which were originally independent (cf. Lk. 11.17–23; 12.10; 6.43–5). The principal themes are the Kingdom divided against itself (25–31) and the tree and its fruit (33, cf. 7.16–20) with two parallel images: verses 36–7 form the conclusion.

25–6. The point of this illustration is that internal strife, if carried sufficiently far, makes the continued existence of any movement or organization impossible. The power of Satan is here described as a kingdom (*basileia*); the world is the theatre of a conflict between the Kingdom (or reign) of God and that of Satan. Jesus' actions are either Satanic or divine. The terms **city** and **house** are to be regarded as indicating units of organization or power.

27. This and the following verse are not found in Mark: they belong to the stock of Jesus' words in the Q tradition. The argument is developed *ad hominem*. By whom do the Jewish exorcists cast out devils? If not by Beelzebul, then it must be by God's power. The sons of the Pharisees (i.e. their disciples or pupils) would be the first to condemn the intransigent attitude shown to Jesus because it implied that they were in league with Satan. For Jewish exorcism, see Ac. 19.13; Josephus *Ant.* VIII.ii.5; *BJ* VII. vi.3; Tob. 8.1–5.

28. by the Spirit of God: Luke has 'by the finger of God'. Both have ultimately the same meaning (cf. Exod. 8.19; Dt. 9.10; Ps. 8.3): they refer to the mighty power of God which inspires Jesus in his exorcisms. It is unlikely that Luke, with his interest in the Holy Spirit, would have changed the reference to 'finger': the Matthean form may be an alteration which made the polemic against the Pharisees more effective (were they challenging God's spirit?) and which, at the same time, gave the evangelist a convenient introduction to the saying on blasphemy against the Spirit. It also links this passage to the quotation from Isa. 42 (in 12.18). **the Kingdom of God has come upon you:** The word used here (*ephthasen*) affirms much the same thing as *ēngiken* ('is at hand',

3.2) but it is more explicit. The Kingdom is not just pressing in upon men: it has come. (For the use of the verb, cf. Rom. 9.31; 2 C. 10.14; and I Th. 2.16; 4.15, where it is employed in an apocalyptic sense.) In the person and, especially, in the action of Jesus the sovereign authority of God has been manifested among men, and in particular to Jesus' adversaries (**upon you**): 'the Kingdom is not a matter of pious hope or religious nostalgia: it has become, in the activity of Jesus, an object of discernment and faith' (Bonnard, p. 181). Cf. Kümmel, pp. 105ff. Only here and in 19.24; 21.31, 43 does Matthew use 'Kingdom of God' instead of his usual 'Kingdom of heaven'.

29. This saying, which may originally have been a detached *logion*, is given in the same context (though not in exactly the same form) by Matthew and Mk 3.27. The picture of the theft in the strong man's house is metaphorical (cf. LXX of Isa. 49.24f.): Satan is the strong man, and Jesus is the stronger one (cf. Lk. 11.22) who takes away from him those whom he dominates. The defeat of Satan is taking place in Jesus' exorcisms, for sickness was one of Satan's great provinces of power. Since it was a Jewish expectation that, in the last days, Satan would be bound (Ass. Mos. 10.1; Test. Levi 18.1, cf. Rev. 20.2), this pronouncement means that the eschatological Kingdom of God has begun its work.

30. This saying was apparently joined to the preceding one in the tradition, though its logical connection is not clear. It simply means that neutrality with reference to Jesus is impossible—and that affirmation is hardly likely to have been addressed to implacable opponents such as the Pharisees! The theme of gathering and scattering is found in the *OT* with reference to the people of God (Ezek. 34.13, 16; Isa. 40.11; 49.6); but here Jesus is the great gatherer (Shepherd) of the last days. In Mk 9.40 (cf. Lk. 9.50) the saying occurs in inverted form ('he that is not against us is for us'), again in connection with casting out demons; 'the sayings are not contradictory', says McNeile (p. 177), 'if the one was spoken to the indifferent about themselves, and the other to the disciples about someone else'.

31. Cf. Mk 3.28–29. Blasphemy in the LXX usually denotes blasphemy of God. Every such blasphemy or sin will be forgiven, but not **blasphemy against the Spirit**. If the saying is based on Mark, then the meaning of this is the attributing of Jesus' actions to diabolical inspiration, the assertion that he cast out demons by being in league with the demonic power. The unforgivable 'blasphemy against the Spirit' is the affirmation that the divine presence and power which inspires the work of Jesus is demonic. The context suggests that this is the correct interpretation.

32. This seems to be the Q form of the preceding saying. Luke gives it at 12.10, though in a different context which it does not easily fit. In Matthew's version, the contrast is between speaking **against the Holy Spirit** ('blasphemy' in Luke), which will never be forgiven, and speaking **against the Son of Man**, which can be forgiven. This may mean that, while an attack on Jesus' own person, as Son of Man and therefore 'hidden', is pardonable, any speaking against the *power* by which he works (i.e. the divine endowment for the messianic ministry) will not be pardoned. The difficulty involved in drawing the distinction between the person and the power of Jesus has led to the view that the saying reflects the Church's consciousness of itself as the Spirit-filled community. After Pentecost, the Spirit became the constitutive factor in the Church's life: to speak against that Spirit would have been tantamount to apostasy. 'Blasphemy against the Son of Man' would then be a sin committed apart from the Christian fellowship—a man might pardonably and understandably fail to recognize Jesus as Messiah during his ministry or outside the Church—but, after the Pentecostal outpouring, 'speaking against the Spirit' would be a denial of the very source of the Messianic community's existence (cf. Stendahl, in *Peake*, 684q). The first explanation is probably best and enables verses 31-2 to be interpreted by one another.

in this age or in the age to come: common phrases in Jewish (apocalyptic) literature and in the rabbis. The expression is equivalent to 'never'.

Words reveal character **33-7**

The point of this section is clear: the blasphemy of the Pharisees and their attack on Jesus are not accidental; they reveal what these adversaries are—viz. evil (34), and evil-speaking. It is by their words—especially on Jesus—that they will be judged.

33. Cf. Mt. 7.17-18. The meaning is this: it is by the fruits of a life, the results in action, that the quality of a life is to be judged. This applies to Jesus and his good works as well as to the Pharisees and their activities. The Greek idiom **make the tree good** could be rendered 'suppose the tree is good'.

34. brood of vipers: a phrase used in 3.7 (by John) and again in 23.33, with a stinging rebuke to Pharisaic hypocrisy; cf. Sir. 27.6.

out of the abundance of the heart the mouth speaks: the word is important for what it expresses about a man's basic attitude and orientation; the heart designates the centre of personality and of a man's psychological integration.

35. Luke has 'from the good treasure of his heart', and this is the meaning of Matthew's words also. It is not a treasure of culture or of goods, but of the heart, which directs life.

36-7. Peculiar to Matthew. Again it is emphasized that words are of critical importance: it is on the basis of his words (in which he may or may not confess Jesus) that a man will be accepted finally (for the saying has an eschatological reference) or condemned by God. There is rabbinic evidence for the belief that a man's record, kept in heaven, included his words as well as his deeds, *SB*, 1, pp. 639f. The unexpected change to the second person singular in verse 37 suggests that the saying may be proverbial. The adjective *argos* (*RSV* 'careless') indicates what is 'casual', 'ineffective', perhaps (so Stendahl) 'insignificant': *JB.* has 'unfounded'.

THE SIGN OF JONAH 12.38-42

This section has a parallel in Lk. 11.29-32 and a partial doublet in 16.1, 2, 4. The Marcan form (8.11-12) gives a firm refusal of any sign, and the Semitic idiom ('if . . .': strong negative) guarantees the soundness of the tradition. It may be that this idiom was the starting point for the tradition in Matthew and Luke: 'except (i.e. if not) the sign of Jonah' (so Stendahl); this would mean that the Q version was a later development. On the other hand, it seems plausible to suggest that Mark's is an abbreviated form of the original, offering a flat refusal in the interests of consistency with the idea of the concealment of Jesus' Messiahship from the people and their religious leaders (see Taylor, p. 363).

38. some of the scribes and Pharisees: in Mark the request comes from the Pharisees and in Mt. 16 from the Pharisees and Sadducees. At this point in Matthew, the identification of the questioners as 'scribes and Pharisees' links the section to the preceding attack by the Pharisees on Jesus and his counter-attack on them and their scribes (12.22-36).

a sign: what is asked for is an authentication of Jesus' authority and mission, not just a miracle: the Synoptics do not use 'sign' to mean 'miracle' in the way John does. The desire for a convincing display of supernatural power was said by Paul (1 C. 1.22) to be characteristic of the Jews. It was expected that the Messiah would be recognized and accredited by certain signs (cf. 16.1).

39. An evil and adulterous generation: this appears to refer to the scribes and Pharisees who represent their generation: 'adulterous' means 'unfaithful to God', 'apostate' (cf. Isa. 57.3, and especially Hosea's conception of Israel as an unfaithful bride).

except the sign of the prophet Jonah: in Luke the 'sign of Jonah' is interpreted as the prophet's preaching which evoked the response of repentance. This would seem to be how verse 41 (with its natural parallel in 42) understands the sign. According to Bultmann (*HST*, p. 118), the meaning of the sign for Luke is that, as Jonah came from a distant land to the Ninevites, so will the Son of Man come from heaven to this generation. But as Manson (*Sayings*, p. 90) points out, the analogy is then not close, for Jonah came preaching repentance but the Son of Man comes in judgment.

40. Here the sign of Jonah is interpreted with reference to the death of Jesus. The period during which Jonah was inside the great fish was three days and three nights, but Jesus' period in the grave was at most three days and *two* nights: therefore, although the Greek version of the Jonah psalm presents the idea of escape from death and distress, it is unlikely that this verse represents a *post eventum* prophecy of Jesus' resurrection: it is incorrect in the details. It is probable that the Jonah reference and its application to Jesus is not concerned with the idea of deliverance or resurrection, but only with the idea of judgment and death. The death of the Son of Man (i.e. Jesus as representative of the true people of God) is the only sign that will be given. It may be that in this Matthean view of the sign there is an even deeper significance. The symbolic significance of the Jonah story has to do with the obligation laid on Israel to bring the knowledge of God to all nations, i.e. to fulfil the rôle of God's Servant and be 'a light to the Gentiles'. If this is the underlying meaning of the Jonah sign for the evangelists, then Luke is declaring that the sign to Jesus' generation is that of the Son of Man, as Servant, bearing a message of mercy to men before judgment, while Matthew goes further and emphasizes that it is *in his suffering* that this 'Son of Man' will fulfil the destiny of Israel to be the Servant. Justin (*Dial.* cvii.1-2) gives the interpretation of the sign as referring to the Resurrection, but does not quote verse 40.

41. This generation has not repented, although **something greater than Jonah** is present—and that 'something' is either the Son of Man or the Kingdom of God which he brings (cf. on 12.6), and which is evidenced by Jesus' activity. Black (*Aramaic Approach*, p. 134) suggests that the phrase **arise . . . with** in verses 41-2 represents a Semitic idiom for 'dispute', and that the words **at the judgment** are a purely Greek addition to make the idiom intelligible. In this case, we should translate 'will rise in judgment with', there being no reference to the final judgment.

42. Likewise **the queen of the South** (i.e. the queen of Sheba, 1 Kg. 10.1-13) may condemn this generation; she came from afar to hear Solomon's wisdom, but this generation has refused to attend to the proclamation and coming of the Kingdom in the person and work of Jesus.

THE RETURN OF THE UNCLEAN SPIRIT **12.43-5**

The Lucan version of this *logion* occurs in the same literary context of a conflict between Jesus and the Pharisees (11.24-6), but there it is attached to the words: 'He that is not with me is against me', and so can be interpreted of the individual. Matthew links it with the condemnation of this generation (verse 45). It is probable that the first evangelist understands the saying as a warning about the future: Jesus' own generation, now purified by his ministry, is menaced by a greater power of evil. The piece reflects the spirit of Jewish folklore and the common ideas about demon possession and exorcism which Jesus shared with his contemporaries.

43. unclean spirit: a Jewish synonym for 'demon'.
through waterless places: it was popularly believed that demons inhabited deserts or ruins (Tob. 8.3). But this demon does not remain content with his bedouin life; he wishes to return to his old quarters and enjoy a settled life.

44. Matthew alone adds that the demon's former dwelling is vacant. Emptiness invites occupation.

45. The idea behind the first part of the verse is that the eight devils will have a better chance of forcing an entry into the house and of resisting successfully a second expulsion. But the real point of the tale is in the second part of the statement: as the man's last state is worse than the first, so with this generation (of Jews) on which John the Baptist and Jesus have had some, if only transitory, effect. It has not been radically reformed or possessed by the power of God, and its end will be unutterably tragic.

THE TRUE FAMILY OF JESUS 12.46–50

Following Mark's order, Matthew has placed this *pericope* at the end of the series of conflicts between Jesus and the Pharisees and this generation. His purpose is to highlight the dramatic break on the part of Jesus with his contemporaries, the Pharisees, and his own family.

46. The introductory words do not fit neatly with what precedes, and are probably just a formula used in the linking of passages. The identity of Jesus' brothers (cf. also 13.55) is disputed. Roman Catholic exegetes regard them as 'half-brothers' (sons of Joseph by a former marriage) or 'cousins' (sons of Mary's sister). It is true that in Hebrew and Aramaic the word for 'brother' has a wider range of meanings than in Greek (cf. also *adelphos* in LXX), and this could be reflected in the Synoptics; nevertheless the texts of Paul, of Acts, and of John also mention Jesus' brothers *in Greek* to Greek-speaking readers, and it is likely that they meant the term *adelphos* to be understood as 'brother' in the accepted sense of the word. The theory of the perpetual virginity of Mary had not arisen when the Gospel was written.

47. This verse is missing from certain important MSS., including the Codices Vaticanus and Sinaiticus. It is unlike Matthew to add words which contribute so little. They may have been inserted under the influence of Mk 3.32 and because of the appearance in verse 48 of 'the man who told him'.

49–50. The disciples (and therefore for Matthew the members of the Christian community) constitute the real family of Jesus, and their kinship to him is created not by physical relationship but by reason of the fact that they do God's will. The content of this will is not indicated, but the sense which Matthew gives to the term (6.10; 7.21; 12.50; 18.14) allows it to be understood in terms of obedience to the Law as reinterpreted by Jesus, an attitude which necessarily involves belief in and commitment to Jesus.

PARABLES OF THE KINGDOM 13.1–52

Of the seven parables recorded in this chapter, which forms the
third Matthean discourse, two are found also in Mark and Luke
—viz. the Sower and its interpretation (Mk 4.1–9, 13–20; Lk.
8.5–15) and the Mustard-Seed (Mk 4.30–32; Lk. 13.18–19). The
parable of the Leaven is found in Lk. 13.20–1, and the remaining
four (the Weeds and its interpretation, the Pearl of Great Value,
the Hidden Treasure, and the Net) are peculiar to Matthew. The
parables are presented as having been spoken in public, with interpretations given privately for the disciples to whom **it has been
given to know the secrets of the kingdom of heaven** (verse
11). Matthew states that others (and especially Jews) do not understand the message of the Kingdom, implying that even the parabolic teaching on the Kingdom will not enlighten them (see the
comments on verses 11ff.).

The works of Dodd and of Jeremias are indispensable for the
help they give in recovering the original tradition of parabolic
teaching and its *Sitz im Leben* and meaning in the ministry of
Jesus. They build on the fundamental thesis of A. Jülicher (*Die
Gleichnisreden Jesu*, 1899–1910) that the Gospel parables are not
allegories whose tiniest details must be interpreted, but didactic
stories which make one decisive point. Dodd and Jeremias affirm
that that main point is not a general ethical truth, but is ultimately
connected with the Kingdom of God inaugurated in Jesus; it
ought to be added, however, that the element of allegory is not
entirely absent from the parabolic teaching; see M. Black, *BJRL*,
XLII, 1959–60, pp. 273–87, and R. E. Brown, *NT*, v, 1962, pp.
36–46, reprinted in Brown, pp. 254–64).

In dealing with this chapter of Matthew's Gospel, we must
bear in mind, not only the setting of the parables in the ministry
of Jesus, but also their place and meaning in the context of this
Gospel. Bonnard (pp. 189–190) suggests that the frequent distinction between 'disciples' and 'Pharisees' (or 'scribes and Pharisees') may be understood in terms of the conflict between the
Syrian Palestinian church of A.D. 80–90 and the orthodox
Judaism of the time. In this kind of perspective the parables of this
chapter, following as they do on conflict narratives in chapter 12,
take on a two-fold significance: to the 'disciples' (i.e. to the
Church) they are the means of explaining why the Kingdom,

inaugurated by Jesus, has not yet arrived in glory, and why, in particular, its results in Jesus' ministry are at this point without grandeur and power: and for 'those outside' (verse 11 and Mk 4.11)—after the break described in 12.38–50—they will be the means of affirming chiefly that what they can see of the Kingdom from the outside is sufficient to confirm them in the refusal to believe in Jesus' authority, and that that is in fact part of the mystery, the scheme of God for the growth and revelation of his Kingdom. (Other literature: A. M. Hunter, *Interpreting the Parables*, 1960; Eta Linnemann, *The Parables of Jesus*, 1966, and Dan O. Via, jr., *The Parables, their Literary and Existential Dimension*, 1967.)

THE PARABLE OF THE SOWER 13.1-9

1-2. These verses form an editorial link with what precedes. The indications of time and place are imprecise. After the break with the Pharisees, the preaching of the Kingdom is made to the multitudes (cf. Mk 4.1; Lk. 8.4), but only the disciples understand. This is not a case of esoteric instruction reserved for initiates (as in Essenism) nor of the proclamation of general spiritual truths easily assimilated by the crowds.

3. in parables: the key to the understanding of *parabolē* in the Synoptic Gospels is the use of the Hebrew word *māšāl* in the *OT* and (together with its Aramaic equivalent *mᵉṭal, maṭlaʾ*) in the rabbinic literature. In twenty-eight out of thirty-three times the word *parabolē* appears in the canonical books of the LXX, it represents *māšāl*. This word covers a wide range of meanings, including the ethical maxim, proverb, by-word, comparison, allegory, fable, riddle (cf. Ps. 49.4; 78.2; Prov. 1.6; Ezek. 17.2 where *māšāl* (translated by *parabolē*) is synonymous with *ḥîḏāh*), and parable proper (i.e. truth embodied in a tale). Many of these meanings belong to *parabolē* in the *NT*—proverb (Lk. 4.23), comparison (10.24f.) a story drawn from nature or human life (13.3–9, 25.1–12). Thus the word in the Greek *NT* has a much wider range of meanings than it does in ordinary Greek literature, where its sense is 'comparison' (the placing of one thing by the side of another). The parabolic method of teaching was characteristic of Jesus. This does not mean that he invented it or was the only one among his contemporaries who used it: it was a common method of illustration among Jewish teachers, and the Gospel parables are similar in form to those of the rabbis. The fact that parables are illustrations of religious truth, and that their meaning is not on the surface (i.e. in the actual illustration), but is found in that to which they point, led scholars—ancient and fairly modern (including Archbishop Trench)—to regard them as allegorical cryptograms. The accepted view today is that *in the main* the parables make one major point and that point concerns the Kingdom of God.

3b–8. The centre of interest is neither the sower, nor the seed, but the various soils. The seed which accidentally falls on the path which borders or crosses the field cannot penetrate the hard-trodden ground, and is picked up by birds: on rocky ground, where the soil was thin, the seed cannot send down deep roots, and the weak plants soon wither and die; seed that falls among thorns is deprived of light, air and nourishment, and so yields no fruit. In good, deep, thorn-free soil the plants produce an amazing result.

9. Cf. 11.15. An impressive formula which marks out what has been said as especially important. But what ought the hearers to hear? In seeking the original meaning of the parable, we must disregard the interpretation (to be considered later). It seems that the message is as follows: Just as every (Palestinian) sower does his work in spite of many frustrations, so the Kingdom of God, inaugurated by Jesus, makes its way, and will be established in its fulness only after much apparent loss. But there will be a sure and glorious harvest; the Kingdom does come at last. That there should be set-backs and apparent failures in the course of its coming is just what many could not understand; they expected the instant triumph of the Kingdom. The accent of the parable, then, is not on how people should hear the word of God (*contra* Hunter), but on the fact that the Kingdom of God will certainly come, with a harvest beyond all expectation, but by way of failure, disappointment and loss.

THE REASON FOR EMPLOYING THE PARABOLIC METHOD OF TEACHING 13.10–17

Comparison of the three Synoptic texts concerning the use of parables (cf. Mk 4.10ff.; Lk. 8.9f.; 10.23f.) reveals that: (a) Matthew's statement on the 'mysteries of the Kingdom' is more precise and polemical than that of Mark and Luke; (b) Mt. 13.12 belongs to different contexts in Mark and Luke; (c) Mt. 13.13 (corresponding to Mk 4.11b–12) has been significantly modified

H

by Matthew; and (d) as in 12.15ff., Matthew gives a full quotation from Isa. 6.9–10, which is hinted at in the preceding verse by all three Synoptics.

10. According to Matthew it is only the disciples who question Jesus (Mark has the complicated phrase, 'those who were about him with the Twelve'), and their question (unlike that in the other Synoptics) is a general and basic one: why does Jesus speak to **them** (the crowds) in parables, when presumably it would be easier to be simple and direct!

11. The answer of Jesus is made explicit in Matthew: the reason why Jesus speaks to others in parables is because the disciples have been given to know **the secrets of the kingdom**. (Mark's form of words is 'to you has been given the secret . . .'.) The expression 'the secret(s) of the kingdom' was common in Jewish apocalyptic (Enoch literature, and 4 Ezra): it appears in the *Apoc.* (Wis. 2.22; Tob. 12.7, 11; Sir. 22.22; etc.) but only in Dan. 2 within the *OT*; there it represents the Aramaic *rāz*, a term which appears frequently in the *DSS*: see Bruce, pp. 8f. and B. Rigaux, *NTS*, IV, 1957–8, pp. 237ff. The 'mystery' is the divine plan or decree, especially as it touches human history; and it is known only to the privileged.

In view of this background, it is not necessary to appeal to the influence of the Hellenistic mystery cults to explain the presence of the word *mystērion* in this passage (its only appearance in the Gospels). Paul uses the term for what cannot be known by men except by divine revelation, which is now made known in Christ. Here the 'secret' is the purpose of God concerning his Kingdom—that it is inaugurated in the person, words and work of Jesus of Nazareth, and also (according to Bonnard, p. 194, and in keeping with the above interpretation of the parables) that it is established only after loss and disappointment. Knowledge of this is given to disciples, but it is not given to others. At this point, Matthew is more precise and firm than Luke or Mark, who says: 'for those outside everything is in parables'; this originally may have meant 'everything is obscure' (so Jeremias, *Parables*, p. 16), *māšāl* (*parabolē*) being synonymous with *ḥîḏāh* ('riddle, enigma'): Mark narrowed the meaning to 'parable' in the technical sense.

12. This saying, proverbial in character, is found again at 25.29 as a warning against taking spiritual privileges for granted; it has a similar meaning in Mk 4.25 and Lk. 8.16, but here it is

used to increase the sense of privilege: to those who have received
knowledge of the Kingdom (i.e. the disciples) more will be given,
while those who have not accepted this knowledge (Jews, and
particularly the Pharisees) will be deprived even of what they
possess (the Law perhaps) in the judgment.

13. The reference is to what precedes. Because it is recognition
of the Kingdom in Jesus that separates and judges men, he speaks
to non-disciples in parables: they neither see, hear nor understand;
they are in process of losing what 'they have'. It might be argued
that Matthew's language 'I speak in parables because (*hoti*) they
do not see . . .' suggests that Jesus employed the parabolic method
to make his point plain and simple, whereas Mark's 'in order that'
(*hina*, an alternative rendering of the underlying Aramaic *dᵉ*)
makes of parables (or riddles) a means of veiling truth. However,
the sterner understanding of the reason for the use of the parables
of the Kingdom seems to be right for Matthew, by reason of the
presence of verse 12 and of the fact that he gives to the quotation
from Isaiah the same sense as Mark. This interpretation is
strengthened also by Matthew's use of the *logion* in verses 16–17 at
this point. Parabolic teaching enables Jesus to produce and preserve the division among his hearers, and so God's word through
Isaiah is not falsified. From the point of view of the Church
situation for which Matthew wrote, the 'disciples' are the believers
who understand the mystery of the Kingdom, but the 'others' are
the Jews who, by their attitudes, have shown that they are not
among those who will see and repent; their obduracy will not be
penetrated by any teaching.

14–15. The citation (Isa. 6.9–20) follows the LXX exactly, as
in Ac. 28.26f. Although the passage is suggested by Mark's
language in 4.12, neither he nor Luke quote it; Matthew gives it
in extenso. It could be a later expansion of verse 13 prefaced by an
unusual version of the formula of fulfilment (see Stendahl, pp.
129–33). If it is original to Matthew, then it shows that for Matthew
the employment of parables was not just a useful pedagogical
method, but was part of the divine plan of God; the mass of the
Jewish people will not understand or receive Jesus' teaching and
the inbreaking of the Kingdom in his word and works. Israel's
resistance to repentance is presented, not as the result of Jesus'
ministry, but as its precondition; their opposition seems to be
thought of as foreordained (**it has not been given** (verse 11);

cf. Rom. 11.7f.). (For discussion of the use of Isa. 6.9ff. in the Synoptics, John and Acts, see Lindars, pp. 159–67.)

16–17. These words appear in Lk. 10.23f. after the great thanksgiving, and are concerned with the blessedness of the present generation which sees the Kingdom of God breaking in, in contrast to the unfulfilled hopes of earlier generations. The Matthean setting refers them to the disciples' understanding of Jesus' purpose or message: they are blessed in that they see *and hear* (not as in Luke, 'Blessed are the eyes which see what you see'). In this way, the saying emphasizes the good fortune of the disciples as a privileged group. Verse 17 is closer to Luke: many of ancient time—the **prophets and righteous** (Luke has 'kings')— desired to see what disciples see and hear (i.e. the effective reign of God in their midst), but did not receive it. Who are these **righteous**? The term denotes more than the saintly and upright who desired the Kingdom of God; it may suggest those who followed the prophets in seeking the purpose of God and disclosed their understanding of it to an unheeding audience—perhaps such a group as the Qumran 'sons of righteousness'; cf. D. Hill, *NTS*, XI, 1965, pp. 296ff.

THE INTERPRETATION OF THE PARABLE OF THE SOWER **13.18–23**

It is widely assumed that this allegorizing interpretation of the parable of the Sower is a product of the early Church which misses the eschatological point of the story in the intention of Jesus. 'In the interpretation the parable has become an exhortation to converts to examine themselves and test the sincerity of their conversion' (Jeremias, *Parables*, p. 62). However, it should be remembered that the *entire* Matthean narrative (i.e. both parable and interpretation) is presented by Matthew from within the faith of the Church of A.D. 80–90 (cf. Bonnard, p. 196). Therefore there is no impediment to believing that both parable and interpretation can bring us *echoes* of the authentic teaching of Jesus: but, as Bonnard remarks, it is impossible to prove this, and impossible to deny it absolutely. The presence of these verses in all three Synoptics, despite the differences from one Gospel to another, makes it certain that the explanation of the parable was widespread in early Christianity.

The interpretation is the only place in Matthew where the phrase **the word of the Kingdom** appears. While this clearly indicates later ecclesiastical redaction, it also affirms what is the point of the parable, and indeed of the entire Matthean narrative —namely, that the Sower and the message of the Kingdom (verses 10–12) are identifiable with the actual person of Jesus. It is worth noticing that the interpretation does not actually make Jesus the sower. If the verses were consciously allegorizing the parable, this would be a surprising omission; in fact, the interpretation is not elaborately detailed at all. Matthew links the interpretation of the parable to what precedes (verses 10–16) by stressing the importance of 'understanding' the words (verses 19 and 23), which is equivalent to knowing 'the secrets of the kingdom of heaven' (verse 11).

19. When anyone hears the word of the kingdom: with much greater explicitness, Mark begins the interpretation with: 'The sower sows the word' (4.14), while Luke has: 'the seed is the word of God'. Matthew assumes that the seed is the 'word'. It is sown **in his heart**—i.e. the place of decision. Lack of reception and understanding is due to the intervention of the 'evil one' (Mark has 'Satan').

this is what was sown along the path: lit. 'this is he who was sown along the path'. *JB*. renders 'the one who received the seed along the path', and this permissible translation of the passive participle avoids the difficulty of making what is sown represent the kind of hearer rather than 'the word'. The more usual rendering, which identifies the seed with the hearers (not the soil), is explained in terms of the human character and conduct which grows from the seed (so Box, p. 221, and McNeile, p. 193).

20–1. The second type of reception is that which is characterized by shallowness: the man who lacks roots ('the man of the moment', *JB*) and who, when tribulation or persecution arises because of the message of the Kingdom, **falls away** (lit. 'is caused to stumble'). Phrases like 'receive the word with joy', 'tribulation or persecution on account of the word', and the use of the word 'root' to suggest inward stability and earnestness—these features (which belong to the language and literature of the apostolic age, and not to any other part of the *NT*) confirm Jeremias in his opinion that the interpretation must be ascribed to the primitive Church. There is no doubt that the phraseology of the verses reflects later experience, but this would inevitably be the case as the parable was applied to life; it does not necessarily imply that the entire interpretation is pure invention.

22. cares of the world: i.e. the cares and anxieties which flourish in the world, and therefore 'worldly concerns and interests'. **the delight in riches:** the word *apatē* could mean 'seductiveness' or 'deceitfulness', but the later meaning 'pleasure' (cf. Polybius, II.lvi.12; 2 Pet. 2.13; and the papyri) is preferred by *RSV*, and may be correct.

23. The man who hears and understands (cf. verse 19 and the vocabulary of Isa. 6.9f.) is 'the one who receives the seed (word) in rich soil' (*JB*), or the **good soil** (*RSV*). This man 'bears fruit' (cf., for this metaphorical use, Rom. 7.4; Col. 1.6, 10), i.e. he yields a harvest of worship and obedience, although the amount of fruit may vary with the individual disciple. Despite the fact that much of the seed is lost in unresponsive people, there *is* an abundant harvest.

THE PARABLE OF THE WEEDS 13.24–30

This parable (and its interpretation in verses 36–43) is found only in Matthew's Gospel. It takes the place of the parable of the Seed Growing Secretly and of its own accord in Mk 4.26–9, to which it has a certain resemblance in its reference to what happens while the farmer sleeps and in its urging of patience. The reason for Matthew's omission of the Marcan parable may have been the fact that it gives the impression of uninterrupted progress and growth on the part of the Kingdom, whereas Matthew is concerned at this point to affirm the eventual harvest of the Kingdom *in spite of* disappointments, setbacks and loss. This is the essential message in the parable of the Sower and also of the Weeds, which affirms that the day of harvest must not be brought forward. Both parables combat messianic (even eschatological) impatience.

According to Kümmel (p. 136) this parable shows that 'in Jesus' view a separation is taking place in the present, the result of which will only be brought to light by the coming judgment. The disciples are to know about this eschatological significance of the present, but they are not to make the separation themselves.' Both Dodd and Jeremias accept the parable as genuine (while rejecting the interpretation), but Bacon and Manson (*Sayings*, p. 193) deny this. The latter says that 'Mt. 13.24–30 is an allegory constructed out of material supplied by Mark's parable (4.26–9) combined with the eschatological teaching of the Baptist (Mt. 3.12). The story as it stands is an allegory composed for the sake

of the explanation which is to follow.' It is too sweeping to claim
that a parable is not genuine because it has elements of allegory
in it: 'an allegory is the expansion of a metaphor; if Jesus employs
metaphors, which no one doubts, it is arbitrary to deny that He
could expand them' (McNeile, p. 195). Furthermore, the fact that
the parable of the Weeds is found in Matthew instead of the Marcan
parable of the Seed Growing Secretly is not conclusive evidence
for the rejection of the former: the evangelist may have found this
parable in his own source material (M), and may have preferred
it to the Marcan story (as hinted above) because it suited his
theme better. The parable contains a number of Aramaisms,
which may be held to be evidence pointing in the direction of
authenticity: the text in Codex Bezae (D) has three asyndeta in
verses 28-9, although Sinaiticus and Vaticanus (B) have the
idiomatic Greek with particles: verse 28b (in D) has an Aramaic
word-order (verb first); the words *echthros anthrōpos* and *ho
echthros* in verse 25 suggest a Semitic original. See Black, *Aramaic
Approach*, pp. 59, 106, and Jeremias, *Parables*, p. 224. The parable
may have a kernel of authentic dominical teaching.

24. The kingdom of heaven may be compared: the Greek
aorist 'likened' represents the Semitic perfect expressing a general
truth. This is a regular form of expression employed in introducing
a parable (cf. verses 31, 33, 44, 45, 47, etc.). Strictly speaking, the
Kingdom is not 'like a man . . .', but what will happen in the
Kingdom is like what happens when a man . . .

25. while men were sleeping: it is not necessary to see in this
a reference to those charged with the care and cultivation of the
seed: the meaning is 'while people were sleeping, an enemy of
his came'.
sowed weeds: these are perhaps the *lolium temulentum*, 'a poisonous
. . . weed which, botanically, is closely related to bearded wheat,
and in the early stages of growth is hard to distinguish from it'
(Jeremias, *Parables*, p. 224).

27. the servants of the householder: in 10.24f. it is implied
that the householder (master of the house) is Jesus, and the disciples are his servants.
did you not sow good seed in your field? The question—
although quite natural in this context, from the agricultural
point of view—may also indicate the application of the parable to
the situation of the Matthean church: it was probably experiencing

concern at the apparent lack of triumph and progress in the world
of the Kingdom inaugurated by Jesus.

28. The reply of the householder agrees with the theme of the
parable of the Sower: the set-backs and disappointments in the
growth of the Kingdom are due to the action of the evil one, Satan.
The servants propose to do what was normal, by gathering together (*sullegō*, the key word of the parable) the weeds for destruction.

29–30. The risk of pulling up the wheat with the weeds was a
real one. We should not suppose that even in the time of harvest
the weeds were rooted out before the reaping of the grain; rather,
as the reaper cut the grain with his sickle, he let the weeds fall so
that they were not gathered into the sheaves, but collected into
separate bundles to be dried and used for fuel (Jeremias, *Parables*,
p. 225). The owner—who is also the sower (see Hoskyns and Davey
p. 111)—is the only one who may put into operation the process
of division; and the time for this is not yet, but at harvest. Harvest
is a common metaphor for the Last Judgment in Biblical literature
(Jer. 51.53; Jl 3.12; Hos. 6.11. etc.). That the meaning of this
parable is a warning against premature judgment in matters of
church discipline is unlikely. It is chapter 18 of this gospel which
is concerned with ecclesiastical discipline; this chapter is concerned
with the growth of the Kingdom in the world.

Therefore the message of the parable refers to the situation
within Jesus' ministry (and applicable later to the progress of the
Church's mission): the time for drawing ultimate dividing lines
was not yet. The Pharisees were at this time regarding themselves
as the New Israel (Ps. Sol. 2.38, 4.7); the Essene community at
Qumran sought to define the true people of God by a strict process
of selection and rejection. But the Kingdom of God, says Jesus
(and also the Church), is not the exclusive coterie of self-elected
saints: God, in his time (that is, in the harvest which, despite all
appearances to the contrary, will come), will separate the pure
community (Jeremias, *Parables*, pp. 223f.). It will be seen later that
the interpretation of the parable (verses 36–43) emphasizes this
main point. 'All false zeal must be checked, the field must be left
to ripen in patience, . . . and everything else left to God in faith,
until his hour comes' (Jeremias, p. 227).

THE PARABLE OF THE MUSTARD SEED 13.31–2

This short parable appears in Luke in a different context (13.18f.);
as in the other Gospels, it is here concerned to answer those who
are surprised to see the Kingdom of God 'sown' in the world with
so little power. Two closely related ideas are presented in it: that of
an historical event or happening—viz. the sowing of a seed in a field
(an idea found in the two preceding parables); and that of a very
tiny beginning leading to a great result. The Kingdom 'sown' by
Jesus (in himself) in the field of the world has a small beginning,
but, one day, it will become something immense, though not totally
different: the end product is the realized potential of the tiny seed.

31. Note that the Kingdom is not like a grain of mustard seed
in itself, but like a grain of mustard seed which a man sowed, with
all its potentialities for growth. The phrase 'which taking (aorist
participle) a man sowed' (cf. 'which taking a woman hid' (verse
33); 'which finding a man hid' (verse 44)) represents an idiomatic
Semitic auxiliary usage.

32. The common rabbinic proverb 'according to the quantity
of a grain of mustard' expressed the smallest thing or tiniest
quantity (M. Niddah, v.2). But the tiniest seed becomes a tree large
enough to provide a lodging for the birds: it could reach a height
of eight to twelve feet in Palestine. The tree in which birds nest is
a common symbol of a great kingdom which protects its vassal
states (cf. Dodd, *Parables*, p. 190, which alludes to Dan. 4.7–24,
especially verses 12 and 21; Ezek. 17.23, and 31.6). Manson
(*Teaching*, p. 133, n. 1) points out that in apocalyptic and rabbinic
literature 'the birds of heaven' stand for Gentile nations. The
parable may therefore have been used to stress again (as in the
parable of the Weeds) that the Kingdom of God is not narrowly
exclusive; but that was not its primary significance.

THE PARABLE OF THE LEAVEN 13.33

The same points are expressed here as with the mustard-seed.
'Once the leaven has been put into the dough, the leavening
process goes on inevitably till the whole is leavened; and this
although there is no comparison between the mass of dough and
the small quantity of leaven' (Manson, *Sayings*, p. 123). From
hidden beginnings in Jesus' ministry, which must have caused
many to be impatient, God causes his Kingdom to grow.

33. In Jewish imagery **leaven** refers to what is unclean or evil (16.6–12; cf. Gal. 5.9; 1 C. 5.6–8; Exod. 12.15ff.). If this were the significance of 'leaven' here, then the parable would signify that a little evil can corrupt a whole life or the whole of humanity. But the context prevents this interpretation. The verb **hid** is important (cf. 13.35 and 44): the Kingdom was inaugurated without display or pomp; its silent, secret character must have surprised those who were zealously impatient for its expected manifestation in power and glory.

ON THE USE OF PARABLES **13.34–5**

The Marcan form of this summarizing statement concludes his chapter on parables (4.33f.). Since Matthew has already departed from Mark in introducing verses 16–17 and 24–30 and in omitting most of Mk 4.21–9, we may assume some independence on his part in the formation of this chapter. This seems a more satisfactory solution of the matter than the assumption that Matthew is following an earlier form of Mark (so Schniewind). Mark's form of the statement is difficult, even ambiguous; but Matthew's version is clearer. Jesus spoke to the crowds only in parables; there is no mention of private explanation to the disciples (and this reduces the emphasis on their privileged position); instead, Matthew adds one of his formula quotations (Ps. 78.2) in which it is 'prophesied' that the secrets which have been concealed from the beginning of the world will be revealed in parables.

34. The arrangement of the clauses is in chiastic parallelism. What has been taught on the Kingdom in the preceding parables was given *to the crowds*, including the disciples. The remainder of the chapter seems to have been addressed to disciples only.

35. Some MSS. refer the quotation to 'the prophet Isaiah', but it is in fact from Ps. 78.2. (For the use of Ps. 110 as prophecy, see 20.43f. All the *OT* scriptures have, for Matthew, a prophetic value.) The first line follows the LXX exactly, and *en parabolais*—the keyword for Matthew—represents *bᵉmāšāl*. The second line is an independent rendering of the Hebrew text, in which the most interesting feature is the translation by *kekrummena* ('things kept hidden': note the interest in hiddenness in 13.33, 44) of the Hebrew *ḥîdot* (= 'riddles', LXX *problēmata*, Aq. *ainigmata*). Both Hebrew words are roughly equivalent in meaning, but Matthew's rendering enables him to stress the hidden character of the message of the Kingdom which is being revealed, but in a veiled way ('in parables'), by Jesus. On the use of Ps. 78 and the translation of *ḥiḏot*, see Lindars, pp. 156–8.

THE INTERPRETATION OF THE PARABLE OF THE WEEDS 13.36–43

Both Dodd (*Parables*, pp. 183–4) and Jeremias (*Parables*, pp. 81–85) regard this section as a later allegorical interpretation of the parable, reflecting the developed eschatology of the Church, and representing the work of the evangelist himself. Jeremias rightly points out certain peculiarities in the language and content of the passage, and declares that it contains thirty-six linguistic characteristics of Matthew. This is undoubtedly an impressive argument for rejecting the authenticity of the passage; but, nevertheless, there are certain features of these verses which make the claim for their partial genuineness at least reasonable. (Cf. M. de Goedt, *RB*, LXVI, 1959, pp. 32–54.) It is possible that in this passage we have an example of the *free* adaptation of Jesus' own teaching to the needs and conditions of the early Christian communities; but, in the application, the authentic kernel is not lost. The important point about the interpretation is its dependence (in verse 41) on Zeph. 1.3. It would seem at first sight that the parable is actually summed up in terms of this verse (and its expansion). But this is not the usual way in which Matthew uses the *OT*: for this evangelist Scripture does not provide convenient summaries, but is rather the source and inspiration of teaching. In fact, the parable of the Weeds functions as an illustration of the Zephaniah text; parable and interpretation belong, and stand or fall, together. If we argue for the authenticity of the parable, we must be prepared to admit the possibility (or even likelihood) that Zeph. 1.3 is the real starting-point of the original parable, and has been preserved, in later editing, within the interpretation. In short, in this *pericope* the evangelist may be editing (and applying to his own time) earlier genuine material, rather than creating a wholly allegorical interpretation. The *elaboration* of the meaning of the parable may be Matthew's own work, but it is carried out from (but does not include) the reminiscence of Zeph. 1. The point of the interpretation, then, is exactly that of the parable itself: only God himself may distinguish the good from the evil: it is God's business alone to decide who belongs to the Kingdom.

36. The place of the explanation is **the house** apart from the crowds, where Jesus is alone with his disciples and can answer their questions (as he answers the problems of the Matthean church).

37. This verse, which interprets Jesus' teaching as 'the sowing of good seed by the Son of Man', begins the allegorizing of the parable. The good seed is personified: it becomes the 'sons of the Kingdom'. At 8.12 this phrase designates the Jews as the traditional heirs of the Kingdom, who are ejected because of unbelief: here it refers to the true heirs, the faithful disciples, as distinct from 'the sons of evil (or the Devil)', a title not found elsewhere in the *NT*, but which obviously denotes those who are controlled by evil. The division of people into two radically opposed groups was common in Judaism, and nowhere more so than at Qumran (cf. 1QS ii.4; iv.17) where 'the good' were identified with the sectaries, and 'the evil' with those outside. The parable differs from the Qumran literature in reserving to the last day and to God the separation of men.

39. the harvest is the close of the age: 'the close of the age' (lit. 'consummation of (the) age', the omission of the article on the analogy of the Hebrew construct state being a common Semitism in Matthew) is a Jewish idea found in the *NT* only in Matthew's gospel (verse 40, 49; 24.3; 28.20). For the idea of the end of the world as a harvest, see Jl 3.13; Jer. 51.33; Hos. 6.11; 4 Ezra. 4.28f.; 2 Bar. 70.2. The eschatological and judging function of angels is described in Enoch 46.5; 63.1. It is striking that the conversation between the householders and the servants, so important in the parable, is omitted from the interpretation altogether: allegorical value is not given to all the ideas present in the story.

40. With this verse we pass from allegory to a description of the Last Judgment in traditional apocalyptic terms. This is not an explanation of verse 30b, but its development in terms of the teaching of Zeph. 1.3. Notice the way in which the key-word of the parable and interpretation, 'gather' (*sullegō*), is taken up again.

41. they will gather out of his kingdom all causes of sin and all evildoers: the verb *sullegō* adequately represents the Hebrew '*āsēp* in Zeph. 1.3. with the meaning 'gather together for destruction' (LXX *exairein*; Vulg. *congregabo*). The Hebrew words *hammakšēlôṭ eṭ-hārᵉšaᶜîm* (lit. 'the stumbling-blocks with the wicked') —a phrase so difficult that emendations are often suggested, though the original text of Washington papyrus of LXX reads *skandala sun* *ois asebesin*—may be represented by Matthew's 'all causes of sin *(skandala)* and all evildoers (those who do lawlessness, *anomia*)'. God, through his agents, carries out judgment. The 'kingdom of the Son of Man' would be, for Matthew, the Church on earth (*TIM*, p. 44) requiring to be cleansed of 'weeds' at the harvest; at an earlier stage of tradition (if such there was in the case of any of the details of this passage) the reference would have been to the 'true Israel'. See Jeremias, *Parables*, p. 82, and C. H. Dodd, *ET*, LVIII, 1947, pp. 294ff., on the eschatology of these verses.

42. The 'furnace' and the 'weeping and gnashing of teeth' are characteristic features of apocalyptic doom. Cf. Dan. 3.6; 4 Ezra 7.36, and the note on 8.12.

43. the righteous will shine . . . Father: the words recall Dan. 12.3, which promises that in the Resurrection 'those who are wise (*hammaśkîlîm*, LXX *hoi sunientes*) shall shine like the brightness of the firmament, and those who turn many to righteousness like the stars for ever and ever'. The *maśkîlîm*—here represented by 'the righteous'—are 'those who understand' (a term prominent in this chapter), and who make others understand (Dan. 11.33) by instruction and example, thereby turning them to righteousness; see D. Hill, *NTS* XI, p. 299. It is possible that in an early stage of tradition there was a word-play in verse 41 between *maśkîlîm* (Aramaic *maśkîlîn*) and *makśēlōṭ* (Aramaic *makśelān*) from Zeph. 1.3. 'The Father's kingdom' is not identified with the Son of Man's; it is the eternal Kingdom of the Father (1 C. 15.24 and Mt. 25.34) to which the Son hands over the elect who are saved; see Dodd, *ET*, LVIII, pp. 294ff.

THE PARABLES OF THE TREASURE AND THE PEARL 13.44-6

These two little parables belong to Matthew's special tradition. Double parables and metaphors are commonly used in the Gospels as a means of emphasizing an idea, and the fact that these form a naturally contrasted pair argues for their originality and unity, though the change of tense raises a question about their belonging together. There are points common to the parables and the context in which they found here: the theme of concealment (verses 44 and 33, 35); the presence of a field in the story (verses 24, 36, 38); these may explain why the two parables appear in this chapter, for their main point does not fit with the themes of the preceding parables—viz. the triumphant growth of the Kingdom in spite of resistance and disappointment, and the necessity for patience in judgment (a theme which is taken up again in verses 47–50). The parables of the Treasure and of the Pearl concern the inestimable worth of the Kingdom, and imply the need for urgency and even sacrifice in entering it: the emphasis lies on 'selling all to possess it' (cf. Dodd, *Parables*, pp. 112f.).

44. Underlying the common beginning to parables (**the kingdom of heaven is like . . .**) is the Aramaic *lᵉ*, which has the force of 'it is the case with . . . as with . . .'. The Kingdom is not directly compared to **treasure** (or a pearl), but what happens when a man finds treasure is compared with what happens (or ought to happen) when a man finds the Kingdom: he will *with joy* make any sacrifice whatsoever to possess it. In the Palestine of Jesus' day, infested with brigands and rapacious soldiers, the best way to ensure the safety of treasure was to bury it; the Qumran discoveries have illustrated this. Attention is not being drawn to the morality of the man's hiding the treasure until he can buy the field where he has put it, only to the enormous worth of what he has found.

45–6. The point is the same as in the previous verse. That the merchant 'seeks' pearls should not be construed as praise for religious efforts: like the first man, he too *finds* his treasure. The pearl, as a symbol of something very precious, is illustrated from the *OT* (Prov. 3.15) and from the famous Gnostic *Hymn of the Pearl* (see *NT Apocrypha*, ii, pp. 433ff., 498ff.), in which the king's son goes to Egypt to win the pearl, his true and original soul.

THE PARABLE OF THE NET **13.47–50**

This, like the two short parables preceding it, is found only in Matthew. We have already pointed out that it naturally follows on the parable of the Weeds and its interpretation by reason of its message and the remarkable similarity of its language. The interpretation of the Net (verses 49–50) is almost a mechanical repetition of verses 40b–42 from the interpretation of the Weeds, and it is not a suitable ending, for the furnace is hardly the place for bad fish. The point of the parable is that the situation at the coming of the Kingdom resembles the sorting of a catch of fish: although bad and good may be mixed together now, their separation will eventually come, and it will be God's doing. The brief interpretation uses the message of the parable as an occasion to describe the

Last Judgment. The identification of the **net** with the Church may
be suggested in the explanation (by the separation of the evil from
the righteous), but the parable itself is about the Kingdom, not the
Church. Manson (*Sayings*, p. 197) notes that in the parable the
fishermen sort the fish, and he identifies them with the missionary
disciples of Jesus: but this may be to press too much (allegorical)
detail from the words of verse 48.

47. The picture is of the drag-net, either drawn between two
boats or laid out by one boat and drawn to land with ropes. The
expression **fish of every kind** in this context may mean simply
'bad and good', or it may imply the universal character of the
Kingdom (cf. Jn 21.11).

48. sorted: note the use of the verb *sullego* here, as in verses
29, 30, 41.
bad: the fish would be those unsuitable for eating—not rotten
ones, for all of them had just been caught.

49–50. These verses (which are probably secondary) repeat the
theme of verses 40b–42, and relate the message of the parable to
the end of the world. The introduction of the angels is necessary
for the Last Judgment scene but hardly suitable in the explanation
of this parable, where the fishermen both caught and sorted the
fish. It might be argued that, if the fishermen represent the apostles,
then verse 49 suggests that there is delegated to the Church on
earth the power of selection and judgment. This idea could be
supported from certain *NT* passages, but it is unlikely here. It
would be contrary to the point of the parable of the Weeds, which
insists that, when the time is fulfilled, God himself will separate
the evil from the good. Till then, this parable may be saying, false
zeal must be checked and the net cast widely.

THE SCRIBE AND THE KINGDOM **13.51–2**

In order to bring to a conclusion the series of parables, Matthew
has placed here an enigmatic word of Jesus which many have
taken to be a clue to the entire work of this evangelist. Some have
thought that the saying belongs to another context (for instance,
on the relation of the new teaching to the Jewish Law, as McNeile,
p. 205), but it should be noted that the verses take up words (e.g.
'householder') and themes ('Kingdom', 'understanding') which
are prominent in this chapter.

51. To 'understand' (verses 13, 14, 15, etc.) means to grasp the mystery of the Kingdom (declared in parabolic revelation), and especially that it is inaugurated by Jesus and will evoke resistance and misunderstanding before its eventual triumph.

52. every scribe who has been trained for the kingdom of heaven: lit. 'become a disciple' (*mathēteutheis*) with respect to the kingdom. Who is the scribe? Any listener who became a disciple; or the evangelist? Many interpreters claim that this is a discreet signature of the Gospel-writer (or redactor), since it seems to sum up so admirably his approach and attitude. Is there even a pun on Matthew's name (*Matthaios, mathēteutheis*)? The scribe, in the technical sense, appeared in Judaism after the Exile: far from being a mere copyist or secretary, he was an expert in the Law, the authorized rabbi (the 'ordained', or commissioned, theologian, Bonnard, p. 210): he was, according to Josephus, the 'interpreter of the ancestral Law'. The scribes formed a group which was the trustee of the Mosaic succession, exercising great influence over the people. Most of them belonged to the Pharisaic party. The existence of 'Christian' scribes (with teaching functions) is suggested by 23.34: cf. Kilpatrick, pp. 110ff. and Strecker, pp. 37–8.

what is new and what is old: these phrases probably connote either traditional Jewish teaching on the Kingdom of God which had now been renewed completely by the presence of Jesus, or the ancient *OT* promises which had found fulfilment in Jesus' person and teaching. The 'things new and old' are not opposed to one another, or simply added to one another: the new things *are* also the old, as Matthew demonstrates throughout his Gospel by constant reference to the *OT*: what was once regarded as old is now new, fresh, relevant and actual, thanks to the coming of Messiah.

THE COMMUNITY OF THE KINGDOM: FAITH AND PRACTICE 13.53–18.35

In the plan of Matthew's Gospel, the fourth section begins at this point. The usual formula of conclusion (cf. 7.28; 11.1; and 19.1; 26.1) is here integrally related to what follows. In this fourth section—which comprises narrative (13.54–17.27) followed by instruction—Matthew follows Mk 6–9 quite closely until the point is reached where he elaborates Mk 9.33 into a lengthy discourse on the discipline of life in the Kingdom (18.1–35).

The emphasis in this section lies increasingly on the attitude
of Jesus' disciples. They are shown as confessing Jesus' authority,
although with the risk of misunderstanding (16.13ff.); as hearing,
but failing to appreciate, the first two announcements of the
Passion (16.21f. and 17.22), and as receiving instruction from Jesus
on the necessary characteristics of life in the Kingdom he has
inaugurated, namely, humility (18.1–4), mercy (18.21ff.) and
care of the weak (18.5ff.)—all of which are themes uncharacteris-
tic of Judaism, both in its orthodox and sectarian forms.

JESUS IS REJECTED AT NAZARETH 13.53–8

This *pericope* follows naturally on the parabolic teaching which implied the rejection of the Kingdom by the religion of Pharisaism
(13.11ff.). This is the position in which the event would now
appear to Matthew in Mark's work, since the intervening incidents after the parables in Mark (4.35–5.43) have been placed
earlier in Matthew (chapters 8 and 9). Luke places the rejection
at a different point in Jesus' ministry, and makes the appearance
at Nazareth the occasion of a declaration of the fulfilment of
prophecy (Lk. 4.21). The key-phrase, 'they took offence at him',
common to Mark and Matthew, is not found in the Lucan account.

53. The Matthean editorial formula suggests that Jesus spoke
all the preceding parables at once, which is unlikely; but the
contents of chapter 13 do form a distinct block in the thought of
this evangelist and in the composition of his book.

54. coming to his own country: i.e. to the land of his parents,
the place of his origin where his family was living. Luke gives its
name, Nazareth; this is presupposed by Mark and Matthew (cf.
Mt. 2.23; 4.13).
he taught them in their synagogue: Mark makes precise
what is implied in Matthew, that the teaching was given on the
Sabbath. The Gospel tradition unanimously relates that Jesus
taught in the synagogues of his people: he purposed to base his
teaching on the normal religious life of his contemporaries, and
it was in their synagogues that he could communicate with those
to whom he was sent. In any case, Jesus was not concerned to
create a new party or religion, but to confront his own people with
his own person.
**Where did this man get this wisdom and these mighty
works?** The Greek adverb *pothen* means 'from where?' or 'from

whom?': the question is concerned with origins, and therefore with authority. Did Jesus receive his power from God, or from the Devil? The two terms 'wisdom' and 'mighty works' refer to the two main aspects of Jesus' ministry: his teaching and his miracles —the main themes of sections 3 and 2, respectively, of this Gospel.

55. Is not this the carpenter's son? Mark has 'Is not this the carpenter?', a form which makes Jesus himself, rather than Joseph (who may have been dead by this time), the carpenter. The word *tektōn* would be better rendered 'builder', or perhaps 'mason'. The dearth of timber in Palestine, and the fact that houses there were usually built of stone, might be taken to suggest that the occupation of carpenter would not be common (E. Lohmeyer, *Das Evangelium des Markus*, 1951, p. 110). On the brothers and sisters of Jesus, see 12.46–50.

57. they took offence at him: lit. 'they were scandalized in him'. They were not only upset in their beliefs by Jesus, but (as their questions imply) they were disturbed at the influence of his person and power. To be offended in or by Jesus amounts to refusing to believe in him.

'A prophet is not without honour' . . . Cf. Jn 6.43 and Pap. Oxy. i, ll. 31–6, (in *NT Apocrypha*, 1, p. 109): 'A prophet is not acceptable in his own country, neither does a physician work cures on those who know him.' The saying may have been proverbial.

58. It is usually claimed that Matthew softens Mark's expression: 'and he could do no mighty works there'; but actually Mark follows this by saying that some healings did take place. Matthew may just be combining the two parts of Mark's verse. The word *apistia* ('unbelief')—found only here and at Mk 6.6 and 9.24—is more than inability to believe: it is wilful refusal to have faith in Jesus.

HEROD AND JESUS **14.1–2**

These two verses in Mark and Matthew form the introduction to the account of John's death, but verses 3–12 belong to a different period in the sequence of Jesus' life, and are omitted by Luke altogether. Consequently we may separate the two opening verses from the following narrative. Jesus has been rejected by his own people at Nazareth: now the Jewish court refuses to believe in him for what he was.

1. At that time: a vague editorial formula. Herod Antipas,

correctly called 'tetrarch' by Matthew and Luke (Mark has
'king', which may reproduce a popular title), was the son of Herod
the Great, and inherited Galilee and Perea from his father. He
married first a daughter of the Arabian king, Aretas, and later
Herodias. This second marriage was within degrees prohibited by
Jewish law (Lev. 20.21). Josephus tells of this marriage and of the
death of John the Baptist at the hands of Herod Antipas (*Ant.*
xviii.5), but he does not connect the two incidents.

2. Herod's belief that Jesus is John the Baptist risen from the
dead may indicate knowledge of the Pharisaic doctrine of the
resurrection of the dead or the Hellenistic belief in the reappear-
ance of dead persons. The idea that it is by reason of John's
resurrection that the powers (miraculous powers) are at work in
him is of interest. In fact, Stendahl (in *Peake*, 686d) claims that
the verse should be noted as significant for early interpretations
of Jesus' resurrection and the miracles performed in his name
(Ac. 2-3).

THE DEATH OF JOHN 14.3-12

The mention of a resurrected John leads naturally to an account
of his death. The details of the event are reduced to a minimum
in Matthew. The *pericope* is in a sense parenthetical, but it does
serve to provide the reason for Jesus' withdrawal from the public
eye into remote areas. Bultmann and others regard the story as
legendary, and there are undoubtedly difficulties within it,
especially in relation to the account by Josephus, the later historian
of the period. It is possible that the Gospel accounts represent
what was widely and popularly said at the time (see Rawlinson,
p. 82).

3. The imprisonment of John (according to Josephus, in the
fortress of Machaerus on the east of the Dead Sea) was because of
Herodias, the wife of Herod's brother. The name Philip is found
in many MSS., but D and the Latin versions (with Vulg.) omit it.
Mark makes Herodias the wife of Philip, but in fact (Josephus,
Ant. xviii.i.4) she was married to another brother of Herod
Antipas, Herod Boethus, son of Herod the Great and Mariamne
II. It was the daughter of Herodias (by Boethus), Salome, who
was married to Philip the tetrarch.

4. Herod's divorce of his first wife (the daughter of Aretas) was,
by Jewish law, legal, but it was contrary to the Law for him to

marry the wife of his brother while that brother was still alive
(Lev. 18.16 and 20.21), although, in the case of a brother who had
died, the Law (in certain cases) required such a marriage. Herod
Antipas, like the other members of his family who governed
Jewish communities, posed as a conforming Jew; therefore he
could rightly be criticized by John. In his account of the event,
Josephus suggests that John's arrest was due to Herod's jealousy
of his influence over the people. This is contrary to Mark, where
Herod is presented as respecting John and even liking to talk with
him, and where it is Herodias who goads a reluctant husband into
executing him. Mark does not harmonize with verse 5 in Matthew's
account, where it is Herod who wishes to be rid of John but fears
a riot if he executes a popular prophet. Matthew's version of the
affair is closer to Josephus.

6. Herod's birthday: perhaps better, 'Herod's birthday
feast'.

the daughter of Herodias danced: this is presumably Salome,
Herodias' daughter by her first marriage, and the only daughter
of hers that we know of. There is difficulty in imagining that a
member of the reigning household would have danced, because
the status of dancing-women at the time was extremely low.
Rawlinson (p. 82) maintains that Salome's dance is 'not wholly
incredible, however outrageous, to those who know anything of
the morals of oriental courts, and of Herod's family in particular.'

7. Mark adds 'even half of my kingdom', a phrase which
strongly recalls Esther 5.3 in a story which may have exercised a
formative influence on his narrative.

8. on a platter: the Greek word *pinax* originally meant a
'board', 'plank', or anything flat like a tablet or plate, and later
'a dish'.

9. The grief of the king is in harmony with Mark's account of
his attitude to John rather than with verse 5. But Herod's fear of
his guests overcame his scruples.

10. It was contrary to Jewish law to put a man to death without trial; nor was execution by beheading allowed, although it was
sanctioned by Roman and Greek custom.

11. the girl: the Greek has the diminutive, 'little girl', although
Salome (born A.D. 10) must have been at least 18 or 19 years old
at the time of this incident. The word *korasion* is found in 9.24 to
describe Jairus' daughter, a girl of 12 years.

12. Both Mark and Matthew mention John's disciples and the fact that they buried the Baptist's body, but only Matthew adds that they told Jesus what had happened. This is in keeping with Matthew's desire to underline the contact between Jesus and John and the relation of their two ministries.

THE FEEDING OF THE FIVE THOUSAND 14.13–21

Within the Gospels there are six accounts of miraculous multiplication of loaves (cf. the parallels, Mk 6.30–44, Lk. 9.10–17, Jn 6.1–13; and Mt. 15.32–9, Mk 8.1–10). Bonnard (p. 217) points out that this fact suggests that the first Christian communities attached very great importance to this episode in Jesus' life, to the extent of not even being embarrassed by having two accounts (although somewhat different) in Mark and Matthew. This may be due to its symbolic relevance to the Eucharist (cf. Benoit, p. 101). Many interpretations have been offered by commentators. That it is a tale about people sharing their lunches after the example of Jesus and his disciples is too facile to account for the narrative and its preservation. There is possibly some influence from 2 Kg. 4.42–44 (concerning Elisha) and Exod. 16 (concerning manna) but that need not require us to view the story as entirely mythical. Lohmeyer thinks that the main point is the idea of Christ gathering together the people of God as the true Shepherd of Israel. Schweitzer suggested that the meaning of the story is Jesus' giving to his followers a foretaste of the messianic banquet in the coming Kingdom. That Jesus could have anticipated the messianic feast would not be out of keeping with his teaching and with Jewish custom and thought. (It is interesting to note that recently Jeremias, *EW*, pp. 231ff., 261, has suggested that the Last Supper was regarded as an anticipatory gift, or 'antedonation', of the consummation.) The adoption of this kind of view necessitates the assumption that the actual event (for surely there must have been *some* action or incident) was not miraculous, and that the numbers have been greatly exaggerated. The idea that the bread was multiplied for the satisfaction of many may have followed when the true nature of the event became obscure, and its meaning (in the Church and in the minds of the Gospel writers) very significant. The 'anticipatory' view would bring together original event, Eucharist, and messianic banquet; see further, Nineham, pp. 178–9.

13. The time reference is to verse 12. The murder of John the Baptist occasioned the withdrawal. The sequence of events in Mark is different, and the withdrawal to a quiet area appears to have been caused by Jesus' desire that he and his disciples should rest.

14. Mark says that the people hurried round the lake, and were assembled at the landing place when the boat arrived. The reason for Jesus' compassion on the crowds is not clearly stated by Matthew here (cf. 9.36), but Mk 6.34 says that on this occasion it was evoked by the fact that 'they were like sheep without a shepherd' (6.34; cf. Num. 27.17 and 1 Kg. 22.17).

15. the day is now over: lit. 'the hour (for the evening meal) has passed'.

16. you: an emphatic pronoun. This phrase—indeed the whole narrative—recalls the story of Elisha (2 Kg. 4.42ff.).

17. Bread and fish formed the basic diet of the poor of Galilee. In early Christian frescoes, bread and fish appear frequently as symbols of the Eucharist; cf. Jn 21.4-14. There is no satisfactory explanation of the numbers 'five' and 'two'.

19. to sit down: the verb *anaklithēnai* means 'to take one's place' (at table), 'to eat' (of any meal). The word does not seem to have formed part of the terminology of the early Eucharist. Matthew omits the details in Mark about the group squatting in groups of hundreds and fifties and the greenness of the grass.

he looked up to heaven, and blessed, and broke and gave the loaves to the disciples: the words reappear in the accounts of the Last Supper (26.26; cf. 1 C. 11.24, and Ac. 2.46; 20.7, 11; 27.35). One also recalls the actions performed daily by the father of the Jewish family: taking the bread into his hands, thanking God for the gift of food, breaking the loaf, and giving each person present a piece to eat. When large numbers were present, the distribution might be undertaken by a companion or servants of the host. (The verb 'blessed' must therefore mean 'blessed God in thanksgiving'.) This daily act in a Jewish household, the Lord's Supper, and the Eucharistic celebration of the early Church (all of which may be regarded as foretastes of the messianic banquet) would all be evoked in the minds of readers by this narrative, and probably all contributed to its formation.

20. The satisfaction of the people's hunger may reflect the expected state of affairs in the Kingdom when established (cf.

5.6). Then God would satisfy all the legitimate needs of men. The
twelve baskets may be related to the twelve disciples (who, in
Matthew's narrative, play an important part in the incident related,
and so illustrate the responsible rôle of disciples in the Church;
cf. Held, in *TIM*, pp. 182f.) or, more probably, to the twelve
tribes of Israel; the blessings of Jesus' work extend to the entire
people of God.

21. Matthew adds, as at 15.38, a reference to the presence of
women and children. The company is completely representative:
the dispersed and 'shepherdless' (Mark) crowd is gathered together
and nourished by Christ, as they will be in the Kingdom.

THE WALKING ON THE WATER 14.22–33

As in the preceding *pericope*, the disciples are here confronted by
a situation with which they must try to cope on their own, and
they are again saved from failure by a sovereign act of authority
on the part of Jesus. According to Mk 6.52, the attitude of the
disciples to Jesus when he appears reflects their lack of understanding; but Matthew presents them in a rather different light:
they experience fear and lack of faith at the beginning, but at the
end stands their confession of Jesus as Son of God. 'The theme
of discipleship has been determinative of the way Matthew has
shaped his narrative, and he has done this by adhering closely to
the *pericope* as he received it. . . . He shows Jesus as the Lord who
gives to his disciples the power to follow him, and interprets the
motive of the uncomprehending horror of the disciples from the
point of view of fear and their little faith' (Held, in *TIM*, p. 206).
The story is closely related in type and meaning to the stilling of
the storm (8.18–27). Both illustrate the difficulties facing disciples
(the Church) in the world, and their triumph through faith in
Christ. The character of this faith is shown in the verses Matthew
has added (28–31), an insertion (see Held, op. cit., p. 205) which
may go back to a cycle of oral tradition concerning Peter (so
Kilpatrick, pp. 38–44). The faith of disciples must be adventurous
and overcome fear, even though it may falter in the face of extreme
danger. 'The scene of Peter walking to the sea contains something
entirely unique: it shows the greatness of the promise made to
faith within discipleship (14.28, 29), but does not remain silent
about the inability of the disciple to hold firmly to this promise
during a time of testing (verse 30)' (Held, op. cit. p. 206).

22. Jesus obliges, even forces, the disciples to go across the lake ('to Bethsaida', according to Mark) without him. This sets the scene for what follows. The 'event' and its meaning have to do with the disciples and discipleship.

23. In Matthew the mention of Jesus engaging in prayer before or after important events in his ministry is less frequent than in Mark or in Luke. Apart from the Gethsemane prayer (Mt. 26.39), the Synoptics (unlike the Fourth Gospel) say nothing about the content of Jesus' prayers.

24. the boat . . . was many furlongs distant from the land: this is the reading of B, and is to be preferred; but other authorities have 'was in the midst of the sea'. The Greek *stadion* ('furlong') was about 200 yards: the lake of Galilee was (according to Josephus) nearly 4½ miles wide.

25. the fourth watch of the night: i.e. between 3 a.m. and 6 a.m. The Romans divided the period 6 p.m. till 6 a.m. into four equal periods, or 'watches'.

26. a ghost: Greek *phantasma*, used of any apparition, particularly that of a spirit. The occurrence of this word and the general atmosphere of the narrative have led some to think that we are here dealing with a misplaced story about an appearance of the risen Christ, but there is no need to assume this: the theme dominant in the story is quite in keeping with its place in Matthew's structure.

27. The words *egō eimi*, **It is I,** may have a numinous quality in this context—not 'It is I', but 'I AM', the Living One, master of wind and wave; cf. Exod. 3.14 and Isa. 43.10; 51.12.

28–31. This small section is undoubtedly Matthean. The use of **the water** for the Sea of Galilee (*thalassa*, in verse 26), and of *katapontizein* ('sink') and *distazō* ('doubt'), which are found only in Matthew (here and 18.6 and 28.17), point to the fact that the insertion comes from the hand of the evangelist, from some peculiarly Petrine tradition. Some exegetes argue that the meaning of the section (like 16.17–19; 17.14–17—also from Matthew's Petrine source) is to indicate the primacy of Peter over the other disciples (so Benoit, p. 10); if so, it is a primacy which reveals weakness of faith! It is more probable that Peter is taken as representative of the disciples (with Jesus, and in the Matthean church) in his enthusiastic love and insufficient faith.

33. In his simplified conclusion to the incident, Matthew suppresses any reference to the multiplication of the loaves (which, Mk 6.52 suggests, ought to have prepared the minds of disciples for the intervention of Jesus) and, instead of mentioning the disciples' astonishment (so Mark), he records their reverential confession of Jesus as truly **the Son of God.** This profession of faith anticipates the words of confession in 16.16. The phrase could be interpreted as 'a son of God'—i.e. a divine being; this is unlikely, for in this Matthean addition there will be reflected the rather more developed faith of the Church (cf. 4.3).

HEALINGS AT GENNESARET **14.34-6**

In this short section Matthew has simplified and abbreviated the version in Mk 6.53-6, but has retained the description of the manner in which the healings were carried out—by touching the fringe of Jesus' garment. The tradition that Jesus healed people *en masse*, though not prominent in the Gospels, demonstrates the evangelists' concern to present him as one who had a ministry to exercise towards the entire people and not just a privileged group. To allow oneself to be touched by large groups of people was an abomination from the point of view of both Pharisees and Essenes. As Bonnard points out (p. 224), it is not surprising that the following sections discuss the subjects of purity and impurity.

34. Gennesaret: a small fertile plain, NW. of the Lake of Galilee, between Capernaum and Tiberias, and also a Roman town built on the site of the ancient Chinnereth (Dt. 3.17). The town and area sometimes gave its name to the Lake.

36. Cf. 8.3 and 9.20. Touching played an important rôle in the ancient rites and legends of blessing and healing. It is not strictly true that Jesus always required an explicit (verbal) confession of faith from those who sought healing; faith is here expressed in the categories of popular magic.

JESUS AND THE TRADITION OF THE ELDERS **15.1-20**

There is no time reference to connect this section with the immediate context. It may be (as Stendahl suggests, *Peake*, 686g) that the notice of a stay in the area of Gennesaret (14.34) supplies a more natural scene for an encounter with officials from Jerusalem. It is possible, however, that the link with what precedes is the continuing interest in the disciples. Although Jesus himself is the focal point of this passage, the question he answers was raised with reference to *disciples'* behaviour (2a); and that, for Matthew, reflects more than merely a biographical concern. The questions are also those of the debate (A.D. 80–90) between the Matthean church and Judaism, from which it had perhaps not entirely parted. The material in Mk 7.1–23 has been rearranged, omitting two verses which explained the customs of the Jews (an explanation which was necessary for Mark's readers who were presumably not in touch with Jews, but superfluous for Matthew's readers) and in verses 12–14 the evangelist has inserted the word on the blind leaders of the blind (cf. Lk. 6.39). This last-mentioned addition does not make the *pericope* an attack on the Pharisees rather than on the oral tradition (*contra* Kilpatrick, p. 108).

Many scholars have argued that in the Marcan parallel (7.1–23) Jesus annuls the written Law, since the injunction concerning things clean and unclean was written. That this is not Matthew's meaning is clear: he omits the words in Mk 7.19 to the effect that Jesus intended to declare all foods clean (whether or not this is dominical is another matter), and he ends the section with the words (not in Mark): 'to eat with unwashed hands does not defile a man'. These points have the effect of making the entire discussion move around the question of the oral tradition, rather than the written Law, in which the washing of hands before meals was not enjoined; cf. Davies, *SSM*, p. 104. Barth (*TIM*, pp. 86–9) suggests that Matthew rejects the washing of hands, not on the basis of a rejection of the rabbinic tradition in principle and *in toto*, but on the basis of a different interpretation of the Law— namely, in terms of the supremacy of the love-commandment, which, in effect, breaks through the whole idea of the rabbinic tradition.

1. There were scribes and Pharisees throughout the whole land, but these came from Jerusalem. Is this a way of suggesting that this was an official deputation from the headquarters of Judaism? Not all Pharisees were scribes, but the majority of the scribes belonged to the Pharisaic party.

2. the tradition of the elders: the body of commentary added to the Law and transmitted orally, over the generations, in the rabbinic schools. It was variously known, as 'the tradition of men' (Mk 7.8), 'your tradition' (Mk 7.9, 13; Mt. 15.3, 6), and by Josephus as 'the tradition of the fathers'. The scribes and Pharisees regarded it as of equal importance with the Law, but

the Sadducees rejected it. It was later written and codified by R.
Judah ha-Nasi (A.D. 135-*c*.220), and formed the Mishnah.
wash their hands: this act was intended to remove ceremonial
defilement caused by contact with things unclean. Ablutions
played a part in the early faith and religion of Israel (Exod.
30.8ff.; Dt. 21.6), and were common among the Qumran sectaries
(1QS v.13-14). Matthew omits the drastic expression 'they eat
with hands defiled' (Mk 7.5).

3. Jesus does not answer the question directed to him, but
counter-attacks: 'If the disciples transgress the unwritten tradition,
the scribes and Pharisees do more—they transgress God's
commandment.' The tradition which ought to explain and apply
the Law has been allowed (by the scribes) to assume precedence
over it.

4. This and the following verses illustrate the charge made in
verse 3. The Law, or will, of God concerning care of parents is
expressed in terms of Exod. 20.12, reinforced by Exod. 21.17.

5. The words **given to God** reproduce the Greek *dōron* ('gift'
or 'offering'). As the parallel at Mk 7.11 says explicitly, Jesus is
here referring to the practice of *korbān*. This signified 'a gift to a
deity' (Ezek. 20.28 and 40.43), then 'a votive offering' in the
Temple, and later the practice whereby a man could set apart his
property for God, and so withdraw its availability from those who
had a legitimate claim for assistance by means of it; see M. Ned.
i, ix, xi. In the Mishnah (Ned. ix.1) it seems to be implied that, in
the event of a conflict over the *korbān* vow and duty to one's parents,
the vow is annulled: but in the time of Jesus it is likely that the
strict view on the binding character of vows (itself set forth in Dt.
23.21ff. and Num. 30.2ff.) was maintained by the Pharisaic party.

7. The hypocrisy of the Pharisees is characterized by a quotation from Isa. 29.13; their sincere and serious regard for externals
and outward piety in fact removes them far from God. They still
pay respect to the command 'with the lips', but their hearts (i.e.
thoughts and motives, the seat of action) are directed to themselves,
under the appearance of fidelity to the divine will. The quotation
as given almost entirely accords with the LXX, which differs
significantly from the Hebrew; cf. Isa. 29.13 (*RSV*).

11. Mark's more general form of the saying ('the things which
come out of a man') is particularized by Matthew's **what comes
out of the mouth,** a phrase which could be construed as limiting

the principle to food (or words), but which, in fact, ought to be interpreted in terms of verse 18. What comes out of the mouth proceeds from the heart, and the heart is the ultimate source of defilement.

12–14. An editorial addition. The question of the disciples implies that the Pharisees understood the saying (in verse 11) which they themselves now require to have explained. Jesus' answer to the question states that the Pharisees (rather than their regulations) do not constitute the true **plant** (or 'plantation') of God, though they think they do. The concept is derived from Isa. 60.21, and was widespread in late Judaism, especially among the Qumran sect, 1QS viii.5; xi.8; CD i.7 (cf. Enoch 10.16 and Ps. Sol. 14.2). The **blind guides** are lit. 'blind leaders of blind people'. 'Leader of the blind' was a title of honour claimed by Jewish rabbis (Rom. 2.19; cf. Lk. 6.39), but, according to Jesus, those who profess to be able to guide the blind are themselves blind. 'Their blindness shows itself in the tradition of the elders with which they conceal the actual will of God' (Barth, in *TIM*, p. 88).

15. The request to have the parable explained relates to the saying in verse 11, not to verses 12–14.

16. The word *akmēn* (**still**) is a late Greek adverbial accusative which places emphasis at the beginning of a sentence. 'Even at this critical juncture, are you without understanding?'

17. whatever goes into the mouth (verse 11) is now explained as food, but Matthew omits the words of Mark which explicitly denied that food can defile a man.
passes on: lit. 'is cast out into the latrine'. The Marcan addition *katharizōn panta ta brōmata* ('declaring all foods clean') is omitted.

19. Matthew's list of vices which originate within a man is shorter than Mark's: after the first one (**evil thoughts**) the others follow the order of the sixth, seventh, eighth and ninth commandments; **slander** could be interpreted from the Greek as 'blasphemy (in religion)'.

20. The second clause, **to eat with unwashed hands does not defile a man,** returns to the question raised in verse 2 and makes verses 1–20 into a unit. By adding this clause Matthew shows his intention to keep the application of Jesus' word to the *tradition* of the elders, and does not infer from it the abolition of the Mosaic food-laws.

JESUS AND THE CANAANITE WOMAN 15.21-8

The question of clean and unclean (verses 1-20) is closely related
to the matter of Jewish attitudes towards Gentiles, and it is
interesting to note that, according to Paul's letters, it was in the
matter of food laws that the tensions between Jews and Gentiles
(both outside and inside the Church) first presented themselves.
It is therefore likely that this *pericope* was employed for the guidance
of the Matthean church in its relations with Gentiles; the part
played by the disciples in the discussion strengthens this impression.
In this context of thought, the significance of the story would be as
follows: Gentiles could not claim an immediate entry to salvation
(i.e. to the life of the Kingdom), for Jesus insisted that his call was
to the children of Israel. But exceptions could be made; if non-
Jews believed with a faith like that of this woman, access would
not be denied them. The healing is then almost incidental; what
is significant is the attitude to pagan belief. 'The words and actions
of Jesus are narrated to guide the Christian communities in their
present decisions, not to provide sentimental reminiscences about
Jesus' (Bonnard, p. 230). Streeter (*Four Gospels*, p. 260) argues that
at this point Matthew used a version of Mark older than that
known to us; it seems more likely that he rewrote (with additions)
his Marcan source (7.24-30) in order to clarify the point at issue
and emphasize its relevance to the Church of his own time.

21. Tyre and Sidon: towns about 30-50 miles NW. of
Gennesaret on the Mediterranean coast; the two names traditionally designated the (pagan) area NNW. of Palestine. They were
mentioned earlier in 11.21ff. Matthew's interest in them (if such
it is) is due, according to Kilpatrick (pp. 130ff.), to the fact that he
was writing for a church in this area.

22. In Mk 7.26 the woman is called 'a Greek, a Syro-Phoeni-
cian by birth', but **Canaanite** is a term associated with the
Semitic world. In fact, there is some evidence (see Kilpatrick,
p. 132) to suggest that 'Canaan(ite)' was current as the Semitic
way of referring to Phoenicia and its people at the time of Matthew's writing. *RSV* rightly translates '. . . a woman from that
region came out' (of her house?); the rendering '. . . a woman
came out from that region' is used by *JB* to suggest that she
came out of her pagan environment to meet Jesus (in Israel?);
but verse 21 clearly states that it was Jesus who had left his

environment and entered the Phoenician region. The address **C Lord, Son of David** (cf. 12.23) is the language of one who recognizes Jesus as Messiah. The point of Matthew's story, however, i that the woman won acceptance with Jesus, not because of her recognition of his Messiahship, but because of her strong and humble faith.

23. The silence of Jesus and the request of the disciples are Matthean additions, and the second is very characteristic of the evangelist's own interests. The querulous disciples represent the Jewish Christian church who are opposed to (or do not understand) the entry of Gentiles to the Church. The words **Send her away** (*apoluson*) could be interpreted as: 'Give her what she wants, and let her go' (*JB*), and this would alter greatly the meaning of the narrative.

24. Another Matthean addition, recalling 10.6. Bultmann (*HST*, p. 155) argues that the form **I was sent** (i.e. by God) shows traces of the Johannine theme of Christ's divinely-given mission and that, consequently, the *logion* is late. But, although Matthew alone has the saying, its undoubted particularism argues for its authenticity. The Church, even before the time of Paul, had engaged in missionary activity among the Gentiles: they would not have created such a saying (see Jeremias, *Promise*, pp. 26–8). It is difficult to be certain whether 'the lost sheep of the house of Israel' means the lost among Israel, or all Israel regarded as lost; the latter interpretation is perhaps more likely (cf. 10.6).

26. The distinction between **dogs** (a Jewish way of referring to the Gentiles) and 'children' or 'masters' emphasizes precedence only: the children get their food first, the household dogs afterwards. It is wrong to suggest that **crumbs** implies that the Gentiles receive only a fragment of what is given to Israel. The point is that their needs are adequately met. 'Just as no one would think of feeding the dogs with the children's food, so Jesus could not entertain the proposal to give Israel's food to Gentiles; . . . Jesus does not grant her request until she has recognized the divinely ordained division between God's people and the Gentiles' (Jeremias, *Promise*, pp. 29, 30).

27. The woman's faith—which wins her request—is not belief in Jesus as Israel's Messiah, but the persevering faith which admits humbly that she has no right to immediate help but is prepared to take second place to Israel(ites).

A GREAT NUMBER HEALED **15.29-31**

It is possible that, in the structure of the Gospel, this summary (which, though certainly redactional, witnesses to the fact of Jesus' healing ministry) is intended to generalize what has been affirmed in the preceding narrative—namely, a ministry among, and even to, Gentiles. On all sides of the Sea of Galilee (a name used only here and at 4.18, where it follows the Isaianic prophecy which promised light to Galilee of the Gentiles), and especially on its Eastern shore, there were many non-Jewish settlements. Moreover, the crowd **glorified the God of Israel,** which suggests that they were not themselves of Israel. At this point in Mark there stands the story of the healing of the man who was deaf and had an impediment in his speech (*kōphon kai mōgilalon*): the second adjective is an extremely rare one, but it is found in the LXX of Isa. 35.5.: the 'eyes of the blind shall be opened, the ears of the deaf unstopped: then shall the lame man leap like a hart, and the tongue of the dumb sing for joy'. It is possible that Matthew has picked up Mark's reference back to Isaiah, and has introduced into his summary the kinds of sickness mentioned there: (the lame, blind, dumb (or deaf = *kōphous*), adding the maimed (*kyllous*)). Cf. Fenton, p. 257.

THE FEEDING OF THE FOUR THOUSAND **15.32-9**

Matthew shares with Mark the tradition having two accounts of feeding the multitude, while Luke has only one (Lk. 9.10-17, cf. Mt. 14.13ff.); the account of the feeding in Jn 6 shows signs of being a combination of both. It is possible that all six narratives stem from a single tradition; it should be noted that they all conclude with a voyage across the lake. Many theories have been put forward to account for the duplication in Mark and its retention by Matthew—e.g. P. Carrington's lectionary hypothesis, which would require a second such story (*The Primitive Christian Calendar*, 1952, p. 16). The fact that Mark (followed by Matthew) locates the incident in a Gentile area supports the solution proposed by Lohmeyer, that the second account relates to the Gentiles, a view which he regarded as strengthened by the reference to **seven baskets** (representing the seven deacons of Ac. 6.1ff.), contrasted with twelve baskets in 14.20 (referring to the twelve disciples as representative of the tribes of Israel); see

E. Lohmeyer, *JBL*, LVI, 1937, pp. 235ff., and Richardson, p. 98. The setting of the story after the incident in Syro-Phoenicia (and especially in view of Matthew's verse 27) would be appropriate. Gentiles enjoy the anticipation of the messianic banquet, as well as Israel. The repetition of the story therefore serves theology, not history.

33. If this event had actually occurred before, it would be quite incredible for the disciples to be so astonished on the second occasion.

34. The number of **loaves** is **seven** (in the other account five). The variation in the numbers in the stories suggests that the evangelists may intend them to be understood symbolically.

36. The word for 'give thanks' here is *eucharisteō*, not *eulogeō* as in 14.19, and it is the same participle as is found at 1C. 11.24. That the Church saw in the feeding miracles the prototype of the Lord's Supper and their own Eucharistic celebrations is certain; these, in turn, were regarded also as 'antedonations' of the messianic banquet.

37. The word used for basket here is *sphuris*, an ordinary kind of flexible basket for food or fish. There is some evidence (cited from Juvenal in Rawlinson, p. 87) which suggests that the word *kōphinos* used in the earlier narrative (14.20 and Mk 6.43) denotes a basket commonly used by Jews, particularly in Rome; cf. Arndt, p. 448. Is the change of term a further hint of Gentile interest here?

39. the region of Magadan: Mark has 'the district of Dalmanutha'. Neither place can be identified. Some manuscripts read 'Magdala' (cf. LXX of Jos. 15.37, where Migdal is reproduced in Codex Vaticanus (B) as 'Magada', and in Codex Alexandrinus (A) as 'Magadal'), the name of a place not far from Tiberias, on the eastern shore of the lake; but a place on the western shore is probably meant.

THE DEMAND FOR A SIGN 16.1–4

Matthew follows Mark (8.11ff.) in narrating how the second miraculous feeding prompted a request for a sign from heaven (cf. also Jn 6.20), although he has already dealt with this event in 12.38–9. The influence of his earlier account causes him to reintroduce the allusion to Jonah here, although that does not feature in Mark. The response of Jesus, according to Mark, was entirely negative. Verses 2b and 3 are missing from the best manuscripts (B, Syr. Sin.): it is likely that they were copied into Matthew at an early date from Lk. 12.54–6.

1. The Pharisees and Sadducees are shown as acting in concert, although they were enemies; but they represent official Judaism in its entirety. That there is here an allusion to the situation of Judaism in Matthew's own time is improbable; by A.D. 85 Judaism was dominated by the Pharisees, and the Sadducees had been eclipsed as an effective force. The sign demanded is one accorded by God to Jesus, a miracle which would give him authority in the eyes of the people.

2b–3. The Jews know how to interpret the signs of the weather, but they cannot discern the **signs of the times**—i.e. the person and activity of Jesus in their midst, which signify that these days are decisive for repentance and judgment. They are for his hearers what the days of Jonah were for the Ninevites.

4. Cf. on 12.39ff. Jesus refuses a sign of the kind sought by his adversaries: but he offers the countersign of Jonah.

A DISCOURSE ON LEAVEN 16.5–12

'This short discourse . . . is of interest as an example of how a saying of Jesus could be used on the basis of association (leaven-bread) in relation to the accounts of the feeding of the multitudes and how it thereby was given additional implications in the preaching and interpretation of the Church. Thereby two thoughts were woven together: (*a*) I have taken care of your physical needs; (*b*) don't be deceived by the teaching of the Pharisees and Sadducees' (Stendahl, in *Peake*, 687b).

5. Matthew simplifies Mark's introductory words: 'Now they had forgotten to bring bread; and they had only one loaf with them in the boat' (8.14), and concentrates attention on the teaching of Jesus which follows.

6. Luke interprets the 'leaven of the Pharisees' (probably correctly) in the sense of hypocrisy: Mark gives no explanation and adds the strange words 'the leaven of Herod'. Matthew explicitly interprets the **leaven of the Pharisees and Sadducees** (he adds the second name, see on verse 1) in the sense of their (false) teaching (verse 12). This is perhaps a further indication of Matthew's catechetical or pedagogical interests.

8–10. The faith of the disciples would require perception and

I

remembrance, not just of the events mentioned, but also of their revelatory significance: see N. A. Dahl, *ST*, I, 1948, p. 93, n. 2.

11–12. Matthew elucidates completely the meaning of Jesus' instruction to the disciples; Mark leaves the reader to interpret for himself.

PETER'S CONFESSION AND THE FIRST ANNOUNCEMENT OF THE PASSION **16.13–23**

With a few changes (to be noted below) Matthew follows Mk 8.27–33 in narrating how Jesus first asks his disciples for their sentiments about him; how Peter speaks for them and confesses that Jesus is the Christ-Messiah; and how this leads to the first prediction of the Passion—a theme which thenceforward receives increasing emphasis (17.22f.; 20.17–19).

There is no doubt that the *pericope* marks a turning point in all the Gospels, but at the same time it fits well into the context in which it is found here. It forms an integral and important part of the narrative (13.53–17.27) which leads up to Jesus' teaching to his disciples on humility, love and forgiveness (chapter 18). The relation of the *pericope* to what follows might be summed up in Bonnard's words (p. 241): 'Because the disciples follow a suffering Messiah and not a triumphant one, they must know how to accept the little ones and to forgive one another.'

To the Petrine confession and the announcement of the Passion, Matthew has added a third focus of interest—the 'majestic statement' (Stendahl) about Peter himself (17–20), which is not found anywhere in Mark or Luke. On the question of the genuineness of this *logion*, there is no consensus of opinion among Protestant scholars: a review of thirty-four modern authors has shown that they divide into two approximately equal groups (A. Oepke, *ST*, II, 1948–50, p. 111, n. 1). The history of interpretation of the *logion* is set out in Cullmann (*Peter*, pp. 158–69), and the affirmation is made that the confessional standpoint of the interpreter has quite often coloured his exegesis. Cullmann himself (with Oepke, and against Kümmel, p. 139, and Bultmann *TB*, 1941, pp. 265ff., and *TNT*, p. 45) defends the genuineness of the saying, but claims that it was uttered during the Passion period in a setting similar to that of Lk. 22.31ff. It was originally transmitted in connection with the prediction of Peter's denial, but was placed by Matthew in a different context (*Peter*, pp. 170–84). Stauffer pp. 32f.) thinks it belongs to a post-Resurrection scene. Although t is difficult to be certain and unwise to be dogmatic, we take the position that verses 17–19 represent an early (Palestinian) Matthean tradition (perhaps an oral Petrine tradition when Peter was still head of the Jerusalem church), but do not form a genuine saying of Jesus; they reflect the post-Easter situation. Whatever be the Aramaic which lies behind *ekklēsia* in verse 18 (a word which is found here and at Mt. 18.17 in the gospels)—whether it refers to the Remnant, the synagogue, or the people of God (cf. K. L. Schmidt, *The Church* (*BKW*))—there is in the saying an element of institutionalism (represented by the authority, in doctrine and discipline, of a particular apostle) which is not easily contained within the traditional thought of the Jewish 'people of God'—which was, in any case, the creation of God (not of the Messiah, or Son of God) and was ruled solely by God, not by an apostle. Furthermore, the suggested association (if not identification) of Church (or community) and Kingdom is post-Easter (Matthean and Pauline) theology; see on 13.36ff.

13. Caesarea Philippi: the city built by Herod Philip and named Caesarea in honour of the Emperor, and Philippi to distinguish it from the seaport of the same name. It was situated about 25 miles north of the Sea of Galilee.

Whom do men say that the Son of man is ?: both Mark and Luke have 'Whom do men say that I am?' To interpret this as meaning that Jesus inquired about the 'Son of Man' still to come is impossible, in view of the parallelism offered in verse 15 and because elsewhere Matthew uses 'Son of Man' as Jesus' self-designation (8.20).

14. Herod Antipas (14.2) thought that Jesus was John the Baptist risen from the dead. Elijah was one of the classic figures of Jewish apocalyptic. In rabbinic teaching he was to fulfil the rôle of High Priest, to anoint the messiah, to promote Israel's repentance, and to bring about the resurrection of the dead. The Baptist was believed to be Elijah returned from heaven (11.4; 17.10ff.). Matthew alone mentions Jeremiah by name; he was often listed first among the so-called 'latter prophets' in the Jewish canon, but no record of his death is found in scripture: presumably he was conceived as having ascended to heaven, like Moses and Isaiah (in *The Assumption of Moses* and *The Ascension of Isaiah*) and as having joined the company of Messiah's immortal companions (cf. 2 Mac. 2.1–12; 15.14f.). Bonnard (p. 243) asks the intriguin question: Had some contemporaries of Jesus already been struc by the mixture of authority and suffering that characterized bot his life and that of Jeremiah?

15. you: emphatic, contrasting the opinions of the common ma with those of the intimate disciples.

16. The answer of Simon Peter adds to Mark's 'the Christ' th words 'the Son of the living God'. **Christ** is a title, the Gree translation of the Hebrew 'Messiah' ('anointed one'). It has alread appeared in Matthew (1.1, 16f., 18; 11.1), but this occasion i depicted as the first on which it came to open expression by Jesu disciples. The addition **Son of the living God** (a form of addres already found on the lips of the disciples at 14.33) is a Matthea explanation, based on a later and more fully elaborated faith 'Son of God' had probably come into use as a messianic title i pre-Christian Judaism (cf. 4QFlor. 10–14; Fuller, *Foundation* p. 32) with the meaning of 'God's adopted vicegerent in his King dom'; but in later Christian thought it was used as a title affirmin Jesus' divine origin and nature.

17. The Semitic character of the following verses (which argue for their Palestinian origin) appears in the first word. **Blessed–** cf. 5.3–12; **flesh and blood** is a Jewish way of referring to man i his entirety, but in his natural weakness (cf. 1 C. 15.50; Gal. 1.16) **Bar-Jona** ('son of Jonah') can with some difficulty be made t mean 'son of John' (*bar-Johanan*). R. Eisler (*Iesous basileus*, 1929 p. 67) gives to the Aramaic *bar-jona* the meaning of 'anarchist' o 'revolutionary' (corresponding to the epithet 'Canaanite' give to a 'Simon' in Mt. 10.4; Mk 3.18), and so makes Peter a Zealot Cullmann thinks that the absence of the object 'this' in the Gree supports the view that the words did not originally stand in thi context, but in another *with* an object, or where they had at leas another introduction. The expressions **blessed** and **my Fathe who is in heaven** are characteristically Matthean.

18. you are Peter: Matthew's list of the disciples (10.2f. cf. Mk 3.16) omits the words 'and he added the name Peter t Simon' in Mark's list. It seems as if this verse is substituted. Ther is no evidence that the Greek word *petros* or its Aramaic equivalen *kēpā(s)* (a feminine word, and therefore rightly translated *petra* but for a man's name changed to *petros*) was used as a persona name before Christian times. It should be translated 'rock'; bu

has nothing to do with indicating the disciple's stability of
haracter. Verse 17 clearly affirms that Peter's personal qualities
nd qualifications matter little. To be open to God's revelation is
verything.

n this rock I will build my church: the word-play goes back to
\ramaic tradition. It is on Peter himself, the confessor of his
Λessiahship, that Jesus will build the Church. The disciple be-
omes, as it were, the foundation stone of the community. Attempts
o interpret the 'rock' as something other than Peter in person (e.g.
is faith, the truth revealed to him) are due to Protestant bias, and
ntroduce to the statement a degree of subtlety which is highly
unlikely. In favour of interpreting the word-play as a personal
eference is the rabbinic saying about Abraham: 'when the Holy
ne wanted to create the world, he passed over the generations of
_noch and of the Flood; but when he saw Abraham who was to
rise, he said: "Behold, I have found a rock on which I can build
nd found the world": therefore he called Abraham rock, as it is
aid [Isa. 51.1]: "Look to the rock from which you were hewn." '
iimilar metaphors are applied to apostles in Gal. 2.9 and Eph.
.20.

ny church: the word *ekklēsia* (used here and again only at 18.17,
. passage whose genuineness is disputed) is used in the LXX for
the people', 'the assembly', 'the congregation'. It is not certain
vhat Aramaic word lies behind the term here: it may be *kahᵃla*, or
nore probably *kᵉništa'* (so Schmidt, *The Church*), which can refer
ither to the people of God or to a separate synagogue—perhaps
iere with special reference to the remnant of Israel, though
Iare (p. 160) argues for radical discontinuity between Jesus'
kklēsia and Israel. In Judaism the concept was always that of the
eople of God, the *ekklēsia* of the Lord, the congregation of the
ovenant (at Qumran); but Matthew makes it Messiah's com-
nunity (cf. 13.41: 'the Kingdom of the Son of Man'). The identi-
ication of Kingdom and Church is characteristic of certain trends
n post-Easter theology; see C. H. Dodd, *ET*, LVIII, 1947, pp. 296ff.

he powers of death shall not prevail against it: lit. 'the
;ates of Hades', which will not close to imprison (in death) those
vho belong to the messianic community, cf. the description of the
ouncil of the community (at Qumran) in the eschatological
)eriod as an edifice securely founded (1QS viii.7). The view that
gates of Hades' actually denotes Hades, the abode of evil spirits,

and that the meaning of the phrase is that the organized power o
evil will not prevail against the organized Christian society, seem
forced and unnatural. An Aramaic fragment of Test. Levi 2.3-
found at Qumran offers certain parallels to this passage, and ever
to its connection with the locality of Caesarea Philippi, on the
slopes of Mt Hermon and near the source of the Jordan. This area
was associated with apocalypticism, as a place of revelation and a
a meeting place for the upper (mountainous) and the lowe
(watery abyss) worlds; cf. J. T. Milik, *RB*, LXII, 1955, pp. 398-
406, esp. p. 405, and J. M. Allegro, *The Dead Sea Scrolls*, pp. 142ff

19. keys of the kingdom of heaven: this is depicted as a
place to be entered, cf. 7.21. The keys are a symbol of Peter'
authority as leader of the Church after the Resurrection (**I wil
give**); he may admit or refuse admittance to the Kingdom. To
bind and to **loose** may refer either to the authority to lay down
binding rules (*halokōth*) and exempt from them, or to the power to
practise discipline in the Church (notice the close association o
authority and the Kingdom in verse 18), including the right to
condemn or acquit (18.18). Both interpretations amount to much
the same thing in the end: Peter has authority to make pronounce
ments (whether legislative, as 'chief rabbi' (so Stendahl, in *Peake*
687f.), or disciplinary) and these will be ratified by God in the
Last Judgment. The rôle of Peter is here understood as unique a
a specific juncture of God's history, and its repetition in the bishop
of Rome is quite another matter and hardly a legitimate deduc
tion (cf. *JB*).

20. The command to keep silent is taken from Mark, with the
addition of the words 'that he was the Christ'. Silence abou
Jesus being Messiah was required, not because Jesus had renounce
all messianic dignity, nor because the early Church had placed or
Jesus' lips a later explanation of his status, nor because the know
ledge of his Messiahship would have caused nationalistic fervour
but—as the following verses show—because knowledge of thi
particular messiahship could only be given to those who were
prepared to accept a share in Jesus' sufferings. A true and ful
understanding of Jesus' person was not achieved quickly or or
superficial impressions; to this extent the Gospel 'secrecy motif
preserves a necessary historical truth about the significance o
Jesus' ministry.

21. From that time: a new phase is marked in the Gospel (a

fact which suggests that the reading 'Jesus Christ' may be original
here). The necessity (*dei*) of suffering lies, not in Jesus' heroic
determination, nor in the opposition of his enemies, nor in a blind
fate, but in the will of God, known to faith and expressed in the
Scriptures.

Although it is unlikely that Jesus spoke about his sufferings and
death with the precision indicated here, this does not take away all
historical value from the passage. That Jesus should have wanted
(and felt urgency) to go to Jerusalem and confront the authorities
there, and if necessary suffer for it, seems quite possible (*contra*
Bultmann, *HST*, p. 151).

This verse deals with what for the early Church was of immense
significance in its apologetic and missionary work—a crucified
(martyred) Messiah rejected by the Jewish authorities in Jerusalem
—the **elders and chief priests and scribes** constituted the
Sanhedrin. Even if there was a place in Jewish thought for an
expected 'suffering Messiah' (see Jeremias, *Servant*, pp. 57ff.), the
Gospels all indicate that the disciples did not think of Jesus in
these terms. If it is possible that Jesus foresaw his sufferings and
death, can he have predicted his resurrection? Or is this a *vaticinium
ex eventu* due to the Church's Passion apologetic?

third day: a phrase traditionally associated with Hos. 6.2; Lindars
(pp. 60ff.) claims that the Resurrection prediction could probably
be original, with the meaning of the Hosea prophecy—that renewal will happen in a short time. Jesus was probably expressing
his belief that his death would quickly prove to be for the lasting
benefit of God's people, in inaugurating the restored, spiritualized
kingdom. In short, the idea of resurrection is being used as a
metaphor of national restoration, just as it is in Hos. 6.2. Another
line of argument is that, since the prediction is made in Mark
regarding the Son of Man (a title ultimately based on Dan. 7), the
fact that the Son of Man there (or the 'saints of the Most High') is
vindicated after trial and suffering implies that the application of
that title to Jesus (indeed, his own application of it) involves his
expectation of victory through suffering, his vindication or exaltation (cf. Mt. 26.64) after defeat (C. F. D. Moule, *Bull. NTS*,
1953, pp. 40ff., esp. p. 46). The presence of the Suffering Servant
theme here is disputed.

22. The words of Peter's rebuke form an exclamation: '(God
be) gracious to you, Lord', and that is equivalent to **God forbid.**

23. Cf. 4.10. To oppose the will of God for his servant is to be the agent of Satan; the words of Peter are a return of the temptation to other ways of fulfilling the messianic rôle than by sacrifice and obedience. Matthew adds: **You are a** stumbling-block (or **hindrance) to me.** The refusal of the Passion would be for Jesus a revolt against God.

you are not on the side of God, but of men: lit. 'you are not concerned with God's affairs, but with men's', which amounts to being an instrument of Satan. Does the presence of this section on Peter mean that the evangelist is trying to counteract Petrine authority (or dominance) in the Church by showing how his confession was linked with a total lack of understanding of Jesus' mission? It seems more likely that the intention is to display, in no less a person than Peter, at the high moment of his confession, the intense power of the Jewish messianic interpretation, which rejected the idea of suffering. A messiah who suffered (on a cross) was indeed a stumbling-block to Jews! (Cf. 1 C. 1.23.)

THE WAY OF DISCIPLESHIP **16.24–8**

Having shown the necessity of his own sufferings, Jesus now calls his disciples to follow in the same path. Matthew has omitted the crowd, or 'multitude', addressed with the disciples in Mark's account (8.34ff.); this is a further example of the first evangelist's preoccupation with the disciples in this section of his work. The substance of the paragraph has appeared before (Mt. 10.38f., 33) in the address to the apostolic messengers of the Gospel. It is significant that Matthew does not retain the saying about the Son of Man being ashamed of those who have not been willing to accept the disgrace of discipleship (Mk 8.38; but see Mt. 10.33); are there none recognized as such among the disciples? In verse 27 Matthew has added a quotation from Ps. 62.12, and he has altered the final clause of the paragraph.

24. If any man would come after me . . .: lit. 'if any man wishes to come . . .' The words are not an expression of doubt: Jesus is addressing men who have engaged themselves to him without fully considering the consequences. The three verbs which follow—**deny himself** (i.e. disown, disclaim, break ties with; cf. 10.33); **take up his cross** (see note on 10.38); and **follow**— describe, not the conditions for discipleship, but the attitudes in which the *whole* life of the disciple must consist. This was the path before Jesus himself: the disciples also will follow it. Bornkamm (*Jesus*, pp. 144f.) points to three characteristics of discipleship which mark it off from Jewish forms: (i) Jesus' disciple does not decide for his master on the basis of personal taste; he is called or chosen by the sovereign word of Christ; (ii) he is not committed to memorizing his master's teaching in order to transmit it to future generations (although the Scandinavian approach to the Gospel tradition would suggest that he was; see Introduction p. 58); (iii) his association with his master is not provisional, until such times as he himself will become a master, but life-long.

25. To 'save one's life' means to abandon Jesus and his messianic pathway: to 'lose one's life for Jesus' sake' means to risk life, to the point of death, in order obediently to witness to Jesus and his gospel. To 'find life' may mean 'obtain or acquire life at the Resurrection'. It could also mean 'discover life'. The true disciple will discover life as it should be now and in the future, i.e. the life of the Kingdom.

26. Cf. 2 Bar. 51.15: 'For what, then, have men lost their life, and for what have those who were on earth exchanged their souls.' 'To gain the whole world' means to possess all its created abundance and richness. The second clause implies that a man's life is more valuable to him than anything else; yet, paradoxically, he must lose this life in order to find it.

27. The reason why disciples must follow in the way of sacrificial living is that there is a coming judgment. The Son of Man will come in the glory of his father with his angels (cf. Mt. 13.41) to repay every man for what he has done. The allusion is to Ps. 62.12; this action of God is not vindictive, but evidence of his steadfast love and faithfulness towards the righteous. While it is generally agreed that Jesus (Christ) was identified with the Son of Man as coming Judge in the faith of the Church, it is sometimes argued that, in Jesus' own usage the title 'Son of Man' was used to point to another than himself: the likelihood of this is greatly minimized by the well-founded argument that Jesus *did* use the title for himself (from Dan. 7.13), and claimed that he had fulfilled it (Mk 14.62). The authority of Jesus as Son of Man will be fully revealed and generally acknowledged only in the future, when he is vindicated; cf. Hooker, *SMM*, pp. 121f.

28. As a means of strengthening the appeal for serious discipleship, this verse claims that the coming in glory is not far off.

Mk 9.1. seems to preserve the most primitive form of the saying: the Kingdom will have come 'in power' within a generation. Matthew alters it to **the Son of Man coming in his Kingdom.** What the Marcan form means is probably 'a visible manifestation of the Rule of God displayed in the life of an Elect Community . . .; but what this means cannot be described in detail because the hope was not fulfilled in the manner in which it presented itself to Him (Jesus), although later it found expression in the life of the Church' (Taylor, p. 386).

Matthew's words may be a legitimate interpretation of Mark, since for the first evangelist the 'Kingdom of the Son of Man' (13.41) seems to be identifiable with the Church, the community of the renewed Israel. Modern exegesis has seen in the Matthean and Marcan *logion* an announcement of the Transfiguration (which may have seemed to the Gospel writers a partial fulfilment) of the Resurrection, of the fall of Jerusalem, of the gift of the Spirit—even of the rapid expansion of the Church throughout the empire! But the statement is concerned to affirm the future vindication of Jesus' rightful authority as Son of Man.

THE TRANSFIGURATION 17.1–8

The three Synoptic writers place this narrative in the same place, following Peter's confession, the first announcement of the Passion, and the words of Jesus on the suffering of disciples and the future glory of the Son of Man (cf. Mk 9.2–8; Lk. 9.28–36). The Transfiguration continues these themes: glory, Sonship, and the necessity of Christ's suffering. The story has been interpreted as a post-Resurrection appearance projected back into Jesus' ministry (so Bultmann, *HST*, p. 259); but this view does not do justice to its careful placing in all three Gospels, nor to its many precise details. On the basis of a form-critical study of the passage Dodd (*SG*, p. 25) declares that 'the *pericope* contrasts with the general type of post-Resurrection narrative in almost every particular'. Some recent studies (particularly H. Riesenfeld, *Jésus Transfiguré*, 1947, and G. H. Boobyer, *St Mark and the Transfiguration Story*, 1942) emphasize the cultic and mythological motifs, mostly drawn from the *OT* and Jewish eschatology, which contribute to the account, but without pronouncing on the documentary value of the narrative itself. Others use all the resources of criticism to try to find the true echo—admittedly overlaid with interpretation for

the Church—of a critical moment in Jesus' life, and among
hypotheses put forward is that of a revelatory or visionary experience granted to the three chosen disciples. The meaning of the
story for the evangelists lies in the revelation of the glory of Jesus
Messiah. Matthew has made a number of changes to embroider
Mark's account, and has placed the fear of the disciples after the
voice from heaven—not after the vision of the transfigured Jesus.

1. after six days: precise indications of time such as this are
unusual in the Gospels before the beginning of the Passion narrative. The reference may be to Exod. 24.16 where 'after six days'
(i.e. on the seventh) God speaks to Moses on Sinai. Bonnard
(p. 254) claims that the allusion is to the six days which separated
the Day of Atonement from the beginning of the Feast of Tabernacles, the actual day being either the first day of Tabernacles
(a day of messianic and nationalist excitement) or the penultimate
day of the week-long feast. There is another allusion to Tabernacles in verse 4.

Peter, James and John: this group forms an inner circle among
the twelve in the Gospels (cf. 20.20; 26.37). Along with Peter and
John, James the Lord's brother forms the three 'pillars' in Gal.
2.9. 'Thus the group of Three, just as that of the Twelve, seems
to have a significance in itself apart from who they may have been,
as both have at Qumran (1QS viii.1-8) (Stendahl, in *Peake*, 687k:
cf. Cross, pp. 174f.).

a high mountain: traditionally Tabor, but some modern exegetes
prefer Hermon. Both Moses and Elijah received revelations from
God on mountains (Exod. 2; 41 Kg. 19).

2. transfigured: Greek *metemorphōthē* ('changed'). The word
occurs again only in 2 C. 3.18 and Rom. 12.2, with reference to
inward and spiritual transformation; but here it has the sense of a
visible transformation (cf. Exod. 34.29; 2. Bar. 51. 3, 5). According to Matthew, Jesus' face shone, as well as his clothes (the latter
only in Mark); cf. Mt. 13.43; Rev. 1.13ff,; and Exod. 34.29f.
concerning Moses. These expressions signify that God himself is
making his glory rest on Jesus and attesting his Messiahship.

3. Elijah was regarded as a forerunner of Messiah (Sir. 48.10;
Mk 9.11; Mt. 17.10): the association of Elijah and Moses in this
capacity is found only rarely in Judaism, perhaps Rev. 11.3 and
Midr. Dt. 201c. It may be that the presence of the two figures is
meant to suggest that the witness of both Law and Prophets is

being borne to Jesus. Luke has added that their conversation was about Jesus' departure (*exodos*) in death.

4. it is well that we are here: this rendering (rather than 'it is good for us to be here') suggests that the disciples are aware of the need to serve Jesus and the heavenly visitors, and not just (selfishly) enjoying their privilege.

I will make . . . : Peter's suggestion implies that he is unaware of what is happening: he wants to provide **booths** (reminiscent of the Tabernacles feast) for the three to spend the night.

5. overshadowed: the word *epeskiasen* recalls the covering of the Tent of Meeting by a cloud (Exod. 40.35) and the *shekinah* ('the divine presence'): cf. 2 Mac. 2.8 for the expectation of the appearance of the cloud and the glory of the Lord in the days of Messiah.

This is my beloved Son: this repeats the testimony to Jesus given at his baptism (see on 3.17).

listen to him: the words probably represent a quotation from Dt. 18.15 (the prediction of a 'prophet like Moses' whom the people must hear and obey), quoted again in Ac. 3.22f.; 7.37. The Moses-like prophet is identified with the beloved Son.

6–7. The description of the effect of the experience on the disciples is strongly reminiscent of Daniel's account of the effects of his vision upon himself (Dan. 10.7ff.).

AFTER THE TRANSFIGURATON **17.9–13**

Matthew has rearranged the Marcan form (9.9–13) to place the emphasis on the explicit identification of Elijah and John the Baptist. The link with the preceding event presumably is that, in the glimpse of glory revealed, Jesus is shown as more than a fore-runner of the Messiah: yet the restoration of all things by Elijah had not taken place as expected (Mal. 4.5). How is this to be explained? The presentation of the conversation (and, in the opinion of many critics, its creation) reflects discussions on the order of Messianic events.

9. This is the fifth and last command to keep silent in the Gospel: it differs from the others in that it permits the disciples to speak of his glory after the Son of Man has been raised. Between Trans-figuration and Resurrection would lie the Cross; that event would destroy all political messianism and all superficial judgments about Jesus' status. If this was not Jesus' own view and attitude, then it represents a true understanding (by the evangelists) of the events of Jesus' life from the point of view of the post-Easter faith: no miracle, and not even the Transfiguration, reveals the full meaning of this life; that can only be known after the 'resurrection'. See on 8.4.

vision: Matthew's word *horama* offers an interpretation of the Transfiguration, and one which the evangelist perhaps uses to help his contemporaries understand the occurrence.

10. On the place of Elijah in Jewish apocalyptic see Mal. 4.5; M. Eduy. viii.7; B. Metzia iii.5. In order to cast doubt on Jesus' Messiahship, the scribes could claim that Elijah, the necessary forerunner, had not yet come.

11. The tradition concerning Elijah is affirmed. He does come, and he will **restore all things** (quoting the LXX of Mal. 4.5), in order that God's curse may be avoided and true religion exist in the land in the days of the Messiah.

12. but I tell you . . . : Jesus corrects the traditional view. The work of Elijah (= John the Baptist) was rejected (**they did not know him** a Matthean addition recalling again the evangelist's interest in faith and understanding), and therefore Messiah comes to an unprepared people. But the plan of God must go forward, although it will now proceed through suffering, and Messiah, or Son of Man, will experience the same fate as the forerunner.

13. An explanatory addition, given for the sake of readers.

THE HEALING OF AN EPILEPTIC BOY **17.14–21**

The three Synoptics place this event after the descent from the mount of Transfiguration (Mk 9.14ff.; Lk. 9.37ff.). Luke omits the discussion about Elijah which intervenes in Mark and Matthew, because it was of no interest to his readers. Matthew's narrative is probably an abbreviation of Mark's, and focuses on the essential point, which (for the first evangelist) is the word of Jesus on faith. This is emphasized by the concluding summary (verse 20), which appears in Mark and Luke in different contexts, and again at Mt. 21.21. (See Intro. pp. 62–3 for a consideration of Matthew's use of miracle stories to centre attention on a saying or pronouncement of Jesus.)

14–15. Mark's detailed introduction (five verses) is shortened considerably, but the phrase **kneeling before him** (sc. as a suppliant) is added. 'Master' (*didaskale*) is changed to **Lord** (*kyrie*), and the description of the symptoms of the boy's illness gives way to the medical diagnosis 'he is a lunatic' (*selēniazetai*); cf. 4.24. Epileptic fits were associated with the changes of the moon.

16. The failure of the disciples is emphasized in this section (14.16ff., 26f., 28ff.; 15.16, 23, 33; 16.5, 22 and 17.4, 10f.). Their inability to heal is strange, for the evangelists all affirm that Jesus gave his disciples power to heal and to exorcise. Perhaps we have here an echo of the situation in the early Church (which is often addressed in the words of Jesus to his disciples), when miracles were lacking.

17. faithless and perverse generation: for 'perverse generation', see the LXX of Dt. 32.5. It is probable that Matthew understood the perversion ('distortion', or even 'tortuousness') to be 'lack of faith'.

How long . . . to bear with you? These words express, not disgust with the people, but the prophetic exasperation of Jesus at the blindness of those who refuse to accept the presence and power of God. A similar idea finds expression in Jn 14.9.

18. The exorcism is narrated with great simplicity and sobriety. If Matthew knew Mark, it is surprising that he did not include Mk 9.23f. Perhaps his interest was concentrated on the disciples' lack of faith, rather than on the struggling faith of the epileptic's father.

19–20. The disciples' (and the Church's) inability to heal is attributed by Jesus to the virtual absence of faith. If they had even the tiniest grain of faith (**mustard seed**), the greatest obstacles could be overcome. 'Removing mountains' (cf. Isa. 40.4; 49.11; 54.10) was a proverbial expression for the overcoming of difficulties. The mighty power of God to change things could be made operative even through weak faith.

21. Missing from the best MSS: it seems to have been due to the influence of Mk 9.29 at a later stage of its textual tradition.

THE SECOND PREDICTION OF THE PASSION **17.22–3**

See on 16.21ff. Cf. also Mk 9.30–32 and Lk. 9.43b–45.

22. be delivered: the verb *paradidosthai*, applied to Jesus, is found frequently in Matthew and in Paul. It belongs to the theological vocabulary of the Passion and its most ancient formulations, and is common in the LXX with reference to the action of God (e.g. Exod. 21.13; Lev. 26.25).

23. they will kill him: omitted by Luke, who in turn omits the mention of the Resurrection. **He will be raised:** (Greek *egerthēsetai*), here replaces Mark's 'will rise' (*anastēsetai*). Although all the details of the predictions of the Passion cannot be held to be authentic, it is likely that there lies behind them a genuine tradition in which Jesus spoke of the likely denouement of his work and life, probably using the title Son of Man; cf. Héring, *Le Royaume*, p. 98, and Bornkamm, *Jesus*, pp. 152ff. The deep sorrow of the disciples indicates that they did not understand the meaning of the announcement of the Resurrection.

THE TEMPLE-TAX 17.24-7

This paragraph is peculiar to Matthew, although the setting is Marcan: the references to Capernaum and to the 'house' (verse 2) are both taken from the verse following the preceding passage (Mk 9.33). The verses offer an important indication of Jesus' attitude (and that of the early Church), not only to the Temple tax, but also to political and social power in general. In verse 24 the interest lies on the payment of the half-shekel Temple tax, but in verse 25 it is on toll or tribute imposed by the State. Therefore the evangelist's concern is not just with Jesus' attitude to the Temple requirements, but to the political power of his time; and the attitude is the same as that in 22.15-22: disciples (and therefore Christians) have a right not to pay taxes because they are free men (i.e. men obedient to God alone), but they will pay in order not to cause offence to others (verse 27). This is an illustration of the teaching which will follow in chapter 18.

The original kernel of the section may have been a saying of Jesus on the payment of the Temple tax, to which Matthew has added guidance on the Christian attitude to taxes in general. Presumably the church of Matthew (being Jewish Christian) continued to pay its dues to Jerusalem, although it knew that its standing and acceptability with God was independent of such obligations.

24. The **half-shekel** (for which the Greek equivalent is *didrachma*) was the amount of the contribution paid annually by every male Jew (even by those outside Palestine) above the age of 19 for the maintenance of the Temple services (Exod. 30.11ff.). Since the *didrachma* was seldom coined in Jesus' time, it is probable that two persons combined to pay a *tetradrachma*, or *statēr* ('shekel',

verse 27). After the destruction of the Temple, the tax was maintained, and the revenue was devoted by the Romans to the temple
of Jupiter Capitolinus (Josephus, *BJ* vii. vi.6.). The *pericope* may
therefore be exhorting against giving offence to the Roman
government; cf. H. W. Montefiore, *NTS*, xi, 1964, pp. 64f.

25–6. Peter's reply in the affirmative (made out of loyalty to
the Law, or because he knew Jesus had paid) must have created
questions at a later date, and these are answered here as Jesus
points out that he does certain things which he is not really obliged
to do as Son of God (cf. 3.15). Jesus' question to Peter takes the
discussion beyond Temple tax to **toll** and **tribute** (i.e. local tax
and poll tax). The governing powers (the **kings of the earth**
(cf. Ps. 2.2) is a Jewish way of describing political authorities)
levy these, but not on **their sons**—i.e. not on their own family or
their court circle—**who** are **free**—i.e. exempt. Because of their
relation of sonship to God, the King of heaven, Jesus and his
disciples are free from obligations to the State.

27. This verse makes it clear that Jesus and his disciples would
submit to the Law—at least to the Temple tax, and, by implication, to State taxation—although they were rightly free from such
duty. Thus they would not give offence to the collectors of taxes,
and avoid being associated in the public mind with agitating
groups like the Zealots. The strange miracle which is added
signifies either that God the Father has paid the tribute to the Law
in the person of Jesus, or, more probably, that he who submits to
the payment of tax is none the less the master of all things.

THE LIFE AND DISCIPLINE OF THE CHRISTIAN COMMUNITY
18.1–19.2

This fourth discourse (which ends with the usual formula) is
concerned with the relations between disciples—the concern
which they must show for one another, and the mutual and unlimited forgiveness they must show. In the study of this chapter,
virtually a manual of church discipline for the Christian community, it is specially important to consider the rule of the sectarian
community at Qumran, the so-called *Manual of Discipline* (1QS).
Care must be taken, however, not to consider mere parallels as
influences or sources. Davies (*SSM*, p. 255) admits that the
Matthean church was open to sectarian influences of an organiza-

tional kind, but goes on to affirm that 'to claim that there was anything like a capture of the Matthean church by Qumran so that it thereby became institutionalized under the peculiarly potent impact of the Essenes after A.D. 68 is to outrun the evidence'.

TRUE GREATNESS **18.1–5**

Matthew has abbreviated the narrative element in Mark (9.33–7), and has concentrated on the question of rank in the Kingdom rather than on the actual rivalry among the Twelve.

1. Matthew has already admitted that there would be distinctions in the Kingdom: some shall be called least in the Kingdom of Heaven, and others shall be called great (5.19). The DSS have revealed the importance which was attached to rank in the structure of the Qumran branch of sectarian Judaism, both in the visions of the heavenly future (1QSa) and in the actual life of the community (1QS ii.19–25, vi.8–13.).

2–3. Jesus hails the child as the ideal, not by reason of its innocence or purity, but because of its humility, lack of pretension, and unconcern with status (cf. Gal. 4.1). The verb **turn** does not mean 'return' (to the state of childhood), but 'change direction and conduct', 'alter the way of conceiving greatness'.

4. This verse repeats, in the positive, what was said in the previous verse, and repeats the words of the question in verse 1; an example of Matthew's use of *inclusio*.

5. This verse may belong to the following *pericope*: the link is the **child**: to 'receive (i.e. welcome and care for) a child', or 'one who has become as a child', constitutes an act of humility, such as is required by Jesus of his disciples (cf. Mt. 25.31–46). The words **in my name** mean 'because of me', or 'because I have commanded it'.

ON STUMBLING-BLOCKS **18.6–9**

This series of sayings is held together by the term *skandalon*, 'stumbling block', Paul's *proskomma* (Rom. 14.13; 1 C. 8.9). It indicates a theme which appears often in the first Gospel (5.29–30; 11.6; 15.12; 16.23; 17.27; 24.10; 26.31f.). Verses 8 and 9 of the section are found again at 5.29–30.

6. causes . . . to sin: the late Greek word *skandalizō* (found in the LXX of Dan. and Sir.) means 'to cause to stumble', 'cause to fall or become apostate'.

little ones: not 'children' in the literal sense, but humble disciples to whom, like the poor, the Kingdom is given.

a great millstone: one driven by an animal, as distinct from the small hand-stone in domestic use.

7. This verse is absent from the parallel passage in Mk 9. 42–8; but cf. Mk 14.21. Offences or stumbling blocks (*RSV* 'temptations to sin') are a means of testing true believers and must come; cf. Mt. 24.10, and Paul's statement in 1 C. 11.19: 'There must be factions among you in order that those who are genuine among you may be recognized.' The responsibility of the individual, however, is not abrogated by the divine necessity: cf. below, on Judas, 26.24.

8–9. (Cf. 5.29–30.) The two verses are an abbreviation of Mk 9.43–8. If the position of these sayings in this context reflects the early application of them to the excommunication of unworthy members (or false teachers) from the Christian body, then (in the opinion of some) Matthew's idea of the Church is very similar to that of Paul (e.g. 1 C. 12.12ff.), although he does not use the word *sōma* ('body').

THE LOST SHEEP 18.10–14

In Luke the parable of the Lost Sheep (together with that of the Lost Coin and the Prodigal Son, which have no parallels) is addressed to Jesus' enemies, the Pharisees and the scribes, in defence of his attitude to sinners among the Jews. In Matthew it is addressed to disciples; it is a call to faithful pastorship in the community, to concern for those who are 'going astray' into sin, and away from the Church. The emphasis does not lie on the shepherd's joy (as in Luke), nor on *repentance* (the actual term is avoided), but on persistent searching for the lost in order to win them back. Most exegetes consider that the Lucan parable and setting are original, but, as Bonnard (p. 271) wisely points out, both texts have been influenced in the oral tradition before their literary fixation, and may have echoes of an authentic parable of Jesus, a parable simple and rich enough to be applied to more than one situation; see Stendahl, p. 27, and Jeremias, *Parables*, pp. 38ff.

10. Peculiar to Matthew. Contempt for childlike believers is condemned because they are specially dear to God. Their guardian angels are of the highest rank and most favoured, in that they **always behold the face of my Father**—i.e. they have unrestricted access to his presence. The DSS witness to the belief in angels as sharing in the community's worship (a mystical communion of the earthly and the heavenly) (1QSa ii.9–10), and also to the idea of angels as the guardians of the meek, the needy, despised and orphans (1QH v.20–2).

11. This verse has weak support in the MS. tradition. It probably derives from Lk. 19.10.

12–13. The lost sheep is described as having **gone astray** (*planasthai*). This is a significant term for Matthew in connection with apostasy (24.4, 5, 11, 24). The 'lost' are lapsed members of the Christian community.

14. So it is not the will of my Father: the Greek phrase *estin thelēma emprosthen* represents the Targumic *ra'ᵃwā min ḳᵒḏām* (Targ. Isa. 53.6, 10). Now, *ra'ᵃwā* may mean 'will' or 'good pleasure'; if the Aramaic had been rendered by a term like *eudokia* instead of *thelēma*, the meaning would have been close to that of Lk. 15.7a: 'there is joy in heaven'; but Matthew's interpretation indicates a different line of tradition and application. Cf. Manson, *Sayings*, p. 208. On the disciples, and Christians, as *mikroi*, see Barth, in *TIM*, pp. 121ff.

TREATMENT OF THE ERRING BROTHER 18.15–20

The parable on seeking the straying sheep leads naturally to more specific regulations on how to deal with matters of discipline. The three-step procedure outlined for the correction of a brother (private, before witnesses, and afterwards before the assembly— the Church) is found in the Qumran *Manual of Discipline* (1QS v.25–vi.1, cf. CD ix.2f.); see Davies, *SSM*, pp. 221ff.: 'the legislation in 18.15ff. is more sectarian in its affinities than rabbinic' (p. 224). There is a partial parallel in thought (though not to the procedure outlined) in 1 C. 5.1ff.

15. against you: the words should probably be omitted, as in some of the most important MSS. They are probably due to Lk. 17.4. The reprimand should first be made in strict privacy; if the brother pays attention and heeds what has been said, he will be won back to the family of the Church. Behind the verse there lies Lev. 19.17f.: 'You shall not hate your brother in your heart, but you shall reason with' (the same Greek word in LXX as 'tell him his fault' here, *elenchō*) 'your neighbour, lest you bear sin because of him. You shall not take vengeance or bear any grudge against the sons of your own people, but you shall love your neighbour as yourself.'

16. If private rebuke fails, then the matter is dealt with before witnesses (one or two) on the basis of Dt. 19.15, which is quoted. The Deuteronomic passage is dealing with procedure in what we would call 'secular' cases, not those which affect the life of a religious community.

17. If the brother is not convinced before witnesses, the matter is brought to the Church (*ekklēsia*)—i.e. a local congregation, or Christian synagogue. The penalty for refusing to heed the Church is 'let him be to you as a Gentile and a tax-collector'—i.e. as one with whom the Church has nothing in common, and therefore probably excommunicated. The phrase—which suggests a Jewish Christian community, sharply distinguished from the outside world—seems strange in a Gospel where these very people put Jews to shame by their faith (8.1–11; 9.9–13; 15.21–8). But, apart from their faith, these people were still of the type of those who would not be interested in the Kingdom of God.

18. To the community of disciples or the local congregation is given the power (bestowed on Peter, 16.19, and therefore not exclusively his) of 'binding and loosing'. This may mean excommunication and absolution, or (according to Bonnard, p. 275) the right to pronounce for or against a disciplinary measure proposed against a brother—i.e. not a definite expulsion on their own authority, but the right of applying or not applying already existing penalties.

19–20. The saying on omnipotent prayer is given with reference to the authority of the witnesses, and the famous **where two or three are gathered together** meant as a promise that Christ himself is acting with the Church in matters of discipline. *Pragma* (as in 1 C. 6.1) denotes 'a case (juridical)'. Church discipline is not an action of merely human administration: it may count on the assistance and ratification of the risen Christ. There is a parallel to verse 20 in P. Aboth iii.2: 'If two sit together and the words of the Law [are spoken] between them, the divine Presence rests between them.' These verses should not be interpreted independently of their context as a general declaration on prayer and worship. They allude to the efficacy of prayer (probably fixed in early liturgies of the time) and the presence of Christ in

his Church with reference to disciplinary decisions such as are
outlined in verses 15–18. See Dodd, *Studies*, pp. 58ff.; and K.
Stendahl, *SEA*, xxii–xxiii, 1957–8, pp. 75–86.

ON FORGIVENESS 18.21-35

The conclusion to Matthew's instructions on Church discipline
is concerned with the pardoning of offences which, on all occasions
when friction occurs between brothers, must take precedence over
orderliness within the Church. The emphasis here (both in the
remark to Peter and in the parable) is on personal issues with a
brother, and not behaviour in general; but these and the lack of
community discipline are closely linked in Matthew, as they were
among the Qumran sectaries. Every 'sin' against a brother involves the congregation, and vice versa. Just as the merciful king
and the heavenly Father have to be severe in their judgment on
the unforgiving, so the Church, though ready to pardon, is forced
to judge sternly those who jeopardize the fellowship by their lack
of mercy towards others. The parable has some affinities with that
of the unjust steward (Lk. 16.1–8), but it is unlikely that they both
spring from a common root; see on the parable, E. Fuchs, *Stud.
Evan.*, i, 1959, pp. 487–94.

21. In rabbinic discussion it was frequently regarded as sufficient to forgive one's brother a maximum of four times. Peter's
'seven times' may represent an attempt to exceed Jewish regulations, but it is not enough within the Christian community.

22. The numbers **seven** and **seventy times seven** are
reminiscent of the words of Gen. 4.24 concerning vengeance: 'If
Cain is avenged seven-fold, truly Lamech seventy-seven-fold.'
'The unlimited revenge of primitive man has given place to the
unlimited forgiveness of Christians' (McNeile, p. 268); but it does
not carry with it unlimited opportunity to sin (cf. the *Gospel of the
Nazaraeans*, in *NT Apocrypha*, i, p. 148.) The Greek words may be
taken as meaning 'seventy-seven times' (*RSV*mg) or 'seventy times
seven'.

23. 'The kingdom is not likened to a king, but in the Kingdom
inaugurated by Jesus things will take place as the parable describes' (Bonnard, p. 278). The oriental king was all-powerful,
possessing the right of life and death over his subjects. (**Therefore**
is a link characteristic of Matthew. It attaches the parable to the
answer to Peter; but probably it did not originally belong there,

since it does not say anything on the necessity for *repeated* for-giveness.)

24–5. The sale of the man's wife, children and possessions would realize only a fraction of a debt of such magnitude. Ten thousand talents represents the largest sum imaginable, something like 'a billion pounds'.

26. The verb *makrothumeō* ('have patience') and its cognates are used in the LXX with reference to God's patience in giving further opportunity for repentance before judgment (cf. Exod. 34.6). The promise to pay is one the servant could not possibly hope to fulfil.

27. The king does much more than show the patience asked for: he remitted (or **forgave**) the debt. On the word describing the king's attitude (*splangchnistheis*), see 9.36; 15.32; 20.34., where it is used of Jesus. The term for **debt**—*daneion*—is found only here in the *NT*, and means strictly 'loan'.

28–30. The attitude of the man to his fellow servant is as astonishing as his master's to him. The sum owed him was insig-nificant ('four' or 'five pounds') compared with his own debt.

33. The duty of the servant to forgive is not dependent on ordinary human feelings, but is linked directly to the attitude shown to him: 'as (or because) I had mercy ... so must you.' This, in a sense, is the real point of the story and the key to the obvious allegorization: the unforgiving will be excluded from God's mercy (verse 35); and those who receive God's pardon must show the same forgiving attitude to others.

JESUS LEAVES GALILEE 19.1–2

The usual sentence ends the discourse (cf. 7.28; 11.1; 13.53; 26.1), and marks the end of the fourth main section of the Gospel and the beginning of the fifth (19.3–26.2). Jesus leaves Galilee to go to Perea on his way to Jerusalem; this common route from Galilee to Jerusalem avoided Samaria.

THE IMMINENCE OF THE KINGDOM: CONTROVERSIES AND ESCHATOLOGY 19.3–25.46

The fifth section of the Gospel is very largely shaped by the Marcan outline, since Mark himself presents a real discourse within this part of his work (Mk 13). The first evangelist makes some alterations (see 21.10–17), introduces substantial additions (20.1–16; 21.28–32; 22.1–14), expands Mk 12.37–40 into a full-length speech against the Pharisees, and gives a series of parables after Mark's eschatological discourse. The narratives and controversies presented in the first half of this section sharpen the issues between Jesus and his opponents, and lead up to his renunciation of Pharisaic Judaism.

The second part of the section contains the discourse on the *Eschaton*, the Parousia and the proper way to wait for its coming.

MARRIAGE AND DIVORCE 19.3–12

The problem of divorce, which had already been touched upon in the Sermon on the Mount (5.32, see commentary *in loc.*) is now dealt with in the context of debate. The rabbinic schools of Hillel and Shammai discussed the matter on the basis of the words *ʿerwaṭ dābār*, which mean, when taken in that order: 'some indecency, or unseemly thing', but which, in reversed order, mean: 'a matter of unchastity'. The words appear in Dt. 24.1, the passage to which Jesus' opponents refer (verse 7), and the variant interpretation of them may account for the exceptive clause in verse 9 (as in 5.32), *porneia* being the 'matter of unchastity' (i.e. adultery or some other marital unfaithfulness, rather than marriage within the prohibited degrees). 'By the addition of the clause "for any cause" to the Marcan version Matthew has brought the question of divorce into the realm of strict legal discussion more closely than has Mark. But his treatment, like that of Mark, in no way can be interpreted as a radical departure from the Law of Moses, but only as a radical interpretation of it . . . To forbid divorce was not to annul the law of divorce, but to intensify it. In any case, it should not be overlooked that Gen. 1.27 to which, like Mark, Matthew appeals is itself a part of the written law' (Davies, *SSM*, pp. 104–5). The form of argumentation employed was acceptable in Jewish exegesis: 'the more original, the weightier'; an appeal to God's intention in creation outweighs (but does not therefore annul) the ordinances of Moses.

Verses 11–12 invite to voluntary self-consecration for the sake of the Kingdom of God. Voluntary celibacy was extremely rare among the Jews, but in Essene (Qumran) Judaism it was very highly regarded (1QSa i.25, ii.11). Indeed, abstinence from marital and sexual relations may have been obligatory on all full

priestly members of the sect under the law of the eschatological
(and spiritual) war. This Essene 'puritanism' may have been
derived from Hasidean asceticism (itself a revival of the ancient
Israelite nomadic idea; see R. de Vaux, *Ancient Israel*, 1961, p. 34;
Black, *Scrolls*, p. 30), and may be related to early Christian forms
of asceticism (Black, 'The Tradition of Hasidean-Essene Asceticism: its Origin and Influence', in *Aspects du Judéo-Christianisme*,
1965, pp. 19ff.) A recent study of this *pericope* by A. Isaksson
(*Marriage and Ministry in the New Temple*, 1965) argues that Jesus,
like the Qumran community, was intensely aware of living in
the end of the Age; that he was conscious of being the fulfilment
of the promise of a New Temple, within which his disciples
would live, like priests, after the rules (on marriage) of Ezek. 44.22;
and that the saying on eunuchs reproduces Jesus' use of Isa. 56.4-5,
where the eunuch's fidelity to the covenant is more important as
a sign of his incorporation in the new Temple worship than to
contribute offspring to the community.

3. for any cause: i.e. 'for any cause you please' (Turner, p.
199). In certain Pharisaic circles, the frequency of divorce was
often an open scandal. In CD iv.21 the ideal of a monogamous
union for life (based on the created order) is stated and supported
by the same text as is used here, Gen. 1.27.

4-5. The creator made the two sexes and made them for marriage, as Gen. 2.24 (quoted in verse 5) affirms. The Matthean
quotation includes **and be joined to his wife,** which serves to
emphasize the ideal of indissolubility.

7-8. The Pharisees refer to the Mosaic injunction of Dt. 24.1.
Matthew makes Jesus refer to it, not as a command, but as a
concession (cf. Mk 10.5) given to men because of their stubborn
disobedience to God's will. In Mark, Jesus appeals to Genesis
against the Deuteronomic command; here the Pharisees appeal to
the Mosaic Law against the order of Creation; but Jesus takes
them back to the weightier authority: **from the beginning it
was not so.**

9. The same exception is found at 5.32 in the words *parektos
logou porneias* which seem close to Dt. 24.1 if taken in the order
dᵉbar 'erwāt, and which indicate some form of sexual unfaithfulness
—probably post-marital—rather than illegal marriage within
prohibited degrees. Most commentators regard these words as
having been added by Matthew out of his experience of the

Church's work as it interpreted and 'legalized' (i.e. made practicable) Jesus' view on marriage. This is not necessary; if *porneia*
means 'adultery', then Jewish law *required* a man to divorce his
wife if she committed that act. Indeed, this fact may be assumed in
the other Gospels (as an understood and accepted part of any
teaching on the subject of divorce), but is spelled out only in
Matthew. An adulterous relationship violated the order of
creation, with its monogamous ideal. Therefore if Jesus upheld the
indissolubility of marriage on the basis of Genesis, he must have
permitted divorce for that, and that alone, which necessarily con-
travened the created order. The variants in the text at this point
reflect attempts to harmonize this with Mk 10.11-12 and with 5.32.

10. This verse links the teaching on marriage and divorce with
further teaching on the subject. Since marriage was almost a duty
to the Jew, the disciples are represented as thinking that to have
such firm restrictions around divorce makes marriage disadvan-
tageous or unwelcome to many. They are virtually making the
attractiveness of marriage contingent upon the possibility of easy
divorce! Their words may reflect the Church's concern about the
frequency of Jewish divorce in certain circles.

11. The reply of Jesus indicates that not everybody can receive
and put into practice **this precept** – i.e. either the disciple's
saying in the previous verse ('it is not expedient to marry'), or the
teaching on marriage in verses 3-9, especially verse 6. If the first
alternative is adopted, then Jesus' answer means that not all are
capable of living by that principle (abstinence from marriage),
but only those who are fitted for, and called, to it; in the second
view, the answer means that the radical demand of marriage and
the prohibition of divorce except on the grounds of unchastity
cannot be made a fixed law at all. The former interpretation is
more plausible (see Davies, *SSM*, pp. 393-5, and *contra*, Bonnard,
p. 284) by reason of the presence of verse 12 and the words: **He
who is able to receive this, let him receive it.** Jesus is com-
mending the unmarried state to those whose 'call' demands it, and
who are fitted for it.

12. Those to whom celibacy is **given** are those born impotent,
those made impotent by physical means, and those who have
voluntarily renounced marriage in order to devote all their time
and energies to the service of the Kingdom. The expression
eunuchs by men is a well-known rabbinical phrase: **eunuchs**

for . . . the kingdom of heaven could be original to Jesus, and
Essene Judaism may have provided the spiritual *milieu* which
nurtured the ideal of a self-consecration to a holy life and warfare
which included celibacy (cf. 1 C. 7.7). Not everyone can practise
that state, but it is difficult to avoid the impression that, by implication, the celibate is exalted above the married.

On the question of the authenticity of this regulatory, casuistical material found in Matthew's special source (of which this
section is an example), Davies judiciously says (*SSM*, p. 398):
'The parallels to it from sectarian and other sources might suggest
that it is a secondary accretion, an imposition on Jesus . . . We can,
however, issue the caveat that it should not be too readily assumed
that Jesus may not in fact have given directions for the actualities
of life as well as words of crisis. Or again, is it quite unthinkable
that Jesus had two kinds of ethical teaching, one radical, critical,
kerygmatic to "the crowds", and another, more applied, to those
who had already responded to his appeal?'

JESUS BLESSES THE CHILDREN 19.13-15

At Mt. 18.3 children were shown as examples of the humility to
be followed by all who would enter the Kingdom. Here the question of the children's place in the Kingdom is treated for its own
sake. There are no grounds for thinking that the disciples represent a common Jewish attitude, and that Jesus is enunciating a
new and more gracious principle.

13. Children were often brought to rabbis and other prominent
teachers to be blessed by the laying-on of hands. The rebuke by
the disciples is not based on jealousy or impatience, but on lack
of understanding of Jesus' ministry; they were annoyed that he was
being stopped on his way to Jerusalem. Were they hastening him
onwards to the city in the hope that he would make a triumphant
messianic display there?

14. do not hinder them: the phrase (*mē kōlyete*) is found in
connection with baptism (3.14; Ac. 8.36; 10.47; 11.17). Cullmann
(*Baptism*, pp. 71–80) suggests that it was a technical term used in
baptismal rites; if so (and the view has been disputed) this *logion*
could be intended to relate to the baptism of infants.

POSSESSIONS AND THE KINGDOM **19.16-30**

The structure of the section is the same in all three Synoptics (cf. Mk 10.17-31; Lk. 18.18-30), but significant differences are found in the details (see below). Here, as often in Matthew, the teaching is directed, not just to any outsider to the Church, but to the disciples—i.e. to the members of the Christian community addressed in the Gospel.

16. Matthew simplifies the introduction in Mark, and makes the questioner a 'young man' (verse 22), whereas in Luke he is a 'ruler'—an important person: the adjective **good** is transferred (by Matthew) from 'Master' to the question: **what good deed?** Some think that the Marcan form, leading to: 'Why do you call me good? No one is good but God alone', was altered to avoid the suggestion that Jesus was not good, and was discriminating between himself and God; but it is unwise to read too much into the change; see Intro. pp. 64-5.

eternal life: a designation of the life approved by God and to which access to the Kingdom (present and eschatological) is promised (cf. the rabbinic 'life of the age to come').

17. God alone is good, and his will, which leads to life, is revealed in the Law.

18. The article (*to*) before the first commandment cited (peculiar to Matthew) may reflect the influence of primitive Christian catachesis, like '*the* Our Father'.

19. The quotations from the latter half of the Decalogue were combined with Lev. 19.18 in Jewish catechism (cf. also Rom. 13.9).

21-2. Jesus does not criticize the man's confession of obedience to the Law by offering a deeper interpretation of the commandments (cf. the *Gospel of the Nazaraeans*, in *NT Apocrypha*, 1, pp. 148-9); he invites him to choose the way that leads to 'perfection', the goal of full Christian development, which involves obedience. Jesus does not here institute a category of 'the perfect', superior to ordinary Christians (cf. Barth, in *TIM*, pp. 95ff.). Following Jesus is the crucial factor. The selling of possessions (which precedes it in the injunction) is a special requirement in circumstances where possessions form a stumbling-block to discipleship. Poverty is not a rule of universal application—Jesus did not make it so in his call to men—but undue concern over wealth, according to the teaching of the Gospels and especially of Luke, could easily impede discipleship. It is more difficult to give wealth to the poor and needy than to surrender it on entry to a religious community for its use; cf. 1QS i.12.

23. The fact that the price was too high for the young man prompts the words on the dangers of wealth.

24. The saying has a proverbial cast, and is quoted in the Koran (vii.38). A very similar saying (with 'elephant' instead of 'camel') is found in the Talmud (B. Berak. 55b). It is a way of indicating something unusually difficult, well-nigh impossible.

25–6. 'To be saved' is equivalent to following Jesus and entering into the kingdom of God. The salvation of rich men, though beyond the ability of men, is within the power of God, who can inspire them with a new sense of values.

27. Peter, as spokesman for the group, asks about the reward for the disciples who had in fact left all and followed Jesus.

28. in the new world: lit. 'in the regeneration' (*en tē palingenesia*). The term occurs only here and at Tit. 3.5, where it refers to baptism. Josephus used it of the restoration of the land of Israel, and it has some of that concrete connotation in Matthew; Jewish hopes awaited a renewal both of the land and of the entire world (cf. Rev. 21. 1–5). But this hope is transformed by the rôle which Jesus plays in it as Son of Man, the vindicated and vindicating judge of the Last Days (cf. 21.31–46), although it is still expressed in the traditional apocalyptic concepts. The twelve disciples will share in the Son of Man's dominion in the new age: **judging** is used in the sense of governing, ruling (cf. the *OT* 'judge'; and Ps. 2.10; 1 Mac. 9.73; Ps. Sol. 17.26). The **twelve tribes** are the new Israel, probably the Church. Kümmel (*Promise*, p. 47) regards this saying in its Matthean form as, in essence, an authentic word of Jesus, a promise to the Twelve which represents Jesus' claim to win the whole nation to whom he has been sent; but see Tödt, pp. 62ff.

29. The promise to all disciples (as distinct from the Twelve) is that those who have sacrificed in order to confess Christ and to be his disciples (**for my name's sake**) will receive 'many times' (the original reading (cf. *RSV* mg); Mark also has 'a hundredfold') the amount they have surrendered. Mark's clear distinction between reward 'already in this age' and reward 'in the age to come' has been omitted; Matthew puts all the reward in the future, and to obtain it is coincident with entering eternal life.

30. There are many people, rich, powerful, and great now,

who will be judged different at the End: and the poor, the meek
and the sinners will be the first in the Kingdom, and will have a
great reward. The statement of the reversal of conditions on earth
is found again (in reverse order) in 20.16, where it is more suitably
placed. Probably Matthew regarded the intervening parable
(20.1ff.) as an illustration or explanation of the saying.

THE PARABLE OF THE WORKERS IN THE VINEYARD 20.1-16

This parable, which is peculiar to Matthew, is explicitly linked to
a theme in the preceding passage. Verse 16 (which probably
forms the right conclusion to the parable) clarifies 19.30: the
workers at the eleventh hour, hired last of all, are called 'first', the
first to experience the generosity of the vineyard owner; those who,
though hired first, grumble at the owner's action, put themselves
in the 'last' rank. The main point of the parable is not concerned
with vocation, nor with the equality of all men before God, nor
with the equal value in God's sight of all work done for the
Kingdom: its main concern is to declare the sovereign grace and
good-will of God, which welcomes (in Jesus) the 'late-comers' into
the Kingdom. It is addressed to those who resembled the grumblers, those who (like the Pharisees) criticized the acceptance of
the despised, the outcasts and sinners, into the Kingdom of God
(cf. Jeremias, *Parables*, pp. 33–8, and Dodd, *Parables*, p. 123). The
theme of the parable is therefore reflected in the parables of Lk.
15 ('Do you begrudge my generosity?' (verse 15)). It is true
that the story is so neatly linked to the 'first–last' concept that there
are grounds for thinking that the parable's real theme is reversal
of human situations in face of the divine judgment: but on the
interpretation outlined above, the parable is an *explanation* of the
'first–last' theme, and not an illustration.

   1. The formula does not mean that the Kingdom is like a householder, but that the grace or good-will which characterizes the
life of the Kingdom (and which is not opposed to justice or right,
but transcends them) is like that shown by this particular householder. The parable therefore allows itself to become an exhortation to disciples, and to the Church. The **vineyard** is a well-known
image from the *OT* and Jewish teaching, and usually connotes
Israel (Isa. 5; Jer. 12.10).

   2. The agreed price, a *denarius* per day (i.e. about 7 pence),
was then a workman's average daily wage.

3–7. The labourers were unemployed, and so loitered or lounged in the market place waiting for someone to hire them. On being hired at various times up until 4 or 5 p.m. (because of the urgency of the work, or possibly because the first groups did not work hard enough) they are promised whatever is right (*dikaion*): this promise is fulfilled in an action of large-hearted generosity. There is no need to suggest a hint of Paulinism here; the story is logical and self-consistent.

8. Some see in the words **when evening came** a veiled allusion to the Judgment. But neither this nor the allegorical explanation of the **steward** as Jesus is necessary: both features form part of the general setting of the story. All the workers are paid 'the wage' (the noun is singular), i.e. the *denarius* agreed on in verse 2.

9–10. It is only when they see the 'last' receive their pay that those hired at the beginning of the day expect to receive more.

11–12. The grumblers complain that the owner has not considered the fact that they have borne **the burden of the day and the scorching heat** which sometimes drove workers from the fields. It is surely straining the parable to find in this an implied complaint that Jesus is not treating fairly those who have borne the burden of the Law, but makes them equal with outcasts and sinners. The verb *epoiēsan* in the sense of 'laboured', or **worked,** may be an Aramaism, but cf. Exod. 36.1 (LXX).

13. Friend: *hetaire*, a term used in friendly remonstrance; cf. 22.12; 26.50.

15. Do you begrudge my generosity? *RSV* mg. 'Is your eye evil because I am good?' renders the Greek in literal fashion, but the interpretation given in the text is correct. The 'evil eye' was an old and well-known Biblical expression (cf. Prov. and Sir.) to designate conditions of envy and jealousy, and lack of generous feeling: cf. 6.22–3.

16. See the introductory note to this passage (p. 285). Some MSS. add here the words of Mt. 22.14; but they do not suit the context, and *RSV* omits them with the best textual authorities.

THE THIRD PREDICTION OF THE PASSION **20.17–19**

Matthew follows Mk 10.32–4 in this third general prediction of the Passion. What has been said on 16.21 and 17.22–3 is, in the main, applicable here. The final journey to Jerusalem, the reference to the Gentiles as tormentors and executioners, and the mention of crucifixion are introduced for the first time. Matthew omits to mention the disciples following behind Jesus in astonishment and fear (Mk 10.32).

17. Before setting out for the city (probably to attend the festival), Jesus takes aside the Twelve from the company of pilgrim disciples so that he may explain to them what is going to happen.

18. The fact that the Son of Man will be condemned to death (*katakrinō* indicates that Jesus' death will follow a trial to establish legal responsibility: it will not be a murder without legal preliminaries.

19. The Jewish authorities will hand over Jesus to the Gentiles (i.e. the Romans), who will mock, scourge and crucify him. This does not imply that the Jewish people, as a whole, are exculpated; they are involved by virtue of the decisions of their leaders. In the other Synoptics death by crucifixion is not mentioned before the actual Passion story; that form of execution was not a Jewish punishment (M. San. vii.1), and some of the details here may well have been added to make the prediction correspond exactly with what took place. As in the other predictions, the mention of the Resurrection is very brief and, in the opinion of many, does not fit into the context well; see the remarks on the question of the authenticity of the Passion predictions in 16.21; 17.22f.

SUFFERING AND SERVICE **20.20-8**

The question of rank in the Kingdom (raised in 18.1-5) is now specifically answered in connection with the request of Zebedee's sons. The words of Jesus make it clear that primacy, or 'greatness', in the Kingdom does not depend on ambition and authority, but on suffering and service. The section finds its unity in verse 28 (cf. Mk 10.45; Lk. 22.27), which presents the Son of Man as the supreme example of the servant figure who suffers for many. It is unlikely that a story so discrediting to two leading apostles is wholly a product of early Christian teaching and piety, and this fact suggests that there is a kernel of historical teaching in the passage.

20. Matthew presents the mother as making the request, whereas, in Mark, James and John speak for themselves. It may be that the first evangelist is attempting to protect the reputation of the disciples, or to suggest that Peter was not actually disregarded

by James and John. Verse 22 shows that the mother's part in
the event is a later addition; only the two sons of Zebedee are
addressed.

21. in your kingdom: cf. Mark's 'in your glory'. The 'kingdom' may be that of Christ (cf. 13.41ff.; 25.31ff.)—namely, the
Church—and that view would support the suggestion that the
original message of the story (or episode) had been applied to
competition for leadership in the early Christian community.

on your right hand . . . your left: such locations on either
side of an important person indicate positions of honour and
authority (cf. Josephus, *Ant.* vi.xi.9).

22. The **cup** here (as in 26.39) is to be interpreted in terms of
OT imagery. It is the cup of judgment or retribution (cf. Ps. 75.9;
Isa. 51.17f.; Jer. 25.15ff.; etc.), the acceptance of which involves
trial and suffering. The saying on baptism (in Mark) is only found
in late mss. of Matthew.

23. James died a martyr's death in Jerusalem around A.D. 44
(Ac. 12.2), but the evidence for John's early martyrdom is extremely dubious. There is therefore no firm ground for regarding
the saying of Jesus as a *vaticinium ex eventu*, when John had been
killed. In any case, it is suffering, not necessarily martyrdom,
which is here envisaged as the fate of the apostles.

24. The indignation of the other disciples (arising probably
from jealousy rather than from humility) provides the setting for
the second part of the *pericope*, dealing with the 'greatness' which
will be characteristic of Jesus' Kingdom.

25–7. Jesus declares that in the community of his disciples
'greatness' will not be demonstrated in terms of power and
authority, as it is among the Gentiles (i.e. among the Romans
primarily), but will he assessed in terms of service.

28. The Matthean and Marcan texts of this *logion* are almost
exactly the same. That it occurs in an ethical setting and not as a
theological or kerygmatic statement should put us on guard
against pressing it too much for christological significance (Stendahl). The word **ransom** (*lutron*) here indicates 'means of emanci-
pation'; only in legal contexts, where the actual price is stated,
does the *lutron* complex of words (and the Hebrew *gā'al* and *pādāh*)
possess the strict 'ransom' significance in the *OT*: in the Psalms
and prophetic literature the words refer to the action of liberating
(see Hill, pp. 53–6). The presence in this saying for **for many**

(*anti pollōn*)—a Semitic way of expressing 'all'—gives to the term *lutron* a substitutionary significance; the death of Jesus will be the means of liberating the whole people (Israel) from captivity and slavery (to sin; cf. 1.21). The atoning value of the sufferings of the righteous martyrs was a theme expressed in the Maccabean writings (2 Mac. 7.37; 4 Mac. 6.28; 17.21f.). This may be the background against which the meaning of this saying is best interpreted. Although the actual language of Isa. 53.11–12 is hardly reflected in the saying (see Barrett, in *NTE*, pp. 1–18), it cannot be doubted that the thought and atmosphere of the passage from the Servant songs has contributed something to this verse.

The genuineness of the saying has been much discussed (see the commentaries on Mk 10.45), but no argument has yet been advanced which is so strong as to make it impossible for us to believe that Jesus could have spoken of his death in the kind of terms reproduced here—of vicarious and representative suffering for his people, in the terms of the old Jewish martyr theology. Perhaps it is the doctrine read into the language that has caused difficulty in the acceptance of the *logion* as dominical; see Taylor, pp. 445f. and Hill, pp. 77–81. The terminology is like that used by Paul to describe the significance of Jesus' death, but it is not completely Pauline.

JESUS HEALS TWO BLIND MEN NEAR JERICHO **20.29–34**

In Mk 10.46ff., and Lk. 18.35ff. there is only one blind man, named Bartimaeus in Mk 10.46. Matthew had *two* demoniacs at 8.28. In all three Gospels the incident occurs in the same place; the significance is probably two-fold: (i) to show that he who goes to Jerusalem to suffer is nevertheless the Son of David, as the blind call him; and (ii) to demonstrate the humility of Jesus in stopping to help needy blind men by the roadside—this Son of David is come 'not to be served, but to serve'. A similar healing incident is narrated by Matthew in 9.27–31 (completing the types of miracle enumerated in 11.4), which many have regarded as a doublet of this *pericope*. There are differences, however. In the earlier story the interest lies on the faith of the blind men, and the healed persons are admonished not to divulge the miracle; here there is no place for secrecy, in spite of the crowd's attitude (verse 31). Each story as presented fits neatly into the place accorded to it in the tradition. On the question of historicity, see Taylor, pp. 446–7.

K

29. Matthew and Mark make the incident occur as Jesus was leaving Jericho, but Luke as he was entering the city. The fact that Jesus is followed by a great crowd suggests that messianic interest and enthusiasm were mounting as Jesus neared Jerusalem.

30. The presence of two blind men, rather than one, may be due to the fact that two persons was the minimum number of witnesses required to authenticate an incident or fact (here Jesus' messiahship, as well as the actual healing). **Son of David** (see note on 9.27) was the most popular name for the Messiah, and implies nationalistic hopes; cf. Ps. Sol. 17. That the restoration of sight was to be a sign of the messianic era is shown in Isa. 29.18; 35.5.

31. The merciful act of Jesus proceeds in spite of the opposition of the crowds (see introductory note on 20.1–16).

32–4. Matthew simplifies the Marcan narrative and introduces the mention of Jesus' active compassion (*splanchnistheis*; cf. 9.36; 14.14; 15.32; 18.27) and his healing by touching (cf. 8.3; 9.20; 14.36; etc.). The healed man's following after Jesus is a sign of discipleship.

THE ENTRY INTO JERUSALEM 21.1–9

Jesus enters Jerusalem from the east (from Jericho), and this brings him over the Mount of Olives, where this messianic manifestation is set. The mount was significant within Jewish eschatology as the place of (messianic) judgment (Zech. 14.4) and of resurrection (cf. 27.52f.). The Gospels present Jesus as arranging the entry himself; all concern for secrecy is gone. The significance of the incident has been variously estimated (e.g., that a spontaneous outburst of acclamation from disciples and pilgrims was later interpreted in a messianic sense under the influence of Zech. 9.9, a messianic cult legend; for other theories, see Taylor, pp. 451ff.). But it does seem certain that the entry was a declaration of messianic dignity which laid claim to the homage of the people, and at the same time revealed Jesus' own conception of that messiahship: those who were able and inclined to understand knew what the 'acted parable' meant. The occasion of the entry may have been the Feast of Dedication (December), or, more probably (with T. W. Manson, *BJRL*, XXXIII, 1951, pp. 271–82), at the time of the Feast of Tabernacles, i.e. six months before the Passover season. The Matthean narrative is distinguished from the other Synoptic accounts by its careful construction and air of solemnity, and by the *OT* quotation in verse 3.

1. Although the village of Bethphage ('house of figs') was separated from Jerusalem by the Kidron valley, it was regarded as part of the suburbs of the city, and was reckoned as being within the city from the point of view of those making arrangements for the Jewish festival.

2. That Jesus speaks of two animals (and later seems to sit on two beasts, verse 7) is due to the care with which Matthew attempts to establish that Zech. 9.9 is fulfilled; but the words of the prophet: **on an ass, and on a colt, the foal of an ass** are an example of Semitic parallelism indicating one animal only. Lindars, p. 114, suggests that the presence of the two animals is not a misunderstanding of a Hebrew parallelism, but a means of emphasizing the immaturity of the colt (cf. Mk 11.2), in that it was not yet separated from its mother, and had to be mentioned in the closest possible relation to her.

3. Lord: the word could refer to Jesus, or to God, or even to the owner of the beast.

4–5. The quotation is from Zech. 9.9, introduced by words from Isa. 62.11. In this *OT* citation Matthew makes explicit what was implicit in the other evangelists: that Jesus acted in deliberate fulfilment of the prophet's words: the Davidic king is 'humble, mounted upon an ass' (contrast Ps. Sol. 17.22ff.). The quotation follows the M.T. and LXX up to **is coming to you,** but then surprisingly omits *dikaios kai sōzōn autos* (Hebrew, *ṣaddîq wᵉnôšāʿ hûʾ*). This has the effect of leaving the emphasis where Matthew desires it to fall—on the Messiah's humility; see Stendahl, pp. 118–20, and Barth, in *TIM*, pp. 129f. Gundry remarks that Matthew may also have reasoned that at this time Jesus was hardly the just and victorious King according to the prevalent Jewish expectation (p. 120).

6–7. Matthew abbreviates the narrative by omitting how Jesus' prediction came true. The garments were put on the animals and Jesus sat **thereon**—on the cloaks, or on the animals.

8. The homage suggested by the spreading of clothes in the road is illustrated in 2 Kg. 9.13. The cutting of branches from the trees would suit the festivities of Tabernacles; cf. 1 Mac. 13.51 and 2 Mac. 10.7 for an account of Simon Maccabaeus' entry to

Jerusalem and the Feast of Dedication in which boughs, palms, and praises are all mentioned.

9. The cry **Hosanna** (late Hebrew for *Hôšî'a-nā*; cf. Ps. 118.25) was both a cry for assistance: 'Save now! Help!' (2 Sam. 14.4; 2 Kg. 6.26), and also an invocation of blessing—even a greeting or acclamation; the latter is emphasized here. The second part of the exclamation comes from verse 26 of Ps. 118 which was used liturgically at the feasts of Tabernacles, Dedication, and Passover. **he who comes** (*ho erchomenos*) may have been a messianic title (cf. 3.11; 11.3); but the psalm cannot have been used at this point as messianic acclamation—the authorities would have been compelled to intervene. The verse was used as a formula of greeting addressed to pilgrims approaching the Temple. **Hosanna in the highest:** perhaps 'May God (in heaven) save him', words which combine prayer, blessing and thanksgiving. This phrase had undoubtedly become part of the liturgical terminology of the early Church at the time of the composition of the first Gospel: then the emphasis was on the acclamation of him who had already come and delivered his people, and who would come with final deliverance at the last day, or in the worship of the Church (cf. Didachē, x.6).

JESUS IN THE TEMPLE **21.10–17**

Following the Marcan sequence of events, Matthew makes the entry and enthusiastic welcome for Jesus in Jerusalem precede the cleansing of the Temple; but he is not so interested, as is Mark, in the actual day of the week on which this latter event took place. According to Mark, Jesus entered the Temple and looked around, and then retired to Bethany, returning on the following morning to cleanse the shrine. Matthew's narrative again simplifies Mark's, and it omits some of the details, especially Mk 11.16 and the reference to the Gentiles in the quotation from Isa. 56.7, which (for Mark) points to Jesus' concern to restore to the Gentiles their rights within the Temple, i.e. in the court of the Gentiles; see Lightfoot, pp. 62–6.

10–11. Matthew alone makes mention of the exceedingly strong emotion (the Greek word *eseisthē* is used elsewhere of earthquakes!) which accompanied the welcome of Jesus to the city. Curiosity is aroused, and the crowds (presumably of Galilean pilgrims) hail him as **the prophet Jesus from Nazareth in**

Galilee. By this address may be meant simply 'a prophet well known in Galilee', and as yet not well known in Jerusalem, and therefore evoking an outburst of local enthusiasm from his home supporters; on the other hand, there may be a reference (on the evangelist's part) to 'the eschatological prophet' of the last days awaited in fufilment of Dt. 18.18, a text which was undoubtedly important in early Christianity (Ac. 3.22; 7.37; Jn 1.21; 7.40), and before that in Qumran circles.

12. Within the Temple area, all kinds of traffic in the necessities for sacrifice (animals, wine, oil, etc.) were apparently authorized. The **money-changers** were engaged in the task of changing the Greek and Roman coins possessed by pilgrims into the standard Temple currency, in which the half-shekel of Temple tax had to be paid. Matthew does not mention the prohibition by Jesus of the carrying of any vessel through the Temple (Mk 11.16), a practice which desecrated the holy place by making it into a short-cut (M. Berak. ix.5).

13. The quotation is from Isa. 56.7 (without the words 'for all nations, or peoples' which are so important for Mark's interpretation), and the last part of the sentence: **a den of robbers** is an allusion to Jer. 7.11. The restoration of the rights of Gentiles in the Temple courts is not emphasized here. It is as purifier of the desecrated Temple that Matthew presents Jesus, not just as an indignant reformer. His action is in fulfilment of Mal. 3.1ff., and therefore is taken as a messianic sign to those who could understand it. The purification of Jerusalem and the Temple formed a striking part of Jewish expectation (cf. Ps. Sol. 17.30) and the action of Jesus poses the question of his eschatological authority over the Holy Place.

Although there are difficulties with the Synoptic dating of the cleansing of the Temple, a time towards the end of Jesus' ministry seems more likely than at the beginning, where John places it. This divergence is very probably due to John's concern to group together at the beginning of his Gospel narratives pointing to the replacement of things Jewish (ritual, Temple and worship) by the new realities in Christ. In John's thought the Temple is not just reformed, but completely transformed, giving way to a new worship 'in Jesus Christ'.

14-15. The healing of the blind and the lame strengthens the messianic impressions of the event—the Lord of the Temple is the

Lord of health. But the presence of the blind and lame in the Temple is itself significant. According to the Qumran *Rule of the Congregation* (1QSa ii.5–22), the lame, blind, deaf and dumb were excluded from the congregation and from the messianic banquet (cf. also 1QM vii.4–5, which excludes the afflicted from taking part in the messianic battle). Pharisaic oral law also excluded the blind and the lame from 'appearing before the Lord in his temple' (to comply with Dt. 16.16) and from making sacrifice (M. Hagig. i.1); cf. Gärtner, *Temple*, p. 111. The violation of Jewish exclusiveness (based on purity laws) and of decorum (children shouting their messianic acclamations in the Temple precincts) would have scandalised the Temple authorities.

16. Matthew cites Ps. 8.3 according to the LXX which had rendered the Hebrew word for 'strength' or 'power' by the word 'glory', or **praise** (*ainos*). Verses 5–7 of this psalm were used in a messianic sense in early Christianity (Heb. 2.6; 1 C. 15.27; Eph. 1.22), but verse 3 is here employed in a polemical fashion. Children sing the glory of God (or of the Messiah Jesus) to confound his enemies.

17. During the Passover festival (and other festivals too) many pilgrims had to lodge outside the crowded city, and so Jesus spent the night at Bethany, on the eastern slopes of the Mount of Olives.

THE CURSING OF THE FIG-TREE AND THE POWER OF FAITH
21.18–22

Matthew presents a version of this story shorter and simpler than that in Mk 11.12ff. The fact that both evangelists place the story in the context of Jesus' visit to the Temple suggests that it is meant to be interpreted as a prophetic action prefiguring the judgment brought by the Messiah upon the Jewish nation and the strictness of Jewish religion, neither of which bore the fruit which by right was expected from them—they gave promise of fulfilment but in fact produced nothing! It has been suggested that the incident is a dramatization of the parable in Lk. 13.6–9; but that story is governed by the theme of delay in judgment, whereas this miracle is concerned with immediate judgment. The fact that the ideas of sterility and the absence of fruit are deeply rooted in the *OT* (cf. Jer. 8.13) as descriptions of the sinful state of God's people may be the clue to the origin of this story as an affirmation of the messianic judgment on an unfruitful Israel. It is likely that the linking of verses 20-2 to the fig-tree incident illustrates another lesson drawn from the story in the teaching and preaching of the early Church—namely, the omnipotence of prayer. The words on prayer were probably separated from the story in the earliest tradition.

18. Matthew seems to locate the event nearer the city and the Temple than does Mark's 'when they came from Bethany'.

19. The first evangelist omits the Marcan statement: 'it was not the season for figs', and this eliminates a difficulty. Matthew assumes that Jesus should have found figs on the tree, as the Messiah ought to have found faith and righteousness among his people. The months of June and September are the usual times of fruit on fig trees, though earlier figs have been discovered. If the latter month is the occasion here, then it supports Manson's dating of the entry and cleansing of the Temple at the Festival of Tabernacles. Jesus' action in cursing the tree seems totally out of character; the only way to preserve some element of historicity here is to assume that it was an act of prophetic symbolism which became interpreted in the tradition as a miracle confirming Jesus' supernatural power.

20. According to Mark, it was the next morning that the disciples discovered the withered tree and Peter remembered the curse: but Matthew emphasizes the immediacy of the results of judgment.

21. The answer of Jesus to the question 'How?' repeats the substance of 17.20, but shifts attention from the smallest effective amount of faith to the opposition of faith to doubt. If disciples do not doubt, they will perform comparable actions—a saying which may reflect concern about the absence of miracles in the early Church. The pictorial saying about 'casting this mountain into the sea' (and if by 'sea' is meant the Lake of Galilee, then the saying probably comes from an earlier period in Jesus' ministry) may be a further illustration of judgment on the Temple: the 'mountain' could be 'the mountain of the Lord of Hosts', the Temple-mountain (Isa. 2.2f.).

22. This saying does not make fulfilment the automatic consequence of praying with faith. Rather it declares that the requests made in prayer must be submitted to a single condition—namely, that they can be, and are, effectively presented with faith—which means, for the *NT*, submission to the sovereign will of God (so Bonnard, p. 309).

THE QUESTION ABOUT AUTHORITY 21.23–7

Between 21.23 and 22.46 there are recorded five controversies between Jesus and the authorities of Israel's religion. They are presented in the form of question and answer, a method used in connection with controversy material in the Talmud. In this first controversy Matthew follows Mk 11.27–33 closely, and the clash with the chief priests and elders is told 'with force and precision' (Stendahl).

23. Jesus is teaching in the Temple, in one of the porticos around the court of the Gentiles, when **the chief priests** (high functionaries of the Temple, former high priests, and members of priestly families—mostly Sadduceean) **and elders** question the nature and source of his authority, presumably for cleansing the Temple (**these things**). Since no particular teaching is mentioned, the question at issue cannot be related to the fact that Jesus was (probably) not an ordained rabbi; it was a question about his competence to *act* as he was doing (in arranging his entry to the city, cleansing the Temple, etc.). Was his authority from God, from men, or from himself? Determining the identity of Jesus is achieved by finding out the justification of, or the final authority for, his activity.

24. To answer with another question is typical of rabbinic debate. It is not necessarily a means of avoiding the issue, but it can be a means of leading to the right answer, or of trapping an opponent into conceding a point which implies the answer to the original question (e.g. verse 41).

25. The question asked by Jesus posed the inevitable alternatives: his authority, like that of John the Baptist before him, is either from God or from men. If the religious authorities could not make up their minds about the one because of acute embarrassment or fear, they were incapable of pronouncing judgment on the other. Their incompetence as teachers had to be admitted ('**We do not know**'). Note that John's significance seems to be dependent on his baptism rather than on his preaching.

THE PARABLE OF THE TWO SONS **21.28-32**

This parable, which is found only in Matthew but may have the
same origin as the story about the two sons (Lk. 15.11–32), forms
part of an important trilogy of parables (21.28–22.14), all of
which deal with the theme of Jesus' rejection by those who ought
to have received him—namely, the leaders of his people. It is
verse 32 which links the story to what precedes by the mention of
John the Baptist (see, especially, verse 25b). Whether verse 32
came to Matthew in the tradition attached to the parable (so
Jeremias, *Parables*, p. 8of.), or whether he added it to the parable
in order to provide it with a setting in the Gospel, is difficult to
say. The first alternative seems more likely, although the application of the parable in verse 31 has the appearance of a conclusion
by reason of the solemn words: 'Truly I say to you.' The word
'repent' is found in verse 29 and again in 32. The historicity of the
parable is not at all impossible. It is a remarkably coherent story;
it does far more than 'vindicate the good news' (Jeremias); it is a
polemic which surely rings true to the situation obtaining in
Jesus' ministry. The publicans and prostitutes who had refused
the will of God expressed in the Law turn now towards God and
enter the Kingdom inaugurated by Jesus, while the leaders of the
people, who officially had always given obedience to God, turn
away now from his messiah.

28. As in 17.25 and 18.12, the words **What do you think?** (a
phrase peculiar to Matthew, and suggesting his own editorial work
in response to the needs and questioning of his own community)
are addressed by Jesus to his adversaries: they introduce a parable
of a polemical nature. The meaning of the parable for Matthew
is that the **man** represents God and the **two sons** are the two
main categories of the Jewish people in the time of Jesus: the
'sinners'—i.e. those who took but slight interest in the Law and
rabbinical prescriptions, and the 'righteous'—i.e. those (especially
the ecclesiastical authorities) who remained faithful to the official
religion. Both classes are 'children' of God, but the difference—
according to this teaching—is assessed in terms, not of piety or of
profession, but of *acts* performed or omitted.

29–30. The manuscript tradition has considerable variation,
but basically they preserve two alternatives: (i) where the son who
said 'No' but repented is mentioned first and regarded as the

obedient one (so most manuscripts); (ii) where the one who said 'Yes' but did not go is said to 'have done the Father's will' (D and other MSS). The second interpretation is probably due to the fact that copyists saw in the story a contrast between Jews (who said 'yes' when the Law was offered to the nations at Sinai) and pagans. But the original emphasis seems to have been on a division of the *Jewish people*, both in the past and in the critical present, and therefore the first alternative is better. Those who once refused God have now repented (and return to God); those who were historically 'righteous' have now rejected the Christ.

31. go . . . before you: probably 'take your place in', rather than 'precede'.

32. This verse recalls Lk. 7.29-30—if not its actual words, at least its sense—and this suggests that here we are in the presence of literary construction, and that the verse did not belong to the original parable. The words **in the way of righteousness** (which some try to interpret as a reference to John's own personal right-eousness) denotes that 'way of righteousness, in obedience to God, which John demanded of those who heard him and which he himself practised': this is the path that leads to the Kingdom; see Hill, pp. 124f., and Benoit, p. 132.

THE PARABLE OF THE VINEYARD 21.33-46

This parable continues the theme of conflict between Jesus and the leaders of his people. Since the details of the story have significance for its understanding (the 'owner of the vineyard' represents God, the 'vineyard' is Israel, the 'tenants' are the leaders of the nation, the 'servants' are the prophets, and the 'son' is Christ), it must be regarded as an allegory (see Black, *BJRL*, XLII, 1959-60, pp. 273-87; Brown, pp. 254-64). Basing his examination of the story on the differences between the Marcan (12.1-12) and Matthean texts and on the fact that pre-Christian Judaism did not apply the title 'Son of God' to the expected messiah, Jeremias (*Parables*, p. 76) claims that the original parable was meant to vindicate the offer of the Gospel to the humble poor **(other tenants,** verse 41); the rebellious leaders of the nation had rejected it. Dodd (*Parables*, pp. 124-32) tries to find the original *milieu* of the story in the revolutionary attitude of Galilean peasants (aroused by Zealotism) towards foreign landlords in the half century before the revolt of A.D. 66.

W. G. Kümmel (in *Aux Sources*, pp. 120–38) argues that it is impossible to work back from the allegorical story to an original simple parable, and that the historical *milieu* is not Galilee during the ministry of Jesus, but the Church of the first century influenced by Isa. 5. This view is probably too negative and drastic. It is certain that Jesus was confronted by opposition from the leaders of his people; and, in speaking of this situation, is it not possible that Isa. 5 was in his mind? An original short parable may well have been built upon by the faith of the early Church as it exploited its allegorical possibilities. It should be noted that the introduction of the 'only' (or 'beloved') son depends on the logic of the story, not on theological motivation. The outrageous behaviour of the tenants must be exhibited; how better than by bringing on to the scene the landlord's son? Probably the Church early identified the 'son' with Christ, but in the suggested original parable the son will have represented simply God's final messenger.

33. The verse quotes Isa. 5.2 rather freely, probably following Mark, who does not follow exactly the LXX. The list of precautions which the owner took underlines his care for his vineyard and his absolute proprietary rights over it (**hedge, tower**). He let it out to tenants, who were to be responsible, in his absence, for its control and its produce, part if not all of which were to be given to him under the contract.

34. Matthew's words: **When the season of fruit drew near** allude clearly (more clearly than Mark or Luke) to the decisive time when God will reckon with his people; *engizō* is a word used often of the Kingdom's near approach or arrival. According to Mark and Luke, only one servant was sent to receive the portion of produce: in Matthew the servants are sent to get the whole crop; in this Mark and Luke are nearer to the realities of agricultural organisation in their time. In Matthew the **servants** represent the prophets, and the allegorical element (already present, of course, in Mark's version) is heightened throughout, providing a sequence of events which is an exact outline of the history of redemption.

35. Again Matthew develops the Marcan tradition. The servants are beaten, killed or stoned (common forms of violence in Jesus' time); the stoning of prophets is noted in Mt. 23.37 and Lk. 13.34. It is of interest to note that the penalty of stoning is meted out to (among others) soothsayers or persons with a familiar spirit (M. San. vii.4). It may be that the implication in the stoning is that the people condemned the genuine prophets, or servants, as *false* prophets.

36. other servants, more than the first: this may contain an allusion to the Jewish classification of prophets into early and latter.

37. Matthew omits Mark's 'beloved'. The son would come vested with the authority of the father, and could be expected to inspire the same respect as would be given to the father. As indicated above, it is widely held that the title 'Son of God' (which is more frequent in Matthew than in Mark or Luke) was not part of Jewish messianic terminology in the time of Jesus: when it does appear (Enoch 105.2; 4 Ezra 7.28f.; 13.13; etc.), it is due to interpolation or to mistranslation into Latin of the Greek 'my servant'. But now we have to bear in mind the evidence of 4QFlor. i.11, which seems to use the idea of (adopted) sonship to God of a messianic figure: see Fuller, *Foundations*, p. 32. In any case, the probing of christological titles may be beside the point here for the original tradition. The introduction of **his son** is logical at this point; the theological identification of him with Jesus Christ would be a natural development in the faith of the Church.

38. The tenants immediately recognize the son as the heir; their crime is not due to misunderstanding. But this was not the case with the adversaries of Jesus who did not recognize him as **heir** of all things. Dodd and Jeremias argue that the law in Galilee in the time of Jesus was such that, in the event of a master's disappearance, property belonged to those who secured immediate possession of it. The fact that the father was still alive (verse 40), and himself owned the vineyard (which could not therefore belong to the tenants, even on the death of his son) is a detail which upsets the development of the story, unless it be assumed (as it was by the tenants, wrongly) that the presence of the son indicated that the master was dead. 'The hope of the workers to inherit the vineyard if they kill the heir is a literary rather than realistic feature in the story' (Stendahl, in *Peake*, 690k).

39. In Mark's story the son is killed and then thrown outside the vineyard; according to Matthew he was killed outside the vineyard, a change probably made to conform with the fact that Jesus died outside the city of Jerusalem (Jn 19.17; Heb. 13.12f.).

41, 43. The phrase **other tenants** is explained by verse 43

where **a nation producing the fruits of it** must mean, not
the Gentiles, but the new people of God—the Church; cf. Hare,
p. 153.

42. The adversaries of Jesus had already (verse 41) drawn the
right conclusion, but now Jesus reveals to them their own responsibility by referring to Ps. 118.22–3 (cf. 1 Pet. 2.6; Ac. 4.11;
Rom. 9.23). The Gospels follow the LXX (Ps. 117), and Luke
adds a rather free version of Isa. 8.14, which appears as verse 44
of Matthew's narrative. (It is missing in the Western text and from
certain versions, and is probably a gloss.) The **stone** prophecy
withdraws the emphasis from the vineyard and tenants, and fixes
attention on the new building—i.e. the Church. It may be a
commentary on the parable created in the early Christian community (but before the time of Mark, for the absence of proof
texts is characteristic of Mark, and when he uses them he follows
earlier tradition), where the parable was allegorically applied to
Christ, and where it was necessary to provide Scriptural support for
the exaltation of the rejected Son.

43. the kingdom of God: not an expression characteristic of
Matthew's Gospel—the usual phrase is 'Kingdom of heaven'.
This suggests either that the verse 43 (interpreting the parable)
was part of the traditional material Matthew inherited, or that
Matthew intentionally differentiates between the eschatological
Kingdom (which the Jews never possessed, in any case) and the
'sovereignty of God' over Israel, expressed in terms of the special
covenantal relationship. The Jewish nation, as a corporate entity,
had now forfeited its elect status.

45–6. These verses return to the distinction already drawn between the apostate leaders of Israel and the multitudes who receive Jesus as a prophet, as they had received John the Baptist
(cf. verse 26).

THE PARABLE OF THE MARRIAGE FEAST **22.1–14**

There can be no doubt that Matthew and Luke (14.16ff.) present
the same parable; the quite significant differences between the two
texts are probably evidence of the freedom with which the oral
tradition transmitted and interpreted the parables of Jesus, relating
them to different circumstances. (This kind of consideration ought
to be borne in mind by those who argue for the fixed character of
traditional material.) The main point of the parable links it with

what precedes: it reveals to the Jews the gravity of their refusal of Jesus. This Matthew presents in a form which is richer in theological allusion, and in language which is more Palestinian, than does Luke. The simplicity of Luke's text could be an indication of its lateness, just as much as the allegorizing tendency in Matthew. To the parable Matthew adds verses 11–13—which are almost a fresh parable—and then verse 14, which seems to fit neatly as a conclusion to 1–10 (rather than to 11–13), although it is possible that it represents an independent parabolic saying.

1. in parables: a stereotyped Matthean formula. The plural includes a reference to the two preceding parables; but at this point it is clumsy.

2. The Kingdom inaugurated by Jesus is not like **a king,** but like what happens in the whole parable. Matthew informs us clearly that it is a royal **marriage feast,** and that gives a more eschatological tone to the story. According to Luke, 'a man once gave a great banquet'; but his preceding verse (14.15) indicates that he has in mind the messianic banquet.

3–4. The succession of servants sent to call those who had been invited recalls the preceding parable (21.36). The theme of the call is characteristically Matthean, and the words 'they were not willing to come' (lit.) emphasize the fact of the (Jews') voluntary decision in refusing.

5. The idea present in *amelēsantes* (**made light of it**) is of culpable negligence or indifference.

6–7. These two verses bring an unexpected tone of violence to the story; they recall the preceding parable (21.35, 39). But they probably represent a later addition to the original story at a time when Christian teachers and preachers were persecuted, and contain an allusion to the Jewish revolt and the fall of Jerusalem in A.D. 70.

9–10. thoroughfares: lit. 'the issues', or 'ends', 'of the roads'; probably the intersections of roads in the centre of a town, where the poor people would gather. The servants are instructed not to make distinctions: whoever they find—whether bad or good— may be invited. There may however be a subtle link here with the verses following, in which the need for discipline in the community is emphasized. Entry into the Kingdom may be gratuitous, but the Kingdom is not characterized by libertinism.

11–13. The **wedding garment** probably symbolizes righteous-

ness (*dikaiosunē*), that faithfulness and obedience which can be
expected of those who are members of the Kingdom, or Church.
The question of how the guests could obtain wedding garments,
since they were just called in from the street, is quite irrelevant to
Matthew.

14. This epigrammatic *logion* may refer to the small number of
Jews who really are the 'chosen ones' (thus completing verses 1–10),
or it may refer more specifically to verses 11–13 to warn Christians
not to trust in their own gratuituous calling in such a way as to be
found unworthy of it, and therefore not to be among the elect.
It should be noted that it is behaviour and action which indicate
whether a man is among the chosen or not: deeds and election are
not set over against one another as in some strands of later
Christian theology (Stendahl, in *Peake*, 690m).

TRIBUTE TO CAESAR 22.15–22

Matthew rejoins Mark at the point where he broke off to insert
the parable of the Marriage Feast. The description of the atmosphere of controversy continues with the discussion of the issues of
tribute (verses 16–22), the Resurrection (verses 23–33), the Great
Commandment (verses 34–40) and the Son of David (verses 41–
46). The mass of the Jewish people (including the Pharisees)
resented paying tribute to the Roman Emperor; it was the supreme
evidence of their subject status. But the Herodians (supporters of
the reigning family of Herod) were well known for their pro-
Roman sympathies, and they would have supported the practice
of tribute payment. Their association with the Pharisees accentu-
ates the political trap which the question opens. If Jesus pronounced
against the tax, he would be in difficulties with the civil authorities; if he approved it, he would incur the hostility of the people.

15–16. According to Matthew, the Pharisees take the initiative
in trying to trap Jesus—a further sign of the anti-Pharisaic bias in
the first Gospel—whereas in Mark 'certain Pharisees and Herodians' are sent, presumably by the Temple authorities. The
introductory words of the deputation are meant to be flattering;
the way of God was a Jewish catechetical term which was taken
up as the early Church's title or 'trade-mark' (Stendahl); cf.
'the Way' (Ac. 9.2; 18.25f.).

17. The question on which Jesus is asked to give an authoritative opinion is not one merely of expediency or civil law, but of a

theological nature: In the eyes of God (i.e. in the light of the Law) is it permissible to pay tribute? That this kind of question exercised the minds of the rabbis is shown by B. Pes. 112b, B. Bab. Kamma 113a.

18–20. Recognizing the deceitful intentions of his questioners, Jesus asked to be shown one of the Roman coins used for the payment of taxes (*dēnarion*). The imperial tax was made more offensive to the Jews because it had to be paid in coins which bore the head of the Emperor and inscriptions which described the religious and cultic claims of the Caesar (e.g. *divus et pontifex maximus* on the coins of Tiberius).

21. The reply of Jesus (lit. 'give back to Caesar . . .') represents a positive and general appreciation of the rôle of the State, in accordance with certain Jewish doctrines which taught that the great owed their authority ultimately to God (cf. Dan. 2.21, 37f.; Prov. 8.15; Wis. 6.1–11; and Rom. 13.1–7; 1 Pet. 2.13–17): this is not incompatible with the claims of the Kingdom of God. In this answer Jesus skilfully avoids tying his mission to current political hopes associated with Zealotism.

CONCERNING THE RESURRECTION **22.23–33**

The question brought by the Sadducees has the same intention as the preceding one—viz. to put Jesus in such a situation that, whatever he says, he will incur the opposition of some of his hearers. The resurrection of the righteous (or of all men) was taught by the Pharisees; scriptural support for their position was found in the apocalyptic expectations in Isa. 26.19 and Dan. 12.2. But the Sadducees, regarding the Torah only as authoritative, did not believe in resurrection; in their view both soul and body perished at death (cf. Ac. 23.8, Josephus, *BJ* II. viii.11–14, and *Ant.* XVIII. i.3–5). In the Qumran writings there are passages which seem to rule out any belief in resurrection (1QS xi.20–2; 1QH xii.25ff.), but there are also verses which suggest some form of resurrection hope (1QH vi.29–34; see Black, *Scrolls*, pp. 141–2).

24. The law of levirate marriage (Latin *levir*, 'husband's brother') required that, if one of brothers living together died leaving a childless widow, then a brother of the deceased must marry the widow to raise up children to his dead brother. The continuation of name and family through offspring was in fact the only answer in early Israelite faith to the search for eternal life.

(Note: **raise up** (*anastēsei*) **children** (*anastasis* = resurrection).)
The quotation from Dt. 25.5–6 is free: the technical term *epigam-breusei* (**must marry**) comes from Gen. 38.8.

25–8. The test case posed by the Sadducees presents the idea
of resurrection as an absurdity. Their argument was probably
effective against the common view that the resurrection life was
merely an extension of the good life of the present (cf. En. 10.17ff.;
1QS iv.7). The Biblical references to resurrection did not give any
indication of the kind of life envisaged.

29. The Sadducees are ignorant of what is in Scripture, as the
appeal to Exod. 3.6 (part of Torah) will show, and ignorant of the
creative power of God, who is able not only to raise the dead
(contrary to Sadducean thought), but to raise them in such a way
that the derisory questions of the Sadducees are made to vanish
(Bonnard, p. 325).

30. In the resurrection (which is spoken of, not so much as an
event, as an enduring state in the life of the Kingdom) there is a
difference in sexual relationships. People do not marry (in sharp
contrast to the expectations of the Pharisees, and cf. 16.18), and
are **like angels** (and angelology was as objectionable to Sadducees
as resurrection teaching!), in that they cannot die but are sons of
God. The Qumran literature and other Jewish writings also speak
of the likeness of the redeemed to angels (1QH iii.21ff., vi.13, on
which see Black, *Scrolls*, pp. 138ff.; also En. 104.4ff.).

31–2. The Sadducees based their teaching and belief on Torah,
and so the quotation by Jesus from Exod. 3 would represent an
appeal to the highest authority. The argument is based on inference: Isaac became patriarch after Abraham, and Jacob after the
death of Isaac; yet God speaks to Moses as if they were contemporary with each other or with Moses. Hence God (who **is not
God of the dead**) regards them as alive, and they become pro-
totypes for **the resurrection of the dead**. (This is the only
passage in the *NT* where this expression is used; elsewhere it is
'resurrection *from* the dead', with the exception of Rom. 1.4; but
that probably represents a Semitic idiom.) The question could be
raised whether the illustration from Exod. 3 'proves' the resurrection of the body, or the fact that personality survives death; but
these would hardly have been alternative answers to the Jewish
mind.

33. It is not said that Jesus' answer convinced the Sadducees, but it did impress the multitudes by reason of its appeal to Biblical teaching.

THE GREAT COMMANDMENT 22.34-40

Here these verses must be understood as yet another attempt to test Jesus. The Pharisees would have been satisfied with his treatment of the question of resurrection, but Matthew now shows them as testing his attitude to the Law (Mk 12.28 says that 'one of the scribes' asked him). Rabbinic teaching tended to emphasize the equal importance of all commandments (Mek. Exod. 6, Sifre Dt. xii.28; xiii.19; xix.11), but the Scriptural passages here cited were probably already regarded as an epitome of the Law (Test. Issachar v.2). It is the supremacy given to the twin ideas of love to God and for one's neighbour, and not the ideas themselves, which constitutes the originality of this piece of teaching. The fact that Matthew and Mark put the summary of the Law on the lips of Jesus, whereas Luke attributes it to the lawyer, suggests that in the early church this resumé was considered, not as an entirely new piece of teaching from Jesus, but as a faithful and acceptable summary of the Law given to Israel.

34. Again the Pharisees are presented by Matthew as the leading opponents of Jesus, as they were of the early Church. They gather together 'to one place'; 'against him' is a secondary reading.

35. lawyer: (*nomikos*, only here in Matthew), a man learned in the law of Moses, i.e. a scribe, belonging to the Pharisaic party.

36. It is sometimes thought strange that the epithet **Teacher** (frequent in Matthew, especially on the lips of his opponents) is given to Jesus, for the function of the teacher or rabbi was to assist his followers to live faithfully by interpreting the Law for them. But this rôle is not inconsistent with Matthew's understanding of Jesus and his relation to the Law.

37. The summary permits of no fulfilment of the Law, which is not, in its very core, obedience to God and service to one's neighbour. The citation is from Dt. 6.5 (according to the M.T., which includes 'heart') and this formed part of the Shema' (Dt. 6.4-9; 11.13-21; Num. 15.36-41), the credo *par excellence* of Judaism.

heart . . . soul . . . mind: the three terms emphasize the totality of the person involved. Any one of them would have been sufficient (in terms of Hebrew anthropology) to denote the entirety

of a man. On the significance of the Shema' and the required areas
of man's repose to it, see B. Gerhardsson, *NTS*, xiv, 1967–8,
pp. 167–9, and Jeremias, *Prayers*, pp. 67ff.

39. a second is like it: not a second in importance, but a
second which is as important, of equal gravity (cf. Arndt, p. 169).
Love of one's neighbour is not identified with love of God, but one
is as urgent as the other. The quotation is from the LXX of Lev.
19.18, where 'neighbour' means 'fellow-Israelite' or 'resident alien
in Israel'. The bringing together of love of God and love of neighbour is attributed to Jesus in Mark and Matthew, but the combination (or at least its essence) was known in Jewish catechesis,
if Test. Issachar v.2 is pre-Christian.

40. depend: Greek *krematai*, which could mean, technically,
'are suspended' (= Hebrew root *tlh*)—i.e. 'derive their authority'.
It is more probable that the expression is meant to indicate
either that the two commandments quoted provide a resumé of,
or give decisive expression to, all the Law and Prophets; or that all
the Law and the Prophets take them as their basis. The essence of
the divine will is expressed in these two commandments (cf. 7.12).
See further *TIM*, pp. 76–8, and Trilling, p. 179.

THE SON OF DAVID 22.41–6

In order to present a continuing discussion, Matthew makes
Jesus direct the question about the Davidic messiah to the Pharisees; Mark and Luke seem to have it addressed to the people.
Here Jesus takes the initiative, and emerges as champion.
Pharisaic Judaism recognized that the Messiah would be a son of
David, and Matthew cannot intend this incident to be a refutation
of a traditional Davidic requirement for Jesus as Messiah, since
elsewhere in his Gospel he stresses the Davidic element. Nor is it
an adequate interpretation to see this discussion as aimed at
deepening or spiritualizing the Jewish conception. The most
likely hypothesis is that the passage is intent on arguing that 'Son
of David' is not an adequate or complete title for Jesus, since
David himself called this son of his 'Lord'. The Messiah has a more
exalted rôle than that of a successor of David, as the Pharisees
regarded him (Ps. Sol. 17); he is 'Son of Man' (or 'Son of God').
Daube (pp. 158–69) argues thus, and shows that the question is
haggadic in nature and involves the reconciliation of apparently
conflicting scriptural propositions.

42. Christ: here 'Messiah' ('Anointed One'), and not a name for Jesus. Belief that the Messiah would be a son of David was widely accepted (cf. Isa. 11.1, 10; Jer. 23.5). The content of the Pharisaic hopes for the Davidic messiah are clearly set forth in Ps. Sol. 17.

43. The Davidic authorship of Ps. 110 (composed for a king) is assumed, and also his inspired (prophetic) condition when composing it. 'Speaking in the spirit' is a typical Rabbinic formula to describe inspired utterance. For the rabbis **the Spirit** tended to be understood almost completely as the 'spirit of prophecy'.

44. The citation is from Ps. 110.1 (mostly according to the LXX Ps. 109), and the words **my Lord** refer to the Messiah. A messianic interpretation of the psalm is not found among the rabbis of the early Christian era, but from the 3rd and 4th centuries it does appear. It could be argued that such an interpretation was common (perhaps even in Jesus' day), but was dropped in reaction to the Christian usage, and introduced again later. The main point of the argument is that, since the Messiah is David's lord, he must be greater and better than a Son of David, just as he was greater than Jonah, Solomon, and the Temple (cf. 12.6f., 41f.).

46. Cf. Mk 12.34b, which concludes the paragraph preceding this incident in Mark. It was omitted by Matthew there, and inserted here to round off the section. Jesus is supreme in the debates with the Jewish leaders of all parties, and their opposition to him now goes underground to reappear later and achieve its purpose.

THE WOES ON THE SCRIBES AND PHARISEES **23.1-36**

This section can be regarded as the opening part—that addressed to the people—of the fifth and final discourse in Matthew; it is followed by a second part for the disciples only (chapters 24 and 25). It may more aptly be considered as a climax to the controversies with the leaders of the people which have been recorded from chapter 21 onwards.

Comparison with the Gospels of Mark and Luke suggests that in this section we are dealing with an original literary creation by the evangelist. The basic ideas of the chapter are found in a few verses of Mark: Mk 12.38-9 contains the essential theme of Mt. 23.1-12, and Mk 12.40 contains a threat which is expanded

in Mt. 23.13–36. Some scholars have thought that Mark has
abbreviated a tradition which was employed in its entirety by
Matthew, as the church for which Mark wrote was not in direct
conflict with Pharisaism when he was writing. Others argue that
the Matthean composition, at this point, developed quite independently of Mark, by reason of the dogmatic interests which find
expression in the first Gospel. It is possible to maintain that this
chapter emerged from a church which was still associated with
Judaism (see especially verses 1–3; cf. Bornkamm, in *TIM*, p.
21), but one would have to add, at the very least, that it was a
church which, having tried to follow both scribal teaching and
Christian catachesis, was now about to definitely sever its union
with Judaism (see Kilpatrick, pp. 101–23 and Bonnard, p. 333).
It is well to bear in mind that the phrases which suggest that the
conflict between the Church and Judaism was, for Matthew,
intra muros may reflect his own careful literary work in putting
these words on Jesus' lips. The impression given by most of Matthew's work is that he appeals to the synagogue from a church
which was outside it. These verses represent Jesus as conceding that
the scribes and Pharisees sit 'in Moses' seat', and that their teaching has authority (verse 23). It is not their doctrine which is
denounced, but their hypocrisy, their failure to maintain (for
themselves) the rigidity of the Law (see E. Haenchen, *ZTK*,
XLVIII, 1951, pp. 38–63). 'In Didache viii.1 "hypocrites" had
become identical with "Jews" . . . , and in this discourse we find
the church on its way to such a clear-cut identification, where
Judaism, and especially Pharisaism, has become somewhat of a
man of straw for self-reassuring attacks. But there is enough of
genuine material, which can well be identified with the actual
teaching of Jesus. He did not enunciate principles, nor did he aim
at a new approach to religion, but he taught with prophetic
consciousness in a nation where he found the strongest resistance
among those who were its spiritual leaders. This must have sharp-
ened his eyes for their shortcomings—most of which they would
admit themselves, at least when they were among themselves . . .'
(Stendahl, in *Peake*, 691b.)

   1. According to all the Synoptics, Jesus does not address himself directly to the Pharisees, but **to the crowds and to his
disciples.** This suggests that Jesus is not attacking Pharisaism in
itself, but is offering himself and his teaching as an alternative to

the leadership of the Pharisees. The **crowds** represent the Syro-Palestinian multitudes, and the **disciples** the Matthean church.

2. Moses' seat: not simply a metaphor. There was an actual stone seat in the front of the synagogue where the authoritative teacher (usually a scribe) sat: cf. E.L. Sukenik, *Ancient Synagogues in Palestine and Greece*, 1934, pp. 57-61).

3. The authority of the rabbis is recognized, and the conclusion is drawn: **practise and observe whatever they tell you.** The word **whatever** would include the rabbinic traditions (*halakoth*), but, in the light of later sayings (verses 15ff.), it is doubtful if this is the intended meaning. The point may be to give the maximum force to the subsequent denunciation of the actions of the scribes. The necessity of combining action and doctrine harmoniously was strongly emphasized by later rabbis.

4. The 'yoke of Torah', or 'of the kingdom of Heaven', which the rabbis placed upon the faithful was burdensome to many. The scribes ordered their lives to suit their own requirements (cf. the Qumran name for the Pharisees: 'the expounders of smooth things'; see Introductions pp. 67-8) but their injunctions were difficult for people in other trades and walks of life. Considerable social tension between the scribes and the people at large is implied in this saying (which may originally have been independent of this context, since it almost contradicts verse 3), and it is further reflected in what follows.

5. Phylacteries: small cases made of parchment or leather containing a piece of vellum on which were inscribed texts of the Law (Dt. 11.13-22; 6.4-9; Exod. 13.11-16; 13.2-10). They were tied to the forehead and left arm in fulfilment of Exod. 13.9, 16; Dt. 6.8; 11.18; the reference here may be to making broad the straps. Such phylacteries have been found at Qumran, but inscribed with slightly different texts. It is not certain that in the time of Jesus Jews called their *tephillim*, or prayer-bands, 'phylacteries' (see J. Bowman, *Stud. Evan.*, 1, 1959, pp. 523ff.): if not, then Jesus may be referring to ostentatious wearing of amulets or charms.

fringes: tassels which the Jew was obliged to wear on the corners of his outer garment in accordance with Num. 15.38f.; Dt. 22.12. Jesus himself wore them (9.20; 14.36), but the Pharisees lengthened theirs in order to draw attention to their piety.

7. The Greek word *rhabbi* is a transcription of the Hebrew for

'my master' (cf. Jn 1.38; 3.26): it was a term of respect applied to
prominent Jewish teachers by their disciples (cf. its use to refer to
Jesus in 26.25, 49). By the time of Matthew's writing, **rabbi** was
an official title for the scribes.

8. This verse introduces a passage addressed to disciples only,
continuing to verse 12. The section may represent the application
of the preceding verses to the situation of the Matthean church,
where a sort of Christian 'rabbinism' may have been developing.
The disciples are not to allow themselves to be called 'my lord', or
'my master', more particularly, perhaps, by people whom they
taught or healed.

9. The title 'Abba' was used in ordinary conversation with old
men, but was not given to rabbis; see Dalman, p. 339, and Jeremias, *Prayers*, pp. 42–3. The disciples, however, are not to address
any man as 'my father' because the honour of the name **Father**
('*ābbā*') is appropriate to God only, and was probably Jesus' own
unique way of addressing God.

10. To some this verse appears as an anticlimax and therefore
it has been regarded as a variant of verse 8. If the Greek word
kathēgētēs ('interpreter', 'expositor') is equivalent to Hebrew
môreh (which is the technical term for the Teacher of Righteousness, the 'right' Teacher, at Qumran), then it is a fitting climax;
'the Christ' is *the* teacher (cf. C. Spicq, *RB*, LXVI, 1959, pp. 387–96).

11, 12. The sayings on humility (a common theme throughout
the Gospels) are directed against the authoritarianism and vanity
of the Pharisees. The idea of abasement in verse 12 must be interpreted in terms of service, not of paralysing self-negation.

13. In Luke's Gospel (11.52) this saying is the climax of the
denunciation of the scribes; in Matthew it is the first of seven woes
(verses 13–31). The significant difference in the presentation of
the denunciation in Matthew and Luke cannot be explained in
terms of their dependence on two sources (Mark and Q); the
variations in oral tradition may be the clue to their divergences.
The meaning seems to be that the scribal teaching and exposition
of Scripture obscured the real issues of belief and conduct;
casuistry was making it virtually impossible for men to fulfil the
Law of God and devote themselves to that fidelity which leads to
the Kingdom of heaven.

14. Omitted in the best MSS. and probably inserted into the
text from Mk. 12.40.

15. A **proselyte** was a pagan converted to Judaism, one who had advanced beyond the stage of being a 'god-fearer' (Ac. 10.2, 13.16), and had become circumcized; only after circumcision would the Pharisees regard a convert as within the true Israel. Josephus, *Ant.*, xx.2.4 illustrates the lengths to which this excessive zeal would go in attempting to convert those who had already become adherents of the Jewish faith under the influence of the more liberal propaganda of Hellenistic Judaism. The making of a convert **twice as much a child of hell** (*Gehenna*) may indicate that some further privilege or requirement was made for proselytes which was not in accordance with the Law (perhaps the opportunity given to a circumcized convert to divorce his wife if she too did not become a convert, a privilege which placed the convert above the Law, which prohibited divorce; so E. Lernle, according to Bonnard, p. 338). Possibly the words are intended simply to suggest, in a dramatic way, that converts tend to be even more zealous than their converters!

16-22. The scribal rulings criticized in this long denunciation illustrate the kind of distinctions which a casuistical system fostered. Oaths by the most holy things were to be avoided because they were as binding as an oath made by God's name; but oaths by less sacred things (i.e. things removed from the centre of holiness) were not matters of such seriousness. This kind of ruling is ridiculed; the scribes and Pharisees are blind to the common hermeneutical rule: 'If the lesser, then also the greater.' Every oath is made before God, and distinctions are out of the question. Oaths 'by the Temple' and 'by the Temple service' are referred to in rabbinic writings.

The mention of these features of Jewish religion does not require us to presuppose a Jerusalem setting and a date before A.D. 70 for the composition of the Gospel; any literary work can contain evidence of a situation and practices which existed earlier than its composition, and this section may be older than the Matthean editorial work. The words **is bound by his oath** renders the Greek *opheilei* which translates the Hebrew *ḥāyaḇ*; and *omnuei en* (**swears by**) must reflect *nišbaᶜbᵉ*, for the Greek verb usually takes the accusative. Are these indications of the early (Semitic) character of the material here set out? On these verses, see Hummel, pp. 79-80.

23. The tithing of vegetables and spices was probably over and

above what was required by the Law (Dt. 14.22–3), but according
to scribal exposition it was necessary. Excessive zeal for minutiae
led to neglect of more important things. The word *krisis* (**justice**)
refers, not to 'condemnation' or 'the Last Judgment', but to that
respect for the rights of others which gives a just judgment; such
justice has the character of mercy. The word *pistis* (**faith**) here
means fidelity to God's will, or trustworthiness. Provided there is
no neglect of the great principles, the observance of minutiae is
not forbidden. 'The former you ought to do, and the latter you
should not neglect' sums up the attitude of Jesus to the Pharisees;
they are criticized for concentrating on what is secondary and
forgetting what is of first importance, and therefore for doing too
little.

24. The same criticism in metaphorical language. The words
of J. Shab. 12a: 'He that kills a flea on the Sabbath is as guilty as
if he killed a camel', gives the background of thought for the
interpretation of this saying. The **gnat** (the Aramaic translation
of which is very like the Aramaic word for **camel**; see Black,
Aramaic Approach, pp. 175f.) is strained out of the wine to make it
pure, but far greater issues are regarded as unimportant.

25–6. The fifth woe focuses attention on the Pharisees' concern
for the ritual purification of kitchen utensils. But the vessel which
is externally clean may be filled (inside) with the results of robbery
and greed. Both the inside (i.e. the contents) and outside must be
clean. Verse 26 applies this to man's life; if the inside is clean (i.e.
if a man is in obedient relation to God and his commandments),
then his outward actions and behaviour will also be pure before
God (cf. 15.11).

27. Sepulchres were whitened each year (before Passover) in
order that passers-by should not inadvertently become polluted
by coming into too close contact with them (cf. Lk. 11.44). But
the cleanliness of graves (like the Pharisees' righteousness) is
merely an external show, and merits the charge of hypocrisy: the
appearance and the underlying reality do not harmonize.

29. The word **tombs** links this saying with the preceding one.
Veneration for the burial-places of saintly men and heroes was,
and is, a common practice in the East. The practice of erecting
monuments to mark the graves of Israel's heroes may have been
initiated by Herod the Great's building of a monument at David's
tomb; such monuments may have been regarded as expiatory in

character as well as a means of honouring the dead (see Jeremias, *Heiligengräber*, pp. 118–21). If Jeremias is correct in his claim that the building of tombs for the prophets occurred as early as Jesus' time, then it may be that a genuine dominical utterance lies behind the woe, evoked, perhaps, by some expression of hostility to Jesus' own prophetic ministry. On **prophets** and **righteous**, see Mt. 13.17: the **righteous** here are the martyrs who by reason of their piety and obedience were persecuted even to death, as were the prophets, according to Jewish tradition.

30–31. The respectful recognition of these martyrs is used to prove continuity in Israel's apostasy, not a change of attitude. ' "Sons" are those who inherit their fathers' character' (McNeile, p. 338). Matthew's **you are sons of . . .** and Luke's 'but you build' (11.48) may represent two translations of one ambiguous Aramaic phrase; see Black, *Aramaic Approach*, pp. 12f.

32. Here the style changes to that of an 'apocalyptic oracle' (Stendahl) which concludes the denunciation of the Pharisees and leads on to the prediction of Jerusalem's destruction (verses 37–9) and the apocalypse proper in chapter 24. This style accounts for the injunction: **Fill up . . . the measure of your fathers**—or: 'complete the works of sin begun by your fathers'. The allusion is to the Jewish view that the final judgment will come only after men have reached the absolute peak of sinfulness.

33. Condemnation to the fires of Gehenna was a common apocalyptic notion in Judaism.

34. By the sending of prophets and others, opportunity will be given to the Jews to complete the measure of their crimes as they again reject the messengers. The first person: **I send**, reflects again the apocalyptic style, as does the word *Idou* ('Behold!'), omitted by *RSV*. The declaration is made on God's behalf by Christ; Lk. 11.45 attributes it to 'the Wisdom of God', and that probably preserves the original character of the saying. The fate of the emissaries of Christ (or of God) is the same as that predicted for disciples in Mt. 10.17, 23; Luke's form of the saying couples 'prophets and apostles'.

It seems certain then that the terms used of the emissaries reflect conditions in the early Church: the **prophets** may have fulfilled a task of proclamation (*kerygma*), and the **wise men and** (Christian) **scribes** a teaching function (see Kilpatrick, pp. 110ff., 126, and D. Hill, *NTS*, 11, 1964–5, pp. 296f.). The details

of the predicted persecution of Jesus' messengers probably reflects
the treatment given to Christian missionaries by Jews; but Jews
never employed crucifixion as a legal form of capital punishment.
The words *kai staurōsete* are really redundant, and may have been
added to the Gospel text by a glossator (see Hare, pp. 88–92).

35–6. righteous: perhaps 'innocent', which is the translation
of *dikaios* when referred to Abel. That which is associated with
martyrdom is both 'righteousness' (i.e. loyalty to God, with
faithfulness and obedience) and 'innocency'.
Zechariah the son of Barachiah: the *OT* minor prophet; but the
Jewish tradition (and the LXX texts about the various Zechariahs)
shows confusion, and the saying could refer to Zechariah the son
of Jehoiada, whose murder is mentioned towards the end of the
last book of the Hebrew canon, 2 Chr. 24.20ff. It could also refer
to Zechariah, son of Baris or Baruch, who was martyred in the
Temple shortly before the fall of the City of Jerusalem in A.D. 70
(Josephus, *BJ* IV.v.4). The description in verse 35b may strengthen
the case for the third alternative, but it could apply in the second
as well.

THE LAMENT OVER JERUSALEM **23.37–9**

Luke (13.34f.) puts these words in a context different from that of
Matthew, and therefore it is possible that they form an independent (and perhaps composite) declaration by Jesus. He 'speaks in
the great style of a prophetic oracle', and therefore the saying
could be a post-Resurrection oracle declared through a Christian
prophet. 'He speaks on behalf of God in first-person singular with
the long history of an apostate Israel in view . . . and at the same
time as the Messiah who is to come in glory . . .' (Stendahl, in
Peake, 691j).

37. The penalty of **stoning** was meted out to idolaters (Dt.
17.5, 7) and sorcerers (Lev. 20.27) and, according to the Mishnah
(San. vii.4), to false prophets. The fate of those sent suggests that
they were rejected outright as false, although they had been sent
by God; cf. on 21.35. **How often** seems to presuppose a repeated
ministry of Jesus in Jerusalem (as John's Gospel suggests), but
your children (i.e. sons of Jerusalem) could refer to the Jewish
people in any part of the land. **You would not** represents the
Greek for 'you were not willing'. Throughout his Gospel Matthew
emphasizes strongly the unwillingness of the Jews to come to Jesus.

38. Some MSS. and versions have **forsaken and desolate:** others omit 'desolate'.

your house: the people in its entirety symbolized by the Temple; cf. Trilling, p. 67.

39. The position of this verse (with its allusion to Ps. 118.26) in Luke (13.35) makes it refer (in history) to the future entry of Jesus to Jerusalem on Palm Sunday. But in Matthew that event is past. It must therefore refer to a later coming of Christ, perhaps at the end of the age. The term 'from now on' (*ap'arti*, **again**)— which is peculiar to and important for Matthean eschatology—is now introduced (and repeated in 26.29, 64), and the great discourse on eschatology immediately follows (chapters 24–5). On his return, Messiah will be recognized by the Jews. But will they know him only as Judge, or is it being hinted that they will acknowledge him as King? The latter possibility (i.e. of an eventual conversion of Israel) is kept open by Bonnard (p. 344) and Benoit (p. 144).

ESCHATOLOGY AND THE EXPECTATION OF THE PAROUSIA 24.1–25.46

Note on the Eschatological Discourse

This lengthy discourse is presented in all three Synoptic Gospels. Discussion of it has been dominated by two main questions: (i) How much of the address is genuine pre-Resurrection prophecy by Jesus, and how much has been created or inserted by later Christian writers? (ii) What is the meaning of the connection between the destruction of Jerusalem and 'the end of all things'? Some scholars of the last century claimed that in the thought of Jesus the destruction of the city was to signal the end of the world, but, because the end did not then occur, they were forced to admit that Jesus was mistaken in his expectation.

In order to avoid a conclusion like this, which cast doubt on the trustworthiness of Jesus, other scholars developed a theory which shifted the responsibility for the error on to the Church. This is the widely-accepted 'little apocalypse' theory, according to which a Jewish or Jewish-Christian 'pamphlet' was the origin of the apocalyptic element in this discourse (i.e. the section predicting the End). This 'apocalyptic news-sheet' was first circulated either when Pilate put Roman ensigns in Jerusalem, or when the emperor Caligula threatened to place his image in the Temple (A.D. 40),

or even when Roman armies moved against the city of Jerusalem
(A.D. 66–70). Such events were considered as 'signs' of the End,
but the prophecy based on some one of them was wrongly attributed to Jesus. Consequently, he was not involved in any prediction
which turned out to be erroneous, and in fact he was not associated
with apocalyptic speculation at all.

Although this ingenious theory has wide support, it is beset by
great difficulties. For instance, when it is sought in the text, the
'little apocalypse' forms no meaningful literary structure (cf. G. R.
Beasley-Murray, *Jesus and the Future*, 1954, pp. 18–21; Kümmel,
pp. 98f.). As far as the interpretation of Matthew's discourse is
concerned, it is well to guard against the unhesitating assumption
that the chapters do advance a thoroughgoing 'apocalyticism'.

In Mt. 24 verses 4–36 answer the question raised by the disciples in verse 3—When will Jesus' Parousia and the End come,
and what will be the signs of these events? The reply given by
Jesus is summed up in three verses which seem designed to calm
apocalytic enthusiasm: 'Take heed that no one leads you astray'
(verse 4); the coming of the Son of Man will be such as to leave no
doubt about its occurrence (verse 27); no one knows the date of it,
except the Father (verse 36). (Matthew is not concerned with the
question as to how far Jesus' predictions were fulfilled in the
events of A.D. 70; for his generation that problem was no longer
vital.)

To these three points there are added two groups of texts whose
significance in the discourse must be carefully considered in relation to the whole. The first group contains the descriptions of the
final tribulations (verses 5–14, 15–25, 29–31). Why are these
included if the whole purpose is to avoid feverish apocalyptic
agitation? Are they included—by Jesus or by Matthew—to
underline the seriousness and importance of the essential teaching
in verses 4, 27, and 36? It seems extremely doubtful that Matthew
gave these highly-coloured pictures from Jewish tradition prominence in his composition. The second group of texts is concerned
with 'enduring to the end' (verse 13): this expression announces
the theme of vigilance, developed from verse 42 onwards. But this
is not the vigilance of excited expectation, but of the active fulfilling of one's given task (24.45–25.30), and especially the task
of helping the little ones (25.31ff.). 'Matthew's purpose in the
last great discourse is . . . to prepare Christians for enduring

faithfulness during the indefinite period that remains' (Hare, p. 178). This kind of teaching is surely part of the attempt to cool down apocalyptic enthusiasm.

In this discourse, Matthew follows Mark both in the importance he gives it in the structure of his Gospel and in the order of the material within it. Yet, as far as the details are concerned, Matthew modifies and completes Mark's text; he employs materials from a source he shared with Luke, which the latter reproduces in Lk. 17.22–37 (cf. Mt. 24.26–8, 37–9, 40–1). There is therefore good reason to think that, as in the other four discourses, so in this fifth and final one, Matthew has grouped together separate elements from oral tradition (or a partially written tradition), and that these have been edited to fit in with his main pre-occupations. It is also likely that the evangelist has grouped together words of Jesus which were spoken on different occasions because he considered that they dealt with the same subject (cf. A. Feuillet, *RB*, LVI, 1949, pp. 343f.).

In the four preceding discourses Matthew has already dealt with several matters: the righteousness of the Kingdom (chapters 5–7); the proclamation of the Kingdom in the world (chapter 10); the mystery of the Kingdom which is provisionally hidden (chapter 13); and the fraternal relations between those who belong to the Kingdom (chapter 18). Now the evangelist announces the cosmic crisis in which the Kingdom (now hidden) will be manifested before the eyes of all (chapter 24), and the active, compassionate vigilance necessary in view of these events (25). Thus these chapters fit into the main purpose of Matthew's Gospel, which is to declare everything consequent for men upon the appearance of the Kingdom of God in the person of Jesus. (On the discourse, see G. R. Beasley-Murray, *Jesus and the Future*; A. Feuillet, in *BNTE*, pp. 261–80; and Bonnard, pp. 347–9, to which this note is indebted.)

JESUS PREDICTS THE DESTRUCTION OF THE TEMPLE 24.1–3

In all three Gospels these verses form the introduction to the eschatological discourse, but Matthew links this opening section more closely with the lament over Jerusalem than does Mark or Luke, by omitting the story of the Widow's Mite (Mk 12. 41-4; Lk. 21.1-4) which continues to inveigh against the ostentatious piety of the Jewish leaders. In prophesying the destruction of the

Temple Jesus stands in line with the *OT* prophets (Mic. 3.12; Jer. 26.6, 18), and it seems certain that the *logion* is authentic. It is found, in one form or another, in all four Gospels. It was the subject of the charge brought against Jesus before Caiaphas (Mk 14.58), and was used as a taunt at the Crucifixion (Mk 15.29). The prophecy provokes the question as to the time and signs of this event, and this leads into the eschatological teaching. In the circles from which Matthew's Gospel emerged, it may have been believed that the destruction of Jerusalem would occur among those cosmic catastrophes expected to herald the final and complete renewal of the world, but Matthew himself seems intent upon differentiating between the events of A.D. 70 and the 'consummation'.

1. Jesus leaves the Temple (which he entered at 21.23) for the last time, and the disciples comment on the complex of buildings.

2. The date of the destruction is not indicated—only that it lies in the future. The word *kataluthēsetai* (**thrown down**) could refer to the results of a military action (like the sack of the Temple by the Romans in A.D. 70,) or to some cosmic catastrophe (apocalyptic rather than natural). If the apocalyptic interpretation is correct, then the argument for dating the composition of the Gospel (or the formation of this saying) after A.D. 70 cannot be based on this verse.

3. Mark and Matthew locate the enquiry by the disciples on the Mount of Olives, a suitable place for discourse on the Parousia (cf. Zech. 14.4), and make the discussion of it a private interview (*kat' idian*). Only in Matthew are the destruction, the return of Jesus, and the end of the world linked together, and the combination of these gives the question a precision not found in Mark. Both 'Parousia' and 'close of the age' are expressions peculiar to Matthew. 'Parousia' does not here refer to Jesus' accession to sovereignty in the Church which has replaced Judaism (Benoit, p. 145), but to his final and glorious coming at the end of history.

THE FINAL TRIBULATION AND THE COMING OF THE SON OF MAN 24.4–36

Although, in its present form, this passage is almost certainly a rather late literary composition, it must be taken as a unit in the Matthean structure. It deals with three main topics: the signs of the final suffering (verses 4–14); the tribulation which leads to the day of the Son of Man (verses 15–28); the Parousia, the parable of the Fig Tree as herald of summer, and the question of the time of these events (verses 29–36).

4–5. The disciples are to guard against being deceived by messianic pretenders, with their apocalyptic assurances. Such pretenders seem to have been known in the first century (Ac. 5.36; 21.38), and again in the time of the second Jewish war, but none of these claimed to be the Messiah Jesus returned, if that is what the words **in my name** mean, rather than denoting the use of the general title 'Messiah'.

6–8. Wars, rumours of wars, and accompanying disasters were regarded as signs of the approaching end in Jewish apocalyptic. In order to curb excited anticipations, Matthew makes two important points: first, these disquieting events must happen according to the purpose of God (cf. Dan. 2.28) and, since history is under the control of God, believers can and should remain calm; and, secondly, these events will be only the **beginning of the sufferings,** lit. 'birth pangs', almost a technical term for the tribulations leading up to the end of the age, which are to be endured by the community of the elect. The disasters experienced are but a prelude, and feverish apocalypticism is out of place.

9–14. Matthew has already used the corresponding paragraph in Mark (13.9–13a) in his second teaching section (10.17–21), and therefore he fills in the gap at this point with a summary which echoes Mk 13.9. The verses relate to persecution of disciples (i.e. all Christians—not missionaries only, as in Mt. 10) which forms part of the messianic woes. Verse 14 indicates that the Gospel will be preached to the entire inhabited world before the End. To interpret this as an allusion to the Christian mission in the Jewish *diaspora*, engaged in ensuring that the Jews in the Graeco-Roman Empire heard the Gospel and had no excuse before God or men (Benoit, pp. 146f.), is unsuitable in the context. It is doubtful, too, whether the verb **preached** refers, not to *human* proclamation, but to an apocalyptic event—i.e. the announcement by an angel of God of the divine act which brings all things to an end (so Jeremias, *Promise*, pp. 22f.); it is much more likely that the word has its usual *NT* sense, and that the idea concerns the plan of God that all nations shall have an opportunity of hearing the Gospel before the end. The word *eis telos* (**to the end**) in verse 13 mean 'finally', 'without breaking down'— not 'to the End'. This passage emphasizes the continuing task and responsibility of the Church in view of an ultimate consummation which is neither especially near nor especially remote (cf. Trilling, p. 30).

The Great Tribulation 15–22

These verses are among the most Jewish in the section. The phrase **desolating sacrilege** comes from Daniel (9.27; 11.31; 12.11), where it refers to the pagan altar set up in the Temple in 168 B.C. by Antiochus Epiphanes (cf. 1 Mac. 1.54ff.); Mk 13.14 may have had in mind Caligula's threat of similar desecration (A.D. 40), while Lk. 21.20 refers it to the siege of Jerusalem. Matthew refers explicitly to the Temple (**the holy place**), 'but he does not have any more explicit references than Mark to the Jewish War or the withdrawing of the Christians from Jerusalem in A.D. 68' (Stendahl, in *Peake*, 692e).

It is probable that the **desolating sacrilege** is a reference to the anti-Christ (2 Th. 2.3f.), whose advent at the End is heralded by a revolt from God. The words **let the reader understand** suggest that there is a hidden meaning in the prediction. Bonnard (p. 351) argues that they are meant to indicate that a special interpretation of the preceding words is to be made by Christians —viz. that the 'holy place' is a veiled allusion to the Church and that in it some abominable sacrilege (idolatry, revolt, or anti-Christ?) will be manifested.

The rest of the section is a vivid portrayal of the crisis evoked by the presence of the anti-Christ. Immediate flight is the only resource, and the slightest delay may bring catastrophe. Expectant and nursing mothers will find it very difficult to make sufficient haste. In winter the rivers and the state of the roads will make speedy travel impossible; and the Sabbath law (which Matthew presumes will be effective when these events take place) forbade any but very short journeys on that day. The shortening of the unprecedented tribulations **for the sake of the elect** (since, if it lasted its fixed period, no living being would survive) is taken from Jewish eschatology (2 Bar. 20.1–2 and 83.1): the phrase *dia tous eklektous* may mean: 'because there is an elect, faithful people in the world' (Bonnard, p. 351), or: 'in order that the elect

L

(i.e. the remnant, those whom God has chosen for his Kingdom, the Christians) may be saved.' It should be noted that these verses and those which follow have the effect of denying the imminence of the End; certain things must happen first.

23–8. Matthew retains Mk 13.21–3, and adds a saying given by Luke in a more general form and in a different context (Lk. 17.23–4, 37). As false claimants to messiahship will accompany the final appearance of Messiah (cf. verses 4–5), so also will false informers about his coming. The false Christs and false prophets offer signs and wonders (perhaps the same signs as the authentic ones, cf. 7.21–23), but their mission is **to lead astray.** 'There is no point in looking for the Messiah in the wilderness (as John the Baptist or the Qumran community), nor in hidden places, as e.g. the Jews could think of Messiah as hidden in the slums of Rome (see E. Sjöberg, *Der verborgene Menschensohn in den Evangelien*, 1955, pp. 72–80; Justin, *Dial.* XLIX. 1)' (Stendahl, *Peake* 629f). The manifestation of the Messiah will not be reserved for a small company of initiates. The Parousia of the Son of Man (who is clearly identified with Messiah) will be clear to all; no doubt will be possible.

28. Probably an echo of a proverb which Luke also associates with this kind of prediction. Birds of prey (eagles, or vultures) gather whenever they have some reason (viz. 'a carcass'); signs as visible and indicative will herald the reality of the Parousia. It is unlikely that *ptōma* (**body**) includes a reference to the crucified body of Jesus or to the city of Jerusalem sacked by Roman legions.

29–31. The appearance of the **Son of man** after the tribulation will be accompanied by cosmic portents described in terms of traditional Jewish apocalyptic (e.g. Isa. 13.9–10; 34.4). There can be no mistaking the event. Here Matthew follows Mk 13.24ff., but he adds two features: (i) when the sign of the Son of Man appears in heaven, **all the tribes of the earth will mourn.** This is an allusion to Zech. 12.10–12 (cf. also Rev. 1.7; Jn 19.37), which speaks of a mourning of repentance granted by God to Jerusalem. But for Matthew it is the lost (i.e. unbelieving Jews) that will mourn when they see the elect being gathered and the Son of Man coming (presumably *from* God) **on the clouds of heaven** (cf. Dan. 7.13, where the coming is *to* a judgment scene *before* God). Although Matthew (following Mark) has understood Dan. 7.13 of the Parousia, the 'arrival of the Son of Man is connected, as in Daniel, with the themes of suffering and vindication—the sufferings of Jesus' disciples and their future vindication' (see Hooker, *SMM*, p. 158. On the 'sign of the Son of Man', see T. F. Glasson, *JTS*, xv, 1964, pp. 299f.); **sign** (*sēmeion*) probably means 'ensign', as in Isa. 11.12, where the context concerns the gathering of the dispersed; 'ensigns' and 'trumpets' are mentioned together in 1QM iii.1–iv.2. (ii) The **trumpet call** is mentioned only in Matthew; cf. Isa. 27.13 with reference to the return from the *Diaspora*. There is no reference to resurrection here, as there is in 1 Th. 4.16; it is a gathering of the elect out of the world at the end-time.

32–3. The little parable of the Fig Tree (which may not here be in its original context) teaches again the lesson of patience: the budding **fig tree** is a sure sign of summer, and the unmistakable signs mentioned herald the arrival of the Son of Man.

34. This verse recalls 16.28, and affirms that some of the disciples would live to see the Parousia. This would presuppose a relatively early date for the event, whereas verse 36 defies all attempts to give a precise chronology.

Was Jesus in error in his prediction of the nearness of the End, if this saying is regarded as authentic? Attempts to explain this difficulty include the arguments: (a) that the reference is not to the End, but to the Fall of Jerusalem. But are not the accompanying words in 35–6 too solemn to refer simply to some specific historical event? (b) that **this generation** indicates 'the people of God' which will survive till the end of time. It is probable that we have here an example of that 'shortening of historical perspective' which is so frequent in the prophets. 'When the profound realities underlying a situation are depicted in the dramatic form of historical prediction, the certainty and inevitability of the spiritual processes involved are expressed in terms of the immediate imminence of the event' (Dodd, *Parables*, p. 71).

35. A repetition—with reference to the preceding prophecy—of a *logion* with far wider implications in 5.17. The validity of Christ's word is eternal.

36. If the words **nor the Son** are retained, then we are confronted with the problem of a declaration of the Son's limited knowledge. This (if the saying is regarded as authentic) can be solved only by supposing with V. Taylor (on Mk 13.32) that 'it is of the glory of the Incarnation that Christ accepted those limitations of knowledge which are inseparable from a true humanity' (p. 523). Others (and there is MS. support here for their position) claim that Jesus did not use the title 'the Son' as a self-description, and that the phrase in question was inserted here because of the need for an explanation of Jesus' supposed miscalculation of the nearness of the End. (The possibility is open, of course, that the omission of the words in the MS. tradition is due to theological embarrassment at the idea of a limitation of Christ's knowledge.) Jeremias (*Prayers*, p. 37) suggests that **the Father** (*ho patēr*) represents the Aramaic *abba*, which could mean 'my Father' (as well as 'the Father'), and that 'nor the Son' is a later addition which made explicit what was implicit (but not expressed in Greek) in the original text. Because he assumed that no Christian would ever have invented such a self-limiting utterance on the lips of Jesus, Schmiedel regarded this as one of his 'pillar passages' for the historical life of Jesus.

EXHORTATION TO VIGILANCE 24.37–51

With verse 37 a fresh note (which has echoes in both Mark and Luke) appears in the discourse—that of 'watchfulness', a word which occurs for the first time in verse 42: the Parousia will be unexpected, therefore vigilance is required. In verses 45–51 this vigilance becomes something active, a faithfulness to responsibilities given and undertaken, and chapter 25 will further elucidate the meaning of watchfulness.

37–41. Matthew emphasizes that **no one knows** (verse 36) by his interpretation of the Noah example: **they did not know until the flood came.** The idea of judgment is associated with the Parousia, but there is no typological use of the Noah story, such as is found in 1 Pet. 3.20f., nor is there any condemnation of the behaviour of the Noachic generation. Verses 40–1 stress the sharp cleavage caused by the coming of the Son of Man, rather than the unexpectedness of the event. The word translated **taken** (*para-lambanetai*; verse 40) has eschatological overtones; 'receive', 'take to oneself' (cf. Jn 14.3). Benoit (p. 151) refers this saying to the destruction of Jerusalem, in which the Jews will be carried away and a small remnant spared. This is surely an unacceptable interpretation in this context; the Parousia and the fall of Jerusalem are not identified in Matthew's thought.

42–4. These verses emphasize the necessity for watchfulness in view of the unexpectedness of the coming of the Son of Man. There is a certain parallelism between these verses and Mk 13.33-6. The exhortation to vigilance is followed in Mark by a parable concerning a householder, but Matthew has a more expanded tradition (cf. Lk. 12.39f.). The comparison of an unexpected event with a thief breaking in is found in 1 Th. 5.2; 2 Pet. 3.10; and in Rev. 3.3; 16.15.

45-51. This parable occurs in another context in Lk. 12.42-6, where it is presented as an interpretation of the preceding saying about the householder. It is possible that in Luke, and *originally* in Matthew also, the parable was addressed to unfaithful leaders of the household of God—i.e. either Jewish or Christian leaders who were abusing their office: the **servant** of God (Luke has 'steward') must be wise and careful of the Master's property, and his faithfulness will lead to higher responsibilities. All this is present in Matthew's form of the story, and possibly emphasized by the mention of **fellow servants**, but the emphasis (in this context) is on watchfulness in view of the unexpected return of the Lord, the Son of Man. The eschatological interpretation of the parable is confirmed by the presence of the idea: **My master is delayed** (Greek *chronizei*). It is possible that we have here an echo of one of the gravest concerns which exercised the minds of Christians in the eighties of the first century. The severity of the punishment inflicted on the unfaithful servant is striking; he merits the same treatment as was promised to the hypocrites (cf. Lk. 12.46) who, in Matthew's view, probably represent the Pharisees. The verb *dichotomein* (**punish**) may mean 'cut in pieces', 'sunder', 'separate', sc. from the company of the faithful. This latter sense, and the use of the word 'lot' (lit. 'put his lot with the hypocrites') in verse 51 recalls the language of the *Manual of Discipline*, 1QS i.10, 11; vi.24f., vii.1, 2, 16, viii.21-23; and especially ii.16-17: 'May he be cut off from the midst of the sons of light because he swerved from following God . . . May He place his lot in the midst of the eternally cursed.' If the language in verse 51 echoes the terminology of church discipline in the Matthean church (cf. 18.15), then that discipline may have been influenced (in its vocabulary at least) by the practice of excommunication in the Qumran community (Hebrew *hibdîl* = Greek *dichotomein*).

THE PARABLE OF THE VIRGINS 25.1-13

This parable, peculiar to Matthew, counsels readiness for the hour in which the 'bridegroom' will come. That the 'bridegroom' is understood (allegorically) as Christ seems certain, unless the words 'and the bride' in verse 1 are part of the original reading. Other allegorical features listed by Jeremias (*Parables*, pp. 51f.) include: the 'ten virgins' as representing the expectant Christian community; the 'tarrying' of the groom which stands for the delay of the Parousia; and the rejection of the foolish virgins, which represents the final Judgment. But the representation of the messiah as bridegroom is unknown in the *OT* and in the literature of late Judaism (except Pesik. 149a), and it makes its first appearance in 2 C. 11.2; therefore it seems improbable that Jesus' hearers would have applied the figure to the messiah. If, then, Jesus was telling a story about the preliminaries to an actual wedding feast, its purpose (stripped of the allegorical accretions) would be to offer a warning in view of the threatened eschatological crisis (Jeremias, p. 53). This the early Church took, and applied to the Parousia, stressing the words 'the bridegroom was delayed', a phrase which may well be simply part of the logical development of the original and authentic (so Jeremias) parable; see also Dodd, *Parables*, pp. 171-4. Not everyone is equally convinced about the entire absence of allegory from the parabolic teaching of Jesus, and some would insist that the idea of the messiah as bridegroom is born out of such *OT* passages as Hos. 2.19; Isa. 54.4ff.; 62.4ff.; and Ezek. 16.7ff., where Yahweh is portrayed as the 'husband' of his people, and that it is implied in Mk 2.19-20 (cf. Mt. 9.15f.). Whether we argue for the genuineness of the allegory or for the authenticity of a non-allegorical kernel not concerned with the Parousia, the essential point of the section is the same: 'Be ready.'

1. The parables of the Kingdom in chapter 13 were introduced in the words: 'The Kingdom of heaven is like . . .'; here we have: **Then the kingdom of heaven shall be compared** to the situation to be described—i.e. when the 'Son of Man' comes in his glory, what happens will be similar to the events described in the story. This means that for Matthew the story is linked to the material which precedes it; the word **Then** and the future tense may be editorial. Certain texts (D, Vulgate, Syriac) read 'the bridegroom and the bride'. If the additional words are original, they make the allegorical interpretation untenable. However, verses 5 and 6 suggest that they are a later addition when the image of 'the bride' was applied to the Church; cf. 2 C. 11.2; Eph. 5.31f. and Rev. 21.2. See further Hoskyns and Davey, pp. 47–8.

2–4. The wisdom of the virgins consists in their taking a supply of oil, i.e. in being prepared for unexpected circumstances. To see in the word **oil** a metaphor for spiritual fervour seems to be a piece of over-interpretation.

5. The delay of the bridegroom may have been a background detail in the original story; but it would certainly have been open to interpretation in terms of the delay of the Parousia, when that fact had to be faced and explained.

9. The answer of the wise virgins in *RSV* reflects the Sinaiticus text; but Codd. B and D have a much more severe answer: 'No, there will certainly not be enough for us and for you.' If that is the correct reading then the point of the parable lies in the absolute untransferability of the oil: 'There can be no loan or gift of that which secures salvation. Here is a terrible sternness: here is no easy humanitarianism' (Hoskyns and Davey, p. 49). Is this not an instance of pressing the utmost in allegory from every detail of the story?

10–12. Sayings about a closed door and the sharp judgment on late-comers are also found in another context; cf. Lk. 13.25; Mt. 7.22, 23. Some have thought that verses 11–12 are a later addition to the parable.

13. The refrain, found in 24.36, 42, 44, 50, is again repeated. Jeremias (*Parables*, p. 52) and others think that this verse, counselling watchfulness, is at variance with the parable, since the wise virgins, as well as the foolish, fell asleep. This is probably to exercise too strict a logic in interpretation. It is unlikely that the exhortation to watchfulness is concerned with the period *immediately* before the feast; preparations have to be made at the right time. The wise could rest peacefully while they waited, because they had done what was necessary in good time. The verse need not be considered as a hortatory addition to the story.

THE PARABLE OF THE TALENTS 25.14–30

This story, in its context, carries on the theme of 24.45–51: watchfulness or preparedness involves faithfulness in the responsibility which is committed to each one; vigilance is not simply a matter of fervour, joy, or even faith—it entails active and responsible service. The present context relates this to preparedness for the Parousia, but in its original form the story may have had another significance. Dodd (*Parables*, pp. 151f.) argues that the condemnation of the servant who buried his talent is an original condemnation of the selfish exclusiveness of legalistic Pharisaism, while Dibelius (*Jesus*, p. 107) considered that it represents the denunciation of the Jewish people as a whole for not making use of what was committed to them. Jeremias (*Parables*, pp. 58ff.) declares that the object of the condemnation was the scribes, who assumed that they could keep the treasure of God's word to themselves by 'hedging the Torah' with many prohibitions.

These attempts to give the parable a setting in the (non-eschatological) teaching of Jesus are necessarily coloured by presuppositions about the person of Jesus, and are therefore partially subjective, though useful. Since Luke also presents the parable in a context concerned with eschatology (19.12–27), it must be interpreted in Matthew with reference to that context. Some have thought that Luke's parable is so different from Matthew's version that it must be considered as a completely independent unit. It is more probable that it is an adaptation by Luke of the Matthean story as it stands, or, possibly, of the original parable which lies behind the Matthean form. The description of the wicked servant (*ponēre doule*) is the same in both Gospels. Another version of the story is found in the later non-canonical *Gospel of the Nazaraeans* (see *NT Apocrypha*, 1, p. 149), but this is undoubtedly a secondary tradition.

The teaching implied in the parable—that active faithfulness in responsibilities allotted is required of those who will be acceptable to God at the end—is in accordance with Matthean ideas; it is not contradictory to Pauline teaching, but rather complementary. No man is saved by works, but the true disciple of Christ will reveal his faith in his life and activity.

14. The story is not introduced by words such as 'The kingdom of heaven will be like . . .'; but it is linked closely with the preceding words: 'You know neither the day nor the hour. For it will be as . . .' i.e. like what happens in the unexpected consequences of reckoning. The man's **going on a journey** and **property** do not require (allegorical) interpretation in terms of

Jesus' ascension and the gifts of the Spirit; they belong to the logical *mise en scène* of the story.

15. The talent was originally a measure of weight, and, later a coin, the highest currency denomination, equivalent to 6,000 denarii (*c.* £400):

to each according to his ability: the master took into careful account what he knew about the servants' aptitudes.

16-18. Many attempts have been made to identify the talents. Suggestions made are that they represent natural endowments, or spiritual gifts, or the Gospel, or the word of God, and even Jesus himself given by God to the disciples. One wonders, however, if these attempts are not really beside the point. The context in chapters 24-5 concentrates on the need for active faithfulness on the part of servants rather than on the explicit content (or limits) of faithfulness. Each person has to decide in what his own personal responsibility or gift consists, and then act upon it.

21. It is doubtful if we should strain to find a meaning for the **much** over which the **good and faithful servant** is set, as Benoit (p. 154) does when he affirms that it is 'a heavenly recompense, and more precisely active participation in ruling in the reign of Christ'. The point made simply is that the reward of responsibility fulfilled is further and greater responsibility.

24-8. The real fault of the third servant is his inaction, which amounted to sheer laziness; he had attempted to evade his responsibility by burying what was given to him. Having no affection for his master (verse 24, though the master does not himself contradict the character sketch, save to omit the word 'hard'), the servant may have imagined that he was better able to look after his own interests than a mere servant was. But he is condemned for not even committing the gift to the bankers to accumulate interest, a result which would have entailed no effort whatever on the part of the servant.

29. With this almost proverbial saying (see Mt. 13.12; Mk 4.25) the emphasis is changed to an exposition of the character of retribution. The passives (*dothēsetai*, *arthēsetai*) may be circumlocutions for the divine name, meaning 'God will give', 'God will take away' (Jeremias, *Parables*, p. 62).

30. Cf. 8.12; 22.13.

THE LAST JUDGMENT 25.31–46

This section, which affirms the ultimate importance of acts of love towards even 'the least of Christ's brethren' (for whom Matthew shows concern elsewhere, 18.6–35), completes the fifth and final discourse of the Gospel. It is thoroughly consistent with what has gone before—instructions to disciples concerning the demands and responsibilities they must face while they are waiting with the Church for the Parousia. See Th. Preiss, *Life in Christ*, 1954, pp. 43–60. Although the story is often referred to as a parable, it cannot really be classified as such. The only parabolic features it contains are the shepherd, the sheep and the goats (verse 33) and these, in fact, are just passing illustrations, probably based on Ezek. 34. The story seems to be a picture of the Last Judgment, an eschatological vision which answers the question: 'How and on what basis is a man to be judged on the final day of reckoning?' The vision has some of the characteristic features of Jewish apocalyptic, e.g. the Son of Man in his glory is King and Judge (cf. Dan. 7.13ff.; 1 En. 40ff.), but it is much more sober and less highly coloured than much apocalyptic material of a visionary kind. Perhaps this is due to the fact that this section stands in Matthew's Gospel as the final words of Jesus to his disciples before the account of the Passion, in which we see the King identifying himself completely with the brother in need. Certain late features are found in the passage (see Jeremias, *Parables*, pp. 206ff.) and therefore its authenticity is rightly questioned; yet, at the same time, the *pericope* contains 'features of such startling originality that it is difficult to credit them to anyone but the Master himself' (Manson, *Sayings*, p. 249).

One might be disposed to ask of this story the questions: 'Does acceptance of Jesus Christ by faith count for nothing at the end?' and 'Is the Matthean Gospel at variance with Paul?' It must be remembered that Matthew was not facing the same problems as Paul (see Intro. pp. 67–8); he was not discussing the conditions for Gentile entry into the Church, but was concerned with the behaviour of 'disciples' already in the Church, while they await the Parousia. And the deeds which achieve acceptance (according to Matthew) are not the 'works of the Law', done to win justification; they are the outcome of faith and love.

31. The title **Son of man** is probably meant to indicate the eschatological Judge: the oldest stratum of tradition, however, does not represent Christ as Judge, but as witness at the final judgment (Mk 10.32f.; 8.38; Lk. 9.26; 12.8f.). However, the Son of Man may not in fact be Judge here. A trial scene is not portrayed, but the pronouncement of a sentence, and the King (= Christ) actually declares the judgment of the Father: 'Come, ye blessed of my Father' (verse 34). The change from 'Son of Man' in verse 31 to 'the King' in verses 34, 40 may be due to the writer's stylized form of introduction.

32-3. 'All the nations' are assembled before the glorified 'Son of Man'. Sentence is being pronounced, not on the elect (i.e. Christians) alone, but on the whole world. Mixed flocks of sheep and goats are common in Palestine; but in the evening they are separated, because goats must be kept warm at night. The fact that sheep are more valuable animals entitles them to the place of chief honour (i.e. on the right hand).

34-6. There is no mystical identification of Christ and the needy. The point is that the Son of Man demands nothing for himself, but with sovereign humility desires to the served only in the service of 'his brethren', and these are not exclusively Christians in need! 'The Son of Man has made himself one with all those who objectively need help, whatever be their subjective dispositions. It is not said that these hungry ones, strangers, prisoners were Christians. The Son of Man sees in any wretch his brother . . . His love as shepherd of Israel claims to be in solidarity with the whole of human misery in all its ranges and ultimate depths' (Preiss, *Life in Christ*, p. 52).

37-40. The righteous (the faithful and vigilant ones of the preceding parables) have not forgotten what they did, but they were unaware that they did it for the Son of Man. The word 'these' in **these my brethren** might give the impression that the reference was to disciples alone; in fact the word probably represents a Semitic superfluous demonstrative: the use of **one** (*heis*) with the meaning 'anyone' (unspecific) may also indicate Semitic influence; see Jeremias, *Parables*, p. 207.

41-6. The condemnation of those who failed to help the brethren of the Son of Man is couched in the imagery of Jewish apocalyptic; see on Mt. 13.41-3. The word **eternal** (with reference to **punishment** and **life**) means 'that which is characteristic of the Age to come'; the emphasis on temporal lastingness is secondary.

THE PASSION AND RESURRECTION 26–8

With chapter 26 we come to the Matthean account of the Passion and Resurrection of Jesus. Although this section seems to fall outside the general structure of the Gospel, in five parts (see Intro. p. 38), it cannot possibly be regarded as an appendix apart from the general pattern of development in the Gospel. Earlier in the work the sufferings of Jesus (16.13.ff.) and the sufferings of the Son of Man (13.1–52) are announced; and the account of these is anticipated.

In his Passion narrative, Matthew follows Mark with remarkable fidelity. All the events of the Marcan story (save Mk 14.51f. and 15.21b) reappear in the same order in Matthew. A significant feature of the Matthean narrative is the transformation into direct speech of reports given in Mark (26.2, 27, 39, 42); see N. A. Dahl, *NTS*, II, 1955, p. 30. This fact may be explained by suggesting that Matthew is drawing upon a tradition based on Mark and employed in the ecclesiastical *milieu* in which he was writing, perhaps even reflecting accepted church practice: cf. the change from Mark's 'they drank of it' (14.23) to 'drink of it, all of you', which probably echoes the eucharistic liturgy.

Important features of Matthew's Passion story are: (i) the interpretation of the events as controlled by God (26.2, 18; 27.62ff.; 28.11ff.); (ii) the fact that it is the Son of God who suffers and dies (27.40, 43), and whose humility is thereby underlined; (iii) this humiliation is voluntary, and therefore an act of obedience fulfilling the will of God; cf. Barth. in *TIM*, pp. 143ff.

THE PLOT AGAINST JESUS 26.1–5

1. For the last time Matthew employs the formula he uses in passing from Jesus' teaching to a narrative section.

2. Jesus now announces his death for the last time, and crucifixion is indicated as the method of death. The Synoptics all associate the death of Jesus with the Passover, but only Matthew makes Jesus explicitly declare the approach of the festival. The **Son of Man** is on the point of being **delivered up**, even before the leaders of the people have taken action; it is as if the Matthean Christ is being pictured as in charge of events, bringing to fulfilment the will of God. The subsequent meeting of the chief priests and elders is treated as if it were effected by Jesus' words.

3-5. Matthew brings together the **chief priests** and **elders** (Mark and Luke have 'the scribes') in the plot. According to Matthew and John (11.49), Caiaphas was High Priest at the time: but Lk. 3.2 and Ac. 4.6 claim that it was Annas. Annas was deposed in A.D. 15, to be replaced in A.D. 18 by Caiaphas, who lived till A.D. 36. Although deposed, Annas still retained great influence. The words **not during the feast** (*en tē heortē*), which conflict with what happened, may mean: 'not in the time of the festival crowd', rather than 'not during the feast', for Passover included the seven-day feast of Unleavened Bread (cf. Jeremias, *EW*, pp. 71-3). On the problems connected with this Passover and the Jewish calendar, see A. Jaubert, *La Date de la Cène*, 1961, and E. Ruckstuhl, *The Chronology of the Last Days of Jesus*, 1966. Recently Mlle Jaubert (*NTS*, XIV, 1967-8, pp. 145-64) has suggested that behind the words of verse 2 lies the correct tradition (witnessed to in later writings) that Jesus was in fact betrayed and delivered up on the Tuesday night (Jewish 'Wednesday') of Passion week.

THE ANOINTING AT BETHANY 26.6-13

All four evangelists recount this story of the anointing of Jesus by a woman, although Luke places it in a totally different context from the others (7.36-50), and uses it to teach a lesson on forgiveness to the Pharisees and to Simon in particular. John locates the incident just before the entry to Jerusalem, and places Mary (the sister of Lazarus) at the centre of the story. Matthew agrees with Mk 14.3ff. in putting the event at the beginning of the Passion narrative, and their accounts agree on all important points. In Matthew it is the disciples (Mark has 'some') who protest against the waste; this difference may indicate that the evangelist is applying the lesson of the story to the Christian community he knows. It is difficult to ascertain the original point of the story (a messianic anointing of Jesus on the threshold of his sufferings? an indication that, by reason of his violent death, Jesus' body would not be embalmed?), but it is possible that, in the hands of the ecclesiastically-inclined Matthew, the story was meant to give support to those who emphasized adoration of Christ in worship, over against those who, in the spirit of Jewish piety, gave supreme value to almsgiving. The message would then be that love for and worship of Christ are superior to almsgiving.

6–7. Matthew, Mark and John locate the event at Bethany (to the E. of the Mount of Olives, on the road from Jerusalem), and John places it in Lazarus' house. Luke locates the story in the house of a Pharisee named Simon, Mark and Matthew in the house of Simon **the leper**, which may indicate a person whom Jesus had healed. The gesture of the woman would not be extraordinary in an eastern home; it could have been dictated by love, joy, or recognition, but Mark and Matthew say nothing about the sentiments which provoked the action. *What* the woman did was important, not *why* she did it.

8–11. The disciples (according to Mark, 'some people', and to John, 'Judas') deplored, not the woman's action, but the financial waste it represented. The reply of Jesus distinguishes between a good work (e.g. almsgiving) and one done with reference to himself while he is present (with his disciples, and also as the 'living Christ' in the Matthean church). The latter is not so much set above the former as considered more urgent (in time).

13. Jeremias interprets the *hopou* (**wherever**), here and at Mk 14.9, in a temporal sense, and the word *euangelion* (**gospel**) as referring to the 'eternal gospel of triumph' (Rev. 14.6ff.); 'when the triumphal news is proclaimed (by God's angel) to all the world, then will her act be remembered (before God), so that he may be gracious to her at the last judgment' (*Promise*, p. 22). He also argues for the genuineness of the utterance in Mark (because of the *amēn legō humin* formula (**Truly, I say to you**); see *Prayers*, pp. 112–24), and overcomes his embarrassment at the prediction by Jesus of a world-wide proclamation of the Gospel by means of the interpretation given. But may not the words **in the whole world** be the simple addition to an original utterance? And the rendering of *eis mnēmosunon autēs* as **in memory of her** is still defensible.

THE TREACHERY OF JUDAS 26.14–16

The Synoptic Gospels give to Judas a considerable part in the Passion narrative, although Matthew alone (with Ac. 1.16–20) recounts his end. All are agreed that he was one of the Twelve, and that his action was to betray (*paradidonai*). But none of them explain why he acted in this way; jealousy, avarice, disappointment with Jesus' rôle have all been suggested, but a motive cannot be affirmed with certainty. The fact that he was thus involved in bringing Jesus to trial and death can hardly be doubted; a scandal so difficult to account for would not have been invented by the early Church.

14. Then in Matthew may be more than a simple connecting link. The action of Judas follows the anointing, which referred forward to death and burial. If Judas was disappointed in Jesus (for not playing the rôle of messianic liberator), then the indication of Jesus' impending death may have been the decisive consideration in convincing Judas that he should act.

Iscariot: four explanations of the name have been given: (i) 'inhabitant of Kariot' (Jn 6.71 in certain MSS.); (ii) transliteration of the Latin *sicarius* (contraction of the Greek *sycharitēs*), a name which would link Judas with the Zealot movement; (iii) 'inhabitant of Jericho', a corruption of the Greek *Ierichōtēs*; and (iv) a transposition of the Aramaic *sheqarya* (= 'false one', 'deceiver'), and therefore a name given by the first Christians to the betrayer (so B. Gärtner, *Die rätselhaften Termini*, 1957). The second interpretation is accepted by many as the most likely.

15-16. Matthew alone mentions the amount of money agreed on by the chief priests: **thirty pieces of silver**, the price of a slave, according to Exod. 21.32. The reference here is probably to Zech. 11.12: 'They weighed out as my wages thirty shekels of silver', a verse acting as the starting-point for the story of Judas' return of the money in 27.3-10 (see below).

PREPARATION FOR THE PASSOVER 26.17-19

In the account of the preparation Matthew abbreviates the Marcan record, but in such a way that it is necessary to presuppose his acquaintance with Mark to understand it. As was the case with the narrative of the entry to Jerusalem, Jesus is presented as being in command. He gives orders, and it is not even necessary for Matthew to affirm that events took place as Jesus said they would. The sequence of narratives here may be meant to suggest that as Judas sets about his preparations, so does Jesus: the betrayer seeks 'an opportunity' (*eukairia*), the Son of Man declares that his 'time' (*kairos*) has come.

17. The three Synoptics place this incident **on the first day of Unleavened Bread**, and Mark and Luke add that it was the day when the Passover sacrifice was made. Matthew omits this detail, possibly because he knew that it created chronological difficulties,

and so approaches the Johannine chronology. The fourth evangelist (Jn 18.28; 19.14, 31) makes the Crucifixion coincide with the
slaughter of the Passover lambs, and, consequently, for him the
Last Supper cannot have been a Passover meal; the Synoptics
think of the Supper as a Passover (see Jeremias, *EW*, pp. 41–62),
which they have dated according to the official Jewish calendar.
Jeremias and others have argued that John has altered the
chronology for a theological purpose; by synchronizing the Crucifixion and the Passover, he sets forth Jesus as the Paschal Lamb
(cf. 1 C. 5.7). Recently G. Ogg (in *HCNT*, pp. 75–96) has argued
that John's chronology is correct, the strongest evidence in its
favour being the incidental comment of Jn 18.28 and the fact that
the Synoptic dating involves the desecration of a Sabbatical
feast-day by such actions as would have made the Sabbath
violations of which Jesus was accused mere trifles (p. 89).

Various attempts have been made to harmonize the Gospel
accounts: that the Supper was a meal without a lamb (not mentioned in the accounts) which, although not a Passover, was later
interpreted as such because it took place at the paschal season;
that a '*Diaspora* Passover' was held on the eve of 14 Nisan, and not
on the regular date of 15 Nisan; suggested differences in the calendars followed in the various parts or sects of Judaism. The most
interesting suggestion in this connection comes from Mlle Jaubert
(*La Date de la Cène*). According to the solar calendar (known from
the book of Jubilees) used at Qumran (and by some Sadducees
and other groups), the Passover always occurred on Tuesday
evening (14–15 Nisan). John's Passover (on Thursday evening)
would represent the official Pharisaic calendar, whereas the
Synoptics hint at the earlier time for Jesus' Supper (cf. on
26.1–2). Chief among these is the fact that there is simply not time
for the Sanhedrin's and for Pilate's activities between a Thursday
night supper and a Friday crucifixion. If the Gospels have con-
densed into one night and morning proceedings which lasted
several days (see M. Black, in *NTE*, pp. 19–33), we would be
brought back to the Tuesday evening for the meal—and a few
Christian traditions do in fact date the Lord's Supper (and Jesus'
arrest) on a Tuesday. If this is the right date, Jesus was celebrating
an unorthodox, if not illegal, (Galilean?) Passover in the Pharisaic
stronghold of Jerusalem.

While the suggestion of Mlle Jaubert solves some of the problems

of the Passion narrative, it must be admitted that it creates
others; chief among them is this question: How could the tradition
of Jesus' celebrating an early Passover be forgotten so completely
that the Synoptic Gospels all conform (or at least appear to
conform) to the official Jewish calendar? An approach to an answer
may come from consideration of the fact that the Eucharist
tradition in early Christian communities (a rite which probably
influenced the presentation of the Gospel account of the Last
Supper) was indebted, not only to the meal which took place
around the Passover season, but more particularly to the first post-
Resurrection celebration of the Passover, when the soteriological
interpretation of Jesus' death was explicitly formulated (cf.
Fuller, *Foundations*, p. 119 and n. 64). To this association of
Passover and Eucharist the account of the Last Supper was made
to conform. The paschal interpretation of the Supper does not
depend solely or directly on the solution of the chronological
problem. See further: E. Ruchstuhl, *Chronology*; A. R. C. Leaney,
Theology, LXX, 1967, pp. 51–62; Preiss, *Life in Christ*, pp. 81ff. (he
argues for an anticipated Passover); A. J. B. Higgins, *The Lord's
Supper in the New Testament*, 1952.

18. The phrase **to such a one** (*pros ton deina*) is a characteristic
piece of Matthean simplification. For clarification we require to
know Mark's story.

time: like 'hour' in John's Gospel, refers to Jesus' death—not to
the meal, nor to his return.

will keep: present tense in Greek (= 'I am to keep'). The usage
indicates a confident assertion which has imminent fulfilment in
mind.

ON THE BETRAYAL **26.20–5**

Matthew follows Mark (14.17ff.) in placing this episode before the
account of the Last Supper. He omits Mark's suggestive allusion
to Ps. 41.9 (in 14.18), but adds the dialogue with Judas in verse
25.

20–1. The reference to **evening** may suggest that Matthew is
thinking of the Passover meal eaten after sunset. Since reclining
was the customary posture at feasts and meals, it cannot be argued
that the verb *anakeimai* (*RSV* **sat**) necessarily makes this a Passover
meal, usually eaten in a reclining position as a sign that the people
were no longer slaves, but free men.

23. The individual is not specified, but he is a friend, eating from the common bowl. This fact aggravates the deceitfulness of the action.

24. Judas' rôle is necessary in the fulfilment of the Scriptural plan, but the enormity of his crime is not thereby lessened. 'What has to happen will happen, but this does not make an excuse, nor is Judas considered a helpless victim for a superimposed fate' (Stendahl, in *Peake*, 693g).

25. You have said so: the words probably represent an Aramaic expression which usually means 'Yes'; they could, however, be interpreted as 'You have said it, not I'.

THE WORDS OF INSTITUTION **26.26–30**

In Matthew's account, the words at the Last Supper follow closely those in Mark. The addition of the verb 'eat' in verse 26 and the alteration of the descriptive phrase 'they all drank of it' to a command, 'Drink of it, all of you' show that the Matthean form is more symmetrical and has a 'liturgical' (Lohmeyer), or 'a more developed liturgical' (Stendahl), accent. Matthew also adds to this saying the words 'for the forgiveness of sins'. These are absent from Mt. 3.2, but Mark and Luke retain them there in relation to John's baptism. For Matthew, apparently, the remission of sins was related to the New Covenant instituted in the death of Christ. On the relation of the version of the words of Institution in Matthew and Mark to that in Luke and in 1 C. 11, see Jeremias, *EW*, pp. 96–105; K.G. Kuhn, in *SNT*, pp. 65–93, and Ellis, pp. 252–5.

26. The words **as they were eating** are found also in verse 21; this suggests that the two *pericopes* 20–5 and 26–30 were separate items in tradition. The blessing is an act of thanksgiving to God ('having said the blessing'), and, according to the usage of pious Jews, would be: 'Blessed art Thou, O Lord our God, king of the universe, who bringest forth bread from the earth'; the blessing over the wine would be: 'Blessed . . . universe, creator of the fruit of the vine'. Such actions in a Passover meal were preceded by a lengthy statement of the meaning of the bread and the lamb, and by the recitation of the first part of the *Hallel* (Ps. 113, or 113–14).

Notice how Jesus presides throughout the meal, as did the father of the Jewish family. The totally new feature of the verse lies in

the last words: **'this is my body.'** In the Aramaic there would be
no copula, though it would be implied. To insert **is** suggests a
relationship of identity which there is no reason to assume,
whereas the rendering 'represents' may convey only a purely
figurative suggestion. Taylor (p. 544) finds least unsatisfactory
Moffatt's rendering 'Take this, it means my body'. What has
happened to the bread (being broken) will happen to Jesus'
body; and, just as the people of Israel had been associated with
the deliverance from Egypt by eating the paschal meal, so the
disciples participate in the beneficial work which is about to be
accomplished in Jesus' death by taking and eating this food. The
meal effectively links the disciples with the results of Christ's
unique sacrifice.

27. It has been suggested that, because the tradition presupposes a common cup, the meal cannot have been a Passover,
at which each man had his own cup; but the evidence for Passover
usage of cups is too uncertain to sustain an argument either way.
There is no clear reason for identifying the **cup** with the third
cup (the 'cup of blessing') drunk at the Paschal feast, unless it be
otherwise certain (which it is not) that the occasion was a Passover
meal (cf. 1 C. 10.16).

28. blood of the covenant: the words recall Exod. 24.8 (used
in the *Haggadah* to interpret the Passover wine as blood which
makes covenant between God and the people, cf. M. Pes. x.6),
where the sprinkling of the dedicated blood means that the people
now share in the blessings of the covenant made at Sinai. So the
death of Jesus inaugurates a new covenant of God with, and in
favour of man—every one, the rest of mankind. The Lucan and
Pauline accounts make clearer reference to Jer. 31.31-4 by speaking
of 'the new covenant'. That that passage is in Matthew's mind is
suggested by the addition of 'for the forgiveness of sins', cf. Jer.
31.34. The event through which God will deliver men from the
power of sin is the death of Jesus, and that deliverance is celebrated
in the meal, just as the escape from Egypt was celebrated (pros-
pectively) in the Passover.

29. fruit of the vine: a liturgical formula for 'wine' which
would be used at Passover (M. Berak. vi.1). This verse, which
follows Mark in all essentials (cf. Lk. 22.17 and the eschatological
interest in 1 Cor. 11.26 'until he comes'), shows that the Supper
points forward to the perfected fellowship of the new Israel in the

messianic age, and that drinking the cup is a present participation in that fellowship; for the idea of the messianic banquet in the kingdom of God, see Isa. 25.6; 1 En. 72.14; Mt. 8.11; Lk. 22.29f. The words 'from now on' (*ap'arti*, RSV **again**) suggest that the non-partaking refers to subsequent Passovers until the consummation in the Kingdom. Jeremias (*EW*, pp. 207-18) argues that Jesus was abstaining from the Passover he was then celebrating, and that this avowal was, like the later fast of the Quartodecimans during the Jewish Passover, an act of intercession for Israel which had rejected her messiah. But was this fast by early Palestinian Christians not in fact a fast in remembrance of Jesus' death (cf. Ogg, in *HCNT*, p. 92)?

30. The second part of the *Hallel* (Pss. 115-18) was sung at the end of Passover, when the last cup of wine had been circulated. On the basis of the late Jewish exegesis of Ps. 118.25f. as an antiphonal song in which the messiah was greeted at his Parousia, Jeremias (*EW*, pp. 255-62) argues that the Lord's Supper was from the beginning an anticipation, or 'antedonation', of the final consummation.

THE PREDICTION OF PETER'S DENIAL 26.31-6

31. As against Mk 14.27, Matthew makes it clear that the disciples will fall away *because of Jesus*, and *on that night*. The sufferings of the master will cause them to stumble or doubt, detach them from his person, and, in the case of Peter, cause him to utter words of denial. The citation of Zech. 13.7 is interesting: the M.T. has: 'Strike the shepherd and the flock will be scattered'; and the LXX reads: 'Strike the shepherd and scatter the sheep'. The first person future in Mark and Matthew suggest that it is God who will smite Jesus, with the result that **the flock** (the band of disciples) will be dispersed.

32. This verse, which is taken from Mark, must be understood as a parenthesis. It is the first prediction of the Resurrection in this chapter, and seems to suggest a return to the old relationship with the disciples after death; Jesus the shepherd will reconstitute his community and lead (**go before**) them into Galilee. (It may have been that Mark introduced the saying at 14.28 to prepare the way for Mk 16.7. The verse is missing from the Fayyum fragment in the Rainer papyri, but this could be due to its difficulty rather than proof of its unoriginality.) Lohmeyer explained the verse in terms of the doctrine that Galilee would be the scene of the Parousia. Is there in this verse an indication that Jesus himself expected the imminent vindication of his cause? On this, see Barrett, *JGT*, pp. 68ff.

34. Cock-crowing was usual at around midnight and at 3.a.m., and the Romans gave the name 'cock-crow' to the watch between these hours. Mark refers to the two crowings, but Matthew regards the second as the only one because it was the main one. To **deny** in this context means 'to disown': if there are associations with a courtroom scene, then the notion of taking up a hostile (or negative) attitude in giving testimony may be present in the term.

JESUS IN GETHSEMANE 26.36–46

This is one of the longest episodes in the Matthean account of the Passion. The narrative is dependent on Mark, but, before being inserted at this point in the first two Gospels, it may have been circulating independently; this would account for its uneasy link with what precedes and follows. There are two strands: one (verses 36, 39, 43, 45) dominated by the idea of Jesus' *hour* (a Christological interest), the other concerned with 'vigilance and temptation', 37, 38, 39b, 40, 41 (parenetic in character).

36. Gethsemane: 'olive-press'. Jn 18.1f. speaks of 'a garden' on the far side of Kidron, and suggests that Jesus often went there with his disciples.

37–8. The group of three (Peter and the sons of Zebedee; cf. 17.1–8) are closer to Jesus in his time of stress than any others. The grief and anguish (*adēmonein* is found only here in Matthew and at Phil. 2.26) is the sorrowful obedience of one who still hopes in God, but knows that a cruel death confronts him. The words addressed to the disciples allude to Ps. 42.6 and 43.5: the addition of **even unto death** denotes anguish that threatens life itself.

39. Mk 14.36 gives the Aramaic 'Abba', the name used by Jesus in prayer to God and retained in the Church's usage (see on 6.9). The **cup** is an *OT* metaphor used of punishment and retribution, but here it involves suffering and death. These Jesus shrinks from, but yet he is wholly dedicated to doing his Father's will, whatever that may entail. Jesus' obedience and loyalty to God is never put in question by the prayer, but its words—if genuine—may imply

that he was at least contemplating the possibility that the establishment of the Kingdom might be achieved without the necessity
of preliminary suffering (see Barrett, *JGT*, p. 46.) The account of
Jesus' praying here has clear allusions to the Lord's Prayer (and
again in verses 41 and 42), and it is possible that the Matthean
form of the story was used for instruction on prayer.

41. The attitude of sleep suggests lethargy towards the peril of
temptation, which here means 'trial', 'assault by the enemy'.
For the suggestion that originally the command to keep awake
was an exhortation to look out for the long-expected fulfilment of
the apocalyptic hope (linked with a Passover night), which was
later mistakenly interpreted as a command to remain physically
awake, see Barrett, *JGT*, p. 47. The contrast between **spirit** and
flesh need not be regarded as Pauline, nor does **spirit** refer to the
Spirit of God imparted to man and fighting against human weakness (Schweizer, *The Spirit of God*, 1960, pp. 24–5): the distinction
is between man's physical weakness and the noble desires of his
will (see Hill, p. 242, and cf. the doctrine of the two Spirits in
Qumran (1QS 3.24ff.))

45. Are you still sleeping and taking your rest? The
Greek could be rendered as a command: 'Sleep on now and take
your rest', and this could imply that the time for watchfulness (for
the hoped-for eschaton) on the disciples' part is over now. The
cup of suffering is not going to be taken from Jesus by a last-
moment intervention; the betrayer is about to come; the 'hour' of
death is about to strike. And all this is according to God's will.

46. Presumably Jesus could see the party approaching, and he
goes to meet the betrayer with a majestic confidence. He has
triumphed over all questionings about the actual form of the
divine plan; he now knows what God's will is, and can go forward
with assurance.

THE ARREST 26.47-56

47. The group accompanying Judas was presumably from the
Temple Guard, although the word *ochlos* (**crowd**) suggests something less formal. There is no indication that Roman soldiers were
involved in this incident. Matthew has omitted the scribes, perhaps
as being unsuitable in this official context.

48-49. A sign to identify Jesus would be necessary because the
area was probably filled with pilgrims bivouacking for the night.

The **kiss** (on hand or foot) was not so much a gesture of affection as a salutation of honour. The words used by Judas: **'Hail, Master** (*lit.* Rabbi)!' confirm this interpretation.

50. The translation of Jesus' words is uncertain. It could be 'Why are you here?': but the tone of Matthew's Passion-narrative suggests that it should be '(Do) what you came for!' (see W. Eltester, in *Neotestamentica*, pp. 70–91, for the rendering: 'May that for which you are here be done!'

51–4. The point of this paragraph (which does not accord well with the restrained spirit of what precedes, and may therefore indicate later tradition) seems to be found in verse 53: if he wished, Jesus had the right and the power to appeal for help and be delivered. It may be that it was in answer to a question about Jesus' power that this incident was created. The difficulties within it are considerable; e.g. Where did the disciple or friend of Jesus get the sword? Why was he not arrested? There is no reference to the healing of the servant (as in Luke and John), nor to his name (as in John). Matthew adds the saying on taking up the sword: to defend the cause of Christ by the sword may be to risk fighting against the will of God. In 1QM vii.6 angels are represented as joining forces with the righteous to win deliverance; but in the mission of Jesus the prophecy of Zech. 13 must be fulfilled (26.31).

55–6. Jesus' words suggest a longer teaching ministry in Jerusalem than the Synoptic accounts imply. He had been there a period of months, as has been suggested by dating his arrival in the city at the feast of Tabernacles. With typical precision, Matthew records that **all the disciples** left Jesus (Mark has 'they all'), and so the attention of the reader is directed again—as it is throughout the Passion narrative—to the person of the one who must suffer alone.

JESUS BEFORE THE SANHEDRIN 26.57–75

The Gospel records of Jesus' trial present a number of important problems, both of a historical and of a juridical nature. On the question of who really bore the responsibility for Jesus' death, the witness of the evangelists is not unanimous. According to the Fourth Gospel, the Roman authorities and the Jewish leaders are involved together from the outset in bringing about the death of Jesus (Jn 18.3, 12), and the leaders are represented as wishing to maintain good relations with their imperial masters; therefore

Jesus is crucified both as a political threat and as an embarrassment to the Jews. In John's narrative it is explicitly pointed out that the Sanhedrin had not the power at this time to inflict the death sentence (18.31); on the other hand, the Synoptics (especially Mark and Matthew) lay the emphasis on the proceedings of the Jewish court. Matthew's only substantial addition to Mark's account of the hearing before Pilate (which does not read like a genuine account of a Roman provincial trial) is the dramatic scene in which the governor washes his hands, leaving the Jews fully and solely responsible for the outcome; obviously the Roman governor is being represented as a mere tool by which the Jewish authorities work their will. But in the presentation of this picture, there is a difficulty. The account of the procedure of the Sanhedrin does not agree with the Mishnaic requirements for legal procedure in capital charges; this had to be carried out in daytime, on two consecutive days, and with private interrogation of the witnesses (see M. Sanhedrin).

Even if all the regulations found in the Mishnah were not in force as early as A.D. 30, the Gospel narrative of the trial gives the impression: (i) of 'telescoping' events (see Black, in *NTE*, pp. 19–33, and above, on 26.17); and (ii) of being determined to make the Jews responsible for the execution of their Messiah. The Marcan and Matthean accounts of the trial may therefore be influenced by theological considerations, and may reflect the situation in the second half of the first century, when the real opponents of the nascent Church were the Jews. Moreover, it is likely that the early Church, seeking to establish itself in the Roman empire, tended to minimize the involvement of the Roman authorities in the execution of the Messiah. But the indisputable fact that Jesus died by crucifixion shows that the formal trial and sentence were the work of a Roman court, for crucifixion was essentially a *Roman* penalty.

Were the proceedings before the Sanhedrin preliminary to the preparation of the case for submission to the Roman procurator for formal trial? Many commentators explain the matter in this way, although the actual charge brought against Jesus by the Jews before Pilate bears little relation to the earlier proceedings. The account of the trial before the Sanhedrin may represent an attempt by the Church, in the absence of precise information, to set forth the grounds on which Jesus was believed to have been condemned by

the Jewish leaders and handed over to Pilate—an account which
clearly implies the responsibility of the Jews, and their deliberate
rejection of the Messiah.

Whatever be the precise relation of the trials in the Passion
narrative, it cannot seriously be doubted that both the Jewish
religious authorities and the Romans were involved in bringing
Jesus to the Cross. A legal issue—probably related to misunderstood 'kingship'—lay between Jesus and Pilate; and a religious
issue brought the Jewish leaders and Jesus into open conflict.
On the problems of the trial narrative, see Barrett, *JGT*, pp.
53–67; Paul Winter, *On the Trial of Jesus*, 1961; A. N. Sherwin-
White, *Roman Society and Roman Law in the New Testament*, 1963;
Nineham, pp. 398–405; and the books on *The Trial of Jesus* by
J. Blinzler, 1959, and G. D. Kilpatrick 1953.

57-8. It is implied that the proceedings were held in the High
Priest's house, and this (if a real trial is meant) is an irregularity,
for the court could not meet there. Nor could a trial involving a
capital charge take place at night; it had to take place by day
with a second session the following day before conviction could be
pronounced. No such trial could commence, therefore, before a
Sabbath or feast-day, because automatically a second session
would be prevented on the day following. If this was not a trial,
but an informal, preliminary investigation (later understood by
the evangelists as a full trial), would the Sanhedrin have met for
it in the middle of Passover night; or, if the Synoptic chronology
is wrong, in the middle of a night just before Passover? A formal
trial and a preliminary hearing both seem unlikely at such a time.
Probably there was only one meeting before the Jewish authorities
in the morning (27.1). The officers with whom Peter sat would be
the High Priest's servants, including, perhaps, the Temple police.

59. The impression given is certainly of a formal session of the
Sanhedrin. In the time of Jesus the council was composed of the
elders, the chief priests (with former chief priests and their
families), and the scribes (usually Pharisaic). It numbered seventy
one members, of whom twenty-three formed a quorum. Is this
night session being confused with, or created out of, the nocturnal
examination at Annas' house (Jn 18.12ff.)? If this was a regularly
constituted meeting of the Sanhedrin, would the members have
been seeking false (i.e. inadmissible) testimony against Jesus?
Again, would the evidence not have been prepared in advance?

Jewish rules regarding the assessing of evidence were strict and fair towards the accused; but here the court appears as prosecutor and judge in a way contrary to legal practice.

61. Two witnesses (the number required if evidence was to be treated seriously) claim that Jesus said that he was **able** (only Matthew has *dunamai*) **to destroy the temple of God, and to build it in three days.** According to Jn 2.19ff., Jesus did utter a saying like this (although John himself interprets it allegorically), and Ac. 6.14 seems to point in the same direction. Probably, therefore, some words on the end of the existing Temple were uttered by Jesus (though originally they may simply have referred to the destruction of the Temple by others; cf. Mt. 24.1–2), and were used against him in his trial. If Jesus said: 'I can (or shall) destroy the Temple', he was setting himself above one of the 'ultimates' of Judaism, and that indeed could be taken as blasphemy, although it did not involve a definite railing against the divine name; and the punishment for blasphemy was death by stoning. Either the Jews were unable to carry out capital sentences (cf. Jn 18.31), or, if they had the power of life and death, they either were required or had chosen to have the death sentence ratified and executed by the Roman procurator.

62–3. The silence of Jesus recalls Isa. 53.7 and Ps. 38.12–14. The question asked by the High Priest may originally have been: 'Art thou the Christ (Messiah)?'; and, in asking it, he may have been relying on information known or revealed about Jesus' claims. Jesus' messiahship was probably an important issue in the actual trial, and it was the decisive issue between the Church and Jewish authorities in the time of the evangelists. The phrase 'Son of God' is unlikely to have been used by a High Priest of the Saducean party with the meaning of 'Messiah'; the title belongs to the language of the Church rather than to the Jewish leaders.

64–6. In his reply (which is less positive here than in Mark), Jesus does not use the titles 'Messiah' or 'Son of God'; but, as elsewhere in the Gospels, the Danielic Son of Man (with Ps. 110.1), and the identification of the speaker with this figure is implicit. Caiaphas could not fail to realize this, and the evangelist is certain of it. M. San. vi.5 prescribes that the judge shall tear his garments on hearing blasphemy; but the blasphemer was not guilty of death unless he used the divine name. In his answer, Jesus used **Power** instead of 'Yahweh', and so he ought to have escaped the charge; but the claim that he would 'sit at God's right hand', in fulfilment of Dan. 7.13–14, must have been regarded as tantamount to blasphemy. Originally, the saying may have referred to Jesus' vindication (as Son of Man), but it was interpreted (in the Church) as referring to his exaltation and Parousia.

67–8. The messianic character of the accused did not impress the court. Jesus is subjected to indignities by which it is thought the hollowness of his claim will be revealed. The Messiah was expected to have power to vanquish his enemies, and to be possessed of prophetic discernment (Ps. Sol. 17.37ff.)

69–75. The account of Peter's denial raises few problems. Some of the details (the servant girl, the Galilean accent of the disciple, Peter's repeated imprecations) give to the narrative the appearance of historical accuracy. In any case, there seems no cultic or apologetic motive which would have led to the invention of the incident. The fact of a three-fold denial and the crowing of the cock at the right time, in fulfilment of Jesus' words (verses 30–5), indicates, not that the story is legendary, but that it had been in process of formation in the oral tradition for a long time before receiving its fixed literary form.

JESUS IS DELIVERED TO PILATE **27.1–2**

1. This second meeting of the Sanhedrin (lit. 'they held a council') convened in the morning (but not complying with the legal requirement that a sunset should intervene before a second session) does not give any hint of a previous meeting. Perhaps this was the only meeting held, and the previous section may record what actually belonged to this session; or it may represent a Christian reconstruction of what was thought likely to have taken place. There must, of course, have been at least one meeting of the Sanhedrin; the Roman governor would not have taken the initiative in arresting and trying Jesus.

2. Pontius Pilatus, the fifth procurator of Judea, held office in A.D. 26–36. From the information we have concerning him (Philo, *Leg. ad Gaium* 38, Josephus, *Ant.* XVIII.ii.2; XVIII.iii.1f.; XVIII.vi.5; *BJ* II.ix.2–4) it seems that he was a cruel and inflexible man, given to corruption and violence. Even allowing for exaggeration in these Jewish works, their portrayal of Pilate is not easily compatible with the weak, vacillating (but fair) character portrayed in the Gospels. It is likely that the evangelists are guilty of whitewashing Pilate because of their desire to exculpate the Romans and put the full responsibility on the Jews for the death of Jesus.

THE DEATH OF JUDAS 27.3-10

The account of Judas' death inserted here presupposes the earlier account—i.e. that Judas was paid (Mk 14.11 and Mt. 26.15), and that his action was necessary for the fulfilment of Scripture (Mk 14.21 and Mt. 26.24); but it attempts to answer the question of Judas' fate. The narrative is based on Ac. 1.16-20 (a pre-Matthean tradition which connected the traitor's death with a grave-yard called 'The Field of Blood'), and on Zech. 11.12-13 (with allusions to Jer. 18.2-3 and 32.6-15). Matthew's use of this quotation depends on a confusion of the Hebrew '*ôṣār* (= 'treasury') and M.T. *yôṣēr* (= 'potter'), a confusion which is witnessed to in the *OT* Peshitta and implied in the Targum. The priests, who recognize that Judas' money could not be put into the treasury without causing defilement, buy **the potter's field,** and so, without being aware of it, bring Zechariah's words to fulfilment; see Stendahl, pp. 120-7, B. Gärtner, *ST*, VIII, 1954, pp. 16-20; and Lindars, pp. 116-22. There are two fixed points in the tradition: the sudden death of Judas, and the purchase of a piece of land called 'the Field of Blood'. 'It may be deduced from the way in which the whole material is handled that, though the story is not created out of the text (Zech. 11.12f.), the text may be freely used to fill up the gaps in the story. This seems to the early Christian exegetes a perfectly legitimate hermeneutical procedure' (Lindars, p. 122.)

3. The fact that Matthew places the account of Judas' death here and declares that the betrayer saw that Jesus had been condemned implies that he understands the decision of the Sanhedrin to have been the crucial one. The Greek word *meta-melētheis* (**repented**) would be better translated 'was seized with remorse'.

4-5. The story seems to presuppose that the High Priests were still in session or within the Temple area; but, according to verse 2, they were at Pilate's residence. This inconsistency suggests that Matthew is deliberately adding this story to Mark's narrative, which he had been following closely. But he does not add the story presented in Acts! Perhaps we may claim (with Bonnard p. 394) that Matthew and the author of Acts are using an oral tradition common in Jerusalem which explained the name of a certain place, 'the Field of Blood'. According to Matthew, Judas hanged himself; according to Acts, he fell down and died from a disease; but it is not impossible that the terms used refer to suicide.

6. It is not lawful to put them into the treasury: according to the M.T. of Zech. 11.13, the prophet's thirty pieces of silver were given to the potter (*yôṣēr*): this form of the text may have influenced verse 7 'the potter's field': the Aramaic *korbanan* (= 'treasury') indicates that the writer either confused *yôṣēr* with *'ôṣār* (= 'treasury') or, more probably, found the reading *'ôṣār* in his own text. (It is the reading of the Peshitta: LXX has 'foundry' —probably the Temple mint.)

7-8. The **potter's field** is the **Field of Blood** because it was bought with blood money. The form of the story in Acts gives the name as *Akeldama* (Aramaic *Haqeldama*), which may be a pun on *'Akeldamak* (= 'place of sleep', 'cemetery'); note verse 7: **to bury strangers in** (lit. 'as a burial place for strangers').

9-10. The quotation is from Zech. 11.13, with the first person ('I took') changed to the third (**they took**), and 'the price at which I was paid off' made to refer to the sum paid for Jesus. Matthew attributes the citation to Jeremiah; Jeremiah did buy a field (36.6-15) and visited a potter (18.2ff.), and words and phrases from the LXX rendering of these incidents have contributed to the quotation given (see Lindars, p. 121).

JESUS BEFORE PILATE 27.11-26

Matthew follows Mark closely throughout this section, but adds some features of his own (verses 19 and 24-5). The scene of this trial was either in the Tower of Antonia (where some think Pilate resided during his stays in Jerusalem) or, more probably, in the old palace of Herod. Josephus (*BJ* ii.xv.5; *Ant.* xx.v.3) and Philo (*Leg. ad Gaium* 38) make the procurator reside at Herod's palace; the word 'praetorium' (verse 27) could be applied to a princely residence (such as Herod's) as well as to a military or judicial seat. If the trial was known to have taken place at Herod's palace, the origin of Luke's special tradition about a hearing before the King might be explained.

11. Pilate asks Jesus about his Kingship. The Sanhedrin presumably brought Jesus' claim to be the Christ (Messiah) before the governor, explaining the title as meaning **King of the Jews**—an appellation calculated to create great anxiety in the mind of the governor of a Roman province. Jesus' reply (as Matthew understands it) seems to be an affirmative.

14. not even to a single charge: or, 'not even one word'. Pilate was impressed and probably embarrassed by the bearing of the prisoner before him.

15. There is no evidence for this custom apart from the Gospels (Mark, Matthew and John). The suggestion that it dated from the Maccabean era, or was introduced by the Romans, is without historical foundation. Josephus had no knowledge of such a practice, and, in any case, if Barabbas was already condemned to death, only the Emperor had the power to release him. The Barabbas incident takes the place of a formal condemnation of Jesus by Pilate, and so ameliorates the impression given of the governor's attitude to the prisoner; it also serves to underline the responsibility of the Jewish leaders for the death of Jesus (verse 20).

16. According to Mk 15.7, Barabbas had committed murder during an insurrection (or 'in the insurrection'. Had there been a revolution or attempted revolt at this time?). In some Greek MSS. the Syriac versions and Origen, the name of the prisoner is 'Jesus Barabbas' and this may well be original; as time wore on, the name 'Jesus' came to be treated as a sacred name, and its application to a criminal would have been specially offensive. (Incidentally, the name 'Barabbas' is very odd: it could only mean 'son of the father'.) If the criminal's name was 'Jesus Barabbas', then there is added point to the tradition: the populace of Jerusalem, by its intervention with Pilate and under the influence of the religious leaders, saved Jesus the criminal, and brought about the execution of Jesus the Messiah.

18. The **envy** must have been on the part of the High Priests (cf. Mk 15.10), caused by Jesus' increasing influence over the people.

19. This verse is peculiar to Matthew, and may represent a tradition (originally from Jerusalem) known only in the circles in which the Gospel received written form. The words of Pilate's wife are not a defence of Jesus; she merely asks her husband not to become involved in the case of a man whom she thinks **righteous** (= innocent). The verse may be an introduction to verses 24f. The allusion to **a dream** is typically Matthean: the opening chapters of the Gospel are held together by dreams.

20–3. Matthew's presentation of the dialogue between Pilate and the people is clearer than Mark's. The responsibility lies with the chief priests and elders, not with the crowds who were simply being used by the authorities.

24–5. Pilate follows his wife's advice to avoid involvement and, by washing his hands, demonstrates that he has no guilt in Jesus' execution. Washing of the hands in this symbolic way was a Jewish custom (Dt. 21.6f, Ps. 26.6), not a Roman one; it is very difficult to imagine that the procurator in fact acted in this way, but the intention of the passage is to exculpate Pilate as far as possible, and to put the full blame for Jesus' death on the Jews. Verse 25b may be understood, from Matthew's point of view, as a prophecy of the judgment which will fall on the Jews in the future, by reason of their rejection of the Messiah. It would be difficult to imagine that the Jews deliberately accepted responsibility for Jesus' death because they viewed it as a sacrifice by which they would be benefited.

26. Scourging was originally a Roman practice but was adopted by the Jews (Mt. 10.17; Ac. 5.40; 22.19; 2 C. 11.25): among the Romans it was a common preliminary to crucifixion, with the object of weakening the prisoner.

THE MOCKING OF JESUS 27.27–31

According to Lk. 23.11 the mocking took place at Herod's palace and came from Herod's soldiers, and this may be more accurate. It is hard to imagine Pilate's soldiers mocking Jesus after having scourged him, for scourging was intended immediately to precede crucifixion. Similar mocking scenes are known (cf. Philo, *Flacc.* 5–6) and they may be distantly related to the Near Eastern New Year rites (see R. Delbruck, *ZNW*, XLI, 1942, pp. 124ff.).

27. Matthew explicitly identifies the soldiers as those of the governor. The **praetorium** most probably indicates the old palace of Herod to the W. of the city (where the procurator resided when he came from Caesarea), rather than some place in the Tower of Antonia. The latter location (to the N. of the Temple) would not fit in with the movements of Pilate and the crowds, as these are shown by the evangelists (especially John) in their Passion narratives; nor would it agree with what is known from other sources (Josephus and Philo) concerning the habits of procurators.

28. According to Mark, the soldiers dressed Jesus in 'purple'— the emperor's colour: Matthew alters this, probably correctly, to **a scarlet robe**—i.e. they put on him one of their own cloaks.

29. a crown of thorns: this may have been designed to cause pain, but it is more likely that the long thorns were used in the form of 'rays' or spikes, as in the radiant crowns pictured on coins of the period (see H. St J. Hart, *JTS*, III, 1952, pp. 66-75).

a reed: given as a staff or sceptre, the symbol of ruling power.

'Hail, King . . .': this corresponds to the usual greeting accorded to the Emperor: 'Hail, Caesar'. The intention throughout seems to be to mock Jesus' claims rather than to inflict pain.

THE CRUCIFIXION 27.32-44

The crucifixion proper is mentioned only briefly in the narrative —almost in passing (verse 35a). The interest and emphasis lies on the division of Jesus' raiment, the inscription on the Cross, and especially on the various taunts made by the witnesses of the event. All the circumstances surrounding the crucifixion are described in words which recall passages from Pss. 22 and 69. As has been his custom throughout his Gospel, Matthew underlines the fulfilment of Scripture; but the ideas and the *OT* allusions were already present in Mark. It seems certain therefore that, before the writing of Mark's Gospel, oral tradition had gone a long way in interpreting the crucifixion with the aid of Pss. 22 and 69, and on this Matthew is building (see Dibelius, p. 184). It must be said, however, that the numerous *OT* allusions do not prove the historical inaccuracy of the events recorded; they only prove— what has been affirmed already—that the Matthean narrative is not primarily an objective chronicle, but a means of instruction on the meaning of Jesus' death.

32. Simon of Cyrene is only a name to Matthew. The Marcan reference to his sons (who may have become Christians; cf. Ac 19.33; Rom. 16.13) is omitted. That another person should carry the prisoner's cross is not exceptional; the rigours of the trial would have drained Jesus of physical strength. (Cf. also on 5.41.)

33. Golgotha: Aramaic, meaning 'skull'. The place was probably so named from a rock of that shape outside the city. The question of the exact location is still open; see A. Parrot, *Golgotha and the Church of the Holy Sepulchre*, 1957.

34. wine . . . mingled with gall: Mark has 'myrrh' instead

of 'gall', the latter having been substituted from Ps. 69.21—'they
gave me poison (LXX, gall) for food and for my thirst they gave
me vinegar to drink'—one of the Psalms used from an early period
in the Church's teaching and liturgy (cf. Jn 2.17; 15.25; 19.28;
Ac. 1.20; Rom. 15.3); cf. Dodd, *Acc. Scrip.*, pp. 57–59. According
to the Talmud (San. 43a, cf. Prov. 31.6–7) a man about to be
executed could beg a 'grain of incense' (a narcotic) in wine in
order to dull his senses and alleviate pain. Jesus refuses the sedative
and heroically endures his sufferings to the end.

35. The simple reference to this most cruel and frightful of
punishments is remarkably restrained. For details of crucifixion
see J. Blinzler, *The Trial of Jesus*, pp. 246ff., and Excursus xii, pp.
263ff. It was usual for the prisoner's clothes to become the per-
quisite of the executioner: the casting of lots for Jesus' clothes is
entirely plausible, but for the early Church its significance lay in
its fulfilment of Ps. 22.18. The exact formula-quotation found in
some manuscripts is likely to be a later accretion to the text (see
Jn 19.23–4).

36. Peculiar to Matthew. The soldiers kept guard to prevent
any attempt at rescue, and Matthew may be countering suggestions that Jesus was removed from the cross before he was dead.

37. When a person was sentenced to death by execution, a
tablet (*titulus*), containing a statement of his crime, was carried in
front of him or hung upon him; when he was crucified, it was
displayed on the cross. John states that Jesus' *titulus* was written
in Hebrew (Aramaic), Latin and Greek—the three languages used
in first century Palestine and symbolic of universality. If the inscription is historical, it means that Jesus was killed for having claimed
kingship—which to the Jews meant Messiahship—and Pilate may
have intended to mock the Jews by allowing such a claim to be
put on the cross.

38. The significance in the crucifixion scene of the two robbers
on either side of Jesus is probably that which a later scribe of
Mark's gospel (Mk 15.28) thought appropriate—viz., Isa. 53.12:
'He was numbered with the transgressors'.

39–44. It is virtually certain that Jesus would have been subjected to taunts and insults from bystanders, but these verses
probably present not so much an accurate historical record as a
tradition which emphasizes again the hostility of the Jews and the
fulfilment of Scripture (cf. the hints of Ps. 22.7 in verse 39, and of

M

Ps. 22.8 and Ps. 69.9 in verse 44). The absence of any independent historical tradition is suggested by the fact that the various taunts merely repeat the two charges (the threat to the Temple and the claim to Messiahship) made before the Sanhedrin. Moreover, the presence of the High Priests and the scribes at a crucifixion during Passover time is highly improbable.

If you are the Son of God: these words recall the Satanic temptation in 4.3, 6, and the phrase brings the whole incident very close to what is described in Wis. 2.6–20, esp. 17ff. (which itself draws on Isa. 53 and Ps. 22); cf. also 1QH ii.8ff., 32ff., and Schweizer, *LD*, pp. 29–30.

THE DEATH OF JESUS 27.45-56

The evangelists do not stress the suffering of Jesus during the time of crucifixion; they have other ways of understanding and declaring the meaning of this event, by their allusions to the Old Testament (see Lindars, pp. 89–93). The unity between this section and what precedes depends on the common use of Ps. 22, some words from which are now found on Jesus' lips. The unexpected feature of the narrative is the mention of the signs following Jesus' death (verses 51–4); these are cultic, cosmic, and eschatological. This conclusion to the narrative is all the more striking when it is recalled that throughout the Passion narrative the evangelists have presented Jesus in all the reality of his humanity. In this section Matthew follows Mark closely, except in verses 51b–3, for which there is no parallel.

45. All the Gospels report the darkness from noon till 3 p.m. and the *Gospel of Peter* elaborates the idea. Whether Matthew means by **all the land** all Palestine or the whole world is uncertain, but the subsequent cosmological effects of the event suggest the latter. In the account of the last plague in Egypt before the death of the first-born 'there was thick darkness in all the land of Egypt for three days' (Exod. 10.22), but the allusion here may well be to the fulfilment of Am. 8.9: '"And on that day, says the Lord GOD, I will make the sun go down at noon, and darken the earth in broad daylight."'

46. The MSS. of Matthew and Mark give the words of Jesus' cry in different forms, but it is probable that Mark wrote *Eloi* (Aramaic) and Matthew *Eli* (the Hebrew version of Ps. 22.1); but only the Hebrew form can explain the misinterpretation of the word as a call to the prophet Elijah (*Elias*). It is possible to take the words of the cry at their face value, and to see in them a cry of utter desolation on the part of Jesus, who felt that he had been abandoned by God in the face of the hostile power of evil. Other commentators argue that the words (from Ps. 22.1) are to be interpreted in terms of the entire Psalm, which is not a cry of despair, but the prayer of a righteous sufferer who still trusts in the protection of God and confidently expects vindication (see Ps. 22.24, 26). There is some evidence that, for the Jews, the opening words of Ps. 22 were interpreted in the light of what follows, and recognized as an effective prayer for succour in time of need (G. F. Dalman, *Jesus-Jeshua*, Eng. Tr., 1929, p. 206). The cry of Jesus raised grave problems in the later development of Christology, and approaches to answers to these are indicated in the MSS. variants and in the *Gospel of Peter* v.19. On the text, see Stendahl, pp. 84–7.

47. According to Old Testament legend Elijah did not die but was taken up into heaven alive (2 Kg. 2.9–12), and it was believed that he would come to rescue the righteous in times of distress (*SB*, IV, 2.769–71).

48. This verse contains a fresh allusion to Ps. 69.21: 'for my thirst they gave me vinegar to drink' (cf. verse 34 for the use of the first part of the verse). Vinegar may have been given as a sedative by one of the soldiers, but in the *Gospel of Peter* (v.16) this drink is understood to have caused premature death (Ps. 69.21a has 'poison' in M.T.).

49. Matthew distinguishes between the person who gave the drink and those who said to him **Wait**; in Mark the same man gives the vinegar and speaks the jeering taunts. The addition in some MSS.: 'And another took a spear and pierced his side, and out came water and blood' is probably due to Jn 19.34.

50. The **spirit** which Jesus yields up is not the divine Spirit, but the 'spirit of life' (Gen. 35.18), without which a man is but dust. Life has now returned to its source in God.

51. There were two curtains in the Temple; an outer one, and a second one before the Holy of Holies (Exod. 26.31–5; 40.21). Probably the inner curtain is meant here, and the evangelist may be alluding to the new approach to God's presence available to men (Gentiles?) by reason of the death of Jesus (cf. Heb. 6.19; 9.12, 24; 10.19–22): it could be that Matthew intends this as a sign of how the Temple and all it stood for will be destroyed. The earthquake may symbolize the demonstration of God's judgment; cf. Josephus, *BJ* vi.v.3 for similar signs before the destruction of the Temple in A.D. 70.

52–3. The eschatological signs recorded here (by Matthew alone) reflect a primitive tradition on the significance of Christ's death and resurrection. The resurrection of the righteous (**the saints**) was expected as one of the great events of the End, which would happen at Jerusalem when the Mount of Olives was parted in two; out of that parting, the dead were to appear. The earthquake at Jesus' death fulfils the first part of this sequence, while the second takes place after his Resurrection. This view of eschatology (in relation to the significance of Jesus' death and resurrection) did not fit into what became the commonly accepted teaching that Christ was 'the first fruits of those who had fallen asleep' (1 C. 15.20), and that all others await the general resurrection; therefore it did not survive in the main stream of tradition. The point being made in this verse is clear: with Christ the general resurrection has begun; the power of death is now vanquished; see Stendahl, in *Peake*, 694 para. 0.

54. It is probable that Matthew intended the Roman centurion's words to be a confession of Jesus' divinity (so *RSV*), though *huios theou* (without article) could mean for a pagan 'a son of God'— i.e. a divine being. The reader of the Gospel would certainly have understood the exclamation as a confession of Christain faith on the lips of a Gentile.

55–6. The women give continuity to the story (verse 61 and 28.1ff.). For **the mother of the sons of Zebedee** Mark has 'Salome'. The second Mary (**the mother of James and Joseph**) can hardly be the mother of Jesus, although in 13.55 two of Jesus' brothers bear those names.

THE BURIAL OF JESUS 27.57–61

The Jews regarded dead bodies, especially the dead bodies of criminals, as unclean. In view of Dt. 21.22f. (a criminal's 'body shall not remain all night upon the tree'), Jesus' body had to be removed before nightfall, especially before the Sabbath; cf. Josephus, *BJ* iv.v.2; on the chronological problems, see Nineham, p. 433. Executed persons were usually buried without honour in a public field (Daube, pp. 310ff.), but Jesus received better treatment at the hands of the otherwise unknown Joseph of Arimathea.

57. Matthew does not present Joseph as an honoured member of the Sanhedrin (as do Mark and Luke), but as a wealthy man who was (lit.) 'discipled' to Jesus (cf. 13.52; 28.19)—i.e. was sympathetically inclined towards Jesus' teaching. Arimathea may be located NW. of Lydda (Ramathaim).

58. The normal Roman custom was to leave the bodies of the crucified on the cross till they decayed, but there is some evidence from the time of Augustus that they were occasionally granted to relatives and friends of the deceased.

59–60. The anointing of Jesus' body is not mentioned specifically, but may be assumed. The details of the tomb are quite natural; the Jews buried the dead outside the city walls in tombs cut out of the rock or formed by natural caves. Bodies were placed in recesses, or on shelves or slabs of stone, and the entrance was usually blocked with a heavy stone. Joseph's tomb was a **new** one; but, if Jesus was buried as a criminal, then the Law forbade the owner of the tomb to use it again. The description of the tomb may simply indicate the honour granted to the body by Joseph.

61. There is a constant watch over what takes place (cf. verses 36, 55). This makes it clear to the readers that there was no mistake about the place or the events.

THE GUARD AT THE TOMB **27.62–6**

This short section is peculiar to Matthew: it probably stems from a cycle of traditions associated with Jerusalem (cf. 27.3–10), and it echoes the kind of objections which may have been made to the faith of the early Church. Having shown that no one could have removed the body from the cross because the soldiers were keeping guard (verses 36, 54), Matthew now adds that the watch on the tomb was kept up over the Sabbath, to prevent the body being stolen and a false claim of resurrection. This paragraph sets the stage for 28.11–15 (also peculiar to Matthew), where the reference to theft of the body appears again. 'This whole tradition is clearly apologetic and is meant to refute the criticism which is mentioned as current among the Jews in 28:15' (Stendahl, in *Peake*, 695c).

62. Next day, . . . after the day of preparation: the Sabbath. The odd fashion of referring thus to the Sabbath is probably due to Matthew's desire to employ the word 'preparation' which he earlier omitted from Mk 15.42. It is extremely difficult to imagine that the chief priests and Pharisees (the latter being hardly mentioned in the Passion narrative, but elsewhere in Matthew the chief opponents of Jesus) went to Pilate on the Sabbath day.

63–4. The leaders of the Jews, as always, are concerned about what would happen to the people; they must not be seduced by a false claim. By **the last fraud** must be meant the acceptance of Jesus' resurrection; and by the **first** belief in his Messiahship.

65–6. The answer put on Pilate's lips has an irony about it which hints at knowledge of the eventual result. The words: **You have a guard of soldiers** (*koustōdia* is a Latinism) may be translated 'Take a guard . . .'

THE EMPTY TOMB 28.1–10

The Matthean account of the Resurrection basically follows that of Mark as against the narratives of Luke and John. Apart from a few abbreviations, Matthew's difference from Mark lies in the addition of verses 2–4 and 9–10; the latter may be compared with the appearance to Mary Magdalene in Jn 20.11–18, and the former is to be understood, not as an attempt to explain exactly how the Resurrection took place (so Stendahl: 'a "description" of the actual resurrection event'), but as a description of how the women were enabled to go into the tomb and affirm that it was empty. In Luke and John the angelic message and the appearances occur in or around Jerusalem, but Matthew locates the decisive, promised manifestation in Galilee.

It should be noted that the Gospels are content to affirm the angelic announcement that Jesus has been raised. They do not describe exactly how this happened, for the primary interest of the first Resurrection accounts was centred on the appearances: the reality of the Resurrection and the appearances was confirmed by the tradition of the empty tomb, which probably grew up and became stronger later (1 Cor. 15, written around A.D. 56, lacks any specific reference to the empty tomb). Nor do the early records offer any description of Jesus' risen appearance; they claim that the continuity of his appearance (before and after the Resurrection) was such as to allow recognition and evoke wonder and worship. Any claim that the story of the Resurrection was a delusion or a fabrication (such as may have been suggested by the Jews) is implicitly denied by the evangelists.

1. Again Matthew's emphasis falls on watching (cf. 27.61).

The sealing of the tomb precludes the anointing of Jesus' body, which is mentioned by Mark as the purpose of the women's visit. The time of their arrival seems to be early on Sunday morning.

2-4. The **angel of the Lord** comes, not to awake or resurrect Jesus, but to open the door of the tomb for the women, show them that the grave is empty and give them instructions. The presence and function of the angel recalls the part played by such beings (especially 'the angel of the Lord') in the opening chapters of the Gospel. The angel at the Birth and at the Resurrection is a witness to the event, explaining its meaning and assigning to others a precise task. In the *Gospel of Peter* (ix.35–xi.44) a detailed description is given of how Jesus walked out of the grave, 'his head overpassing the heavens'. This account serves to demonstrate the sobriety of our Gospel narratives and their reserve about giving a precise account of what took place. Note how the guards are terrorized by the glorious, supernatural appearance. Unlike the women, they do not understand, and there is no message for them.

5-6. The young man dressed in white (Mk 16.5) becomes in Matthew the **angel** of verses 2-4. The words **as he said**, following **he has risen**, are added by Matthew.

7-8. It is surprising that Matthew, who has elsewhere shown a special interest in Peter (10.2; 16.17ff.), does not retain Mark's special mention of him: 'tell his disciples and Peter' (Mk 16.7). Nor does he retain the Marcan statement that Jesus predicted the appearance in Galilee (**Lo, I have told you** replaces 'as he told you'): this may be because Matthew is concerned about the Jewish accusation that the disciples staged what they were expecting to take place (Stendahl, in *Peake*, 695g). Mark's record of the women's total silence (Mk 16.8) becomes the very opposite in Matthew—a joyful proclamation.

9-10. This account of Jesus' appearance to the women looks like a partial doublet of verses 5-7, and may be a later addition to the text. Some have thought that it is a Matthean version of the appearance to Mary Magdalene in Jn 20.11ff. The two post-Resurrection appearances of Jesus recorded by Matthew (here and at verses 16ff.) both refer to the fact that Jesus was **worshipped**. This may well reflect a liturgical setting for the development of the tradition.

THE CHIEF PRIESTS' FRAUD **28.11-15**

These verses (peculiar to Matthew) follow on from 27.62-6. What is narrated here was prompted by the need to answer an actual accusation current in the time of the evangelist. The appalling behaviour of the Jewish leaders is again emphasized. According to Bonnard (p. 414), these five verses confirm the hypothesis locating the redaction of Matthew's Gospel in a Christian *milieu* still in contact with the representatives of official Judaism, ten to fifteen years after the fall of Jerusalem. But is not the story about the Jewish dismissal of Jesus' resurrection as a forgery more likely to have been set down *after* relations between Matthew's church and the Synagogue had been broken off? The interest in the empty tomb (recognized here as a fact) is something of an indication of the lateness of the tradition. As in the case of 27.3-10, 62-6, this story may be based on a special Jerusalem cycle of tradition.

11. According to the *Gospel of Peter* (xi.45-9), the guards reported to Pilate. Here they bear their tidings to the High Priests, presumably because they had been placed at the disposal of the Sanhedrin by the Procurator (27.65).

12-15. In making the priests employ the fraud which they had expected the disciples to perpetrate, Matthew shows them as not at all concerned about the truth of the guard's story, but only about the effect the rumour would have on the people. The event must be explained away. For the presence of this story in the mid-second century, see Justin, *Dial.* 108.

THE RESURRECTED LORD AND HIS DISCIPLES **28.16-20**

The end of the Gospel presents a glorious epiphany of the Risen Christ to his disciples on a mountain in Galilee. Three themes which have been of great importance to Matthew throughout reappear here: (i) the supreme authority which is given to Jesus Christ. (ii) the Matthean church, represented by the disciples is receptive to the ethical and missionary instructions of the Lord. (iii) the eschatological—indeed, universalist—perspective of the instructions given. Therefore, although part of this *pericope* (verse 19) may have taken literary shape at a later time than the rest of the Gospel (see below), the main content of the section is consonant with the work as a whole; and features of the language and style of the verses mark them as having been composed by Matthew himself. See Barth, in *TIM*, pp. 131-7, on this passage.

16. The appearance to the disciples (as representative of the Church) is located in Galilee probably for theological reasons. It ensures that the risen Christ and his teaching are not thought of as a substitute for, but as continuous with, Jesus' ministry and teaching in Galilee (note verse 20a: '. . . to observe all that I have commanded you'). The Resurrection confers on the words of the Galilean teacher an incomparable authority.

No particular mountain was indicated in the earlier tradition of Jesus' sayings. There is no need to regard it as the Mount of the Beatitudes or of Transfiguration; a high place, a mountain, is the place for revelation.

17. The words **but some doubted** are not expanded (cf. the episode regarding Thomas in Jn 20.24-9). Do they refer to some of the disciples not present on this occasion, or to disciples who doubted the reality of some other resurrection appearance? Probably it is best to regard them as some there present (and so within the Christian community); the worship of the group was not without an element of questioning and hesitation. This is in accordance with what is said of christophanies in the *NT* generally; they were not of such a kind as to make doubt utterly impossible. But notice that those who had difficulties received the words of Jesus no less than those who believed.

18. All authority . . .: these words belong to the christology of the Son of Man who, once humiliated and suffering, has now received from God the universal and eternal dominion promised to him in Dan 7.14; cf. Phil. 2.6-11. 'It is not so much a matter here of the resurrection of Jesus from the dead as of his exaltation and establishment as the eschatological ruler and judge of the world' (Barth, in *TIM*, p. 133).

19. Christ has authority on earth as well as in heaven. '*Therefore* the time has come for them [the disciples] to do what he never did except in reluctant anticipation: to go to the Gentiles' (Stendahl, *Peake*, 695k). The proclamation of Christ's Lordship involves making **disciples of all nations**—and that phrase probably includes Jews also (see Intro. p. 71f). Many commentators doubt that the trinitarian formulation was original at this point in Matthew's gospel, since there is no evidence elsewhere in the *NT* of such a formula, and baptism is described as performed 'in the name of the Lord Jesus' (Ac. 2.38; 8.16). Nevertheless, trinitarian formulations (of liturgical and doxological character) are found in Paul's writings (2 C. 13.14; 1 C. 12.4–6), and the formula in this verse cannot be so very late, since it is found in much the same terms in the *Didachē* (vii.1–3), a fact which proves that it was known to the Church at the end of the first century in a *milieu* rather like that of the first Gospel (cf. E. Massaux, *L'Influence de l'Évangile de St Matthieu*, 1950, p. 639). The *Sitz im Leben* of the verse probably lies in the life and work of the Church about fifty years after the death of Jesus. Had Christ given the command to 'make disciples of all nations', the opposition in Paul's time to the admission of Gentiles to the Church would be inexplicable. It must be presumed that the Church, having learned and experienced the universality of the Christian message, assigned that knowledge to a direct command of the living Lord.

20. The teaching of Jesus is here described as **all that I have commanded you**; cf. the terms used of the Law (15.4; 19.7, 17, and Exod. 7.2; 29.35; Dt. 1.41; 4.2; etc.). It is by the disciples' proclamation of Jesus' teaching (including probably for Matthew the orders of Church discipline in 18.15–22) that Christ is made known. Earlier in the Gospel, at 18.20, the presence of Jesus was promised to his Church when they carried out his ordinances: now, in the last words of the Gospel, the same presence is promised to the Church (not the hierarchy) represented by the disciples, as they obey Christ's will and engage in evangelization **to the close of the age** (cf. 13.39f., 49; 24.3). The period indicated—from the Resurrection and enthronement of Christ till the final consummation—is for Matthew the era of the Church's life and mission. It was within the life of the Church and as a contribution to its mission that this Gospel was composed and took on its distinctive character.

INDEX OF MODERN AUTHORS

INDEX OF NAMES AND PLACES

366